JOURNAL FOR THE STUDY OF THE NEW TESTAMENT
SUPPLEMENT SERIES
216

Executive Editor
Stanley E. Porter

STUDIES IN NEW TESTAMENT GREEK
9

Executive Editor
Stanley E. Porter

Sheffield Academic Press
A Continuum imprint

Sentence Conjunction in the Gospel of Matthew

καί, δέ, τότε, γάρ, σὺν and
Asyndeton in Narrative Discourse

Stephanie L. Black

Journal for the Study of the New Testament
Supplement Series 216

Studies in New Testament Greek 9

To Bill—
Partner in faith,
partner in life,
partner in ministry:
Psalm 34.3

Copyright © 2002 Sheffield Academic Press
A Continuum imprint

Published by Sheffield Academic Press Ltd
The Tower Building, 11 York Road, London SE1 7NX
370 Lexington Avenue, New York NY 10017-6550

www.SheffieldAcademicPress.com
www.continuumbooks.com

British Library Cataloguing-in-Publication Data

A catalogue record for this book is available from the British Library

Typeset by Sheffield Academic Press
Printed on acid-free paper in Great Britain by MPG Ltd, Bodmin, Cornwall

ISBN 1-84127-255-8

CONTENTS

Even in a university community, where the people one encounters represent a broad range of academic interests, I've found that professing a passion for Greek grammar is a dinner party conversation stopper. No one seems quite sure what to say next. But if I answer the question 'And what is your field of work?' by explaining that I am fascinated by the ways we human beings use language to communicate with each other, by the ways we construct pictures in our minds of what we hear, and by the ways we use small words like conjunctions to help build and manipulate those pictures in others, and especially that I am intrigued by the possibility of using these ideas to learn more about how an ancient language worked, people respond with enthusiasm. Language is a social function, and people are interested in how other people use and understand language. A grammatical study like this one is essentially a study of human beings using the linguistic means at their disposal to make contact with one another.

At the same time, I do not claim in this research to be a linguist per se. My previous training is in New Testament studies, and I consider myself a New Testament scholar who has a keen interest in how the language of the New Testament functions. My primary motive in exploring the Greek of the New Testament is to arrive at a better understanding of the New Testament documents themselves. The linguistic works cited in this study are merely representative of major trends in linguistic theory and related clinical research in cognitive processing, rather than exhaustive. The linguistic principles incorporated here are chosen for their applicability to the primary topic, an examination of the ways Matthew the Evangelist uses sentence conjunctions in the narrative framework of his Gospel and what meanings those conjunctions convey.

In regard to the sentence conjunctions themselves—καί, δέ, τότε, γάρ and οὖν, plus asyndeton—I have attempted to be more exhaustive, including all of the studies of these forms in the New Testament that I am aware of published in English since 1990 (a surprisingly small collection), as well as significant studies and larger grammatical works from earlier periods, in other languages, or on sentence conjunctions in the Classical period. My survey of works on Matthew's Gospel is more selective, focusing on recent major commentaries such as those by Gundry, Hagner, Davies and Allison, and Luz, and incorporating other works where they are pertinent to the topic under discussion.

In embarking on an investigation of sentence conjunctions in Matthew's narrative framework I proceeded simultaneously along two fronts. On one hand, I made detailed observations of the distribution of καί, δέ, τότε, γάρ, οὖν and asyndeton in Matthew's Gospel, looking particularly for related lexical and syntactical collocations which might characteristically be combined with specific conjunctive choices, or features of discourse context which might help account for such choices. At the same time, I explored in the recent history of linguistic research and in the insights of other Greek grammarians theoretical approaches which offer a fuller appreciation of the semantics of sentence conjunctions in the Greek of the New Testament. As these two starting points converged, I developed descriptions characterizing the use of καί, δέ, τότε, γάρ, οὖν and asyndeton as a conjunctive system in Matthew's narrative framework, as well as outlining a theory of the semantics of sentence conjunctions which accounts for the distribution patterns of these forms in narrative in Matthew's Gospel.

I begin this presentation by surveying existing studies of Greek sentence conjunctions and by summarizing linguistic principles and models which offer a framework for a more adequate understanding of the linguistic function of sentence conjunctions in Matthew's Gospel (Chapter 1). Turning to the question of what sentence conjunctions 'mean', I explain that these forms have a low-level semantic content which can be described as *procedural* rather than *conceptual*—that is, these forms encode instructions about how to relate subsequent propositions to preceding text in constructing a mental representation of the discourse (Chapter 2). Each can be used in a variety of discourse contexts where a range of semantic relations between propositions may actually be present. This distinction between procedural and conceptual meaning is a significant one, as previous studies of sentence conjunctions in the New Testament have tended to treat such forms in terms of their supposed logical values rather than their contribution to discourse processing. Following this theoretical overview, I describe the empirical methods used in my analysis of καί, δέ, τότε, γάρ, οὖν and asyndeton in Matthew's narrative framework (Chapter 3). The methodological chapter is by necessity an extended one. I believe that developing an empirical methodology for the study of sentence conjunctions and related features—a methodology which is also potentially applicable to other lexico-grammatical issues—is one of the significant contributions of this research to the study of the Greek of the New Testament. In subsequent chapters I give the results of my analysis of each sentence conjunction and the procedural role(s) I understand each to play in narrative discourse in Matthew's Gospel: καί as a signal of unmarked continuity (Chapter 4); δέ as a signal of low- to mid-level discontinuity (Chapter 5); asyndeton both at points of tight continuity in dialogue and at mid- to higher-level breaks in the discourse (Chapter 6); τότε—arguably the least 'characterizable' of the sentence conjunctions considered here— as a signal of marked continuity (Chapter 7); and γάρ and οὖν as signals guiding pragmatic inferences related to material which supports the narrative line (Chapter 8). After treating each sentence conjunction individually I show how sentence conjunctions function as a system in Matthew's narrative framework, using Mt. 8.1–9.34 as a passage for extended analysis (Chapter 9). Finally, I summarize this research and suggest avenues of further study (Chapter 10).

Woven throughout this work is the recognition that linguistic communication is rarely merely a matter of one 'signal'—one lexical item or one syntactical structure—at a time. Sentence conjunctions form patterns with choices of other linguistic features, such as constituent order (for example, verb–subject or subject–verb order) or verbal tense-form. These serve as mutually reinforcing signals of continuity or discontinuity, prominence or relative unimportance, as Matthew's narrative unfolds. This volume concludes with an appendix by Elizabeth Allen and Vern Farewell explaining and summarizing their multivariate analysis of my data on sentence conjunctions and related features, which Allen carried out under Farewell's supervision as part of her MSc thesis in the Department of Statistical Science, University College London. Their work contains more mathematical equations than perhaps have ever yet been published in a volume on Greek grammar, and is not for the faint of heart. While the use of complex statistical methods and probabilistic modeling is becoming widespread in corpus linguistics, these methods have not yet influenced the study of Greek. Allen and Farewell are the first to model the ways multiple features from different linguistic systems interact in narrative in the Greek of the New Testament. As such, the combination of my observations and their statistical analysis represents a new generation of linguistic studies, the methods of which will become more familiar to Greek scholars as time goes on and the importance of the interplay of multiple features in language is more widely recognized. Allen and Farewell introduce a number of statistical concepts and attempt to make these methods and their application understandable to the non-specialist. The general reader is encouraged to look especially at the initial overview and at the preliminary comments in each results section, while more detailed explanations are provided for those with an interest in the technical aspects of their analysis.

This volume is a revision of my doctoral thesis at the University of Surrey Roehampton. As most research students discover, the several years of study and writing were by no means a solitary endeavor. I would like to thank Stan Porter, now of McMaster Divinity College, for sharing the wealth of his knowledge during the supervision of this thesis, for his careful review of my work, and for his incisive comments and suggestions. Needless to say, the remaining imperfections are entirely mine. I am indebted as well to my fellow students in the Biblical Studies Cluster at the University of Surrey Roehampton, especially Matt Brook O'Donnell, for their encouragement and exchange of ideas; to Vern Farewell and Elizabeth Allen of University College London for sharing their expertise in statistics and for their enthusiasm in exploring new applications of probabilistic modeling to linguistic issues; to Egbert Bakker of the University of Montreal, and Randall Buth of Jerusalem University College, who each generously gave their time to read and comment on an early version of my chapter on δέ; and to Don Hagner of Fuller Theological Seminary for his thoughtful comments on the final version of the thesis. I am very grateful to Tyndale House Biblical Studies Research Centre in Cambridge for desk space, for access to their outstanding library, and especially for the collegiality of fellow 'readers' and staff. I also want to express my heartfelt thanks to my parents, Jim and Nancy Larsen, and to the many friends, especially the people of First Presbyterian Church of Reading, Pennsylvania, who provided both the loving support and the funding that made it possible for me to spend this time studying the Word of God in new ways.

And most of all, to my family: my husband Bill, who truly believed we could both be research students at the same time, when I doubted it was possible; and Linnea and Caroline, two special daughters who cheerfully endured (usually) two parents pursuing two PhDs across two continents, and who daily kept the rarefied air of academic research 'earthed' in a wonderful way.

Stephanie Black

ABBREVIATIONS

ASCP	Amsterdam Studies in Classical Philology
BDF	F. Blass and A. Debrunner, *A Greek Grammar of the New Testament and Other Early Christian Literature* (trans. R.W. Funk; Chicago: University of Chicago Press, 1961)
BETL	Bibliotheca ephemeridum theologicarum lovaniensium
Bib	*Biblica*
BR	*Bible Review*
CBQ	*Catholic Biblical Quarterly*
CTL	Cambridge Textbooks in Linguistics
EKKNT	Evangelisch-Katholischer Kommentar zum Neuen Testament
ETEL	Edinburgh Textbooks in Empirical Linguistics
FN	*Filología neotestamentaria*
ICC	International Critical Commentary
JBL	*Journal of Biblical Literature*
JSNT	*Journal for the Study of the New Testament*
JSNTSup	*Journal for the Study of the New Testament*, Supplement Series
JTS	*Journal of Theological Studies*
LCL	Loeb Classical Library
NA[27]	E. Nestle and K. Aland (eds.), *Novum Testamentum Graece* (Stuttgart: Deutsche Bibelstiftung, 27th edn, 1993)
Neot	*Neotestamentica*
NovT	*Novum Testamentum*
NovTSup	*Novum Testamentum*, Supplements
NTS	*New Testament Studies*
NTTS	New Testament Tools and Studies
RSV	Revised Standard Version
SBG	Studies in Biblical Greek
SBL	Society of Biblical Literature
SBLDS	SBL Dissertation Series
SBLMS	SBL Monograph Series
SBLRBS	SBL Resources for Biblical Study
SNTG	Studies in New Testament Greek
START	*Selected Technical Articles Related to Translation*
TNTC	Tyndale New Testament Commentaries
TynBul	Tyndale Bulletin

UBS	United Bible Societies
WBC	Word Biblical Commentary
ZNW	*Zeitschrift für die neutestamentliche Wissenschaft*
ZTK	*Zeitschrift für Theologie und Kirche*

Abbreviations for Grammatical Terms

ap	articular pronoun
gen abs	genitive absolute participial construction
SV	subject–verb constituent order
S_1V	subject–verb constituent order, with subject as topical theme
S_2V	subject–verb constituent order, with subject not as topical theme
V	verb-only (monolectic) constituent order
VS	verb–subject constituent order
V(S)	verb–subject constituent order, with subject optional
∅	asyndeton (no conjunction)

Chapter 1

A LINGUISTIC FRAMEWORK

It is the task and the duty of the N.T. student to apply the results of
linguistic research to the Greek of the N.T. But, strange to say, this has not
been adequately done.[1]

The Study of the Gospels Is the Study of Language

The study of the Gospels, as of all of the New Testament, is a study of
linguistic communication. As written texts the New Testament Gospels are
encoded in human language—as it happens, the Greek common to the
Mediterranean world and beyond as a result of the conquests first of Alex-
ander and then of the Roman Empire.[2] Whatever oral traditions, written
sources, or earlier versions they may have drawn from, each a linguistic
object in itself, at some point each of the canonical Gospels was put into
the form we encounter by someone using human language in an attempt to
convey certain things about Jesus of Nazareth.[3] The extent to which we

1. A.T. Robertson, *A Grammar of the Greek New Testament in the Light of
Historical Research* (Nashville: Broadman Press, 4th edn, 1934), p. 3.

2. Louw observes, 'Strictly speaking ... there is no such thing as New Testament
Greek'. Louw compares Greek in the Hellenistic era to English today, 'a language
known and used in most parts of the world, a koine language. Yet, there is no such
thing as Koine English.' Louw warns against assuming that a single form of Greek
appears in the New Testament: 'Rather one should talk of various forms and styles of
Greek within the area of Hellenistic Greek, ranging from fairly highbrow as for
example in 1 Peter and Jude, to quite colloquial in Mark and even substandard in
Revelation' (J.P. Louw, 'New Testament Greek—The Present State of the Art', *Neot*
24 [1990], pp. 167-68). Whether or not one accepts Louw's characterization of the
language of individual books, his warning against assuming that the Greek within the
New Testament is monolithic is well taken.

3. This is admittedly something of an oversimplification which does not do justice
to the question, 'which form?' This study is based on E. Nestle and K. Aland (eds.),
Novum Testamentum Graece (Stuttgart: Deutsche Bibelstiftung, 27th edn, 1993),

understand the characteristics and conventions of human languages in general, and this language in particular, will in large part determine how much of that intended communication we are able to recover.

The interpretative task of the New Testament scholar is complicated by distance in time between the present day and the production of the text. While the Greek language in its various forms and dialects has been continuously in use from pre-Classical times to the modern era, inevitable changes in language conventions over centuries mean that the varieties of Greek found in the New Testament documents have been superseded as a living language by later forms of Greek. Without direct access to native speakers from the Hellenistic period who might highlight the nuances of various words or combinations of words, point out the emphases inherent in a given structure, or suggest what might have been said that was not, scholars are more dependent on general linguistic principles in their attempt to decode the Gospels. The better the linguistic tools and the more carefully they are used, the more closely the contemporary scholar may be able to approximate, out of the range of possible meanings of each text, what each Evangelist hoped to convey.

A wide range of linguistic issues is of interest to the student of the New Testament. The goal of this study is to outline a linguistically based approach which contributes to the understanding of paratactic intersentence conjunctions such as καί, δέ, οὖν, γάρ and (in Matthew's Gospel) τότε, lexical items which connect coordinate sentences or clauses and to which I will refer simply as 'sentence conjunctions'.[4] More specifically, the focus of this study is the attempt to understand how speakers of Greek in the Hellenistic period used and made sense of such conjunctions in the context of narrative discourse. The particular text chosen for this research is the Gospel of Matthew.

because of its widespread availability and use among scholars, but this is not meant to suggest that other text types and critical editions are not potentially useful for the study of the language of the New Testament. (See Chapter 3 for further discussion of the choice of NA[27] as the text for this research.)

4.   'Sentence conjunctions' can be considered either as a subset of 'particles', using more the traditional grammatical categories generally favored by classicists, or as a subset of 'discourse markers' or (more narrowly) 'discourse connectives', using the more recently developed pragmatically oriented categories favored by linguists. On terminology and linguistic treatments see, for example, B. Fraser, 'What Are Discourse Markers?', *Journal of Pragmatics* 31 (1999), pp. 931-52.

Sentence Conjunctions in Matthew's Gospel

English speakers who were told as schoolchildren that it is bad style to begin a sentence with *and* may be surprised by the prevalence of conjunctions beginning sentences in the Greek of the New Testament.[5] The use of paratactic sentence conjunctions in the New Testament varies from author to author, but by my count almost 70% of the sentences in the Gospel of Matthew begin with a conjunction serving as a link to the preceding sentence.[6] Or rather, as forms such as δέ, οὖν and γάρ are invariably postpositives, a conjunction appears in one of the first few 'slots' in the sentence. Of the sentences which function in the narrative framework of Matthew's Gospel—that is, excluding exposition attributed to Jesus, reported speech, and Old Testament quotations—92% begin with a conjunction. Καί and δέ are by far the most common, with one or the other appearing as the sentence conjunction in 50% of the sentences in the Gospel of Matthew and in more than 80% of the sentences in Matthew's narrative framework.[7]

Although καί and δέ are the conjunctions found most frequently, these two represent only part of the system of sentence conjunctions in Matthew's Gospel, that is, the set of conjunctive options from which the Evangelist chooses. In the Gospel of Matthew, the system consists (with a limited number of variations) of the set καί, δέ, τότε, γάρ, οὖν and asyndeton.

5.   Wierzbicka speculates that one reason particles in general received little attention in modern linguistic theory for so long is that 'the majority of the most influential works in modern linguistic theory have been written in English and by native speakers of English. And it just happens to be the case that in English, the role of particles is unusually limited...' (A. Wierzbicka, 'Introduction', in *idem* (ed.), 'Special Issue on "Particles" ', *Journal of Pragmatics* 10 [1986], p. 519).

6.   Counts and statistical comparisons are based on a computer database of Matthew I created for this research. The independent clauses in the Gospel, approximately 2300 in total, were analyzed for factors such as sentence conjunction, constituent order, verbal tense-form, subject reference, discourse type (narrative, exposition, quoted speech), etc. The database is described in detail in Chapter 3.

7.   Καί: 30% (700/2302) of all sentences, 47% (335/720) of sentences in the narrative framework; δέ: 20% (470/2302) of all sentences, 36% (257/720) of sentences in the narrative framework. Mayser reports that καί and δέ are likewise the most common conjunctions in the papyri: 'δέ ist nach καί in allen Perioden der Papyrussprache die weitaus häufigste partikel' (E. Mayser, *Grammatik der Griechischen Papyri aus der Ptolemäerzeit*. II/3. *Satzlehre, Synthetischer Teil* [Berlin and Leipzig: W. de Gruyter, 1934], p. 140).

These six options account for 99% of the sentences in Matthew's narrative framework, and about 90% of the sentences in the rest of the Gospel.[8] Asyndeton, or the lack of a conjunction, is included in the system of sentence conjunctions because it represents an option that alternates with other conjunctive choices.[9]

The set of sentence conjunctions in the Gospel of Matthew is similar to, but reveals certain differences from, conjunctive systems in other Hellenistic Greek texts. For example, Mayser lists καί, δέ, τέ, οὖν and γάρ as the most common particles in the Ptolemaic papyri.[10] As in Mayser's list, καί, δέ, οὖν and γάρ are among the conjunctions found most frequently in Matthew's Gospel. However, τέ appears only three times in the Gospel of Matthew, only two of which are found in the narrative framework where it conjoins participles rather than clauses with finite verbs (27.48; 28.12). In other words, in addition to being relatively rare, τέ does not function as a sentence conjunction in Matthew's Gospel and so τέ is not addressed in this study. On the other hand, in contrast to Mayser's papyri and to the rest of the New Testament, τότε does serve as a sentence conjunction in the Gospel of Matthew, and so is treated here.

Only clause-initial occurrences of καί, functioning as part of the system of sentence conjunctions in Matthew's Gospel, are included in this study. For example, in 9.10b, καὶ ἰδοὺ πολλοὶ τελῶναι καὶ ἁμαρτωλοὶ ἐλθόντες συνανέκειντο τῷ Ἰησοῦ καὶ τοῖς μαθηταῖς αὐτοῦ, the initial καί (καὶ ἰδοὺ ...) is included, but καί in τελῶναι καὶ ἁμαρτωλοί or in τῷ Ἰησοῦ καὶ τοῖς μαθηταῖς αὐτοῦ is not. Finally, although Greek grammarians often discuss ἀλλά alongside δέ, ἀλλά is omitted here because it is not used as a sentence conjunction in Matthew's narrative framework, and appears intersententially fewer than 20 times elsewhere in the Gospel.

In spite of the fact that they appear in nearly every sentence in the Gospel of Matthew, the linguistic function of sentence conjunctions is not

---

8.   Exceptions in the narrative framework consist of πάλιν in 4.8 and 26.42, arguably an instance of asyndeton with πάλιν as an adverb; οὐδέ in 22.46, a variation on δέ accounted for by the presence of οὐδείς in the previous clause; and διό in 27.8, διὸ ἐκλήθη ὁ ἀγρὸς ἐκεῖνος ἀγρὸς αἵματος, the sole occurrence of διό in Matthew's Gospel.

9.   Although the focus of this study is narrative discourse, further details of the distribution of sentence conjunctions across types of discourse in the Gospel of Matthew can be found in the cross-tabulation tables supplied at the end of this volume.

10.   Mayser, *Grammatik der Griechischen Papyri*, p. 121.

well understood. A fuller appreciation of the ways sentence conjunctions are used in discourse is necessary to deepen our understanding of the ways the Evangelist uses language to convey his message.

Previous Studies

The widespread use of sentence conjunctions in the New Testament and the relative paucity of works addressing their use from the standpoint of current linguistic research motivate this study. For particles in the Classical period, Denniston's *The Greek Particles* has become the standard work.[11] Perhaps unfortunately, as Rijksbaron observes, 'the book was so good, in fact, and so much ahead of what was done for other languages, that it...simply became *the* standard reference book, and for a long time there must have been a widespread feeling that improving upon his treatment was not feasible and a waste of time'.[12] Denniston's volume is groundbreaking in the breadth and depth of its discussion of particles, and is particularly helpful in terms of the extensive examples Denniston amasses from Classical literature. However, Denniston follows in the tradition of earlier grammarians in the proliferation of categories under which instances of various particles are handled, so that δέ, for example, is treated separately as continuative and as adversative, as well as under a grouping of 'particular uses'—an exercise which amounts to a comprehensive survey of semantic contexts in which δέ may be found while indicating little about what δέ itself contributes to such a variety of contexts.[13] More significantly for New Testament scholars, Denniston takes 320 BCE as his *terminus ad quem*, and so offers little on particles in the New Testament.[14]

Thrall's study of particles in the New Testament, which treats what she terms the 'degeneration and development' in their use since the Classical era as emblematic of what she sees as wider tendencies in Greek of the Hellenistic period, breaks little new ground in terms of the linguistic function of conjunctions or other particles.[15] Although Thrall addresses

11. J.D. Denniston, *The Greek Particles* (rev. K. Dover; Oxford: Clarendon Press, 2nd edn, 1954).

12. A. Rijksbaron, 'Introduction', in *idem* (ed.), *New Approaches to Greek Particles* (ASCP, 7; Amsterdam: J.C. Gieben, 1997), p. 1.

13. See Denniston, *Greek Particles*, pp. 162-77.

14. See Denniston, *Greek Particles*, p. vii.

15. See M. Thrall, *Greek Particles in the New Testament* (NTTS, 3; Leiden: E.J. Brill, 1962), p. 1.

several suggestions by others which would in today's terms be considered 'pragmatic' or 'discourse-centered' understandings of καί, δέ and γάρ, in her refutation of these ideas she falls back more often than not on a traditional range of categories of use such as those outlined by Denniston.[16] Blomqvist, in his monograph on particles in Hellenistic prose, explicitly adopts Denniston's descriptive categories for the functions of the particles.[17] These two scholars further the study of sentence conjunctions and other particles in the New Testament era by treating them as diachronically separate from the Classical period, but neither of them addresses in a meaningful way how conjunctions actually function in the creation and comprehension of discourse.

In recent decades several articles and monographs addressing sentence conjunctions in the New Testament have appeared which take more notice of developments in linguistic theory than do Thrall and Blomqvist, especially in terms of exploring the function of sentence conjunctions above the level of the sentence, in paragraphs or other units of discourse. Notable among these are the works of scholars associated with the Summer Institute of Linguistics, especially studies by Buth and Levinsohn.[18] Less has been produced by scholars more in the mainstream of

16. See Thrall, *Greek Particles*, pp. 41-67.

17. See J. Blomqvist, *Greek Particles in Hellenistic Prose* (Lund: C.W.K. Gleerup, 1969), pp. 20-21; similarly, his *Das Sogennante KAI Adversativum: Zur Semantik einer griechischen Partikel* (Studia Graeca Upsaliensia, 13; Uppsala: Almqvist and Wiksell, 1979), p. 7 n.1.

18. See, for example, R. Buth, 'Semitic Καί and Greek Δέ', *START* 3 (1981), pp. 12-19; R. Buth, 'On Levinsohn's "Development Units" ', *START* 5 (1981), pp. 53-56; R. Buth, 'Perspective in Gospel Discourse Studies, with Notes on Euthus, Tote and the Temptation Pericopes', *START* 6 (1982), pp. 3-14; S.H. Levinsohn, *Textual Connections in Acts* (SBLMS, 31; Atlanta: Scholars Press, 1987); R. Buth, ' ͻEdayin/Tote— Anatomy of a Semitism in Jewish Greek', *Maarav* 5-6 (1990), pp. 33-48; K. Titrud, 'The Overlooked Καί in the Greek New Testament', *Notes on Translation* 5 (1991), pp. 1-23; I. Larsen, 'Notes on the Function of γάρ, οὖν, μέν, δέ, καί, and τέ in the Greek New Testament', *Notes on Translation* 5 (1991), pp. 35-45; R. Buth, 'Οὖν, Δέ, Καί, and Asyndeton in John's Gospel', in D.A. Black *et al.* (eds.), *Linguistics and New Testament Interpretation: Essays on Discourse Analysis* (Nashville: Broadman, 1992), pp. 144-61; K. Callow, 'The Disappearing Δέ in Corinthians', in Black *et al.* (eds.), *Linguistics*, pp. 183-93; K. Titrud, 'The Function of Καί in the Greek New Testament and an Application to 2 Peter', in Black *et al.* (eds.), *Linguistics*, pp. 240-70; J.A. Heckert, *Discourse Function of Conjoiners in the Pastoral Epistles* (Dallas: Summer Institute of Linguistics, 1996); S.H. Levinsohn, *Discourse Features of New Testament Greek: A Coursebook* (Dallas: Summer Institute of Linguistics, 2nd edn, 2000).

biblical studies, with the notable exception of Poythress's article on sentence conjunctions in the Gospel of John.[19] Each contributes to the study of conjunctions in the Gospels by detailing numerous appearances of individual forms and attempting to describe contextual factors affecting their use. In describing the function of δέ in narrative in John's Gospel Poythress, for example, lists patterns of use which include sentences with ὁ or οἱ as the subject; introducing a sentence or block of sentences which does not continue the main line of events in the narrative 'backbone' (his term), such as parenthetical information, background, or explanation; instances where τοῦτο δέ, οὗτος δέ or the like introduce the significance of a statement or event; and where a temporal ὡς clause begins a new sentence.[20] The identification and summation of this type of data helps to move the study of sentence conjunctions in the New Testament forward. Little work of a similar type has been done on sentence conjunctions as a conjunctive system in the Gospel of Matthew, however.[21] More importantly, as with Denniston, Thrall and Blomqvist, these authors rarely address the theoretical question of what conjunctions 'mean'—that is, their linguistic function in discourse and what they contribute to the communicative intent of a Gospel as a text.

Meanwhile, work on Greek particles in Classical and pre-Classical periods, especially by Dutch scholars, has begun to incorporate insights generated by linguistic research in the pragmatics of discourse comprehension.[22] In fact, as Rijksbaron notes in his introduction to *New*

---

19. V.S. Poythress, 'The Use of the Intersentence Conjunctions *De, Oun, Kai*, and Asyndeton in the Gospel of John', *NovT* 26 (1984), pp. 312-40; see also, for example, R.A. Edwards, 'Narrative Implications of *Gar* in Matthew', *CBQ* 52 (1990), pp. 636-55.

20. Poythress, 'Intersentence Conjunctions', pp. 325-26.

21. Levinsohn gives some attention to sentence conjunctions as a set of choices in the Gospel of Matthew, especially with respect to speech margins (see Levinsohn, *Discourse Features*, pp. 71-80, 235-40). However, his treatment is necessarily limited by the breadth of his study, which covers various discourse features throughout the New Testament.

22. See, for example, C.J. Ruijgh, *Autour de 'Te Épique'* (Amsterdam: Adolph M. Hakkert, 1971); E.J. Bakker, 'Boundaries, Topics, and the Structure of Discourse: An Investigation of the Ancient Greek Particle *De*', *Studies in Language* 17 (1993), pp. 275-311; C.M.J. Sicking and J.M. van Ophuijsen, *Two Studies in Attic Particle Usage: Lysias and Plato* (Leiden: E.J. Brill, 1993); and the collection of studies in Rijksbaron, *New Approaches*. At the same time, Kroon has made similar applications to Latin particles: see, for example, C. Kroon, *Discourse Particles in Latin: A Study of* nam,

Approaches to Greek Particles, the proceedings of a colloquium held in Amsterdam in 1996, 'The "New Approaches" mentioned in the title of this book are…for a large part pragmatically oriented approaches'.[23] For all the benefits of these recent studies, there are several limitations as well. The most obvious for the New Testament scholar is that work done on sentence conjunctions in earlier periods must be tested for its applicability to Hellenistic Greek, given the potential changes in language conventions over time. From a methodological standpoint, these studies tend to be based on relatively small language samples, as in Ruijgh's analysis of δέ and subject switch in 56 sentences from Herodotus,[24] or Sicking's analysis of δέ and related 'boundary' features in 44 sentences from Lysias.[25] The use of larger samples of continuous discourse and a more rigorous application of corpus linguistic techniques, including more developed methods of quantitative analysis, would make this type of research both more representative of language patterns of a given period and statistically more reliable. Finally, although these studies incorporate work linguists have done in the pragmatics of discourse comprehension, few if any make use of recent studies in cognitive aspects of discourse processing, and only a few place themselves within any broader framework of linguistic theory which would help to account for the patterns of use they identify for sentence conjunctions in terms of the roles such forms play in human communication.

enim, autem, vero *and* at (ASCP, 4; Amsterdam: J.C. Gieben, 1995); C. Kroon, 'Discourse Markers, Discourse Structure and Functional Grammar', in J.H. Connolly, R.M. Vismans, C. Butler and R.A. Gatward (eds.), *Discourse and Pragmatics in Functional Grammar* (Berlin: W. de Gruyter, 1997), pp. 17-32; C. Kroon, 'A Framework for the Description of Latin Discourse Markers', *Journal of Pragmatics* 30 (1998), pp. 205-23.

23. Rijksbaron, 'Introduction', pp. 2-3. Van Ophuijsen maintains that in taking a pragmatic approach to the semantics of particles, 'We are thus carried back from the more taxonomic way of 19th and 20th century positivist scholarship to a highly relevant insight expressed over four hundred years ago by Devarius in one of the earliest treatments of the Greek particles [1588]: a word may acquire, in addition to its own meaning (*significatio*), some other force (*vis et qualitas*) from the discourse it forms part of (*ex modo sermonis*)' (J.M. van Ophuijsen, 'ΟΥΝ, ΑΡΑ, ΔΗ, ΤΟΙΝΥΝ: The Linguistic Articulation of Arguments in Plato's Phaedo', in Sicking and van Ophuijsen, *Attic Particle Usage*, p. 80).

24. Ruijgh, *'Te Épique'*, pp. 131-32.

25. See C.M.J. Sicking, 'Devices for Text Articulation in Lysias I and XII', in Sicking and van Ophuijsen, *Attic Particle Usage*, pp. 12-13.

Linguistic Models

Simply to say that this study, by contrast, constitutes a 'linguistic' approach to sentence conjunctions in the Gospel of Matthew is not enough. As in any still emerging field, there seem to be nearly as many methodologies within New Testament Greek linguistics as there are practitioners. These reflect a variety of linguistic models, such as Chomskyan transformational grammar,[26] systemic-functional grammar,[27] case grammar,[28] construction grammar,[29] speech act theory,[30] use of the notion of semantic fields in lexical semantics,[31] corpus linguistics,[32] or general theories of communica-

26. See, for example, D.D. Schmidt, *Hellenistic Greek Grammar and Noam Chomsky: Nominalizing Transformations* (SBLDS, 62; Chico, CA: Scholars Press, 1981); M. Palmer, *Levels of Constituent Structure in New Testament Greek* (SBG, 4; New York: Peter Lang, 1995).

27. See, for example, S.E. Porter, *Verbal Aspect in the Greek of the New Testament, with Reference to Tense and Mood* (SBG, 1; New York: Peter Lang, 2nd edn, 1993); S.E. Porter, 'Word Order and Clause Structure in New Testament Greek: An Unexplored Area of Greek Linguistics Using Philippians as a Test Case', *FN* 6 (1993), pp. 177-205; J.T. Reed, *A Discourse Analysis of Philippians: Method and Rhetoric in the Debate over Literary Integrity* (JSNTSup, 136; Sheffield: Sheffield Academic Press, 1997); G. Martín-Asensio, 'Hallidayan Functional Grammar as Heir to New Testament Rhetorical Criticism', in S.E. Porter and D.L. Stamps (eds.), *The Rhetorical Interpretation of Scripture: Essays from the 1996 Malibu Conference* (JSNTSup, 180; Sheffield: Sheffield Academic Press, 1999), pp. 84-107.

28. See, for example, S. Wong, 'What Case Is This Case? An Application of Semantic Case in Biblical Exegesis', *Jian Dao* 1 (1994), pp. 49-73; S. Wong, *A Classification of Semantic Case-Relations in the Pauline Epistles* (SBG, 9; New York: Peter Lang, 1997). See, also, Porter's response to Wong: S.E. Porter, 'The Case for Case Revisited', *Jian Dao* 6 (1996), pp. 13-28.

29. See, for example, P. Danove, 'The Theory of Construction Grammar and Its Application to New Testament Greek', in S.E. Porter and D.A. Carson (eds.), *Biblical Greek Language and Linguistics: Open Questions in Current Research* (JSNTSup, 80; Sheffield: JSOT Press, 1993), pp. 119-51; P. Danove, *The End of Mark's Story: A Methodological Study* (Biblical Interpretation Series, 3; Leiden: Brill, 1993).

30. See, for example, J.E. Botha, *Jesus and the Samaritan Woman: A Speech Act Reading of John 4.1-42* (NovTSup, 65; Leiden: E.J. Brill, 1991); D. Neufeld, *Reconceiving Texts as Speech Acts: An Analysis of I John* (Biblical Interpretation Series, 7; Leiden: E.J. Brill, 1994).

31. See, for example, J.P. Louw and E.A. Nida (eds.), *Greek–English Lexicon of the New Testament Based on Semantic Domains* (New York: United Bible Societies, 2nd edn, 1989); S.E. Porter and M.B. O'Donnell, 'Semantic Patterns of Argumentation in the Book of Romans: Definitions, Proposals, Data and Experiments', in S.E. Porter

tion such as Gricean pragmatics and Relevance Theory.[33] These models shape the approaches biblical scholars take in their analysis of discourse in the New Testament.[34] Many biblical scholars, myself not excluded, draw from more than one of these streams as they explore the potential for applying new linguistic tools to the study of an ancient language.[35]

My own approach is informed primarily by Halliday's systemic-functional grammar.[36] Before I outline concepts in Halliday's grammar which are applicable to sentence conjunctions in the Gospel of Matthew, it is necessary to describe briefly a paradigm shift in linguistics, usually traced to the influence of de Saussure, which took place at the beginning of the twentieth century—a shift which still has not fully worked its way into the study of the Greek of the New Testament as we enter the twenty-

(ed.), *Diglossia and Other Topics in New Testament Linguistics* (Sheffield: Sheffield Academic Press, forthcoming).

32. See, for example, E.W. Güting and D.L. Mealand, *Asyndeton in Paul: A Text-Critical and Statistical Enquiry into Pauline Style* (Studies in the Bible and Early Christianity, 39; Lewiston, NY: Edwin Mellen, 1998); M.B. O'Donnell, 'The Use of Annotated Corpora for New Testament Discourse Analysis: A Survey of Current Practice and Future Prospects', in S.E. Porter and J.T. Reed (eds.), *Discourse Analysis in the New Testament: Approaches and Results* (JSNTSup, 170; SNTG, 4; Sheffield: Sheffield Academic Press, 1999), pp. 71-117.

33. See, for example, R. Blass, 'Constraints on Relevance in Koine Greek in the Pauline Epistles' (prepublication draft; first presented at the SIL Exegetical Seminar, Nairobi, Kenya, 29 May-19July, 1993 slightly revised March 1998).

34. See, for example, Porter and Reed, *Discourse Analysis*; Black *et al.* (eds.), *Linguistics*; Levinsohn, *Discourse Features*. For an introduction to approaches to discourse analysis with a focus on their implications for study of the Greek of the New Testament, see S.E. Porter, 'Discourse Analysis and New Testament Studies: An Introductory Survey', in S.E. Porter and D.A. Carson (eds.), *Discourse Analysis and Other Topics in Biblical Greek* (JSNTSup, 113; Sheffield: Sheffield Academic Press, 1995), pp. 14-35.

35. For a more detailed survey of contemporary linguistic models and basic assumptions which are common to disparate approaches, see S.E. Porter, 'Studying Ancient Languages from a Modern Linguistic Perspective', *FN* 2 (1989), pp. 147-72.

36. See, for example, M.A.K. Halliday, *Explorations in the Functions of Language* (London: Edward Arnold, 1973); G. Kress (ed.), *Halliday: System and Function in Language* (Oxford: Oxford University Press, 1976); M.A.K. Halliday, *Language as Social Semiotic* (London: Edward Arnold, 1978); M.A.K. Halliday, 'Dimensions of Discourse Analysis: Grammar', in T.A. van Dijk (ed.), *Handbook of Discourse Analysis*. II. *Dimensions of Discourse* (London: Academic Press, 1985), pp. 29-56; M.A.K. Halliday, *An Introduction to Functional Grammar* (London: Edward Arnold, 2nd edn, 1994).

first. Then, following a short outline of Hallidayan systemic-functional grammar, I describe how the rise of discourse analysis provides further opportunity for the study of sentence conjunctions.

A Linguistic Framework

De Saussure

The twentieth century saw a revolution in the study of linguistics, often dated from the appearance of de Saussure's *Cours de linguistique générale* in 1915.

Diachronic vs. synchronic analysis. De Saussure stressed the importance of a synchronic approach to language (looking at a language as spoken at one point in time) over a diachronic approach (tracing the development of a language through time). His classic illustration is that of a chess game in which the preceding sequence of moves has no bearing on the current state of the match.[37] Barr's *Semantics of Biblical Language* makes much the same point for biblical Greek and Hebrew. In his critique of etymological studies Barr writes, 'Words can only be intelligibly interpreted by what they meant at the time of their use by the speaker or writer'.[38] Barr stresses that there is no innate meaning derived from their original forms or 'roots' which adheres to words as they undergo change over time. While Barr addresses only individual words, the principle is equally applicable to grammatical forms and structures: the history of past usage may trace how current usage came about and shed light on what grammatical functions a form or structure emerged to fill, but in the final analysis it is only the current conventional use (and, more particularly, a habit of use by the author in question) that has relevance for the interpretation of a text.[39]

37. F. de Saussure, *Course in General Linguistics* (trans. W. Baskin; London: Collins, 1974), p. 89.

38. J. Barr, *The Semantics of Biblical Language* (Oxford: Oxford University Press, 1961), pp. 139-40.

39. Givón warns, however, that a too-artificial dismissal of diachronic developments is overly reductionistic and may at times hamper linguistic study: 'There is nothing inherently wrong with the structuralists' desire to ignore change under particular conditions... The problem...lies in dismissing the relevance of the data-base of change and variation to our understanding of synchronic structure. By way of analogy, this is akin to suggesting that the evolutionary mechanism that gave rise to a particular life-form is irrelevant to our understanding of that life-form' (T. Givón, *Functionalism and Grammar* [Amsterdam: John Benjamins, 1995], p. 7). Givón's warning about a

The standard New Testament grammars of the twentieth century reveal little awareness of de Saussure and his followers, reflecting for the most part nineteenth-century approaches to language.[40] Winer—among the first to recognize that the language of the New Testament was a variety of the Greek of its historical period rather than a form of Greek unique to the Bible—aimed in his 1822 grammar both 'to check the unbounded arbitrariness with which the language of the New Testament had so long been handled in Commentaries and exegetical prelections', and 'to apply the results of the rational philology...to the Greek of the New Testament'.[41] By 'rational philology' Winer meant a method 'which seeks for the explanation of all the phenomena of languages...in the modes of thought which characterise nations and individual writers...'[42] Winer's was the most widely used New Testament grammar of the nineteenth century. However, as the century continued Winer's 'rational philology' was superseded. A historical-comparative approach to language came to the fore, building on the discovery of the relationship of Sanskrit to Latin and Greek and the subsequent postulation of various 'proto-languages'. Robertson, writing at the turn of the twentieth century, lauds Winer but laments that he 'was not able to rise entirely above the point of view of his time... It is to be borne in mind also that the great science of comparative philology had not revolutionized linguistic study when Winer first wrote.'[43] Grammarians working from the new standpoint of comparative

---

too-artificial distinction is well taken, in that an understanding of past usage may in some cases illuminate aspects of present usage. However, comparing linguistic forms, in which meaning and use are conventional, to biological life-forms, in which function is an inherent property, may be misleading.

40. For surveys of linguistic approaches to New Testament grammar in the nineteenth and twentieth centuries, see D. Schmidt, 'The Study of Hellenistic Greek Grammar in the Light of Contemporary Linguistics', in C.H. Talbert (ed.), *Perspectives on the New Testament: Essays in Honor of Frank Stagg* (Macon, GA: Mercer University Press, 1985), pp. 27-38; Louw, 'Present State'; S.E. Porter and J.T. Reed, 'Greek Grammar since BDF: A Retrospective and Prospective Analysis', *FN* 4 (1991), pp. 143-49; D.A. Black, 'The Study of New Testament Greek in the Light of Ancient and Modern Linguistics', in D.A. Black and D.S. Dockery (eds.), *New Testament Criticism and Interpretation* (Grand Rapids: Zondervan, 1991), pp. 396-405.

41. G.B. Winer, *A Treatise on the Grammar of New Testament Greek* (trans. W.F. Moulton; Edinburgh: T. & T. Clark, 3rd edn, 1882), p. xxi.

42. Winer, *Treatise*, p. 7.

43. Robertson, *Grammar*, pp. 3-4. Robertson's own grammar reflects his primarily historical and comparative concerns.

philology sought to classify and systematize relationships among languages and dialects, demonstrating historical development from one language variety to another.[44] The discovery of the Hellenistic papyri, demonstrating conclusively that the Greek of the New Testament reflected widespread, often non-literary, patterns of then current use, provided new grist for the historical-comparative mill. In 1895 the first of Deissmann's lexical studies, *Bibelstudien*, appeared,[45] followed by *Neue Bibelstudien* in 1897.[46] In 1896 the first edition of Blass's *Grammatik des Neutestamentlichen Griechisch* (revised as Blass and Debrunner in 1913 and subsequently) appeared.[47] Both Deissmann and Blass made extensive use of the new discoveries. Moulton's 1906 *Prolegomena*, confidently asserting that ' "Biblical" Greek, except where it is translation Greek, was simply the vernacular of daily life', an approach which Moulton understood as 'a change in our conceptions of the subject nothing less than revolutionary', was hailed as epoch-making.[48] Ironically, on the eve of the Saussurean

44. As Porter and Reed put it, in comparative philology 'under the influence of Darwinian thought…the internal structure of a given linguistic phenomenon is examined for the light it sheds on the deterministic development of the phenomenon with regard to all other related (usually Indo-European) languages' (Porter and Reed, 'Greek Grammar since BDF', p. 145).

45. A.G. Deissmann, *Bibelstudien: Beiträge, zumeist aus den Papyri und Inschriften, zur Geschichte der Sprache, des Schrifttums und der Religion des hellenistischen Judentums und des Urchristentums* (Marburg: Elwert'sche Verlagsbuchhandlung, 1895).

46. A. Deissmann, *Neue Bibelstudien: Sprachgeschichtliche Beiträge, zumeist aus den Papyri und Inschriften, zur Erklärung des Neuen Testaments* (Marburg: Elwert'sche Verlagsbuchhandlung, 1897). Deissman's *Bibelstudien* and *Neue Bibelstudien* appeared together in English as A. Deissmann, *Bible Studies: Contributions Chiefly from Papyri and Inscriptions to the History of the Language, the Literature, and the Religion of Hellenistic Judaism and Primitive Christianity* (trans. A. Grieve; Edinburgh: T. & T. Clark, 1901). See also A. Deissmann, *Licht vom Osten: Das Neue Testament und die neuentdeckten Texte der hellenistisch-römischen Welt* (Tübingen: J.C.B. Mohr [Paul Siebeck], 1908); English translation, A. Deissmann, *Light from the Ancient East: The New Testament Illustrated by Recently Discovered Texts of the Graeco-Roman World* (trans. L.R.M. Strachan; London: Hodder & Stoughton, 1910).

47. F. Blass, *Grammatik des Neutestamentlichen Griechisch* (Göttingen: Vandenhoeck & Ruprecht, 1896).

48. J.H. Moulton, *A Grammar of New Testament Greek*. I. *Prolegomena* (Edinburgh: T. & T. Clark, 3rd edn, 1908), pp. 1, 4. See also Schmidt, 'Hellenistic Greek Grammar', p. 30.

'revolution', Robertson could write, 'The new era has now fairly begun'.[49]

Botha observes that 'so many of the standard grammars available to New Testament scholars are totally innocent of the precepts of modern linguistics...'[50] Blass and Debrunner in Germany, Moulton, Howard and Turner in Britain, and Robertson in America applied comparative philology to the Greek of the New Testament.[51] The historical-comparative approach of Blass and Debrunner has remained largely unchanged through numerous editions and widespread use both in German (now as Blass, Debrunner and Rehkopf) and in English (now as Blass, Debrunner and Funk). Porter and Reed state that 'BDF was already methodologically outdated when it was published in 1961',[52] while Louw writes, 'Even the 1976 revision of Blass and Debrunner by Rehkopf is amazingly still innocent of linguistics'.[53] Plans are under way to rewrite Blass–Debrunner from an updated linguistic perspective, but that project has not yet been completed.[54] Although an understanding of modern linguistics appears to be slowly growing among New Testament scholars,[55] Louw argues that in comparison to articles, monographs and books revealing an awareness of modern linguistic principles, commentaries and works on biblical theology generally show less acquaintance with twentieth-century developments in linguistics.[56]

As Louw points out, 'Saussure's insistence that a synchronic structural approach to language should be primary and that consequently the historical-comparative method should be supplemental to determining the meaning in a text, was so revolutionary that it took at least half a century to be accepted'.[57] De Saussure's emphasis on synchronic over against diachronic analysis motivates the study of conjunctions in the New

49. Robertson, *Grammar*, p. 5.

50. J.E. Botha, 'Style in the New Testament: The Need for Serious Reconsideration', *JSNT* 43 (1991), pp. 71-87 (reprinted in S.E. Porter and C.A. Evans [eds.], *New Testament Text and Language: A Sheffield Reader* [The Biblical Seminar, 44; Sheffield: Sheffield Academic Press, 1997], p. 115).

51. See Schmidt, 'Hellenistic Greek Grammar', p. 29.

52. Porter and Reed, 'Greek Grammar since BDF', p. 144.

53. Louw, 'Present State', p. 161

54. See Botha, 'Style', p. 116; Porter and Reed, 'Greek Grammar since BDF', pp. 149-63.

55. For an overview of more recent works related to linguistics and the New Testament, see Black, 'New Testament Greek', pp. 401-405.

56. Louw, 'Present State', pp. 163-64.

57. Louw, 'Present State', p. 163.

Testament on their own terms rather than as the development of—or worse, degeneration of—Classical Greek.[58] In the study of conjunctions in the Gospels neither previous usage in Classical Greek nor cross-linguistic borrowing has any necessary bearing on either the semantic content or syntactical function of a given form. Although empirical analysis suggests that there is, in fact, a great deal of continuity in the use of sentence conjunctions and similar particles from the Classical period to the Hellenistic era, there is change as well. Usage in Classical Greek may shed light on sentence conjunctions in the New Testament, but is not always a reliable predictor, nor, more importantly, should Classical usage be treated as a norm or desirable standard for use in the New Testament. The approach I take to sentence conjunctions in this study is essentially synchronic, looking at the patterns of use by one author in one discourse.

Language as system. De Saussure also asserts that in language, 'everything is based on relations'.[59] By this he means that linguistic signs (words and parts of words) convey meaning not primarily in themselves but in relation both to other signs with which they appear in context and to those with which they are associated in the mind.

Linguistic signs form a system of relationships with at least two dimensions. The first, *syntagmatic* relationships, may be described as the horizontal dimension, the elements which are arranged sequentially in a sentence or other unit of discourse. The second dimension, which de Saussure called associative relations but which today is usually referred to as *paradigmatic* relationships, may be described as the vertical dimension. As it has come to be used, this is the relationship a term has with other words, parts of words, or phrases which could acceptably alternate with that term in the same 'slot' in the sentence.

A systemic approach to language has implications, for example, for theories of Semitic influence or the (related) impact of the LXX on the Greek of the New Testament. Comparative philologists tended to treat the development of individual words and grammatical features in isolation, without recognizing relationships to other words and features in the language.[60] But in fact, while ideas about possible Aramaic forms influencing

---

58. This is in contrast to Thrall, who highlights evidence of 'linguistic degeneration' and 'linguistic development' in the particles, even to the extent of suggesting that such 'degeneration' is evidence of overall cultural decline (Thrall, *Greek Particles*, p. 39).

59. De Saussure, *Linguistics*, p. 122.

60. See Porter, 'Ancient Languages', p. 153.

Matthew's use of τότε, for example, may help explain how Matthew came to include this particular form in his set of conjunctive options,[61] Matthew's use of a Greek conjunction is not circumscribed by the use a similar form may have had in another language. Rather, the more significant linguistic issue is how the various conjunctions (whatever their source) alternate with each other and interact with other features of Matthew's Greek—that is, how they function as a system to convey meaning. For example, even if τότε as used by Matthew can be shown to be Semitic in origin, Matthew now uses τότε in opposition to other Greek conjunctions rather than in opposition to other Semitic conjunctions. Τότε's range of use is necessarily affected by the ranges of use of the conjunctions it alternates with, so that Matthew's set of conjunctive choices may be said to be like a pie cut up into pieces which differ in their relative size from the 'pie' of Semitic conjunctions. As Porter writes, 'While the development of a particular linguistic element from its origins and usage through various times to the present and beyond may be very interesting…the relation of this item to other items in the language at the time of its use constitutes the major concern of the modern linguist'.[62]

The approach to linguistics which looks at language as integrated systems of relationships came to be known as 'structuralism', and is the foundation upon which more recent linguists such as Halliday have built.

Halliday

Halliday's notions of system, function and choice offer a framework for the study of sentence conjunctions in Matthew's Gospel.

Function in language. Halliday describes his 'systemic-functional' grammar as following in the European functional tradition, acknowledging his debt to Firth, to Hjelmslev, and to the Prague school of linguists.[63] Functionalist approaches to language place an emphasis on written and spoken

---

61. See, for example, R. Buth, 'Semitic Καί and Greek Δέ', pp. 12-19; and 'Perspective', pp. 3-14, in which Buth outlines his view of Semitic influences on Matthew's use of τότε. See also discussion of possible Semitic antecedents to Matthew's use of τότε in Chapter 7.

62. Porter, 'Ancient Languages', p. 153.

63. See Halliday, *Introduction*, p. xxvi. For an introduction to the Prague school, see P.A. Luelsdorff (ed.), *The Prague School of Structural and Functional Linguistics* (Linguistic and Literary Studies in Eastern Europe, 41; Amsterdam: John Benjamins, 1994); also J. Vachek (ed.), *Praguiana: Some Basic and Less Known Aspects of the Prague Linguistic School* (Prague: Academia, 1983).

language as an instrument of communication in various social contexts and explore ways the structures of language reflect those interactions. Halliday explains that his grammar

> is functional in the sense that it is designed to account for how the language is *used*. Every text—that is, everything that is said or written—unfolds in some context of use; furthermore, it is the uses of language that, over tens of thousands of generations, have shaped the system.[64]

Or, as Halliday puts it more succinctly elsewhere, 'Language is as it is because of what it has to do'.[65]

Halliday identifies three components of meaning, or 'metafunctions', of language. The first two, the ideational and the interpersonal, 'are the manifestations in the linguistic system of the two very general purposes which underlie all uses of language: (i) to understand the environment (ideational), and (ii) to act on the others in it (interpersonal)'.[66] The third, the textual metafunction—within which sentence conjunctions play a part—'fills the requirement that language should be operationally relevant—that it should have a texture, in real contexts of situation that distinguishes a living message from a mere entry in a grammar or a dictionary'.[67] These three types of meaning intertwine in the lexico-grammatical structures of language in use:

> A clause in English is the simultaneous realization of ideational, interpersonal and textual meanings. But these components are not put together in discrete fashion such that we can point to one segment of the clause as expressing one type of meaning and another segment as expressing another. The choice of a word may express one type of meaning, its morphology another and its position in sequence another; and any element is likely to have more than one structural role, like a chord in a polyphonic structure which participates simultaneously in a number of melodic lines.[68]

Choice and system. Central to Halliday's grammar is the notion of choice. He writes,

> The speaker of a language, like a person engaging in any kind of culturally determined behaviour, can be regarded as carrying out simultaneously and

---

64. Halliday, *Introduction*, p. xiii.
65. Halliday, *Explorations*, p. 34.
66. Halliday, *Introduction*, p. xiii.
67. Halliday, *Explorations*, p. 42.
68. Halliday, *Explorations*, p. 42.

successively, a number of distinct choices... It is the system that formalizes
the notion of choice in language.[69]

These choices are functionally motivated, that is, they reflect the use of
language in a particular 'context of situation'.[70]

Using Halliday's notions of system and choice, I begin with the assumption that sentence conjunctions and asyndeton in the Gospel of Matthew
constitute a *paradigmatic system*, a set of 'vertical' relations, or elements
which can alternate in the same 'slot' in the sentence. The Evangelist
makes choices from within this system to connect sentences in the Gospel,
choices which are functionally motivated in the process of constructing the
discourse. As I noted above, in the Gospel of Matthew the Evangelist's set
of conjunctive choices generally consists of καί, δέ, τότε, γάρ and οὖν—
plus asyndeton, which is included in the system of sentence conjunctions
because it represents an option that alternates with other conjunctive
choices.

Halliday recognizes not just one system or set of choices within language, but a network in which choices from various systems (involving,
inter alia, lexical, morphological, syntactical and thematic dimensions)
interact with one another. In the chapters which follow I show that the
system of sentence conjunctions in Matthew's Gospel forms *syntagmatic*
(or 'horizontal') relationships with other linguistic features such as lexical
choice, constituent order, or verbal tense-form.

It is important though to note that when I describe the Evangelist as
'choosing' one form or combination of forms over against another, I
recognize that the degree of intentionality or self-conscious decision
making involved in such choices may reflect any point along a wide spectrum. It is to be assumed that some choices are made with a great deal of
care or deliberation, while some choices are made with no more conscious
thought than the intuitions of a competent storyteller, and some choices
are almost automatic in that they reflect strongly held linguistic conventions for particular contexts and combinations of words. Thompson's
observations on Matthew's redactional activity may be extended to his
lexical and syntactical choices:

> We may wonder how Matthew could have kept all these details in his head,
> as he combined the various stories into one coherent narrative. It seems

---

69. M.A.K. Halliday, 'A Brief Sketch of Systemic Grammar', in Kress (ed.),
System and Function, p. 3.

70. See, for example, Halliday, *Language as Social Semiotic*, pp. 108-26.

somewhat artificial and unrealistic. Perhaps he was not equally aware at all times of each thematic connection or each redactional technique. But the accumulated evidence suggests that such thoroughgoing editorial work cannot be attributed to a mere scribe. Somewhere between these two extremes we find the evangelist, an intelligent man who not only reacted to the material inherited from his sources but also created a new interpretation of the Gospel tradition for the community he served.[71]

Although the idea that Matthew was equally aware of every linguistic choice is similarly, in Thompson's terms, 'somewhat artificial and unrealistic', it is clear that the Gospel itself is the work of a thoughtful author, one who is responsible for the linguistic form in which the narrative reaches us, including choices of words and grammatical structures.

Theme. Within his notions of system and choice, Halliday's concept of thematic choice has particular significance for the study of sentence conjunctions. Using terminology derived from the Prague school, Halliday describes 'theme' as 'the element which serves as the point of departure of the message; it is that with which the clause is concerned'.[72] Halliday states that languages may differ in the way theme is indicated: Japanese, for example, uses the particle *-wa*, while English and many other languages make use of word order.[73] In English a thematic item is usually the first item in the sentence.

Halliday identifies three components of theme: experiential (or topical), interpersonal and textual. These correspond to his three metafunctions of language, the experiential or topical theme to the ideational metafunction, the interpersonal theme to the interpersonal metafunction, and the textual

71. W.G. Thompson, 'Reflections on the Composition of Mt 8.1–9.34', *CBQ* 33 (1971), pp. 387-88.

72. Halliday, *Introduction*, p. 37.

73. Halliday, *Introduction*, p. 37. Li and Thompson report, however, that 'the surface coding of the topic [equivalent to Halliday's "theme"] in all the languages we have examined always involves the sentence-initial position'. Even in Japanese and other languages with morpheme markers like the Japanese *-wa* 'the topic in these languages must remain in sentence-initial position'. They explain, 'The reason that the topic but not the [grammatical] subject must be in sentence-initial position may be understood in terms of discourse strategies. Since speech involves serialization of the information to be communicated, it makes sense that the topic, which represents the discourse theme, should be introduced first. The subject, being a more sentence-oriented notion, need not receive any priority in the serialization process' (C.N. Li and S.A. Thompson, 'Subject and Topic: A New Typology of Language', in C.N. Li [ed.], *Subject and Topic* [New York: Academic Press, 1976], p. 465).

theme to the textual metafunction. Halliday's topical theme is 'the first element that has a function in transitivity'.[74] Within the system of transitivity Halliday includes processes (typically verbal groups), participants (typically nominal groups) and circumstances (typically adverbial groups or prepositional phrases), which may be understood as roughly equivalent to traditional grammatical notions such as verb, subject, object, indirect object and adverb—in short, the 'core' of the sentence. These elements contribute to the clause's ideational (or experiential) function, 'its role as a means of representing patterns of experience'.[75] Halliday writes, 'Usually when people talk about what a word or a sentence "means", it is this kind of meaning they have in mind—meaning in the sense of content'.[76] The topical theme, then, is the first element of this type that appears in the sentence, and every clause has one such thematic element. For example, in the English sentence *Elizabeth wrote them a letter yesterday*, *Elizabeth* (a participant) is both the topical theme and the grammatical subject. In the sentence *Yesterday Elizabeth wrote them a letter*, *yesterday* (a circumstance) is the topical theme although *Elizabeth* is again the grammatical subject.

The clause may also have either an interpersonal theme or a textual theme or both. The interpersonal theme 'is any combination of (i) vocative, (ii) modal, (iii) mood-marking'.[77] It grammaticalizes the interpersonal metafunction of language, the enacting of social relationships, and is of little concern in this study of sentence conjunctions.[78] The textual theme, of prime consideration with respect to sentence conjunctions, 'is any combination of (i) continuative, (ii) structural and (iii) conjunctive, in that order' in English.[79] These elements have a textual metafunction, creating relevance to context.[80] In the sentence *Well anyway, yesterday Elizabeth wrote them a letter*, *well anyway* is the textual theme while *yesterday* remains the topical theme. Sentence conjunctions in the Greek of the New Testament may be described within Halliday's notion of textual theme.

74. Halliday, *Introduction*, p. 53.
75. Halliday, *Introduction*, p. 106.
76. Halliday, *Introduction*, p. 106.
77. Halliday, *Introduction*, p. 53.
78. The particle ἰδού is an example of an item which functions within Halliday's notion of 'interpersonal theme' in Matthew's narrative framework. By using ἰδού the speaker draws the audience's attention to what is being communicated.
79. Halliday, *Introduction*, p. 53.
80. See also Halliday, *Introduction*, pp. 323-30.

Textual theme and textual metafunction. As Halliday explains,

> The 'textual' function is not limited to the establishment of relations between sentences; it is concerned just as much with the internal organization of the sentence, with its meaning as a message both in itself and in relation to the context.[81]

Anyone who has used the 'move' or 'paste' command in a word processing program has no doubt had the experience of moving an existing sentence to a new context and finding that once it has been moved the sentence not only needs a different initial connective (*nevertheless*, for example, rather than *therefore*), but that internal adjustments need to be made as well, perhaps transferring a phrase from the beginning of the sentence to the end, or exchanging a noun for a pronoun or vice versa. This is an example of the textual function of language, whereby ideational components of the sentence, that is, participants, processes and circumstances, are manipulated and arranged to convey meaning as part of a coherent text.

Thus, although Halliday himself does not develop it fully, there is the potential in Hallidayan systemic-functional grammar for a correspondence between textual theme—in this case, sentence conjunctions in Matthew's Gospel—and 'the internal organization of the sentence', with both dimensions serving the same textual function. In fact, such a correspondence does occur in Matthew's narrative framework, as is evidenced in the characteristic collocations I identify in this study between particular conjunctions and systems such as thematization (that is, choice of topical theme), constituent order, and verbal tense-form.

Applicability. There is always some question concerning how transferable linguistic theories may be from one language to the next, in this case from English to Hellenistic Greek. Halliday observes that his *Introduction* is intended as a functional grammar of English, but that the ideas have also been used as a basis for studying other languages. 'But then', he cautions, 'you have to ask yourself: how would I have interpreted the grammar of this language if English had never existed?' Halliday warns against the errors of either extreme: on the one hand finding the same set of categories in other languages that were identified in English ('because if one looks for a particular category in a language one will usually find it: early European grammarians found pluperfect subjunctives in languages the

---

81. Halliday, *Explorations*, p. 107.

world over'), and on the other hand refusing to recognize any common characteristics at all.[82] With respect to thematization, for example, the Greek of the New Testament does appear to function in ways similar to English, exploiting linear word order by placing important elements toward the beginning of the sentence or clause.[83] Of course, there are likely to be differences as well. For example, the role of participles placed before the verb in Greek has yet to be systematically explored in terms of thematization.[84] The fact that speakers of Greek have the option of supplying an explicit subject with a verb or not doing so adds an additional dimension of choice concerning word order which does not occur in English. As well, the position of some sentence conjunctions as post-positives can have an effect on the order of different types of thematic elements in Greek.

Nonetheless, I adopt Halliday's systemic-functional approach as a working model for several reasons. First, his notions of system and choice are productive in identifying the various forms (and asyndeton) conjoining sentences in the Gospel of Matthew as a system of sentence conjunctions which alternate with each other and interact with other systems in the language. Secondly, his notion of multiple themes gives sentence conjunctions a place in the grammar of the sentence, while at the same time recognizing a difference between 'textual theme', or the role of forms like conjunctions in joining a clause to previous discourse, and the experiential component, or the core participants, processes and circumstances which make up the substance of the sentence viewed from a more traditional framework. Other grammarians have struggled to find a place for sentence conjunctions within sentence grammar, as I discuss with respect to

---

82. Halliday, *Introduction*, p. xxxiii.

83. See, for example, C.F.D. Moule, *An Idiom Book of New Testament Greek* (Cambridge: Cambridge University Press, 2nd edn, 1959), p. 166; F. Blass and A. Deb-runner, *A Greek Grammar of the New Testament and Other Early Christian Literature* (trans. R.W. Funk; Chicago: University of Chicago Press, 1961), §472. This is not meant to imply that English and Greek exploit word order in identical ways, but simply that the circumstance that thematization is expressed through word order in both languages allows Halliday's notions to be used as a starting point in investigating Greek syntax.

84. But see, for example, R. Hoyle, 'The "Scenario" Theory of Cognitive Linguistics, Its Relevance for Analysing New Testament Greek and Modern Parkari Texts, and Its Implications for Translation Theory' (PhD thesis, University of Surrey Roehampton, in preparation), who argues that clusters of participles can represent a stereotypical scenario for which the finite verb serves as a 'title'.

discourse analysis below. Thirdly, Halliday's distinction between various types of theme allows me to explore collocations between 'textual theme' (specifically the sentence conjunctions Matthew uses) and 'topical theme', or the first element in the transitivity structure of the sentence. I show that certain sentence conjunctions in Matthew's Gospel tend to combine with certain constituents in thematic position in the transitivity structure. Finally, Halliday's description of the textual metafunction of language, which concerns not just textual theme but the internal organization of the sentence, accounts for other collocations between sentence conjunctions and intrasentential features, such as constituent order and verbal tense-form.

Discourse Analysis

Although Halliday writes with an eye toward discourse function, his grammar is largely a grammar of the sentence. Since the role of sentence conjunctions is to connect clauses to previous text, any analysis of their function and meaning must take place above the sentence level, at the level of discourse. Only in this way does the contribution of sentence conjunctions in guiding the audience's comprehension of the unfolding discourse become apparent. The emergence of discourse analysis in the last 25 years or so has opened the door to the study of linguistic structures above the level of individual sentences and clauses. This has created an environment in which sentence conjunctions can be further explored.

Early discourse analysts recognized that a number of the challenges in explaining the function of various elements, word order choices, and other phenomena within sentences revealed the limitations of the sentence as the basic unit of syntax. Sinclair and Coulthard wrote in 1975, 'The recent progress of work in syntax suggests that an artificial ceiling has been reached. The clause, or the sentence, has had to cope with most of the interesting complexities that research has brought to light'.[85] Sinclair and Coulthard raise the question of where choices determining issues such as active versus passive constructions are 'located', that is, which unit or level of language determines the way clauses are put together. They predict that units above the sentence level will be found to affect many of these choices. Speaking of the choice *passive*, for example, they suggest, 'Maybe in due course some of its sphere of relevance will be located in discourse illocution, where it will be seen as one method of adjusting the

---

85. J.McH. Sinclair and R.M. Coulthard, *Towards an Analysis of Discourse: The English Used by Teachers and Pupils* (London: Oxford University Press, 1975), p. 121.

sequential presentation of information in the sentence and beyond'.[86] Their insight that choices in sentence construction are often determined by discourse-level considerations constraining the way information is presented is especially applicable to sentence conjunctions. Conjunctions signaling continuity, discontinuity or other procedural information are chosen to convey the relationship between preceding text and the sentence or larger discourse unit which follows, even though the conjunction itself lies within the contour of the sentence as traditionally understood.

Discourse analysts were aware from an early date that sentence conjunctions resisted treatment within sentence grammars. Dik (1972) asserts that coordination and coordinating forms cannot be adequately treated in the sentence descriptions of Chomsky and his followers in transformational-generative grammar. Dik suggests that in fact the description of coordination 'may well be regarded as a test-case for transformational theory'.[87] As part of his system for analyzing sentences in their discourse context, Grimes (1975) recommends constructing a separate column which he labels 'the PLP column, for Pesky Little Particle'. He explains, 'Most languages have particles whose use seems to be related to gluing the parts of discourses together but which are never easy to pin down'.[88] Stubbs (1983) also observes that sentence conjunctions are among the issues that cannot be adequately explained within the syntax of the sentence.[89]

> Almost by definition conjunctions cannot be fully dealt with within syntax, since they are not really part of the structure of syntactic units. They have rather a sequencing function of relating syntactic units and fitting them into a textual or discourse context.[90]

Although Halliday manages to describe sentence conjunctions within the grammar of the sentence, he does so through his concept of multiple themes, separating textual theme, or sentence conjunctions and other forms which join the clause to previous discourse, from the experiential component, or the participants, processes and circumstances which make up the referential core of the sentence. Although he recognizes that textual

---

86. Sinclair and Coulthard, *Discourse*, p. 122.

87. S.C. Dik, *Coordination: Its Implications for the Theory of General Linguistics* (Amsterdam: North-Holland Publishing Company, 1972), p. 4.

88. J.E. Grimes, *The Thread of Discourse* (Janua Linguarum Series Minor, 207; The Hague: Moulton, 1975), p. 93.

89. M. Stubbs, *Discourse Analysis: The Sociolinguistic Analysis of Natural Language* (Language in Society, 4; Oxford: Basil Blackwell, 1983), p. 77.

90. Stubbs, *Discourse Analysis*, p. 78.

meaning 'is not limited to the establishment of relations between sentences', but 'is concerned just as much with the internal organization of the
sentence',[91] he does little to develop the integration between textual theme
and other systems within the sentence.

I show that particular sentence conjunctions in Matthew's Gospel (that
is, textual theme in Halliday's terms) tend to combine with particular
thematic choices (that is, Halliday's topical theme) as well as with other
systems within the sentence. I do not believe that sentence conjunction and
thematization, for example, are interacting with each other as much as that
they reflect in parallel ways functional choices made on the basis of
discourse context. Choices both of sentence conjunction and of thematization are located above the sentence, at the level of discourse. Similar
dynamics are in play in choices of, *inter alia*, constituent order and verbal
tense-form. Despite a sometimes bewildering array of approaches, the rise
of discourse analysis with its emphasis on linguistic units above the level
of the sentence and its awareness that sentence conjunctions cannot
adequately be explained merely within sentence grammar offers further
justification for looking at discourse-level issues in describing the function
of sentence conjunctions.

Summary

I have described certain developments in linguistic theory over the past
hundred years and some of the resulting implications for the study of
sentence conjunctions in the New Testament. De Saussure's emphasis on
synchronic over against diachronic analysis motivates the study of conjunctions in Hellenistic Greek on their own terms rather than as merely the
development—or degeneration—of Classical Greek. His understanding of
language as based on relations, both among elements within the sentence
and among elements which alternate with each other in the same 'slot' in
the sentence, provides a foundation for systemic approaches to grammar
such as that developed by Halliday. Linguists in the European functional
tradition of the Prague school also contribute to Halliday's systemic-
functional grammar. Halliday's notions of system and choice, recognizing
that speakers are continually engaged in a series of interrelated, functionally motivated choices, is formalized in the grammar by the concept of
a system network. Halliday's insights lead me to treat sentence conjunctions—plus asyndeton—as a conjunctive system within the Greek of the

---

91. Halliday, *Explorations*, p. 107.

New Testament, under Halliday's notion of 'textual theme', and allow the interaction between this system and other lexico-grammatical systems to be explored. Alongside Halliday, the rise of discourse analysis with its emphasis on linguistic units above the level of the sentence, and its awareness that sentence conjunctions cannot adequately be explained within sentence grammar, offers further justification for looking at discourse-level issues in describing the function of sentence conjunctions.

Each of these streams contributes to an approach to sentence conjunctions which is synchronic, systemic-functional and discourse-centered. In effect they define the parameters within which the study of sentence conjunctions may take place. However, they do little to address the central question, namely, what do various sentence conjunctions 'mean'? In Chapter 2 I address the kind of meaning conveyed by sentence conjunctions.

Chapter 2

WHAT DO SENTENCE CONJUNCTIONS 'MEAN'?

This part of Grammar has been, perhaps, as much neglected, as some others over-diligently cultivated. 'Tis easy for Men to write, one after another, of Cases and Genders, Moods and Tenses, Gerunds and Supines...yet he who would shew the right use of Particles, and what significancy and force they have, must take a little more pains, enter into his own Thoughts, and observe nicely the several Postures of his Mind in discoursing.[1]

Recent Studies

The linguistic streams described in the previous chapter define the parameters within which this study of sentence conjunctions proceeds. The approach to sentence conjunctions taken here is synchronic, systemic-functional and discourse-centered. However, the question remains: what do sentence conjunctions 'mean'?

Only relatively recently have the words which connect propositions in discourse received much attention in general linguistic research. Halliday and Hasan's seminal work, *Cohesion in English* (1976), lists conjunction as one of five types of cohesion, providing 'a set of semantic resources for linking a sentence with what has gone before it' (the others being reference, substitution, ellipsis and lexical cohesion).[2] Van Dijk (1977) comments that 'discourse connectives have hardly been studied in a systematic way', and is himself a pioneer in the recognition that natural language connectives have both semantic and pragmatic dimensions.[3]

1. J. Locke, *An Essay Concerning Human Understanding* (ed. P.H. Nidditch; Oxford: Clarendon Press, 1975), p. 472.

2. M.A.K. Halliday and R. Hasan, *Cohesion in English* (London: Longman, 1976), p. 10.

3. T.A. van Dijk, *Text and Context: Explorations in the Semantics and Pragmatics of Discourse* (Longman Linguistics Library, 12; London: Longman, 1977), pp. 9-10.

Levinson (1983) writes, 'It is generally conceded that [utterance-initial connectives] have at least a component of meaning that resists truth-conditional treatment ... We still await proper studies of these terms'.[4] In the mid-1980s, two important analyses appeared: Schiffrin's study of discourse markers in informal conversation, within which she includes discourse connectives such as *and*, *but* and *or*,[5] and Blakemore's treatment of discourse connectives as 'semantic constraints on relevance', which explores the role of conjunctions such as *but* within the framework of Relevance Theory (more on Relevance Theory and Blakemore's work below).[6]

Subsequently, the 1990s saw a flurry of research on conjunctions and other discourse markers, prompting one linguist to describe their study as a 'growth industry' in linguistic research.[7] A number of studies explore the

4. S.C. Levinson, *Pragmatics* (CTL; Cambridge: Cambridge University Press, 1983), p. 88.

5. See D. Schiffrin, 'Functions of *And* in Discourse', *Journal of Pragmatics* 10 (1986), pp. 41-66; and *Discourse Markers* (Cambridge: Cambridge University Press, 1987).

6. See D. Blakemore, *Semantic Constraints on Relevance* (Oxford: Basil Blackwell, 1987).

7. B. Fraser, 'Contrastive Discourse Markers in English', in A.H. Jucker and Y. Ziv (eds.), *Discourse Markers: Descriptions and Theory* (Pragmatics and Beyond NS 57; Amsterdam: John Benjamins, 1998), p. 301; see also Fraser, 'What Are Discourse Markers?', p. 932. For a recent comprehensive 'tutorial overview' of linguistic studies of discourse markers, see L. Shoroup, 'Discourse Markers', *Lingua* 107 (1999), pp. 227-65. As representative of such studies, see, for example, G. Redeker, 'Ideational and Pragmatic Markers of Discourse Structure', *Journal of Pragmatics* 14 (1990), pp. 367-81; B. Fraser, 'An Approach to Discourse Markers', *Journal of Pragmatics* 14 (1990), pp. 383-95; M.J. Schleppegrell, 'Paratactic *because*', *Journal of Pragmatics* 16 (1991), pp. 323-37; G. Redeker, 'Linguistic Markers of Discourse Structure', *Linguistics* 29 (1991), pp. 1139-72; V. Rouchota, 'Discourse Connectives: What Do They Link?', *UCL Working Papers in Linguistics* 8 (1996), pp. 199-212; C. Unger, 'The Scope of Discourse Connectives: Implications for Discourse Organization', *Journal of Linguistics* 32 (1996), pp. 403-38; Kroon, 'Discourse Markers'; J.D. Murray, 'Connectives and Narrative Text: The Role of Continuity', *Memory & Cognition* 25 (1997), pp. 227-36; R. Risselada and W. Spooren (eds.), 'Special Issue on: "Discourse Markers and Coherence Relations"', *Journal of Pragmatics* 30 (1998); A. Georgakopoulou and D. Goutsos, 'Conjunctions versus Discourse Markers in Greek: The Interaction of Frequency, Position, and Functions in Context', *Linguistics* 36 (1998), pp. 887-917; M.-B.M. Hansen, *The Function of Discourse Particles: A Study with Special Reference to Spoken Standard French* (Pragmatics and Beyond NS 53; Amsterdam: John Benjamins, 1998); M.-B.M. Hansen, 'The Semantics Status of

role connective words play in the cognitive processes of discourse comprehension. Representative of such psycholinguistic research is that of Segal, Duchan and Scott, a series of experiments in which adults were asked to read a set of simple narratives with and without connectives such as *and* and *then* or their logical cognates, 'additive' and 'temporal', supplied between sentences;[8] or the work of Millis and Just, four experiments investigating whether the presence of a connective like *because* between two clauses decreased reading time for the second statement and led to faster and more accurate responses to comprehension questions.[9]

Theorists such as Halliday and Hasan, Schiffrin, Blakemore and others have made significant contributions to the question, 'What do conjunctions in discourse "mean"?', while the work of those such as Segal *et al.*, and Millis and Just has helped to provide an empirical basis for testing and evaluating such theories. Those interested in the Greek of the New Testament must pick their way warily through these studies since, apart from the obvious potential problems in applying work done largely on English to Hellenistic Greek, recent research tends to focus on spontaneous informal conversation or simple narrative and may not be fully applicable to a more complex written text like a Gospel. However, with this caveat, research into whether conjunctions in English and other languages carry meaning of their own, and if so what kind, how much and over what scope, offers a useful starting point for the study of sentence conjunctions in the Gospels.

What Do Conjunctions Add to Discourse?

The most basic issue concerning what sentence conjunctions 'mean' is whether they add anything at all to the total semantic meaning of the propositions they connect, or whether they are merely structural elements of some kind. As Dik observes, 'The question as to whether particles like

Discourse Markers', *Lingua* 104 (1998), pp. 235-60.

8.   E.M. Segal, J.F. Duchan and P.J. Scott, 'The Role of Interclausal Connectives in Narrative Structuring: Evidence From Adults' Interpretations of Simple Stories', *Discourse Processes* 14 (1991), pp. 27-54. See also K.K. Millis, J.M. Golding and G. Barker, 'Causal Connectives Increase Inference Generation', *Discourse Processes* 20 (1995), pp. 29-49.

9.   K.K. Millis and M.A. Just, 'The Influence of Connectives on Sentence Comprehension', *Journal of Memory and Language* 33 (1994), pp. 128-47. See also Millis, Golding and Barker, 'Causal Connectives'.

prepositions, articles, and connectives have meaning (and if so, what kind of meaning) has been a moot point since antiquity', going back at least as far as Aristotle's contention that 'syndesmoi' (used in a much wider sense than 'conjunctions') are 'meaningless sounds'.[10]

Content Words vs. Function Words: 'Truth-conditional' vs. 'Non-truth-conditional'

There has long been an intuitive recognition that words and morphemes fall into two basic categories: forms such as nouns and verbs that convey the ideational or propositional content of a message, and forms such as conjunctions, prepositions and other particles that serve primarily to relate those ideas to each other.[11] As Jespersen puts it, 'Articles, particles, prepositions, auxiliaries … act as policemen and direct each of the other words to its proper place in the brain of the hearer so as to facilitate orderly understanding'.[12] Grammarians have sought to distinguish these

10. Dik, *Coordination*, p. 250. In addition to nominal and verbal forms (ὄνομα and ῥῆμα), Aristotle speaks of σύνδεσμοι, a designation which includes various connective particles as well as prepositions and other unspecified items: Σύνδεσμος δὲ ἐστιν φωνὴ ἄσημος ἢ οὔτε κωλύει οὔτε ποιεῖ φωνὴν μίαν σημαντικὴν ἐκ πλειόνων φωνῶν … 'A σύνδεσμος is a meaningless sound, which neither prevents nor creates a single significant sound out of several sounds' (Aristotle, *Aristotle*. XXIII. *The Poetics*, 20.6-7 [LCL, 199; London: William Heinemann, 1982], pp. 76-77). See also R.H. Robins, *A Short History of Linguistics* (London: Longman, 2nd edn, 1979), p. 26. For an overview of ways particles have been classified by grammarians from antiquity through the sixteenth century, see D.M. Schenkeveld, 'From Particula to Particle—The Genesis of a Class of Words', in I. Rosier (ed.), *L'Héritage des grammairiens latins de l'antiquité aux lumières: Actes du Colloque de Chantilly, 2-4 Septembre 1987* (Paris: Société pour l'information grammaticale, 1988), pp. 81-93.

11. Dionysius Thrax (c. 100 BCE) describes σύνδεσμοι, within which he includes καί, δέ and other conjunctions (συμπλεκτικοί), as words which bind the meaning of a passage together in an orderly way and fill gaps in its interpretation: Σύνδεσμός ἐστι λέξις συνδέουσα διάνοιαν μετὰ τάξεως καὶ τὸ τῆς ἑρμηνείας κεχηνὸς πληροῦσα (Dionysius Thrax, *Grammatike*, 25, in I. Bekkeri, *Anecdota Graeca*. II [Berlin: G. Reimer, 1816], p. 642). See also Robins, *History*, pp. 33-34.

12. O. Jespersen, ' "Monosyllabism in English", the Biennial Lecture on English Philology, read before the British Academy, Nov. 6, 1928', citation in Rijksbaron, 'Introduction', p. 1. Rijksbaron adds, 'Jespersen compared the function of particles and other "grammatical words" with that of policemen controlling the traffic, a daring but appropriate comparison. Without particles human communication would of course still be possible, but soon look like the traffic in Cairo at rush-hour' (Rijksbaron, 'Introduction', p. 14).

aspects of communication in various ways, labeling them 'content-oriented vs. functional', 'lexical vs. grammatical', 'truth-conditional vs. non-truth-conditional', and so on.

Thus in the English sentence, 'You don't know about me without you have read a book by the name of *The Adventures of Tom Sawyer'*, the words *you, know, me, read, book, name, adventures* and *Tom Sawyer* are understood to be truth-conditional.[13] The words *about, without, a, by, the* and *of* are non-truth-conditional, serving to indicate the relations among the concepts implied by the other words.[14] Similarly, in the Greek sentence in Jn 3.16, οὕτως γὰρ ἠγάπησεν ὁ θεὸς τὸν κόσμον, ὥστε τὸν υἱὸν τὸν μονογενῆ ἔδωκεν, ἵνα πᾶς ὁ πιστεύων εἰς αὐτὸν μὴ ἀπόληται ἀλλ᾽ ἔχῃ ζωὴν αἰώνιον, truth-conditional forms include ἠγάπησεν, θεός, κόσμον, υἱόν, μονογενῆ, and ἔδωκεν, while non-truth-conditional forms include γάρ, ὥστε, ἵνα, εἰς, and morphological variations of the article.[15] In this twofold division sentence conjunctions such as καί and δέ are function words rather than content words, that is, non-truth-conditional as opposed to truth-conditional, joining propositions rather than adding propositional substance of their own.

Pragmatic Inferences: Minimalist vs. Maximalist Perspectives
But if the role of sentence conjunctions as 'function' words is to relate ideas in the message rather than add truth-conditional content, the question of how the reader or hearer knows what relationship is being communicated remains. Does the reader recognize a semantic relationship that already exists between the juxtaposed propositions, does the conjunction itself create a relationship, or do context and the specific conjunction work together in some way?

It is now a basic assumption of functionally oriented linguists to recognize the interplay between text and co-text (linguistic context), and between text and context ('real life' situation), in the ways people interpret linguistic communication. Both dimensions may be referred to more generally as 'context'. Schiffrin points out that discourse analysts tend to

13. M. Twain, *The Adventures of Huckleberry Finn* (New York: Grosset & Dunlap, 1994), p. 1.

14. The treatment of verbal auxiliaries such as *don't* and *have* varies among grammarians.

15. To keep this illustration simple, I am ignoring such issues as case endings on nouns, which could be said to be non-truth-conditional, and markers of person and number, in verbs, which could generally be described as truth-conditional.

take either a minimalist or maximalist approach to the semantics of discourse connectives in describing the inferences readers and hearers make on the basis of conjunctions and similar forms, depending on how heavily they weight the role of context.

> These two perspectives differ because they reverse the division of labor inherent in the communication of utterance meaning. The minimalist view reduces the signaling load of the referential meaning of a particular form, and increases the role of pragmatic principles governing use of that form in context. The maximalist view reverses that division of labor.[16]

In other words, a minimalist assigns a smaller role to a particular sentence conjunction, and places more importance on context in working out the semantic relationship between the sentences it conjoins, while a maximalist assumes a more specific or determinative meaning (or a range of possible meanings) for the conjunction, and places relatively less emphasis on the role of context.

The distinction between minimalist and maximalist perspectives becomes important when one tries to describe how a conjunction like καί or δέ contributes to or circumscribes the meaning of conjoined sentences. Take, for example, Mk 12.12, καὶ ἐζήτουν αὐτὸν κρατῆσαι, καὶ ἐφοβήθησαν τὸν ὄχλον ..., where the semantic relationship between the two clauses appears to be adversative: 'And they sought to arrest him, *but* (or *and yet*) they feared the crowd.' While the first καί (καὶ ἐζήτουν) would generally be considered a simple coordinator, the role of the second καί (καὶ ἐφοβήθησαν) would be the subject of some debate. The question for the New Testament exegete is: 'How does one know what the relationship between the two propositions is?' Does the presence of καί as a potentially 'adversative' conjunction cue the audience to look for the possibility of an adversative relationship, or does an adversative relationship between the two propositions lead the audience to assign an adversative sense to καί? Or is something else going on?

A maximalist view would say that καί has a specific meaning which the reader recognizes as defining the semantic relationship between two clauses. In the case of an ambiguous form like καί which the maximalist would say has the potential to indicate several different semantic relations—for example, additive, adjunctive, adversative, or ascensive— the appropriate one is recognized by the reader or hearer as being compatible with the meanings of the sentences it conjoins, which in the

---

16. Schiffrin, '*And*', p. 47.

example above would be 'adversative καί'. A minimalist view would say that καί has a basic low-level content that can be used in a wide range of circumstances with a variety of communicative effects, because pragmatic principles will lead to differing interpretations in different contexts. That καί appears here in a context of contrast does not reflect an ambiguity in the meaning of καί, which simply indicates a conjoined relationship between the two clauses. The conclusion that the two clauses are to some measure in an adversative semantic relationship is worked out by inferences made on the basis of the clauses themselves.[17] Schiffrin notes that both minimalist and maximalist approaches acknowledge that the semantic value of a conjunction and the meanings of the propositions it links interact in some way, so that both the conjunction itself and the context are important in analyzing the total communicative meaning of utterances. The difference lies in their understanding of the role of context in analyzing conjunctions.[18]

Halliday and Hasan take a strongly minimalist perspective that might be described as an 'empty' view of conjunctions. They argue that conjunctions add little or nothing to the combined meaning of two propositions, rather that 'it is the underlying semantic relation ... that actually has the cohesive power'.[19] Schiffrin herself supports a minimalist view, in which 'context is a source of inferences which interact with the minimal (e.g. logical) meaning contributed by the connective; context thus leads to the pairing of *and* with certain speaker-meanings'.[20] However, in her research on discourse connectives in informal conversation in English,

17. See, further, the discussion of 'adversative' καί in Chapter 4.

18. Schiffrin, '*And*', p. 47.

19. Halliday and Hasan, *Cohesion*, p. 229. However, in his *Introduction to Functional Grammar*, Halliday appears to take a more 'maximalist' perspective, writing with respect to conjunction as a means of cohesion in English sentences that a range of possible logical-semantic relations 'is expressed by the choice of a conjunctive Adjunct (an adverbial group or prepositional phrase), or of one of a small set of conjunctions *and, or, nor, but, yet, so, then* ...' (Halliday, *Introduction*, p. 324). He states that 'the headings that may be found useful for most purposes of analysis [of conjunctive relations] are the general ones of appositive, clarificative; additive, adversative, variative; temporal, comparative, causal, conditional, concessive, matter' (Halliday, *Introduction*, p. 330). Schiffrin herself observes that in *Cohesion in English* 'Halliday and Hasan's ... analysis of *and* as a cohesive tie equivocates between minimalist and maximalist views' (Schiffrin, *Discourse Markers*, p. 182; see also, Schiffrin, '*And*', p. 46).

20. Schiffrin, '*And*', p. 47.

Schiffrin comes to the conclusion that rather than merely reflecting semantic relationships, 'markers *select* a meaning relation from whatever potential meanings are provided through the content of talk, and then *display* that relation'.[21] This gives the conjunctive form a larger role than that described by Halliday and Hasan.

Although Schiffrin does not make the idea of selection more explicit, this concept of selection and its implications for authorial intent is important in the study of sentence conjunctions in the New Testament. It is not the words themselves, of course, that 'select' a relationship, it is the speaker or writer who chooses to use one conjunction over against another acceptable alternative, thereby selecting which of the potential relationships within discourse she or he wants to display. In the attempt to recover as much of a Gospel writer's intended meaning as possible, the interpreter seeks to determine which textual relationship the Evangelist has chosen to display in a given context using the conjunctive devices available in Hellenistic Greek and following the habits of his own style.[22]

As Schiffrin's research is specifically oriented toward spontaneous conversation, I turn to Dik's more general work on coordination to articulate a minimalist perspective which may be more broadly applicable. Dik suggests, 'From the point of view of natural language, we can say that a word like *and* is a multiple-purpose tool of low semantic specificity, used to combine semantic aspects which, in their final interpretation, may be characterized by a variety of different relations'.[23] By acknowledging that conjunctions have minimal conventional semantic values which restrict what can be coordinated, Dik's view, as Schiffrin points out, is a somewhat stronger claim than that which Halliday and Hasan make.[24] At the same time, his description of conjunctions as 'multiple-purpose tools of low semantic specificity' allows for each conjunction to be used in a variety of contexts, reflecting the fact that natural language as an open

---

21. Schiffrin, *Discourse Markers*, p. 318 (her emphasis).

22. I will argue that with respect to sentence conjunctions the choice is not between various logical (that is, semantic) relations, but between the portrayal of continuity, discontinuity, or more specialized procedural relations.

23. Dik, *Coordination*, p. 269. Dik goes on to distinguish four basic semantic values for coordinators: combinatory (or copulative), alternative, adversative, and causal (Dik, *Coordination*, pp. 271-81), an approach which differs from the procedural semantics for sentence conjunctions I adopt below.

24. Schiffrin, *'And'*, p. 1.

system 'constitutes a finite means applicable to an infinite variety of different communicative situations'.[25]

Traditional Grammarians
At the risk of reading later linguistic issues back into earlier grammatical studies, a range of minimalist and maximalist perspectives can be observed in the different treatments of sentence conjunctions in the standard reference grammars for the Greek of the New Testament, although the role of context tends to be underdeveloped. Taking something very close to a maximalist approach, Winer writes, 'Conjunctions…are divided into classes according to the kind of connexion expressed. These classes are the same in every cultivated language, and are eight in number.'[26] When Blass, Debrunner and Funk state that coordinating conjunctions may be categorized 'according to the relationships they imply' as copulative, disjunctive, adversative, consecutive, causal or concessive, they also appear to assign the major role in determining the relationship between clauses to the conjunction itself.[27] On the other hand, Dana and Mantey claim that καί is usually 'a mere colorless copulative giving no additional meaning to the words preceding or following', expressing, at least for καί, a strongly minimalist viewpoint similar to that of Halliday and Hasan.[28] At the same time they acknowledge that some conjunctions do add a modest amount of meaning to propositions: 'The meaning of a sentence following a conjunction, and often times of a whole paragraph, is suggested or colored by the connective'.[29] Robertson seems to say that rather than 'suggesting' or 'coloring' relations between clauses, conjunctions make those relationships explicit: 'The Greeks, especially in the literary style, felt the propriety of indicating the inner relation of the various independent sentences that composed a paragraph. This was not merely an artistic device, but a logical expression of coherence of

25. Dik, *Coordination*, p. 251.
26. Winer, *Treatise*, p. 541. In a footnote Moulton observes that Krüger, whom Winer cites in reference to the classification of conjunctions (*Sprachlehre*, 4th edn, 1861-62, p. 345), 'now has *nine* classes,—copulative, disjunctive, adversative, comparative, hypothetical, temporal, final, consecutive, and causal conjunctions' (Winer, *Treatise*, p. 541 n. 1; Moulton's emphasis).
27. BDF, §438.
28. H.E. Dana and J.R. Mantey, *A Manual Grammar of the Greek New Testament* (Toronto: Macmillan, 1927), p. 239.
29. Dana and Mantey, *Grammar*, p. 240.

thought.'[30] Robertson appears to take a more minimalist perspective echoing Schiffrin's 'select and display' approach.[31]

Several recent intermediate grammars assign a relatively large role to conjunctions in conveying logical relations between coordinated sentences. That is, they may be seen as taking a more maximalist approach to sentence conjunctions. Young writes, 'The New Testament writers follow the classical practice of using conjunctions to indicate semantic relations between sentences and paragraphs'.[32] Porter, treating conjunctions as a subset of particles, defines a particle as an indeclinable word 'used for the purpose of introducing subjective semantic nuances (i.e. nuances of meaning) to a clause or to the relationship between clauses'. For each conjunction or other particle he offers one or more classificatory semantic labels—for example, adversative, causal, comparative, conditional, connective, consecutive, emphatic, explanatory, inferential and temporal—indicating the nature of the relationship expressed.[33] Wallace states that 'logical connectives', within which he includes most coordinate conjunctions, 'relate the movement of thought from one passage to another by expressing logical relationships between the connected ideas'. His semantic categories include ascensive, connective, contrastive, correlative, disjunctive, emphatic, explanatory, inferential and transitional.[34] Wallace warns New Testament exegetes, however, that in trying to determine the semantic connection between two sets of ideas linked by a conjunction, it is often the case that 'more than one possible connection exists. When this situation occurs, context and authorial expression are two key ways to determine the most likely connection.' Although Wallace recognizes the role of context, his approach is still essentially maximalist, in that the interpreter seeks to determine *ex post facto* which of the alternative meanings conveyed by a single polysemous conjunction is consistent with the context: 'When there are several possible connections, try to be aware

30. Robertson, *Grammar*, p. 443.

31. 'We moderns do not feel the same need for connecting-particles between independent sentences. The ancient Greeks loved to point out these delicate *nuances*' (Robertson, *Grammar*, p. 1192 [his emphasis]).

32. R.A. Young, *Intermediate New Testament Greek: A Linguistic and Exegetical Approach* (Nashville: Broadman & Holman, 1994), p. 179.

33. S.E. Porter, *Idioms of the Greek New Testament* (Biblical Languages: Greek, 2; Sheffield: Sheffield Academic Press, 2nd edn, 1994), pp. 204-205.

34. D.B. Wallace, *Greek Grammar Beyond the Basics: An Exegetical Syntax of the New Testament* (Grand Rapids: Zondervan, 1996), pp. 670-74.

of the options. Test each option with an interpretive translation in determining the best one.'[35] This leaves Wallace categorizing καί and δέ first as 'connective (continuative, coordinate)' and then as 'contrastive (adversative)' ('if indicated by context'), abandoning the attempt to find a unified function for either which might explain its use in such a variety of contexts.[36]

Summary and Conclusions

I have examined the question of whether sentence conjunctions add anything at all to the total semantic meaning of the propositions they connect. Discourse analysts tend to take either a minimalist or maximalist approach to the semantics of discourse connectives, depending on how heavily they weight the role of context. A minimalist view would say that a form like *and* has a basic low-level content that can be used in a variety of semantic contexts, while a maximalist view would say that a sentence conjunction has a more specific meaning (or several such meanings) which the reader recognizes as defining the semantic relationship between two clauses. A range of minimalist and maximalist perspectives can be found in differing treatments of sentence conjunctions in Greek grammars of the nineteenth and twentieth centuries.

I follow Dik and Schiffrin in taking a minimalist view of the role of sentence conjunctions in discourse, a perspective which acknowledges that some contribution is made by an individual conjunction while recognizing that the minimal semantic value of each form permits it to be used in a range of discourse contexts.[37] This makes allowance for the variety of semantic relationships between conjoined propositions in the New Testament recognized by Greek grammarians and reflected in their wide-

35. Wallace, *Grammar*, p. 668.
36. See Wallace, *Grammar*, p. 671.
37. I do not, however, make the *a priori* assumption that every form must have one and only one minimal semantic value. Empirically this does appear to be the case with Matthew's use of καί, δέ, γάρ, οὖν and (less clearly) τότε, but, as I show in Chapter 6, asyndetic sentences fall into two broad groups, suggesting that asyndeton in Matthew's narrative framework can have either of two minimal semantic values, when combined with differing contextual features. In allowing for the possibility of multiple meanings, I am in sympathy with Hansen's proposal of a 'third alternative' to minimalism and maximalism, which she refers to as 'polysemy' or a kind of 'methodical minimalism', seeking 'as far as possible to maintain the minimalist assumption of a common core meaning, while aiming for relative precision of description' (Hansen, *Discourse Particles*, pp. 87-88).

ranging characterizations of words like καί and δέ. I will adopt Dik's brief definition of coordinators as 'multiple-purpose tools of low semantic specificity' as a basis for my analysis of sentence conjunctions in the Gospel of Matthew. I accept that sentence conjunctions in Matthew's Gospel do add meaning to discourse, but that hearers and readers use both a particular conjunctive form and the linguistic co-text in which it appears to generate inferences about the Evangelist's total communicative intent.

Assuming that sentence conjunctions do carry some meaning, even if minimal, the next question is what the nature of that meaning may be.

What Kind of Meaning Do Conjunctions Convey?

Procedural vs. Conceptual Meaning

As I described above, grammarians have long recognized that words and morphemes fall into two basic categories: forms such as nouns and verbs that convey the ideational or propositional content of a message, and forms including sentence conjunctions that serve primarily to relate those ideas to each other. These aspects of communication have been labeled 'content-oriented vs. functional', 'lexical vs. grammatical', 'truth-conditional vs. non-truth-conditional', and so on. 'Function' words like sentence conjunctions are understood to be non-truth-conditional or non-conceptual, which may suggest that they have little or no semantic value. However, sentence conjunctions do carry meaning—although they have 'low semantic specificity'—which allows readers or hearers to make different pragmatic inferences about the author's communicative intent in different contexts. If, then, sentence conjunctions have semantic value but are not truth-conditional or conceptual, what kind of meaning do they convey?

Blakemore breaks new ground by pointing out that communicators can use particles such as conjunctions to guide the ways their hearers make inferences in processing discourse. She develops a distinction in lexical semantics between 'conceptual' and 'procedural' meaning, describing discourse connectives such as *but*, *and*, *moreover*, or *so* as non-truth-conditional forms whose contribution to discourse is to provide processing instructions rather than propositional content. She suggests a 'non-unitary theory of linguistic semantics':

> On the one hand, there is the essentially *conceptual* theory that deals with
> the way in which elements of linguistic structure map onto concepts—that
> is, onto constituents of propositional representations that undergo

computations. On the other, there is the essentially *procedural* theory that deals with the way in which elements of linguistic structure map directly onto computations themselves—that is, onto mental processes.[38]

In this schema the semantic value of sentence conjunctions is procedural, making a contribution to mental processes in discourse comprehension. Blakemore observes that in pragmatic theories of communication there can be a tendency to describe linguistic content as contributing conceptual or propositional meaning while assuming that inferences about the interdependence of propositions are derived from extra-linguistic input.[39] She is at pains to point out that linguistic forms can in fact encode either conceptual input (truth-conditional meaning) or information about how to process or relate concepts to each other (non-truth-conditional).

Developing this distinction further, Wilson and Sperber maintain that discourse connectives should be described more specifically as both procedural *and* non-truth-conditional since it is possible for a form to be one but not the other.[40] They argue that conceptual/procedural and truth-conditional/non-truth-conditional distinctions do not describe the same things, but that both should be applied to linguistic forms, and further that the two distinctions 'cross-cut' each other, so that four combinations are possible.[41] The idea of procedural as opposed to conceptual meaning will

38. Blakemore, *Semantic Constraints*, p. 144 (her emphasis). See also R. Blass, *Relevance Relations in Discourse: A Study with Special Reference to Sissala* (Cambridge: Cambridge University Press, 1990), especially Chapter 4, 'Constraints on relevance and particle typology'.

39. '[T]he idea that there are aspects of utterance interpretation that are determined by general pragmatic principles has often led to the conflation of linguistic semantics and propositional (or truth-conditional) semantics so that, on the one hand it is assumed that linguistic meaning cannot determine non-truth-conditional aspects of utterance interpretations, while on the other, it is assumed that pragmatic principles cannot play a role in determining the propositional content of utterances' (Blakemore, *Semantic Constraints*, p. 72).

40. See D. Wilson and D. Sperber, 'Linguistic Form and Relevance', *Lingua* 90 (1993), pp. 1-2, 19-20.

41. Their four logically possible types of meaning and examples of each include: conceptual and truth-conditional (most regular 'content' words, for example, nouns, verbs and adjectives); conceptual and non-truth-conditional (various types of sentence adverbials, such as *seriously* or *frankly*, as in *Seriously, I thought the play was too long*, 'elements of conceptual representations which can be true or false in their own right'—that is, the speaker may or may not actually be serious—but which encode concepts that are not part of the sentence they modify); procedural and truth-conditional (personal pronouns such as *I* and *you*, which 'guide the search for the

be developed further in the following sections. But simply stated, in Wilson and Sperber's terms sentence-initial καί would be one of those 'expressions whose function is not so much to encode a concept as to indicate how to "take" the sentence or phrase in which they occur...'[42]

Relevance Theory. Blakemore's analysis rests on the framework of Relevance Theory developed by Wilson and Sperber.[43] They in turn build on the work of Grice, who was one of the first to suggest that much of the process of making sense of conversation—and, by extension, other discourse—relies on the hearer making a number of pragmatic inferences not about the linguistic content of individual propositions (the logical content, one might say, of sentences), but about how the speaker intends his or her statements to be taken. In Grice's view, both the speaker and the

intended referent', that is, which provide procedural information leading the audience to access the correct person or thing for which the form stands in that particular context); and procedural and non-truth-conditional (discourse connectives—of which sentence conjunctions are a type—which 'guide the search for intended contexts and contextual effects'). Words in the last category help hearers recognize which relationships between propositions are intended by the speaker, but they do not add conceptual content to those propositions (Wilson and Sperber, 'Linguistic Form and Relevance', pp. 16-21).

42. Wilson and Sperber, 'Linguistic Form and Relevance', p. 11.

43. See D. Sperber and D. Wilson, *Relevance: Communication and Cognition* (Oxford: Basil Blackwell, 2nd edn, 1995). As I stated earlier, those interested in the Greek of the New Testament must be discriminating about applying to biblical texts research such as that of Sperber and Wilson which tends to focus on spontaneous informal conversation or simple narrative. A more serious concern is that Relevance Theory, as its authors acknowledge, 'has been developed from the point of view of the *audience* of communicative acts... The cognitive processes at work in the *communicator* ... are, of course, essential to the wider picture ...' (Sperber and Wilson, *Relevance*, p. 279; my emphases). It is my assumption that in the study of the Gospels methodological priority should be given to the attempt to recover the communicative intent of the author(s) or redactor(s). In this study I am not as interested in the inferential processes audiences may have undertaken in reading Matthew's Gospel at various points in history, as I am in the inferential processes the author *expected* his intended audience to undertake based on the conventions of the language as then in use. In particular I am interested in the ways he may have used sentence conjunctions as part of the linguistic code available to him to guide those inferences. Fortunately the New Testament scholar need not adopt all the fine points of Relevance Theory—nor perhaps even the basic formulation that *all* communication is geared to the maximization of relevance—to benefit from the insights it offers into the ways an author conveys his or her intent.

hearer share certain expectations about how conversation should proceed. Grice summarizes these expectations in his Cooperative Principle—*Make your conversational contribution such as is required, at the state at which it occurs, by the accepted purpose or direction of the talk exchange in which you are engaged*—and its related maxims of quantity, quality, relation and manner.[44]

Wilson and Sperber take up Grice's concept of relation or relevance and develop it in new ways until it becomes the overriding dynamic in their theory of inferential processes in communication.[45] Their First (or Cognitive) Principle of Relevance is this: *Human cognition tends to be geared to the maximisation of relevance.*[46] By this they mean that since there is a cost (in terms of time and effort) in processing information, hearers pay attention to and process the information which appears to be the most relevant to them at the least cost. When new information comes

---

44. H.P. Grice, 'Logic and Conversation', in P. Cole and J.L. Morgan (eds.), *Syntax and Semantics*. III. *Speech Acts* (New York: Academic Press, 1975), pp. 41-58. See also H.P. Grice, *Studies in the Way of Words* (Cambridge, MA: Harvard University Press, 1989). Concerning the issue of relation or relevance, Grice writes, 'Under the category of Relation I place a single maxim, namely, "Be relevant".' Though the maxim itself is terse, its formulation conceals a number of problems that exercise me a good deal: questions about what different kinds and focuses of relevance there may be, how these shift in the course of a talk exchange, how to allow for the fact that subjects of conversation are legitimately changed, and so on. I find the treatment of such questions exceedingly difficult and I hope to revert to them in a later work' (Grice, 'Logic and Conversation', p. 46).

45. While Grice's Cooperative Principle and its maxims are understood as norms shared between communicator and audience, Sperber and Wilson believe that communication does not require shared assumptions or a common purpose between communicator and audience beyond the shared goal of having the audience recognize the communicator's 'informative intention'. Their two principles of relevance are offered as a generalized description of human communication. 'Communicators and audience', they claim, 'need no more know the principle of relevance to communicate than they need to know the principles of genetics to reproduce' (Sperber and Wilson, *Relevance*, p. 162). Sperber and Wilson see a richer role for inference in communication in general than does Grice, including the process of making sense of the conventional meanings of words. See Sperber and Wilson, *Relevance*, pp. 161-63, for a more detailed discussion of their understanding of the differences between Grice's approach and Relevance Theory.

46. Sperber and Wilson, *Relevance*, p. 260. This is the first of two 'Principles of Relevance', the other being *Every act of ostensive communication communicates a presumption of its own optimal relevance*.

their way, hearers generally are not willing to devote more time and effort to process it than is required by how relevant they believe it to be. Input which takes little processing effort (whatever is readily recoverable from what is said in context) will likely be processed, as well as input which may require more processing effort (that which is more difficult to recover from what is said in context) if it is believed to be relevant enough. As Blakemore writes in an overview of Relevance Theory,

> The point is that hearers are not prepared to spend any amount of time and effort in the recovery of contextual effects. If they were, there would be nothing to stop them from continuing to process new information bringing more and more contextual assumptions to bear on its interpretation...[47]

Blakemore states, 'Within this framework the sole concern of pragmatic theory is the explanation of how the hearer recovers not just any interpretation, but the one the speaker intended'.[48] Blakemore's work offers a description of the role sentence conjunctions play in this process.

Semantic Constraints on Relevance. Blakemore argues that discourse connectives such as *but*, *and*, *moreover*, or *so* function as 'semantic constraints on relevance'. Their presence is best explained 'in terms of the speaker's goal of optimizing relevance in accordance with the Principle of Relevance, or in other words, of ensuring correct context selection at minimal processing cost'.[49]

Blakemore observes that Relevance Theory places the responsibility for success in communication solely on the speaker.[50] She explains that communicators can use particles such as conjunctions or other connectives to maximize relevance in two related ways: first, in guiding the audience to select the correct context within which to generate inferences about the intended meaning; and secondly, in minimizing the processing effort involved by providing such cues. To restate Blakemore's theory in more general terms, conjunctions and similar connective words are supplied by a speaker to help keep an audience from wandering too far from the speaker's intended meaning (limiting or 'constraining' what possibilities the audience will consider in searching for a context that makes sense of

47. D. Blakemore, 'Relevance Theory', in J. Verschueren, J. Ostman and J. Blommaert (eds.), *Handbook of Pragmatics: Manual* (Amsterdam: John Benjamins, 1995), p. 446.
   48. Blakemore, *Semantic Constraints*, p. 63.
   49. Blakemore, *Semantic Constraints*, p. 123.
   50. Blakemore, *Semantic Constraints*, p. 63.

the speaker's message), while at the same time making it easier, simply by their presence, for the audience to recognize how the speaker intends for one statement to relate to a previous one (reducing 'processing effort'). In this way discourse connectives function as non-truth-conditional forms whose contribution to discourse is to provide procedural information rather than propositional content. Blakemore argues not only that such particles function as 'semantic constraints on relevance', but that the speaker's goal of optimizing relevance—that is, 'ensuring correct context selection at minimal processing cost'—explains the very existence of such forms.[51]

Mental Representations in Discourse Processing

Blakemore observes that:

> if a speaker wishes to constrain the interpretation recovered by a hearer, he must constrain the hearer's choice of context. And since the constructions we are considering ensure correct context selection at minimal processing cost, they can be regarded as effective means for constraining the interpretation of utterances in accordance with the principle of relevance.[52]

While Blakemore goes on to speak in relevance-theoretic terms of modified assumptions and contextual implications,[53] I will turn to a more general view of discourse processing based on mental representations to develop further the role of sentence conjunctions in guiding the comprehension of discourse.

Johnson-Laird. Work in artificial intelligence has led linguistics to become increasingly aware that discourse comprehension relies on encyclopedic knowledge stored in memory in integrated 'chunks', variously referred to as 'scripts', 'scenarios', 'frames' and so on.[54] Johnson-Laird points out

---

51. Blakemore, *Semantic Constraints*, p. 123.

52. D. Blakemore, *Understanding Utterances* (Oxford: Basil Blackwell, 1992), p. 137.

53. See Blakemore, *Understanding Utterances*, pp. 137-41.

54. See, for example, M. Minsky, 'A Framework for Representing Knowledge', in P.H. Winston (ed.), *The Psychology of Computer Vision* (New York: McGraw–Hill, 1975), pp. 211-77; R.C. Schank and R.P. Abelson, *Scripts, Plans, Goals and Understanding* (Hillsdale, NJ: Lawrence Erlbaum, 1977). For a brief introduction to the use of scripts in artificial intelligence, see R.C. Schank and M. Burstein, 'Artificial Intelligence: Modeling Memory for Language Understanding', in T.A. van Dijk (ed.), *Handbook of Discourse Analysis*. I. *Disciplines of Discourse* (London: Academic

that even when no ready-made script exists—that is, when the discourse topic is not as stereotyped as is assumed in, for example, a 'restaurant script', a stored set of expectations about what generally happens in a restaurant—hearers or readers will create a mental representation based on the content of the discourse, which they will then continue, modify, or abandon based on subsequent propositions.[55] He theorizes that the cognitive mechanism enabling the implicit inferences involved in the comprehension of discourse is 'a device that constructs a single mental model on the basis of the discourse, its context, and background knowledge'.[56]

Simply put, theories of mental representations posit that when human beings process discourse they do not remember—or remember only briefly—the actual form of the words and sentences used.[57] Instead they store and manipulate what they take in in the form of a mental 'picture' they create. This picture or model incorporates what is explicitly said in the discourse and what is implicit in the discourse from contextual cues and/or inferences they make, as well as general knowledge of the world they already have.[58]

Press, 1985), pp. 145-66.

55. See P.N. Johnson-Laird, *Mental Models: Toward a Cognitive Science of Language, Inference, and Consciousness* (Cambridge: Cambridge University Press, 1983), p. 371.

56. Johnson-Laird, *Mental Models*, p. 128. See also W. Kintsch and T.A. van Dijk, 'Towards a Model of Text Comprehension and Production', *Psychological Review* 85 (1978), pp. 363-94; T.A. van Dijk and W. Kintsch, *Strategies of Discourse Comprehension* (New York: Academic Press, 1983); R.M. Kempson (ed.), *Mental Representations: The Interface between Language and Reality* (Cambridge: Cambridge University Press, 1988); Givón, *Functionalism*, pp. 343-44. For studies of discourse processing which rely on theories of mental representations, see, for example, C.A. Weaver, S. Mannes and C.R. Fletcher (eds.), *Discourse Comprehension: Essays in Honor of Walter Kintsch* (Hillsdale, NJ: Lawrence Erlbaum Associates, 1995); G. Rickheit and C. Habel (eds.), *Focus and Coherence in Discourse Processing* (New York: W. de Gruyter, 1995); S.R. Goldman, A.C. Graesser and P. van den Broek (eds.), *Narrative Comprehension, Causality, and Coherence: Essays in Honor of Tom Trabasso* (Hillsdale, NJ: Lawrence Erlbaum Associates, 1999).

57. Surveying clinical studies by a number of cognitive psychologists, Givón writes, 'It is fairly well established that the working memory buffer for text is severely limited, perhaps retaining no more than 2-5 clauses at a time, or roughly 8-20 seconds of verbatim text … By "verbatim" one means not only the vocabulary but also the surface grammatical form of utterances' (Givón, *Functionalism*, p. 344).

58. While the existence of non-propositional mental representations in the

Johnson-Laird identifies several ways in which hearers can adapt to 'indeterminacies', or ways in which subsequent propositions appear to be inconsistent with the current mental model.[59] However, appealing to Grice's Cooperative Principle and its maxims, he claims that the radical reconstruction of a mental model is rarely necessary in everyday discourse because communicators tend to be orderly in their communication.

> In other words, if you construct a mental model on the basis of my discourse, then I am likely to order the information in my description so as to prevent you from going astray. I owe you an account that you can represent in a single model without running into a conflict with information that I only subsequently divulge.[60]

Although Johnson-Laird does not identify a role for discourse connectives in the construction and manipulation of mental models,[61] Blakemore's concept of semantic constraints on relevance can be adapted to account for the role of sentence conjunctions in ordering the presentation of discourse. Rather than speaking in relevance-theoretic terms of modified assumptions and contextual implications, we can simply say that communicators use sentence conjunctions like καί and δέ to help guide the mental representations constructed by their audience. This approach is consistent with Blakemore's contention that communicators make use of particles such as conjunctions or other connectives both to guide the audience to select the correct context within which to generate inferences about the intended meaning, and to reduce the processing effort involved by providing linguistic cues.[62]

comprehension of discourse is widely accepted, differing theories abound regarding their exact nature and function. Kempson writes, '[T]he present state of the art [regarding mental representations] is in general unrelentingly tribal...each researcher articulating and evaluating solutions within the confines of their own selected paradigm' (Kempson, *Mental Representations*, p. 21).

59. Johnson-Laird, *Mental Models*, p. 164.

60. Johnson-Laird, *Mental Models*, p. 165.

61. Johnson-Laird discusses conjunctions such as *and* and *or* chiefly in terms of logical value or truth-functions: 'The use of connectives in mental models is straightforward if their truth conditions are elementary' (Johnson-Laird, *Mental Models*, p. 424).

62. Of course, it may be that such forms are present merely as indicators of the communicator's own mental representation of the discourse, what Bestgen calls a 'trace' of the difficulty a communicator encounters, for example, in the introduction of a change in topic. Bestgen warns that it is difficult to distinguish between connectives which are signals and those which are traces because it is difficult to find a form which

Similarly, Hansen builds on the notion of mental representations in developing the theoretical basis for her treatment of discourse particles in spoken French. She defines discourse markers (within which she includes sentence conjunctions) as 'non-propositional linguistic items whose primary function is connective' and which moreover 'function as instructions from the speaker to the hearer on how to integrate the host unit into a coherent mental representation of the discourse'.[63] She agrees that the semantic value of such markers is procedural rather than conceptual, noting that this 'has the advantage of making individual items compatible with a large number of different contexts...'[64]

The role of sentence conjunctions and other discourse connectives in the construction of mental representations is also recognized in the work of linguists such as Givón and in recent research in cognitive psychology.

Givón. Givón is one functional linguist who attempts to integrate the role of sentence conjunctions (among other grammatical features) with the construction of mental representations of discourse, within the larger issue of the cognitive processing of language. Taking his own advice that 'in formulating our hypothesis about the functional correlates of grammar, we must begin to pay attention to relevant work on the cognition and neurology of language, memory and attention', he draws widely from research done in these fields.[65] Givón warns that 'transforming the study of text into the study of mind is a delicate and complex undertaking'. He contends, however, that:

> this progression—from text-centered to mind-centered method and theory—is both natural and necessary... As elsewhere in science, the theory that one constructs is not about the visible artifacts, but rather about the invisible process responsible for them.[66]

functions exclusively as one or the other (Y. Bestgen, 'Segmentation Markers as Trace and Signal of Discourse Structure', *Journal of Pragmatics* 29 [1998], pp. 753-56). But even if discourse connectives arise as traces of the process of discourse production—and this is less likely to be the case in as carefully edited a text as one may assume a Gospel to be—once present in the discourse these forms then serve as cues guiding the readers' mental representations as they seek to comprehend the author's meaning.

63. Hansen, *Discourse Particles,* pp. 73-75.

64. Hansen, *Discourse Particles,* p. 75.

65. Givón, *Functionalism,* p. 16. See, for example, his discussion of what he terms 'the co-evolution of language, mind and brain' (Givón, *Functionalism,* pp. 393-445).

66. Givón, *Functionalism,* p. 389. Chafe similarly affirms that 'we can never really understand language without understanding the human mind, and vice versa' (W.

Givón speaks of two 'processing channels' in human discourse production and comprehension: one 'knowledge-driven' (which he also
describes as 'vocabulary-driven'), and another 'grammar-driven'.[67]
Speaking of the second, 'grammar-driven', channel he continues, 'For the
text comprehender, overt grammatical signals—syntactic constructions,
morphology, intonation—*cue* the text processor, they *guide* him/her in the
construction of a coherent mental representation of the text; and this is a
vital cognitive boost'.[68] I understand Givón's distinction between
knowledge-driven and grammar-driven channels of discourse production
and comprehension to correlate to a large extent with Blakemore's notions
of conceptual and procedural meaning. This is all the more evident when
Givón explains that 'one may consider the grammatical signals associated
with natural language clauses as the *mental processing instructions* that
guide the speech comprehender toward constructing a coherent, structured
mental representation of the text'.[69] Givón describes sentence conjunctions
as part of a grammatical sub-system along with intonation, pauses, and
paragraph indentation, devices which 'are inherently cataphoric [that is,
related to subsequent elements in a text]: The grammatical cue is placed
between the two clauses, signalling the degree of thematic continuity of
the next clause'.[70]

Chafe, *Discourse, Consciousness, and Time: The Flow and Displacement of Conscious
Experience in Speaking and Writing* [Chicago: University of Chicago Press, 1994], p.
iv). Chafe asserts, 'If I am right, there will sooner or later be a broader recognition of
the fact that neither language nor consciousness can be adequately understood until we
succeed in combining them within a more comprehensive picture in which the nature
of each will shed crucial light on the nature of the other' (Chafe, *Discourse*, p. 4). Even
John Locke, in a chapter on particles in *An Essay Concerning Human Understanding*
(1690), suggests that it is not enough 'for the explaining of these Words, to render
them, as is usually in Dictionaries, by Words of another Tongue which came nearest to
their signification: For what is meant by them, is commonly as hard to be understood in
one, as another Language. They are all *marks of some Action, or Intimation of the
Mind*; and therefore to understand them rightly, the several views, postures, stands,
turns, limitations, and exceptions, and several other Thoughts of the Mind, for which
we have either none, or very deficient Names, are diligently to be studied' (Locke,
Human Understanding, p. 472; his emphasis).
   67. Givón, *Functionalism*, p. 342.
   68. Givón, *Functionalism*, p. 343 (his emphasis).
   69. Givón, *Functionalism*, p. 344 (his emphasis).
   70. Givón, *Functionalism*, p. 373.

Insights from cognitive psychology. Cognitive psychologists and linguistic researchers in related fields have attempted to measure the effect of sentence conjunctions and similar markers on discourse processing speed and comprehension. Surveying the work of others, Murray reports,

> Experiments have shown that the presence of a connective between adjacent clauses reduces the reading time of the second clause…enhances memory for the clauses…increases accuracy in response to comprehension questions, and decreases question-answering time…[71]

For the most part these researchers assume some form of a theory of mental representations in discourse processing, with sentence conjunctions and other markers as signals of continuity or discontinuity in the integration of successive sentences into the mental model. Murray summarizes, 'According to mental model theory, readers' memory representation of a narrative is composed of an interpretation of the text events being depicted rather than a strictly linguistically based representation'.[72] Bestgen and Vonk write,

> Understanding a text is generally seen as an incremental process in which new sentences are integrated, by default, with the preceding ones … The integration process is facilitated when writers linguistically express the relations that link two contiguous statements…[73]

Bestgen explains,

> Oral and written discourse contains numerous linguistic and paralinguistic devices, like punctuation, pauses, connectives, adverbial phrases, and referential expressions, that specifically mark continuity and discontinuity…[74]

Murray's experimental data lead him to conclude that 'connectives are powerful indicators of continuity and discontinuity in text' and furthermore that specific 'connectives clearly differ in terms of whether they predominately signal continuity or discontinuity'.[75]

Among these researchers there is a shared assumption that continuity is the expected, or 'default', condition in discourse. In asserting that 'new sentences are integrated, by default, with the preceding ones', Bestgen and

---

71. Murray, 'Role of Continuity', p. 227.

72. Murray, 'Role of Continuity', p. 228; see also Segal *et al.*, 'Interclausal Connectives', pp. 27-28.

73. Y. Bestgen and W. Vonk, 'The Role of Temporal Segmentation Markers in Discourse Processing', *Discourse Processes* 19 (1995), pp. 385-406 (388).

74. Bestgen, 'Trace and Signal', p. 754.

75. Murray, 'Role of Continuity', p. 231.

Vonk make use of a 'nextness principle' earlier proposed by Ochs.[76] Ochs writes that in making sense of discourse, 'We use the principle of "nextness"... We may link one proposition to another because they appear next to one another and because we expect sequentially expressed propositions to be relevant to one another.'[77] Segal *et al.* articulate an updated 'principle of continuity' for narrative based on a theory of mental representations:

> *A new sentence in the text is interpreted in terms of an ongoing construction of an integrated component of the narrative's meaning. Unless specifically marked, the new meaning is incorporated into, and regarded as continuous with, the current ongoing construction.*[78]

They explain that 'only if there is a textual cue that the new text is discontinuous with the old, or if attempts at continuous integration cannot be maintained, does the reader interpret new information as discontinuous ...'[79] In other words, unless readers or hearers are told otherwise, they assume that the events, participants, time and setting of the next sentence in the narrative are consistent with the one preceding. As Murray puts it, 'As readers progress through a narrative, they assume that the events will follow in a linear fashion'.[80]

Where there is some element of discontinuity in the narrative, the audience expects to be told. Bestgen explains that

> authors are expected to produce their discourse in such a way that readers can apply the nextness principle. However, each time a new topic is introduced in the discourse, they have to explicitly prevent the application of this principle. According to the Gricean maxims of communication, speakers and writers are expected to inform the addressees that continuity is not preserved, that there is a topic shift, and that specific action should be taken ...[81]

---

76. See Bestgen and Vonk, 'Temporal Segmentation Markers', p. 388; also Bestgen, 'Trace and Signal', p. 755.

77. E. Ochs, 'Planned and Unplanned Discourse', in T. Givón (ed.), *Syntax and Semantics. XII. Discourse and Syntax* (New York: Academic Press, 1979), pp. 65-66.

78. Segal *et al.*, 'Interclausal Connectives', p. 32 (their emphasis). Murray ('Role of Continuity', p. 228) and Bestgen ('Trace and Signal', p. 775) make use of the 'principle of continuity' developed by Segal *et al.*

79. Segal *et al.*, 'Interclausal Connectives', p. 32.

80. Murray, 'Role of Continuity', p. 228.

81. Bestgen, 'Trace and Signal', p. 775.

Segal *et al.* include the introduction of a new character or a shift in time or place as examples of narrative discontinuity.[82] Murray also identifies 'reversions to an earlier setting or scene (such as a flashback), an abrupt topic change, a surprising turn of events, a character moving away from what he/she is currently doing, or a violation of an expectation created in the previous text' as among numerous examples of discontinuity in narrative.[83]

Sentence conjunctions are one means of informing the audience whether continuity is or is not being maintained at any point in the narrative. Recent work on sentence conjunctions and other particles in Classical Greek recognizes their procedural role in conveying continuity and discontinuity in discourse.[84] Sicking writes, for example, 'It is here assumed that the particles discussed do not convey information about relations—adversative, causal, consecutive, inferential, &c.—between sentence *contents*'.[85] Rather, Sicking explains:

> What is at stake is not the connecting (or leaving unconnected) of sentences—and a fortiori not that of 'sentence contents'—but the articulating the discourse in question and marking the relation between the successive sections within the narrower or wider context which they form part of. Such relations between what precedes and what follows may occupy any point on a scale ranging between the extremes of continuity and discontinuity, and the single word 'connexion' cannot do justice to the fact that one of the characteristics distinguishing between these particles is precisely in the definition of the range of possible values on this scale of continuity which is peculiar to each of them.[86]

In the chapters which follow I argue that Matthew uses καί to signal that what follows is continuous with the audience's ongoing mental representations of the narrative, while δέ informs the audience that a low- to mid-level discontinuity occurs at that point in the discourse. The other sentence conjunctions in Matthew's Gospel likewise serve as procedural signals as the audience construct and modify mental representations.

---

82. Segal *et al.*, 'Interclausal Connectives', p. 50.
83. Murray, 'Role of Continuity', p. 228.
84. See, for example, the studies in Rijksbaron (ed.), *New Approaches*, as well as the monographs by Sicking and van Ophuijsen in Sicking and van Ophuijsen, *Attic Particle Usage*.
85. Sicking, 'Devices for Text Articulation', p. 45.
86. Sicking, 'Devices for Text Articulation', p. 45.

Markedness and Prominence

The assumption of continuity as the default condition in narrative—that audiences assume continuity of events, participants, time and setting unless signaled otherwise—is a significant psycholinguistic notion in describing the function of sentence conjunctions. Another important linguistic notion is the concept of 'markedness', first elucidated by phonologists of the Prague school,[87] and developed as a language universal by Greenberg and others,[88] although as Givón observes, 'The notion of markedness has been implicit, under one guise or another, in linguistic analysis since antiquity...'[89] Comrie explains,

> The intuition behind the notion of markedness in linguistics is that, where we have an opposition with two or more members...it is often the case that one member of the opposition is felt to be more usual, more normal, less specific than the other (in markedness terminology, it is unmarked, the others are marked).[90]

Thus the distinction between continuity and discontinuity in narrative described above, in which continuity is understood to be the default condition, may be restated in terms of markedness: continuity is 'unmarked' in narrative discourse, while discontinuity is to some degree 'marked'.

87. Greenberg states that Trubetzkoy first introduced the terminology 'marked' and 'unmarked' with respect to phonology in 1931, while its first explicit use for grammatical categories is probably by Jakobson in 1932 (J.H. Greenberg, *Language Universals: With Special Reference to Feature Hierarchies* [The Hague: Mouton, 1966], p. 11 n. 3). For an introduction to the work of Jakobson and Trubetzkoy, in the context of general introductions to markedness theory, see E. Andrews, *Markedness Theory: The Union of Asymmetry and Semiosis in Language* (Durham, NC, and London: Duke University Press, 1990), pp. 9-43; E.L. Battistella, *Markedness: The Evaluative Superstructure of Language* (Albany: State University of New York Press, 1990), pp. 1-22.

88. 'The concept of the marked and unmarked will be shown to possess a high degree of generality in that it is applicable to the phonological, the grammatical, and the semantic aspects of language ... In particular, it will be shown that the concept of marked and unmarked categories provides the possibility of formulating higher level hypotheses with deductive consequences in the form of more specific universals commonly arrived at by a more purely empirical consideration of the evidence' (Greenberg, *Language Universals*, pp. 10-11).

89. Givón, *Functionalism*, p. 25.

90. B. Comrie, *Aspect: An Introduction to the Study of Verbal Aspect and Related Problems* (CTL; Cambridge: Cambridge University Press, 1976), p. 111.

The notion of markedness can be applied to oppositions among sentence conjunctions as well as to the opposition between continuous and discontinuous narrative contexts in which they are found. I will argue, for example, that as a signal of discontinuity δέ is a marked sentence conjunction in comparison with καί—that is, that δέ occurs as a relatively marked choice in Matthew's narrative framework against the more 'usual' or 'normal' background of καί and continuous narrative. This use of δέ is 'unusual' not primarily in that it occurs more rarely (although it is in fact less frequent than the unmarked καί), but in that it stands out to some degree against what the audience recognizes as the unmarked or default choice. Battistella writes, 'The marked/unmarked relation is sometimes compared to the relation between figure and ground or between abnormal and normal'.[91] He continues:

> Since the unmarked or unspecified term of an opposition carries less information, it appears as the ground against which the marked term appears as a figure; the unmarked is a conceptual default value that is assumed unless the marked term is specifically indicated or chosen. Of course, the notions figure/ground and abnormal/normal are relative ones; what is the figure and what is ground depends on the construal of a situation.[92]

Battistella and other linguists warn that what is marked or unmarked in a given opposition is not absolute, but may be highly context-dependent. Battistella observes, 'Like the figure/ground relation, markedness too has a contingent, contextually determined aspect. Markedness relations are not fixed, but rather depend on the language-internal evaluation of the terms of an opposition.'[93] Not only are markedness relations language-specific (or language-internal in Battistella's terms), but such relations may vary from one discourse context to another within a language. Comrie points out that it is 'possible that in certain circumstances one member of an opposition will be unmarked, while in other circumstances the other member (or one of the other members) will be unmarked'.[94] As Givón puts it, 'Markedness is a context-dependent phenomenon par excellence. The very same structure may be marked in one context and unmarked in another.'[95]

That markedness relations may vary from context to context motivates,

91. Battistella, *Markedness*, p. 4. See also Greenberg, *Language Universals*, p. 60.
92. Battistella, *Markedness*, p. 4.
93. Battistella, *Markedness*, p. 4.
94. Comrie, *Aspect*, p. 118.
95. Givón, *Functionalism*, p. 27.

for example, my specifying that the functions of sentence conjunction described here apply to their use in narrative, as opposed to other discourse types—that is, other contexts—where they may or may not reflect similar markedness relations. Similarly, in my comments on discourse functions of sentence conjunctions in Mt. 8.1–9.34 (Chapter 9), I argue that Matthew's use of δέ to signal the discontinuity of units larger than a single sentence varies in its degree of markedness relative to the patterns of use of other sentence conjunctions in each context.

While markedness is a broad concept incorporating a variety of linguistic issues, for the purposes of this study the focus will be on two facets of markedness: first, frequency distributions of marked and unmarked forms; and secondly, the congruence between marked forms and marked contexts and between unmarked forms and unmarked contexts. Frequency of distribution is one of several criteria contributing to a determination of markedness for a particular form or structure.[96] There is a consensus among linguists that no single characteristic automatically identifies a form as marked in relation to other choices, but that a number of factors may come into play—with the tendency being for a cluster of criteria to coincide, such as structural complexity, frequency of distribution, and cognitive complexity (to use Givón's schema as an example).[97] Sentence conjunctions in Matthew's narrative framework appear to follow the tendency that the marked form will also be the one which occurs less often.[98] Καί, understood here to be unmarked, is by far the most common sentence conjunction in the narrative framework, appearing 335 times in 720 sentences, or in 47% of the narrative sentences in Matthew's Gospel. Δέ, marked in relation to καί, is used less often: only 257 times, or in 36% of the sentences in Matthew's narrative framework. This can be carried further, characterizing καί and δέ together as the usual or unmarked narrative conjunctions in Matthew's Gospel, appearing significantly more

---

96. But see Comrie (*Aspect*, pp. 116-17) and Andrews (*Markedness Theory*, p. 137), who question the value of statistical frequency in determining markedness.

97. See Givón, *Functionalism*, p. 28. See also Comrie, *Aspect*, p. 111; Battistella, *Markedness*, pp. 25-26.

98. Halliday asserts, 'An unmarked term is a default condition: that which is selected unless there is good reason for selecting some other term. It is not *defined* by frequency, but it is likely to correspond to the more probable term in a system whose probabilities are skew' (M.A.K. Halliday, 'Corpus Studies and Probabilistic Grammar', in K. Aijmer and B. Altenberg [eds.], *English Corpus Linguistics: Studies in Honour of Jan Svartvik* [London: Longman, 1991], p. 35).

frequently than do other more marked or unusual narrative connectors—that is, τότε, γάρ, οὖν or asyndeton—which collectively appear in only 17% (124/720) of narrative sentences. In this study frequency of distribution is taken as an important indicator of markedness, so that an item or combination of items is generally referred to as marked if it is statistically less frequent, although at the same time it is understood that as a linguistic concept markedness involves more than simply frequency or infrequency of use.[99]

The idea that there is a congruence between the markedness of forms and the markedness of the contexts in which they are used helps to explain the collocation of sentence conjunctions as procedural signals in Matthew's narrative framework with other indicators of discourse continuity and discontinuity. Regarding the principle of 'markedness assimilation' Battistella writes:

> This principle suggests that marked elements tend to occur in marked contexts while unmarked elements occur in unmarked contexts. It involves the claim that there is an iconic diagrammatization between linguistic elements and the contexts in which they occur ... Markedness assimilation ...provides a semiotic organization to the facts of language according to which units and contexts and expressions and meanings are patterned together in a single superstructure.[100]

In analyzing Matthew's patterns of use of sentence conjunctions I find that the unmarked form, καί, is used in the context of continuous (that is, unmarked) narrative, while the more marked form, δέ, is used in the context of discontinuous (that is, relatively marked) narrative. As I will argue in subsequent chapters, I also find that the unmarked sentence conjunction καί is used more frequently with relatively unmarked syntactical structures such as monolectic verbs (Chapter 4), while the more marked sentence conjunction δέ tends to be used with more marked syntactical structures such as subject–verb constituent order (Chapter 5). A similar example is the increased frequency of τότε, a signal of marked

---

99. 'If it turns out that in fact frequency is an adequate unifying principle for the domain of the marked and unmarked in semantics and grammar, a great over-all simplification will have been achieved. But frequency is itself but a symptom and the consistent relative frequency relations which appear to hold for lexical items and grammatical categories are themselves in need of explanation. Such explanations will not, in all probability, arise from a single principle' (Greenberg, *Language Universals*, p. 70).

100. Battistella, *Markedness*, p. 7.

continuity, with present tense-form finite verbs (the so-called 'historic present'), which may be understood as a more marked tense-form in past-referring narrative (Chapter 7). This clustering of marked sentence conjunctions with marked contexts and collocating features, and of unmarked sentence conjunctions with unmarked contexts and collocating features, gives a tantalizing glimpse of the ways these and other components from various linguistic systems function together in the Greek of the New Testament in 'a single superstructure' incorporating form and meaning.

In an early essay Halliday puts the notion of markedness into a literary context useful to the discourse analyst, although he does not use the term 'markedness' at this point. He relates markedness to literary criticism via his understanding of prominence and of foregrounding or highlighting.[101] In stylistic studies of individual authors Halliday is eager to distinguish 'true foregrounding from mere prominence of a statistical or an absolute kind'.[102] What Halliday calls 'prominence' shares with the linguistic notion of markedness the idea of distinguishing the relative 'usualness' or 'normalness' of elements in a text. He writes, 'I have used the term *prominence* as a general name for the phenomenon of linguistic highlighting, whereby some feature of the language of a text stands out in some way'.[103] According to Halliday, prominence of this type is quantifiable, in a manner analogous to the use of frequency distributions in determining markedness. Halliday explains that 'prominence may be of a probabilistic kind'. He asserts that 'we are dealing with a type of phenomenon that is expressible in quantitative terms, to which statistical concepts may be applied'.[104]

But the simple fact that a particular linguistic choice is statistically less frequent and thus stands out from the rest of the text in some way does not insure that it is significant in the author's construction of a discourse, or, in Halliday's terms, that it is 'foregrounded'. He explains, 'Foregrounding, as I understand it, is prominence that is motivated'.[105] Halliday suggests that quantitative analysis has value in pointing to potentially highlighted or foregrounded features, but that it cannot guarantee whether such features are important at the level of discourse: 'What cannot be expressed statistically is foregrounding: figures do not tell us whether a particular

101. See Halliday, *Explorations*, pp. 112-17.
102. Halliday, *Explorations*, p. 112.
103. Halliday, *Explorations*, p. 113.
104. Halliday, *Explorations*, p. 115.
105. Halliday, *Explorations*, p. 112.

pattern has or has not "value in the game".'[106] Quantitative analysis is only one factor in recognizing what features an author is using stylistically, but it is useful. 'A rough indication of frequencies is often just what is needed: enough to suggest why we should accept the writer's assertion'—the assertion, that is, of a literary critic or discourse analyst—'that some feature is prominent in the text, and to allow us to check his statements. The figures, obviously, in no way constitute an analysis, interpretation or evaluation of the style.'[107]

In this study I use the term 'prominence' in a different way than Halliday does in his essay, with a stronger meaning similar to Halliday's 'foregrounding'. If Halliday can say that 'foregrounding is prominence that is motivated', my approach is that 'prominence is markedness that is motivated'. I use quantitative analysis to identify relative frequencies of sentence conjunctions, along with features which tend to collocate with given sentence conjunctions and the various discourse contexts in which particular sentence conjunctions tend to appear. Where the Evangelist chooses a sentence conjunction, or a combination of sentence conjunction and collocating features, that is statistically less frequent, or where a conjunctive choice appears to stand out from expected default choices on some other basis, I refer to it as relatively marked in that context. As a marked linguistic choice it points to elements which are *potentially* prominent in the narrative the Evangelist is constructing.[108] These marked choices are important data in the exegesis of Matthew's Gospel. However, a more thorough reading which takes into account factors such as literary, historical-cultural and theological dimensions of the text is often needed to determine whether such a choice ultimately has 'value in the game'—that is, that in making this choice the Evangelist is conveying the relative importance of some element in his Gospel.

Summary and Conclusion

Halliday's systemic-functional grammar, introduced in the previous chapter, provides a framework for notions such as choice and system, the textual function of language, and textual versus topical theme—notions

---

106. Halliday, *Explorations*, p. 116.

107. Halliday, *Explorations*, p. 117.

108. As Porter notes regarding word order, 'When the marked order is found the interpreter is free to ask whether prominence is being established' (Porter, *Idioms*, p. 303).

which play a significant role in the understanding of sentence conjunctions. Halliday does not offer a full exposition of the discourse function of sentence conjunctions, but drawing from other linguists I have argued that sentence conjunctions have a low level of semantic specificity, that is, a minimal semantic value allowing their use in a range of discourse contexts where there may be a variety of semantic relationships between propositions. These forms encode procedural and non-truth-conditional meaning, indicating the ways the sentences they introduce are to be related to preceding discourse. Sentence conjunctions can be used by communicators to facilitate the audience's comprehension of discourse in two related ways: in guiding hearers or readers as they construct or modify mental representations they make of discourse, and in reducing processing effort by providing such cues. In narrative discourse sentence conjunctions may help to indicate continuity (the default or unmarked condition in narrative) or some measure of discontinuity.

In the remainder of this study I hold this theoretical framework of sentence conjunctions as procedural signals which contribute to the construction and manipulation of mental representations of discourse in one hand, as it were, while carrying out empirical studies in Matthew's Gospel with the other hand. I find, for example, that in Matthew's narrative framework sentence-initial καί—collocating with other features of discourse continuity—generally signals that a representation of the discourse is to be continued without significant change, while δέ, alongside its collocating features, warns of some low- to mid-level adjustment in the representation, perhaps in terms of a change in actor or some degree of temporal discontinuity. The remaining sentence conjunctions, τότε, γάρ and οὖν, plus asyndeton, are similarly characterized in terms of the procedural meanings they convey and the features with which they tend to appear. But first, the empirical methods and procedures used in these investigations are detailed in the following chapter.

Chapter 3

METHODOLOGY

I find it helpful to think of linguistic form as if it were located in a pane of glass through which ideas are transmitted from speaker to listener. Under ordinary circumstances language users are not conscious of the glass itself, but only of the ideas that pass through it. The form of language is transparent, and it takes a special act of will to focus on the glass and not the ideas… [T]he experience of becoming conscious of previously unconscious phenomena is one of the principal joys of linguistic work.[1]

Introduction: Probabilistic Grammar

Using Halliday's notions of system and choice, I begin with the assumption that sentence conjunctions and asyndeton in the Gospel of Matthew constitute a *paradigmatic system* (a set of 'vertical' relations, or elements which can alternate in the same 'slot' in the sentence). The Evangelist makes choices from within this system to connect sentences in the Gospel. Halliday recognizes that there are networks of systems in language, and that choices from various systems interact with one another in intricate ways. Thus the system of sentence conjunctions in Matthew's Gospel forms *syntagmatic* (or 'horizontal') relationships with other linguistic features such as lexical choice, constituent order, or verbal tense-form.

Halliday himself points out that the notion of system in language opens the way for a probabilistic treatment of choices made within a system. He writes, 'It had always seemed to me that the linguistic system was inherently probabilistic, and that frequency in text was the instantiation of probability in the grammar'.[2] As Nesbitt and Plum (building on Halliday's foundation) explain:

---

1. Chafe, *Discourse*, p. 38.
2. Halliday, 'Probabilistic Grammar', p. 31.

What is said is not only interpreted against a background of what could have been said but was not; it is also interpreted against the background of expectancies, against the background of what was more likely and what was less likely to be said. The grammar of a language is not only the grammar of what is possible but also the grammar of what is probable.[3]

Nesbitt and Plum make clear that 'the incorporation into grammatical descriptions of information on the actual patterns of choice realized in text [is] the motivation for working towards the probabilistic modelling of language'.[4] Hallidayan systemic-functional grammar provides a theoretical framework within which the relative frequencies of sentence conjunctions in the Gospel of Matthew, along with the relative frequencies of their collocations with other lexical and syntactical features, can be quantitatively described and modeled.

Thus for procedural aspects of this study I draw heavily from recent developments in corpus linguistics with its emphasis on quantitative analysis.[5] Although Matthew's Gospel is a far smaller corpus than those usually used in corpus studies—in fact, it is properly described only as a single text and not as a corpus or 'a large and principled collection of natural texts'[6]—a number of the concerns of corpus linguistics are applicable here. As Biber *et al.* observe:

The essential characteristics of corpus-based analysis are:
- it is empirical, analyzing the actual patterns of use in natural texts;
- it utilizes a large and principled collection of natural texts, known as a 'corpus', as the basis for analysis;

3. C. Nesbitt and G. Plum, 'Probabilities in a Systemic-Functional Grammar: The Clause Complex in English', in R.P. Fawcett and D. Young (eds.), *New Developments in Systemic Linguistics*. II. *Theory and Application* (Open Linguistics Series; London and New York: Pinter Publishers, 1988), p. 9.

4. Nesbitt and Plum, 'Probabilities', pp. 6-7.

5. See, for example, Aijmer and Altenberg (eds.), *English Corpus Linguistics;* J. Svartvik (ed.), *Directions in Corpus Linguistics: Proceedings of Nobel Symposium 82, Stockholm, 4-8 August 1991* (Berlin and New York: Mouton de Gruyter, 1992); T. McEnery and A. Wilson, *Corpus Linguistics* (ETEL; Edinburgh: Edinburgh University Press, 1996); D. Biber, S. Conrad and R. Reppen, *Corpus Linguistics: Investigating Language Structure and Use* (Cambridge Approaches to Linguistics; Cambridge: Cambridge University Press, 1998).

6. Biber *et al.*, *Corpus Linguistics*, p. 4; see also O'Donnell, 'Annotated Corpora', p. 73.

- it makes extensive use of computers for analysis, using both automatic and interactive techniques;
- it depends on both quantitative and qualitative analytical techniques.[7]

This study is both empirical and exhaustive, identifying all the occurrences of paratactic sentence conjunctions in Matthew's Gospel, and analyzing all those in the narrative framework, the focus of this research. I offer both quantitative and qualitative analyses of the patterns of use of sentence conjunctions in the Gospel of Matthew. In order to keep track of the large amount of data I utilize a computer. In fact, in practical terms it is the computer which makes such an approach possible. As Leech observes,

> The computer's ability to search, retrieve, sort, and calculate the contents of vast corpora of text, and to do all these things at an immense speed, give us the ability to *comprehend*, and to *account for*, the contents of such corpora in a way which was not dreamed of in the pre-computational era of corpus linguistics...[8]

While this is even more true of analysis of the huge corpora with which many corpus linguists work, which can comprise tens of millions of words, it is also true of lexico-grammatical studies in the New Testament. The computer's ability to store, sort, search and quantify data allows a scope of study that was beyond the practical reach of earlier grammarians.

Research Design

My specific methods in this study originate from two starting points: first, a general interest in Greek discourse structure in the Gospels which led to my framing a more specific question, 'Where do connective words—specifically, paratactic sentence conjunctions—occur between sentences in Matthew's Gospel and why?'; and secondly, the use of a computer and commercially available database software as an aid to recording and analyzing my observations of these forms. Each of these starting points has its own ramifications in shaping this study.

Form-to-function Approach
My basic question, 'Where do paratactic sentence conjunctions occur in Matthew's Gospel and why?', led me to design a research project that is

---

7.   Biber *et al.*, *Corpus Linguistics*, p. 4.
8.   G. Leech, 'Corpora and Theories of Linguistic Performance', in Svartvik (ed.), *Directions in Corpus Linguistics*, p. 106.

essentially formal in its focus and scope. In other words, I first chose a set of forms—sentence conjunctions—and then began to look for their contribution to discourse in Matthew's Gospel.

Of course, the study of form does not exclude the study of meaning. In fact, meaning is communicated through linguistic form, and differences in form constitute differences in meaning. This is in direct contrast to the assumptions of some transformational grammarians and others who treat the 'deep structure' or underlying meaning of language as distinct from variations in sentence structure.[9] Bolinger observes,

> Differences in the arrangement of words and in the presence or absence of certain elements are often assumed not to count. What is supposed to matter is the underlying deep structure, which is capable of producing, through transformations, divergent structures that mean exactly the same thing.[10]

Bolinger disagrees with this assumption, arguing that 'there is no such thing as two different surface structures with the same deep structure (that is, with the same meaning)'.[11] He asserts the principle of 'one meaning, one form', or, that different forms convey different meanings.[12] Thus formal choices made by the Evangelist, not only in the choice of a sentence conjunction or asyndeton but also in the selection of other collocating features and the arrangement of sentences and larger units, convey meaning in Matthew's Gospel.

A different approach than beginning with a set of linguistic forms would have been to start with a general inquiry into the means of connection between clauses or sentences in the Gospel of Matthew and then investigate the lexical and syntactical forms which share this textual function. This is not to say that a form-to-function study is always to be preferred over one that moves from textual function to form, or vice versa. It is to say that the study which follows is inevitably shaped by the starting point. For example, limiting my study to paratactic conjunctions led me from the beginning to omit subordinating particles such as ἵνα or ὅπως.

---

9. A classic example of the relation between 'deep structure' and 'surface structure' is the active-passive transformation, in which *John kicked the ball* and *the ball was kicked by John* are assumed to be identical in meaning although differing in surface structure. For an application of transformational-generative grammar to the Greek of the New Testament, see Schmidt, *Hellenistic Greek Grammar*, pp. 41-65.

10. D. Bolinger, *Meaning and Form* (London: Longman, 1977), p. 3.

11. Bolinger, *Meaning and Form*, p. 4.

12. Bolinger, *Meaning and Form*, p. 19.

Nor is it the case that a formally based study cannot take place within a functional framework. I have already shown that Halliday brings form and function together in systemic-functional grammar. Within a theoretical approach which assumes a close relationship both between form and meaning and between form and function, I focus primarily on formal syntactical analysis, specifically the interaction of sentence conjunctions with other syntactical features such as constituent order and thematization or verbal tense-form. Other than the semantics of sentence conjunctions (which I understand to convey procedural meaning), I deal only sparingly with other non-formal issues. Throughout the study I identify formal features from various systems within the grammar which appear to collocate with sentence conjunctions as mutually reinforcing elements in discourse.

Text-based Quantitative Approach

The second starting point, the decision to use a computer to record my initial observations of sentence conjunctions in Matthew's Gospel, also served to shape the study itself. Although my original intent was to use software with a simple database (Microsoft Works 4.0) merely to keep track of the sentence conjunction in each clause in the Gospel, it soon became apparent that I would need to record other contextual variables as well. Once I began to do that—and the identification of relevant variables itself became an important theoretical and methodological issue—the search functions and filters built into the software allowed me to manipulate the data in ways I had not previously considered. As a result, the study became more quantitatively focused with, I believe, significant results. In particular, quantitative analysis allowed me to recognize the interplay of multiple features such as sentence conjunction, thematization, verbal tense-form, and sentence constituent order (that is, subject–verb, verb–subject, verb-only or verbless) in narrative structure in Matthew's Gospel.

The type of formal approach outlined above is particularly suited to the quantitative techniques of corpus linguistics. Sigurd observes that in addition to its empirical, descriptive and quantitative characteristics, computer-based corpus linguistics 'tends to focus on form rather than meaning'. By this Sigurd means that computer-based corpus linguistics 'has to start from the graphic objects: letters, capital letters, word spaces, commas etc. and keeps this focus on form even when it looks for meaning. I admit that meaning is treated in corpus linguistics, but one always has to look for a formal marker of it, e.g. certain words denoting modality, certain words marking coordination...'[13]

In the sections below I detail the fields and variables that I developed in the database as well as some issues regarding the use of methods from corpus linguistics on a relatively small corpus such as Matthew's Gospel. What is important to note at this juncture is that my database records a variety of features related to clause or sentence structure rather than just the parsing of individual words. Along the way a number of colleagues asked why I did not simply make use of existing tagged New Testament texts such as those in the GRAMCORD project or BibleWorks. Although I did occasionally use GRAMCORD's excellent Accordance program for word searches, the existing resources—tagged texts with search functions— are primarily designed to provide morphological information about individual words rather than syntactical information about the function of words or word groups in a clause or larger discourse unit.[14]

For this research, however, I needed information at clause and sentence level rather than just word level. For example, I did not merely need to know that καί appears 1194 times in the Gospel of Matthew, something which a package like Accordance quickly indicates. I needed to know how often καί appears in initial position in an independent clause and what percentage of those occurrences are in narrative discourse as opposed to other discourse types, along with patterns of use (if any) with particular lexical items, verbal tense-forms, sentence constituent order, and other features. I needed to look at thematic elements in sentences beginning with καί and what the sentences before and after a particular example of καί were like.[15]

The ability to create automatically generated clause- or discourse-level tags for machine-readable texts of the New Testament—that is, clause- or discourse-level parsing software—is beyond the reach of Greek linguistics at present, and few if any manually tagged texts exist for the New

13. B. Sigurd, 'Comments', in Svartvik (ed.), *Directions in Corpus Linguistics*, p. 123.

14. For a survey of existing machine-readable tagged texts of the New Testament, see O'Donnell, 'Annotated Corpora', pp. 93-95.

15. For an introduction to types of text annotation relevant to the study of the New Testament—orthographic, morphological, grammatical, syntactical, semantic and discourse—see O'Donnell, 'Annotated Corpora', pp. 74-92; see also R. Garside, G. Leech and A. McEnery (eds.), *Corpus Annotation: Linguistic Information from Computer Text Corpora* (London: Longman, 1997), pp. 19-101.

Testament or other Hellenistic Greek texts.[16] In fact, linguists in general find it difficult to use automated corpus techniques to study clause-level features. Halliday himself remarks on this problem:

> I cannot even today ask the system to retrieve for me all clauses of mental process or marked circumstantial theme or high obligation modality. I have to choose, between working on just those systems that can be retrieved by parsing...and doing a massive job of manual analysis and simply using the system to crunch the numbers afterwards, which of course severely limits the size of the available sample.[17]

As Halliday suggests, I had to rely extensively on manual analysis of the text to identify sentence-level features relevant to the function of sentence conjunctions in Matthew's Gospel. To record these features, I developed a database specific to this research. That is, rather than attempting to design a system of computer-readable tags related to clause-level features in the Gospel and tagging a Greek text directly, I took the approach of constructing a database in which each line represents the occurrence of a sentence conjunction in the Gospel and each column or 'field' represents a contextual variable. Manually collected information was entered into the database. That the Gospel of Matthew is a relatively short text means that the manual analysis of sentence-level features such as sentence conjunctions and various contextual variables is more manageable than would be the case with huge corpora, although for all practical purposes a computer is still required for storing, sorting, searching and quantifying data. As an alternative to directly parsing and tagging the text, the database approach offers a method which, although representing a level of abstraction from the text itself, allows the quantification and analysis of clause-level features.[18]

16. One such project currently under way, the Hellenistic Greek Text Annotation Project of the Centre for Advanced Theological Research, University of Surrey Roehampton (S.E. Porter, Project Director; M.B. O'Donnell, Project Manager), has as its goal the creation of a machine-readable corpus comprising the Greek New Testament and related texts from the Hellenistic world, tagged at levels from morphology to discourse. The first major body of texts is scheduled for completion in two to three years, with other texts expected to follow.

17. M.A.K. Halliday, 'Language as System and Language as Instance: The Corpus as a Theoretical Construct', in Svartvik (ed.), *Directions in Corpus Linguistics*, p. 64.

18. For a brief overview of technical issues regarding databases in linguistic research and the potential future usefulness of linguistic databases, see J. Nerbonne, 'Introduction', in *idem* (ed.), *Linguistic Databases* (Stanford, CA: CSLI Publications, 1998), pp. 1-12. Concerning the pros and cons of databases versus annotated corpora,

Text. A corpus-based study necessitates a corpus. This research is based on the Gospel κατὰ Ματθαῖον in E. Nestle and K. Aland (eds.), *Novum Testamentum Graece* (Stuttgart: Deutsche Bibelstiftung, 27th edn, 1993). There are potential difficulties with this choice, given that as a critical edition NA[27] is an eclectic text, with the result that what appears in NA[27] does not correspond exactly to any extant manuscript of Matthew's Gospel. Or in other words, NA[27] as it stands does not represent an instance of naturally occurring text. This introduces a certain element of artificiality into the study which could have been avoided had I chosen instead any of the existing manuscripts of Matthew as a basis for analysis.[19] However, I believe that the potential drawbacks to using NA[27] are outweighed by the advantages of using a standard text which has widespread availability and current use among scholars who can then interact with this research. This decision also bypasses the theoretical problem of determining *which* manuscript of Matthew's Gospel would be chosen as most representative of his style for use in such a study, as well as the difficulty of establishing the text of a particular manuscript with respect to word divisions, clause boundaries, and punctuation.

This is not meant to suggest that other manuscripts and/or critical editions are not useful for the study of sentence conjunctions in the Gospel of Matthew. In fact, having developed initial conclusions about Matthew's use of sentence conjunctions based on NA[27], it could be profitable in subsequent research to test these against various other manuscripts with an eye to the possibility of particular manuscripts or families of manuscripts demonstrating differing patterns of use. In the meantime, NA[27] forms the corpus for this initial inquiry.

Although in this study I speak of 'Matthew', the 'Gospel of Matthew' and 'Matthew's narrative framework', there is of course no certainty regarding who authored the Gospel 'according to Matthew'. The broad outlines of the so-called two-source theory—that the Gospel of Matthew

---

Nerbonne writes that among researchers, 'The tendency [is] less to ask which is correct, and more to ask how we can have both' (Nerbonne, 'Introduction', p. 3).

19. For a listing of Greek manuscript evidence for the Gospel of Matthew and other New Testament documents, see B. and K. Aland, J. Karavidopoulos, C.M. Martini and B.M. Metzger (eds.), *The Greek New Testament* (Stuttgart: United Bible Societies, 4th edn, 1993), pp. xiii-xxxi. For significant variants among Matthew manuscripts, see R.J. Swanson (ed.), *New Testament Greek Manuscripts: Matthew: Variant Readings Arranged in Horizontal Lines against Codex Vaticanus* (Sheffield: Sheffield Academic Press, 1995).

draws both from Mark's Gospel and from additional material, much of which is shared with the Gospel of Luke—are accepted here as a working hypothesis, as they are by most contemporary New Testament scholars.[20] Whatever its sources, it appears that sometime between 70 CE (or earlier, according to some scholars) and about 100 CE a presumably Greek-speaking Christian of Jewish heritage, possibly in Syria, produced the form of the Gospel which we now have.[21]

In this research, however, I am not so much concerned with who the author/redactor of the Gospel may have been or with the history of its compilation per se as I am with the resulting text itself. Specifically I am

20. Luz asserts, 'To question this hypothesis is to refute a large part of the post-1945 redaction-critical research in the Synoptics, a truly daring undertaking which seems to me to be neither necessary nor possible' (U. Luz, *Matthew 1–7* [trans. W.C. Linss; Minneapolis: Augsburg, 1989], p. 46). This is not to say, however, that there is unanimity on this point among New Testament scholars. Wright describes Farmer's *The Synoptic Problem* (1964), in which Farmer argues that Mark is the latest of the three Synoptic Gospels, as a work 'in which one of the most "assured results" of a century of research was painstakingly dismantled, leaving (so it appeared) scarcely one stone upon another' (S. Neill and T. Wright, *The Interpretation of the New Testament, 1861–1986* [Oxford: Oxford University Press, 2nd edn, 1988], p. 360); see W.R. Farmer, *The Synoptic Problem: A Critical Analysis* (New York: Macmillan, 1964). France observes, 'If it was once possible to use the classical "Two-Document Hypothesis" as a non-negotiable framework for the study of the gospels, that time is now past', but France adopts the assumption that 'where Matthew and Mark run parallel it is more likely that the Marcan version is the earlier, and that therefore it is possible to discern Matthew's special interests in the differences between his version and Mark's, even if it would be over-simple to speak baldly of his "altering the Marcan text"' (R.T. France, *The Gospel According to Matthew: An Introduction and Commentary* [TNTC; Leicester: Inter-Varsity Press, 1985], pp. 37-38). For a brief introduction to the two-source theory and challenges to it, see D. Senior, *What Are They Saying about Matthew?* (New York: Paulist Press, revd edn, 1996), pp. 21-25.

21. See, for example, W.C. Allen, *A Critical and Exegetical Commentary on the Gospel According to S. Matthew* (ICC; Edinburgh: T. & T. Clark, 3rd edn, 1912), pp. lxxxiv-lxxxv; A.H. McNeile, *The Gospel According to St Matthew* (London: Macmillan, 1938), p. xxviii; E. Schweizer, 'Matthew's Church', in G. Stanton (ed.), *The Interpretation of Matthew* (Studies in New Testament Interpretation; Edinburgh: T. & T. Clark, 2nd edn, 1995), pp. 149-50; Luz, *Matthew 1–7*, pp. 82, 90-93; D.A. Hagner, *Matthew 1–13* (WBC, 33A; Dallas: Word Books, 1993), pp. lxxiii-lxxvii. See also the extensive and helpful introduction in W.D. Davies and D.C. Allison, *A Critical and Exegetical Commentary on the Gospel According to Saint Matthew*. I. *Introduction and Commentary on Matthew I–VII* (ICC; Edinburgh: T. & T. Clark, 1988), pp. 7-58, 127-47.

interested in what a direct analysis of the text may reveal about linguistic choices made during its construction. 'Matthew' and 'Matthew's Gospel' will be used in the discussion to refer to the author/redactor and to the canonical text as a matter of convention, without intending to imply a more precise identification of the Evangelist.

Focus on narrative. Although I am interested in all discourse types in the Gospel of Matthew, this study focuses primarily on Matthew's narrative framework. There are two important reasons for this. First, in the rather small corpus which this Gospel represents the narrative component offers the largest amount of relatively homogenous data for linguistic analysis. Approximately one-third of the sentences in Matthew's Gospel can be characterized as forming the narrative framework (720 of 2302 sentences in the database), one-third as quoted speech or dialogue (733/2302), and one-third as more extended exposition attributed to Jesus (768/2302). However, the sentences I have designated as speech and expository discourse actually incorporate a wide range of discourse types: statements of fact, questions, commands, pronouncements of blessing or woe, prayer, parables and so on. It is unlikely that there are enough examples among these discourse types to yield statistically meaningful results about the use of sentence conjunctions in various linguistic contexts. On the other hand, sentences in the narrative framework are more similar in structure and purpose, and together form a large enough body of comparable data to generate meaningful results.

Secondly and just as importantly, Matthew's narrative framework is both essential to his portrayal of Jesus and fundamental to his unique contribution among the Synoptic Gospels. As Luz writes,

> Several signs indicate that the Gospel of Matthew was intended to be primarily a *narrative book*. Matthew made a decision to this effect by using the Gospel of Mark as the basis for his own presentation, even though in several points it was not close to him theologically.[22]

Luz describes Matthew's choice of Mark as the basis for his Gospel as the most important theological decision he makes. 'This means theologically: *He has tied the ethical proclamation of Jesus concerning the kingdom of God to the history of God's actions with Jesus*.'[23] Luz's point holds whether or not one accepts that Matthew is directly dependent on Mark:

---

22. Luz, *Matthew 1–7*, p. 42 (his emphasis).
23. Luz, *Matthew 1–7*, p. 44 (his emphasis).

Matthew ties his report of what Jesus said to a description of what Jesus and others purportedly did in an historical context. Thus the ways in which Matthew structures his narrative framework, rearranging Mark's account (if one accepts the hypothesis of Markan priority) and incorporating material unique to his Gospel, comprise a great deal of what the text conveys about Jesus. Linguistic insights into narrative structure in Matthew's Gospel can make a significant contribution to the study of Matthean theology.

The Database

As Biber *et al.* explain, 'Corpus-based studies usually have one of two primary research goals: describing a linguistic structure and its variants ... or describing some group of texts'.[24] This study describes a linguistic structure—or, more precisely, the linguistic *system* of paratactic sentence conjunctions in the Gospel of Matthew, especially in the narrative framework—and variants within the system. Biber *et al.* outline the basic method used in such studies:

> The unit[s] of analysis in corpus-based studies…are called the 'observations' for the study. Each observation is an occurrence of the structure in question… There are a number of contextual factors that might be influential in making the choice between…variants… To investigate the relative influence of these contextual factors, we would code a large sample of…constructions, where each clause constitutes a separate observation… Each line represents the information about a single observation—i.e., a single occurrence… Each column represents the values for a different variable… Using data such as these, we are able to carry out a number of quantitative analyses to determine the association of different contextual factors with the…structural variants. The simplest of these is to produce cross-tabulation tables, which display the frequency counts for each combination of values across variables… Given a large enough data set, we could also consider the influence of multiple factors at the same time… Statistical techniques can also be used to analyze the significance and strength of these associations.[25]

These are essentially the methods I employ in analyzing patterns of use of sentence conjunctions in Matthew's Gospel. I code a large sample of constructions, in fact all of the occurrences of paratactic sentence conjunctions and asyndeton in the Gospel of Matthew—more than 2300

24. Biber *et al.*, *Corpus Linguistics*, p. 269.
25. Biber *et al.*, *Corpus Linguistics*, pp. 269-73.

'observations'. Each line in the database represents the occurrence of a sentence conjunction or asyndeton in the Gospel, and each column (that is, each database field) represents a contextual variable. In the chapters which follow I offer cross-tabulation tables displaying collocations between particular conjunctions and contextual variables. Where possible I attempt to identify the interaction of multiple variables. I utilize statistical techniques to analyze the significance and strength of various collocations.

The major point at which I differ from the methodological paradigm above is in treating sentence conjunctions as a system in the Hallidayan sense. I am interested not merely in describing contextual variables that collocate with a single structure, but in trying to explain how contextual variables interact with multiple options within a system.

Fields and Variables
A number of fields and variables are defined in the database. By 'fields' I mean the information grouped in columns, sets of related items which often correspond to systems within the grammar (for example, verbal tense-form or subject reference). By 'variables' I mean the specific items grouped within these sets, such as *present*, *aorist*, *imperfect* and so on in the verbal tense-form field.

The identification of meaningful fields and variables relating to Matthew's use of sentence conjunctions is one of the problems which this research addresses. The search for syntactical or lexical elements within sentences which may have significant correlations with the sentence conjunctions beginning those sentences, along with features above sentence level which may also correlate with the choice of sentence conjunction (for example, a change in grammatical subject from one sentence to another), is at the heart of my attempt to identify formal dimensions of discourse structure. Further research may determine additional fields and/or variables which collocate with sentence conjunctions, or may suggest ways to refine the fields and variables identified here.

Chapter, verse, clause. Fields for chapter, verse and clause primarily serve to designate the various sentences in the database, allowing the data to be identified and sorted easily. (The field for 'clause' indicates which sentence in the verse—designated *a, b, c* and so on—is meant if more than one occurs.) However, the deceptively simple exercise of listing the sentences in the Gospel of Matthew forces the more difficult decision of which clauses will be included for analysis.

As in many languages, determining the boundaries of a sentence in the Greek of the New Testament is not always straightforward. Bloomfield's now classic definition of the sentence as 'an independent linguistic form, not included by virtue of any grammatical construction in any larger linguistic form', raises difficulties for this research, as sentence conjunctions themselves could be understood as grammatical constructions which link the sentence to a larger linguistic form, a discourse.[26] In his study of δέ, οὖν, καί and asyndeton in John's Gospel, Poythress defines a sentence as a 'maximal clause', 'not embedded in or modifying a still larger clause, together with the sentence conjunction (if any) at its beginning'. He admits a certain degree of circularity, since a sentence is being defined in terms of sentence conjunctions, but notes that sentences are also characterized by grammatical 'closure' and that 'an entire discourse can be analyzed into a string of sentences with no remainder'.[27] Although no definition is completely satisfying, Poythress's general approach is adopted here.

This study treats all independent clauses as separate sentences. In other words, all clauses with verbs which can stand independently—that is, finite verbs marked for person, thus omitting participles (including 'genitive absolute' participles) and infinitives—plus verbless equative or attributive clauses are treated as sentences. A sentence is defined as having one and only one such finite verb (or verbless equative construction). The terms 'sentence', 'independent clause', and 'clause' are used interchangeably in the discussion, unless a distinction is made in a particular context. When two or more finite verbs are so closely linked that they could arguably be described as one sentence rather than two clauses (usually having the same implied subject and joined by καί with no intervening words), I treat the second verbal 'clause' as a sentence with a separate entry in the database—and likewise for the third, if applicable—but also

26. L. Bloomfield, *Language* (London: George Allen & Unwin, 1935), p. 170. Crystal observes that while there are 'innumerable' attempts to define the sentence, 'most linguistic definitions of the sentence show the influence of … Bloomfield' (D. Crystal, *A Dictionary of Linguistics and Phonetics* [Oxford: Basil Blackwell, 4th edn, 1997], p. 347).

27. Poythress, 'Intersentence Conjunctions', p. 315. Abbott similarly suggests that the presence of a conjunction 'often helps us discern the beginning of a sentence' in Greek (E.A. Abbot, *Johannine Grammar* [London: Adam & Charles Black, 1906], p. 69). Buth makes use of Poythress's definition of the sentence as a 'maximal clause'; see Buth, 'Οὖν, Δέ, Καί, and Asyndeton', p. 144 n. 2.

indicate in another field that this is potentially part of a compound sentence.[28] This determination represents a judgment call on my part. I have used this designation fewer than ten times in narrative clauses in the database.[29]

Sentences which begin with γάρ are also included, although there may be room for debate concerning whether some of these are properly coordinate (paratactic) or subordinate (hypotactic) clauses. Γάρ begins sentences only ten times in Matthew's narrative framework.[30] Ότι is included in the database in only three types of context in which it is found: following and related to an imperative; following a speech margin to introduce direct speech;[31] and in combination with μακάριος and οὐαί. The difficulty of deciding whether or not to include various ὅτι clauses and similar clauses, for example those with ἵνα and μήποτε which seem to alternate with ὅτι and γάρ following imperatives, suggests that the distinction between coordinate and subordinate clauses may be far from absolute or that these forms may be used in both paratactic and hypotactic contexts.

On the basis of these guidelines, 2302 independent clauses—that is, sentences—in Matthew's Gospel are identified in the database.

Discourse type. Each sentence is designated as one of four discourse types: narrative (events recounted from the narrator's viewpoint in roughly temporal order, forming the framework for the discourse), exposition (longer discourse sections attributed to Jesus, including parables), speech (conversation between Jesus and others, or among other characters; short statements attributed to Jesus, especially as a reply to another's question or statement), or Old Testament quotation (longer citations as indicated in

---

28. Buth takes a similar approach in 'ambiguous situations where two clauses joined together could be thought of as two maximal clauses, yet semantically they seem to be one compound maximal clause'. In such situations he treats the clauses as maximal and as sentences. 'Such a definition does justice to the surface structure since a writer has a choice of using subordination or two coordinated sentences' (Buth, 'Οὖν, Δέ, Καί, and Asyndeton', p. 144 n. 2).

29. Mt. 4.11, 14.3, 17.24, 20.32, 26.50, 27.30, 28.9; for a similar construction with three verbless clauses, see 1.17.

30. Mt. 4.18, 7.29, 9.21, 14.3, 14.4, 14.24, 19.22, 26.43, 27.18, 28.2.

31. The term 'speech margin' refers to syntactical structures used to introduce direct speech, whether conversation or monologue, and to set it into the narrative framework. A speech margin usually, but not necessarily, includes a verb of speaking such as λέγω, either in a finite form or as a participle.

NA[27]—only sentence conjunction, discourse type and whether the sentence is the first in a quoted sequence are noted for these). These distinctions allow me to isolate the narrative sentences, dropping out the intervening speech and expository segments to follow more closely the underlying structure of Matthew's storytelling.

Mode. For the purposes of this study four sentence-types, or 'modes', are identified: declarative, modulated declarative, imperatival, and interrogative.[32] In treating issues of mood and modality, the following principles are followed in the database: [33]

- Declarative sentences are those with indicative verbs, verbless sentences, and sentences with μή and a subjunctive verb used to express negation. In these sentences the speaker expresses an attitude of definiteness or certainty toward the content of the sentence.
- Modulated declarative sentences have a modulating element containing ἄν or one of its compounds. They may have an indicative or subjunctive verb form or be verbless. In these sentences the speaker expresses an attitude of indefiniteness, uncertainty or possibility toward the content of the sentence.
- Imperatival sentences are those with imperative verbal forms, as well as some sentences with subjunctive or future verb forms used with imperatival force.

Except for sentences with μή and a subjunctive verb used to express negation and sentences with subjunctive or future forms functioning as imperatives, these determinations were made formally, based on the main verb of the sentence or on the presence of ἄν, rather than by analyzing speech acts.

- Interrogative sentences are classified as such based on their punctuation as questions by NA[27]. They are considered interrogative sentences regardless of which of the other three sentence-types they might have been designated without such punctuation.

---

32. 'Mode' is not used here in Halliday's sense of 'mode' as a component of context alongside 'field' and 'tenor'; see, for example, M.A.K. Halliday and R. Hasan, *Language, Context, and Text: Aspects of Language in a Social-Semiotic Perspective* (Victoria, Australia: Deakin University, 1985), pp. 24-28.

33. See also the entry on 'mood (modal, -ity)' in Crystal, *Dictionary*, pp. 247-48.

In addition, a few sentences which do not easily fit into the above categories, such as pronouncements of blessing or woe (μακάριος or οὐαί), are designated 'other'. Declarative sentences, either with finite verbs or verbless, constitute the only mode in this schema which occurs in the narrative framework, except for the unique aside to the reader, ὁ ἀναγινώσκων νοείτω, in 24.15.

Sentence conjunction. As discussed in Chapter 1, Halliday describes 'theme' as 'the element which serves as the point of departure of the message; it is that with which the clause is concerned'.[34] It appears to be the case that in the Greek of the New Testament, as in many languages, thematic elements are placed at or near the beginning of the sentence.[35]

To reiterate, Halliday identifies several components of theme, not all of which are present in all clauses: textual, interpersonal and experiential (or topical), usually in that order in English. The textual theme 'is any combination of (i) continuative, (ii) structural and (iii) conjunctive' in English.[36] Halliday describes these elements as having a textual metafunction, creating relevance to context.[37] In this study sentence conjunctions in the Gospel of Matthew are treated within Halliday's notion of textual theme.

In the Greek of the New Testament the sentence conjunction appears either as the first word in the sentence or, in the case of postpositive forms like δέ, as the second or even the third, fourth, or fifth word in the sentence.[38] Seventeen sentence conjunctions plus similar particles or particle combinations in the Gospel of Matthew are identified in the database—ἀλλά, ἄρα, γάρ, δέ, διὰ τοῦτο, διό, εἰ δὲ μή γε, ἤ, καί, μηδέ, μέν, ὅτι, οὐδέ, οὖν, πάλιν, πλήν and τότε—as well as numerous instances of asyndeton. Of these, γάρ, δέ, καί, οὖν, τότε and asyndeton are by far the most common, together accounting for 93% of the sentences in Matthew's Gospel and 99% of those in the narrative framework. On this basis γάρ, δέ, καί, οὖν, τότε and asyndeton were selected for detailed analysis.

34. Halliday, *Introduction*, p. 37.
35. See, for example, Moule, *Idiom Book*, p. 166; BDF, §472.
36. Halliday, *Introduction*, p. 53.
37. Halliday, *Introduction*, pp. 33-34.
38. Robertson observes that postpositive words commonly appear in second position in the New Testament, but can be found further along in the sentence. He notes that δέ, for example, appears in fourth place in Jn 8.16 and in fifth place in 1 Jn 2.2 (Robertson, *Grammar*, p. 424). See also BDF, §475.

Other textual theme. In addition to the sentence conjunctions recorded in the previous field, this field identifies 75 instances in which other words toward the beginning of a sentence also appear to be elements of textual theme, functioning primarily to tie the sentence to preceding text. These include 13 instances of εὐθέως and 2 of εὐθύς; forms which combine with καί, such as instances of καὶ τότε, and 1 use each of καὶ ἀπὸ τότε (26.16) and καὶ διὰ τοῦτο (14.2); words and phrases such as ὁμοίως καί, οὕτως, οὕτως καί and ὡσαύτως, which point directly to previous text; and other forms with similar cohesive functions.

Interpersonal theme and modulation. In Halliday's terms the clause may also have an interpersonal theme. The interpersonal theme 'is any combination of (i) vocative, (ii) modal, (iii) mood-marking'.[39] It grammaticalizes the interpersonal metafunction of language, the enacting of social relationships.[40]

This database field covers a range of features found at or near the beginning of the sentence which generally correspond with Halliday's notion of interpersonal theme. Included in the field are vocative elements and interpersonal lexical items such as ἀμήν, ἰδού, οὐαί and χαῖρε. Also included are a variety of modal elements and other elements which play a role in the attitude toward reality expressed in the sentence: interrogative pronouns, particles, or phrases; indefinite relative clauses, with or without ἄν and its compounds; indefinite temporal clauses with ὅταν or similar forms; conditional clauses with εἰ or ἐάν; ὥσπερ, usually followed by οὕτως; and negative particles.

Topical theme. As explained in Chapter 1, Halliday's experiential or topical theme is 'the first element that has a function in transitivity'.[41] Within the system of transitivity Halliday includes processes (typically verbal groups), participants (typically nominal groups), and circumstances (typically adverbial groups or prepositional phrases), which may be understood as roughly equivalent to traditional grammatical notions of verb, subject, object, indirect object, or adverb—the conceptual 'core' of the sentence. These elements contribute to the clause's 'ideational function, its role as a means of representing patterns of experience'. As Halliday writes, 'Usually when people talk about what a word or a

---

39. Halliday, *Introduction*, p. 53.
40. See Halliday, *Introduction*, pp. 33-34.
41. Halliday, *Introduction*, p. 53.

sentence "means", it is this kind of meaning they have in mind—meaning in the sense of content'.[42] The topical theme, then, is the first element of this type which appears in the sentence, usually following any textual or interpersonal theme.

A variety of items occurs in the position of topical theme in Matthew's Gospel: verbs, participles (usually aorist nominative), subjects (nominative case), direct objects (usually accusative case), indirect objects (dative case), prepositional phrases (generally with time or place reference), adverbs (also generally time or place reference), temporal phrases with ὅτε, genitive modifiers, predicate nominative constructions in copulative or verbless clauses, and hanging nominative constructions. Genitive absolute participial constructions are also treated as topical theme when they appear in this position.

I have treated an interrogative particle or phrase as the topical theme if it also functions as part of the transitivity structure and is the first element with such a function. Thus in 3.7, τίς ὑπέδειξεν ὑμῖν φυγεῖν ἀπὸ τῆς μελλούσης ὀργῆς;, τίς is noted in two fields: as the topical theme (an interrogative pronoun functioning as the grammatical subject) and in the field for 'interpersonal theme and modulation' as a marker of mode (interrogative).

Halliday observes that a conditional clause can function thematically if it precedes the clause it modifies.[43] In modulated declarative sentences I treat clauses including ἄν or one of its compounds, other conditional clauses, and indefinite relative clauses as topical theme if they occur before the finite verb, as well as noting in a separate field their role in modality. For example, in 6.14, ἐὰν γὰρ ἀφῆτε τοῖς ἀνθρώποις τὰ παραπτώματα αὐτῶν, ἀφήσει καὶ ὑμῖν ὁ πατὴρ ὑμῶν ὁ οὐράνιος, the conditional clause ἐὰν γὰρ ἀφῆτε τοῖς ἀνθρώποις τὰ παραπτώματα αὐτῶν is treated both as the topical theme and in the field for 'interpersonal theme and modulation' as a marker of mode (modulated declarative) because of the ἄν compound, ἐάν. Identifying the theme in such clause complexes can occasionally be an intricate process, as is evident even in Halliday's multi-layered analysis of similar constructions.[44] It is worth noting that none of the sentences in the narrative framework, which forms the main focus of this research, includes

42. Halliday, *Introduction*, p. 106.
43. See Halliday, *Introduction*, pp. 56-57.
44. See, for example, Halliday, *Introduction*, pp. 56-57.

interrogative or modulating elements, so these more complex examples do not affect the analysis of narrative structure.

Fronted participle. Circumstantial participles which occur before the main verb, whether as the topical theme or as another fronted constituent (that is, as another element appearing before the verb), are identified and parsed in this field. Tense-form and case are noted, as well as whether the participle is part of a genitive absolute construction.

Other fronted elements. This field includes any other elements in the transitivity structure which appear before the verb but after the topical theme. Items include participles, subjects, direct objects, indirect objects, prepositional phrases, adverbs, temporal phrases with ὅτε, and genitive modifiers.

Verbal tense-form. The tense-form of the main verb is identified here: aorist, imperfect, present, future, perfect, or pluperfect. Imperatives are noted. Although present and aorist tense-form imperatives originally were not distinguished in the database, notes concerning tense-forms of imperatives in exposition were later added in the 'other' field (see below). Subjunctive forms in prohibitions are included and identified as such. Instances of εἰμί are noted in order to facilitate their omission in quantitative analyses involving verbal tense-form, to allow for the aspectual vagueness of εἰμί.[45] Verbless clauses are indicated by '0'.

Subject. The notional subject of the sentence is identified, even if the verb is monolectic (that is, the verb does not have a grammaticalized subject) and an implied subject has to be sought in surrounding text. Thus this field is semantic rather than merely formal.

Subject reference. The maximal reference to the grammatical subject within the sentence is noted, even if it appears outside the independent clause (for example, in a conditional clause or subordinate clause). This may be a proper noun, noun phrase, pronoun, relative clause, pronominal article, or a lexical item such as αὐτός, οὗτος, πάντες, or ἄλλοι. Sentences with no grammaticalized subject are indicated by '0'. In

---

45. For a discussion of the aspectual vagueness of verbs which, like εἰμί, do not evidence fully developed morphological distinctions between tense-forms, see Porter, *Verbal Aspect*, pp. 442-47.

combinations of more than one type of reference both are indicated, joined by '+'.

Agent. Active, middle and passive forms of verbs are not distinguished in the database. If the agent of the action of the verb is the same as the notional subject (grammaticalized or implied), 's' for 'same' appears in this field. Otherwise a full reference to the implied agent is given, even if this has to be sought in surrounding text. Thus this field, too, is semantic rather than formal, and occasionally it is not possible to make a definitive identification of the implied agent.

Other. Several other features were noted in this field, most importantly whether the sentence functions as a speech margin, with or without forms of λέγω or φημί. Sentences in which a second (or third) clause has a verb so closely linked to the preceding clause that they might best be described as forming one compound sentence (see 'Chapter, verse, clause' above) are identified here. Succeeding clauses in such a cluster are indicated by '+2' in this field. Tense-forms of imperatives in exposition are also noted here.

Notes. Miscellaneous observations on various sentences and combinations of sentences are also recorded. These include instances of recurrent phrases or unusual grammatical constructions; various subgroupings within discourse types, such as parable, genealogy, or prayer; incidents of ellipsis; contextual information about usage of lexical items like ἰδού, μακάριος or οὐαί; and other general observations.

Constituent order. Two additional fields were created for sentences of narrative discourse type only. The first, constituent order, was syntheti- cally derived from information in the fields for topical theme, other fronted elements, and subject reference, rather than by direct observation. Only two elements are considered in this simplified analysis of constituent order: the main verb (if any), and the grammaticalized subject (if any), in relation to each other. Other predicate or complement elements are not considered. Specifically, the presence of any direct object is not included in the description of constituent order, even though most studies of constituent order in language typology identify subject, verb and object: VSO, SOV, SVO and so forth. (However, thematic direct objects are identified in the field for topical theme and included in analyses of sentence conjunction and theme.) Grammaticalized subjects appearing before the main verb are distinguished in terms of whether they function as the topical theme or as a subsequent fronted element.

For the purposes of this study, six constituent orders are delineated: verbless sentences ('0'); sentences with an explicit subject as the first, or thematic, element in the transitivity structure of the sentence ('S_1V'); sentences with an explicit subject preceding the verb, but not in thematic position ('S_2V'); sentences with an explicit subject appearing after the verb ('VS'); monolectic verbs, or sentences in which no subject is grammaticalized ('V'); and clauses which contain the second (or third) verb in a sequence which could be described as forming one compound sentence with the preceding clause ('+2').[46]

Analysis of various constituent orders yielded significant correlations with specific sentence conjunctions, as will be shown in the following chapters.

Subject switch. The second field added for narrative discourse only, 'subject switch', is defined as a change in the notional subject—that is, the grammaticalized subject if any, or the equivalent participant as understood from context if there is no explicit subject—from the previous sentence in the narrative framework. This field is thus semantic rather than formal. In earlier stages of the research this field was given the name 'topic switch' to reflect usage of the notion of 'topic' by other linguists, and that designation is retained in the original report of the multivariate statistical analysis done on my behalf by Elizabeth Allen (more on Allen's work below).[47] However, 'topic switch' was later changed to 'subject switch'

---

46. I found no example of VS constituent order with a thematic nominative participle in Matthew's narrative framework, that is, sentences of the structure <nominative participle + verb + subject>. This raises questions concerning the interaction of participles and finite verbs in Greek narrative syntax which are beyond the scope of the simplified analysis of constituent order undertaken here. Further research on the role of participles in discourse structure in the Greek of the New Testament is needed to address this issue. See, for example, Hoyle, ' "Scenario" Theory'.

47. See, for example, J. Lyons, *Introduction to Theoretical Linguistics* (Cambridge: Cambridge University Press, 1968), pp. 334-37; Li (ed.), *Subject and Topic*; van Dijk, *Text and Context,* pp. 114-16; T. Givón, 'Topic Continuity in Discourse: An Introduction', in *idem* (ed.), *Topic Continuity in Discourse: A Quantitative Cross-Language Study* (Amsterdam and Philadelphia: John Benjamins, 1983), pp. 1-42. See also E. Allen, 'Greek Syntactical Analysis: An Investigation into the Relationship

both to clarify the focus on the syntactical subject as opposed to other notions of discourse topic, and to eliminate possible confusion with Halliday's notion of topical theme.

In a few instances the database may not reveal clearly whether a subject switch has taken place. This indeterminacy arises if a change in the notional subject occurs between the current sentence and a preceding subordinate clause or a participial phrase (including a genitive absolute construction) which is not included among the independent coordinate clauses which make up the database. So, for example, 14.6-8:

14.6 ... ὠρχήσατο ἡ θυγάτηρ τῆς Ἡρῳδιάδος ...
14.7 ὅθεν μεθ' ὅρκου ὡμολόγησεν αὐτῇ δοῦναι ὃ ἐὰν αἰτήσεται.
14.8 ἡ δὲ ... φησίν ...

In this instance, the central clause, 14.7, ὅθεν μεθ' ὅρκου ὡμολόγησεν αὐτῇ δοῦναι ὃ ἐὰν αἰτήσεται, is omitted from the database because it is treated as a subordinate clause beginning with ὅθεν. As a result, the database indicates only the continuity between 14.6 and 14.8 with Herodias's daughter as the subject, and not the intervening action by Herod in 14.7. As there are very few such examples in the narrative framework, they were not deemed numerous enough to affect adversely the general patterns reflected in the analysis of subject switch.

Examples
Although some of the elements in more complex sentences in exposition or speech are difficult to classify, the 'parsing' of sentences in the narrative framework is relatively straightforward. The following illustrates how a few representative sentences from Matthew's narrative framework are handled:

2.19 τελευτήσαντος δὲ τοῦ Ἡρῴδου ἰδοὺ ἄγγελος κυρίου φαίνεται κατ' ὄναρ τῷ Ἰωσὴφ ἐν Αἰγύπτῳ λέγων· ...

The *sentence conjunction* is δέ; the *topical theme* is the genitive absolute participial phrase τελευτήσαντος... τοῦ Ἡρῴδου; ἰδού is treated as an *interpersonal theme*; the grammaticalized subject, ἄγγελος κυρίου, appears before the verb but after the topical theme, so *constituent order* is S$_2$V; *verbal tense-form* is present

between Conjunctions and Contextual Variables in the Gospel of Matthew' (unpublished MSc thesis, University College London, September 1999).

(φαίνεται); the sentence functions as a *speech margin* with a participial form of λέγω; there is *subject switch* from τὸ ῥηθέν in the previous narrative sentence (2.17).

13.1 ἐν τῇ ἡμέρᾳ ἐκείνῃ ἐξελθὼν ὁ Ἰησοῦς τῆς οἰκίας ἐκάθητο παρὰ τὴν θάλασσαν.

There is no *sentence conjunction* (asyndeton); the *topical theme* is the temporal prepositional phrase ἐν τῇ ἡμέρᾳ ἐκείνῃ; there is an additional fronted element, the participial phrase ἐξελθὼν ... τῆς οἰκίας; the grammaticalized subject, ὁ Ἰησοῦς, appears after the topical theme but before the verb so *constituent order* is again S₂V;[48] *verbal tense-form* is imperfect (ἐκάθητο); there is continuity of subject (no *subject switch*) with the previous narrative sentence (12.49).

26.40 καὶ ἔρχεται πρὸς τοὺς μαθητὰς καὶ εὑρίσκει αὐτοὺς καθεύδοντας, καὶ λέγει τῷ Πέτρῳ·...

This is handled as three separate 'sentences', each with καί as the *sentence conjunction*, a present tense-form verb as the *topical theme*, and monolectic (V) *constituent order*; there is continuity of subject (no *subject switch*) of the first sentence with the previous narrative sentence (26.39), and of each of the two subsequent sentences with the one before it; the third sentence functions as a *speech margin* with λέγω.

Evaluating the Data

Once the fields and variables to be analyzed have been determined, the text is then parsed and the manually collected data are recorded in the database. The next step is to count and compare the relative frequencies of different variables, looking for features which show a tendency to collocate with particular sentence conjunctions.

48. If the prepositional phrase were absent, i.e. if the sentence began ἐξελθὼν ὁ Ἰησοῦς τῆς οἰκίας ἐκάθητο... the participial phrase would be considered the topical theme because it is the first element in the sentence, and ὁ Ἰησοῦς treated as the second element, in spite of the fact that ὁ Ἰησοῦς is found within the participial phrase.

At this point the question of what constitutes a 'meaningful' numerical result arises. If καί, for example, is the sentence conjunction in almost half (47%) of narrative sentences in the Gospel of Matthew, but in less than a third (30%) of sentences with present tense-form finite verbs (the so-called 'historic present'), how does one determine whether this is a meaningful difference? Or similarly, if δέ is the sentence conjunction in only about a third (36%) of sentences in Matthew's narrative framework, but appears in almost eight out of ten instances (79%) in which the grammatical subject is the topical theme in the sentence, how confident can one be that this represents a meaningful pattern in sentences of this type rather than just a random result?

Z-scores

I use z-scores as a test of statistical significance in most such comparisons. Although what follows by no means represents an exhaustive or theoretically adequate description of the mathematical properties involved, the rationale and use of z-scores can be described here briefly.[49]

The z-score is based on a standard normal distribution, the so-called 'bell curve'. Statisticians have found that the standard normal distribution is so predictable in its symmetrical bell shape that for randomly distributed data they can speak of 'a sort of typical distance from the mean', which is referred to as a 'standard deviation'.[50] The 'mean' is the center of the curve, at its highest point, representing the outcome that occurs most frequently. Statisticians have found that about 68% of randomly distributed data will fall within one standard deviation on either side of the mean, more than 95% of the data will fall within two standard deviations of the mean, and approximately 99.7% of the data will fall within three standard deviations of the mean.[51]

A z-score is just a way of expressing the distance from a mean in terms

---

49. For a more detailed introduction to z-scores, see L.B. Christensen and C.M. Stoup, *Introduction to Statistics for the Social and Behavioral Sciences* (Pacific Grove, CA: Brooks/Cole, 2nd edn, 1991), pp. 88-94; W. Chase and F. Brown, *General Statistics* (New York: John Wiley & Sons, 2nd edn, 1992), pp. 95-97; G. Barnbrook, *Language and Computers: A Practical Introduction to the Computer Analysis of Language* (ETEL; Edinburgh: Edinburgh University Press, 1996), pp. 95-97; M.P. Oakes, *Statistics for Corpus Linguistics* (ETEL; Edinburgh: Edinburgh University Press, 1998), pp. 7-8.

50. Chase and Brown, *General Statistics*, p. 82.

51. Chase and Brown, *General Statistics*, p. 87.

of standard deviations. To say, for example, that a value has a *z*-score of 1.68 is another way of saying that the value lies 1.68 standard deviations above the mean on a particular normal distribution. Similarly, to refer to a *z*-score of −2.28 is another way of saying that a value lies −2.28 standard deviations below the mean on a particular normal distribution. The essential point for the application of *z*-scores as a test of significance is that only a very small amount of data (less than 5%, or 1–95%) will fall more than two standard deviations from the mean, and only a negligible amount (0.3%, or 1–99.7%) will fall more than three standard deviations from the mean. Thus a *z*-score equal to or greater than ±2—a value that falls two standard deviations or more from the mean—suggests a non-random occurrence, or in other words, an outcome occurring less than 5% of the time in randomly distributed data. For this reason, a *z*-score of ±2 is often chosen as a cut-off point for significance in statistical analysis, and is said to represent a 5% 'confidence level'.

In this study *z*-scores are used to express a sentence conjunction's frequency in a particular context, in comparison to the frequency that would be expected based on that conjunction's distribution in the narrative framework as a whole. For example, while δέ is the sentence conjunction in 36% of all sentences in Matthew's narrative framework, I find that in a particular set of sentences, the 149 narrative sentences with VS (verb–subject) constituent order, δέ is the conjunction in only 19%. A *z*-score of −4.13 indicates that this result falls more than four standard deviations below the mean that would be expected if samples of 149 sentences were selected randomly from the narrative framework, suggesting that there is a statistically significant disassociation between δέ and VS sentences.[52] I have chosen a *z*-score of ±3 as the cut-off point for significance in my analyses rather than the more widely used ±2. This higher threshold makes a conservative adjustment for the fact that there are actually multiple tests

---

52. To calculate *z*-scores I have used the following formula:

$$z = \frac{O-E}{\sigma}, \text{ that is, } z = \frac{O-E}{\sqrt{n \cdot p(1-p)}}$$

where *O* is the *observed value*, in this case the actual number of VS sentences having δέ as the sentence conjunction (29). *E* is the *expected value*, the number that would be expected if δέ had the same frequency of use in VS sentences as in the narrative framework overall (53.18). σ is the standard deviation (5.85). In the calculation of the standard deviation *p* represents the probability of δέ occurring (257/720, or 0.357), and *n* is the number of sentences in the sample (149).

involved in most of these analyses. That is, several sentence conjunctions in Matthew's narrative framework (καί, δέ, τότε, γάρ, οὖν and asyndeton) are being compared to each other in several linguistic contexts (for example, S_1V, S_2V, VS or V constituent order) at the same time, rather than just the two possible outcomes—as, for example, 'heads' or 'tails' in a coin toss—assumed in the standard normal distribution. Used in this somewhat *ad hoc* way, a z-score of ±3 can be said to represent a 5% confidence level for up to about 20 tests at a time.[53]

It is also important to note that because z-scores are expressed in units of standard deviations, and because one of the factors in the calculation of the standard deviation is the size of the sample, z-scores can indicate whether a value is statistically significant *for that size sample*. As an indicator of statistical significance z-scores yield less meaningful results when sample sizes are less than 30. For this reason, t-scores are sometimes used in statistical analysis instead of z-scores when the sample size is less than 30.[54] The t-score is similar to the z-score in representing a typical distance from a mean, but there are differences between z-scores and t-scores in calculating both the standard deviation and the test statistic itself. In this study I have chosen to use z-scores only, both to maintain consistency among comparisons and because few of the relevant samples have fewer than 30 items, but I note where smaller sample sizes limit the reliability of a z-score as a measure of statistical significance.

While z-scores are a less sophisticated measure of significance than the approach taken by Allen and Farewell in their analysis of my data from Matthew's narrative framework (see below), z-scores are relatively simple for the lay person to understand and use in comparing quantitative results, and so form a useful starting point for evaluating the significance and strength of various combinations of features in this study of Matthew's sentence conjunctions.

53. V. Farewell, personal communication.

54. In a paper published in 1908, Gosset described the probability distribution of data in smaller samples. Gosset found that the t-distribution resembles the standard normal distribution—the so-called bell curve—except that it is flatter and more spread out. In fact, the curve of the t-distribution varies with the size of the samples involved. With very small samples the curve is flattest and most widely spread; with increasingly larger sample sizes, the curve gets closer and closer to the standard normal distribution. With sample sizes of 30 or more, the curve is approximately the same as the standard normal distribution. For a more extensive introduction to the t-distribution, see Christensen and Stoup, *Introduction to Statistics*, pp. 234-39; Chase and Brown, *General Statistics*, pp. 354-70; Oakes, *Statistics for Corpus Linguistics*, pp. 11-14.

Multivariate Analysis

Comparing two variables—for example, one sentence conjunction and one collocating feature—is a relatively straightforward process. Comparing more than two variables simultaneously in the search for a more nuanced model of linguistic interaction is a much more complex endeavor which, depending on how many variables are involved, may in practical terms be impossible without computer software packages designed for statistical analysis. However, as Halliday asserts, human language involves networks of systems, or, in other words, simultaneous choices among multiple variables. For help in analyzing the interaction of multiple variables in Matthew's narrative framework I am indebted to Vern Farewell and Elizabeth Allen of the Department of Statistical Science, University College London. Under the supervision of Professor Farewell, Allen developed logistic regression models based on my data, relating sentence conjunctions to the collocating features I identified in the narrative framework of Matthew's Gospel.[55] A summary by Allen and Farewell of this analysis appears as the appendix to this volume.[56]

As Allen explains,

> Logistic regression is a mathematical modeling approach that can be used to describe the relationship of several predictor variables $X_1, X_2, X_3 \ldots X_k$ to a *dichotomous* dependent variable Y, where Y is typically coded 1 or 0 for its two possible categories.[57]

In Allen's analysis of these data the dependent variable (Y) is the choice of sentence conjunction, and the two possible categories are the choice of καί (the default sentence conjunction) or the choice of another conjunction or asyndeton. The independent, or predictor, variables—also referred to as 'fields'—that I chose to have Allen include in her analysis are topical theme, verbal tense-form, subject reference, use as a speech margin, constituent order, and topic switch (= subject switch). 'Default' values were assigned as follows:

Field		*Default value*
sentence conjunction	⇒	καί
topical theme	⇒	thematic verb
verbal tense-form	⇒	aorist finite verb

55. See Allen, 'Greek Syntactical Analysis'.
56. See E. Allen and V. Farewell, 'Statistical Analysis of the Choice of Conjunction in the Gospel of Matthew', this volume.
57. Allen, 'Greek Syntactical Analysis', p. 7.

subject reference	⇒	no grammaticalized subject
use as a speech margin	⇒	not used as a speech margin
constituent order	⇒	monolectic verb
topic switch (= subject switch)	⇒	no subject switch

In other words, the default or most unmarked sentence structure in Matthew's narrative framework is considered to be a sentence which includes καί and a thematic aorist tense-form finite verb with no grammaticalized subject, which is not used as a speech margin, and which continues the notional subject of the preceding narrative sentence—for example the three sentences in 1.24b-25, καὶ παρέλαβεν τὴν γυναῖκα αὐτοῦ, καὶ οὐκ ἐγίνωσκεν αὐτὴν ἕως οὗ ἔτεκεν υἱόν· καὶ ἐκάλεσεν τὸ ὄνομα αὐτοῦ Ἰησοῦν (the negative particle οὐκ is ignored).[58] Any difference in sentence conjunction, specifically the choice of δέ, τότε, or asyndeton rather than καί, is analyzed in terms of variations from these default values.

The goal of logistic regression is to develop a mathematical model, incorporating any or all of these predictor variables, which maximizes the probability of obtaining the observed set of data, specifically in this case the sentence conjunctions I observed in Matthew's narrative framework. 'This involves testing a statistical hypothesis to determine whether the independent variables in the model are "significantly" related to the outcome variable. The question to be asked is "does the model that includes the variable in question tell us more about the outcome variable, than a model that does not include that variable".'[59]

---

58. This is not, of course, necessarily the most frequent sentence structure in Matthew's narrative framework. Only 42 narrative sentences in the database share all these features.

59. Allen, 'Greek Syntactical Analysis', p. 10; see also Allen and Farewell, this volume, §2.1. Allen warns, 'It is important, however, not to base the model solely on tests of statistical significance. Numerous other considerations should influence the decision to include or exclude variables from a model' (Allen, 'Greek Syntactical Analysis', p. 10).

On the use of multiple regression and modeling in language studies, see also A. Woods, P. Fletcher and A. Hughes, *Statistics in Languages Studies* (CTL; Cambridge: Cambridge University Press, 1986), pp. 237-48; Oakes, *Statistics for Corpus Linguistics*, pp. 33-39. See also Nesbitt and Plum's use of loglinear modeling to 'progressively build up models of the data testing the fit between these models and the data itself' in their study of clause relations (parataxis or hypotaxis) across register and genre (Nesbitt and Plum, 'Probabilities', pp. 27-29).

Based on a logistic regression model, the relationships of the predictors in the model to the dependent variable—in this case the relationships of collocating linguistic features or combinations of such features to the choice of sentence conjunction—can be quantified in terms of an 'odds ratio'. This is 'a widely used measure of effect (i.e. a measure that compares two or more groups in predicting the outcome (dependent) variable)'. 'Odds' is defined as 'the ratio of the probability that some event will occur divided by the probability that the same event will not occur'.[60] An 'odds ratio' compares the probabilities or odds of two or more groups of features. For example, in analyzing δέ versus καί, an odds ratio of 51.49 for S_1V constituent order should be interpreted as indicating that a sentence with S_1V constituent order is 51.49 times as likely to have the conjunction δέ (rather than καί) as is a sentence with V constituent order (the default value).[61]

Not only are the effects of individual predictor variables on the likelihood of a given sentence conjunction evaluated, but their combined effects and the interactions of those effects are analyzed. Allen points out that a logistic regression model can be used 'to "statistically adjust" the estimated effects of each variable in the model for associations with the other independent variables'. When this is done, adjusted odds ratios for sentence conjunctions in Matthew's narrative framework can express the impact of collocating linguistic features or combinations of such features, 'adjusting for all other variables in the model'.[62]

Allen initially undertook three analyses of the data I provided from Matthew's narrative framework: δέ vs. καί, τότε vs. καί, and asyndeton vs. καί. Initial univariate analyses were carried out, followed by multivariate analyses allowing not only for the estimation of adjusted odds ratios, but also for investigations into possible interactions between variables.[63] These findings are integrated into my discussion of δέ, asyndeton and τότε in Chapters 5–7, and summarized in the appendix by Allen and Farewell. Overall, Allen found that:

---

60. Allen, 'Greek Syntactical Analysis', p. 11; see also Allen and Farewell, this volume, §2.2.

61. E. Allen, personal communication.

62. Allen, 'Greek Syntactical Analysis', p. 13.

63. Allen, 'Greek Syntactical Analysis', p. 14. An interaction can be understood as the presence of one variable noticeably modifying the effect of another (E. Allen, personal communication).

the structures of clauses with different conjunctions are quite distinct:
Variables that affect the choice of 'de' over 'kai' do not necessarily play
any part in the choice of 'no conjunction' or 'tote'. There are however
certain features that have a noticeable effect on the choice of more than one
conjunction over the standard form 'kai'.[64]

'Rules' vs. 'Regularities'

My reliance on the quantitative techniques described above does not
amount to a view that lexico-grammatical phenomena are fully quantifiable, nor, more importantly, a belief that full quantification is a desirable
or appropriate goal. Robertson's warning of almost a century ago against a
prescriptive approach to grammar is applicable here: 'As far as possible
principles and not rules will be sought. The Greek grammarian is an
interpreter of the facts, not a regulator of the facts.'[65] Even more to the
point, Brown and Yule affirm that the discourse analyst is concerned not
with 'rules' but with 'regularities', 'simply because his data constantly
exemplifies non-categorial phenomena. The regularities which the analyst
describes are based on the frequency with which a particular linguistic
feature occurs under certain conditions in his discourse data.'[66]

I have already mentioned Halliday's belief that linguistic systems are
inherently probabilistic, with frequency in text being 'the instantiation of
probability in the grammar'.[67] He continues:

> It is clear that the significance of such probabilities is not that they predict
> single instances. What is predicted is the general pattern ... [I]ts relevance
> lies not in predicting but in interpreting. Part of the meaning of choosing
> any term is the probability with which that term is chosen; thus the meaning
> of negative is not simply 'not positive' but 'not positive, against odds of
> nine to one'.[68]

Determining on the basis of overall frequencies the probability that a form
will appear in a given context helps to shed light on choices the author
makes to use that form or not to use it at any particular point. The less
probable a form is to be used in a certain way, the more significant a

---

64. Allen, 'Greek Syntactical Analysis', p. 46; see also Allen and Farewell, this
volume, §5.1.

65. Robertson, *Grammar*, p. 387.

66. G. Brown and G. Yule, *Discourse Analysis* (CTL; Cambridge: Cambridge
University Press, 1983), p. 22.

67. Halliday, 'Probabilistic Grammar', p. 31.

68. Halliday, 'Probabilistic Grammar', p. 32.

choice it may represent when it is used.[69] This is consistent with Lyons's dictum that 'the "meaningfulness" of utterances, and parts of utterances, varies in inverse proportion to their degree of "expectancy" in context'.[70]

The relation between quantitative data and qualitative analysis in this research thus becomes clear. While quantitative descriptions of linguistic patterns are useful in understanding narrative syntax in Matthew's Gospel, they do not tell the whole story. Quantitative data contribute to an awareness of probabilities in Matthew's narrative framework, to an expectation of what features are likely to be combined in any given context. This forms a background against which one can begin to recognize the impact of linguistic choices the Evangelist makes at specific points in the Gospel. Or, using the notions of markedness and prominence introduced in the previous chapter, statistically unlikely choices may be understood as marked in terms of their frequency distribution, raising the possibility that such choices indicate prominence in the discourse—in Halliday's phrase, that they have 'value in the game' as significant elements in the narrative the Evangelist is constructing.[71]

In terms of quantifiability and expectancy, time and again in this research I came up against what I have come to call the '80% rule'. I found that a number of features or combinations of features occur with roughly an 80% frequency in a given context. For example, together καί and δέ, the unmarked sentence conjunctions in narrative compared to the relatively rare conjunctive choices τότε, γάρ, οὖν or asyndeton, account for just over 80% of the sentences in the narrative framework (592/720; 82%). Of the sentences in Matthew's narrative framework, nearly 80% (553/720; 77%) have finite verbs with aorist tense-forms, the unmarked form in past-referring narrative. Καί appears in something short of 80% of narrative sentences with monolectic verbs (191/263; 73%), considered the least marked constituent order (see Chapter 4), while δέ appears in very close to 80% of narrative sentences with thematic subjects (155/195; 79%), considered the most marked constituent order. While no features or combinations of features show a 100% frequency in a particular context (with the exception of the consistent use of δέ with a pronominal article—

---

69. But it is important to bear in mind Halliday's caveat that 'grammatical choices may mean different things in different registers, where the odds may be found to vary' (Halliday, 'Probabilistic Grammar', p. 33).

70. Lyons, *Introduction*, p. 415.

71. See Halliday, *Explorations*, p. 116.

ὁ δέ, οἱ δέ, and so on), 'regularities' of about 80% are not uncommon. In considering what features might qualify as regularities in discourse, Brown and Yule suggest that 'the frequency of occurrence need not be as high as 90%'.[72] They write, 'The discourse analyst, like the experimental psychologist, is mainly interested in the level of frequency which reaches significance in perceptual terms. Thus, a regularity in discourse is a linguistic feature which occurs in a definable environment with a significant frequency.'[73]

Corpus Linguistics and Gospel Studies

Some legitimate questions remain to be addressed about the usefulness of corpus linguistics, especially its reliance on quantitative methods, in analyzing the Greek of the New Testament. On the one hand, a systemic-functional approach to language recognizes that choice within a system—specifically here the system of sentence conjunctions in Matthew's Gospel—lends itself to the assignment of percentages, or 'odds ratios' in Allen's logistic regression models, on the basis of observed frequencies. These numerical figures can then provide a foundation for comparisons.

At the same time, several factors necessitate caution. The first is the relatively small database involved in corpus studies of the language of the New Testament. Compared to the hundreds of millions of words amassed in the major English language text collections used in corpus linguistics,[74] the New Testament contains only about 137,500 words and the Gospel of Matthew only about 18,300.[75] Secondly, because little if any of the New Testament is available in a machine-readable form suitable for discourse studies (as opposed to GRAMCORD's word-level tagging), the database for a research project like this one must be created independently, with the

---

72. Brown and Yule, *Discourse Analysis*, p. 22.
73. Brown and Yule, *Discourse Analysis*, p. 22.
74. 'Machine-readable text collections have grown from one million to almost a thousand million words in thirty years, so it would not be impossible to imagine a commensurate thousand-fold increase to one million million word corpora before 2021' (G. Leech, 'The State of the Art in Corpus Linguistics', in Aijmer and Altenberg [eds.], *English Corpus Linguistics*, p. 10). The 1998 release of the Bank of English contained about 329 million words (see Garside *et al.* [eds.], *Corpus Annotation*, pp. 2, 16).
75. See R. Morgenthaler, *Statistik des Neutestamentlichen Wortschatzes* (Zürich: Gotthelf-Verlag, 1958), p. 164.

result that its design and content are circumscribed by the needs of the research at hand. Once constructed, the narrow scope and small size of this database restrict its generalizability, and the conclusions derived from its use are limited by the lack of broader data for comparison.

Thirdly, a methodological question arises when patterns derived from a relatively small database are reapplied to that same small database and used interpretively, thus incorporating a certain degree of circularity into the analysis. In other words, when I find (as I show in the following chapter) that καί appears as the sentence-initial conjunction in 30% of Matthew's sentences, but in 46% of the sentences in his narrative framework, and in 50% of narrative sentences with aorist tense-form finite verbs, each succeeding set (*Matthew, narrative, aorist*) is a subset of the preceding set and incorporates the conditions of the larger set in itself. The question is whether this significantly distorts the findings. As one of my colleagues has suggested, ideally one would have two 'Matthews' to work with: one to use initially to analyze and describe patterns of use and a second on which to test the accuracy of those descriptions. Or, for want of a better option, one might divide Matthew's Gospel in two, using one half for description and the second for testing.[76]

However, for the purposes of this type of study the fact that increasingly concentrated uses of a form such as καί are found in smaller and smaller subsets of the larger database does not seem to be an insurmountable methodological obstacle. The necessary task is to identify at an acceptable level of confidence the factor within each subset that accounts for the increased frequency. When a subset has been selected for a single property (in this case narrative discourse type or aorist tense-form) and that subset shows variation from the larger set, especially when corroborated by an accepted test of statistical significance like a z-score, one can be reasonably confident that a meaningful factor has been discovered—but of course not absolutely certain that all relevant factors have been identified, as there is always the possibility that some other as yet unrecognized element is also at work.

Even with the current hindrance of a relatively small database, there is reason to be cautiously optimistic about the use of corpus linguistic methods in analyzing the Greek of the New Testament. First, some areas of research will be less constrained by the present size of the database than others. In lexical studies, for example, few words are used even 50 times

---

76. I am indebted to M.B. O'Donnell (personal communication) for raising these issues.

in the entire New Testament, making it all the more important to incorporate data from outside the New Testament if it exists. However, in a syntactical study such as this one, frequencies like 700 uses of sentence-initial καί in Matthew's Gospel and 553 uses of the aorist indicative in the narrative framework allow more detailed patterns to emerge within a single Gospel. Certainly additional data would be desirable, but where they are unavailable much can still be learned from the discourse itself.

The development of databases and tagged texts of the New Testament suitable for discourse studies must begin somewhere. No New Testament database was found relevant to this research into sentence conjunctions in Matthew, so I created one for the Gospel. The fact that currently there appears to be no equivalent database for other New Testament books with which to compare patterns found here reduces this research for the present to a *de facto* study of Matthean style rather than of sentence conjunctions in the New Testament, but it need not remain so. Only as similar research is carried out on the other Gospels and on a larger corpus of Hellenistic texts of similar discourse type, register and date, will it become apparent how Matthew's use of various forms compares to that of other authors.[77] We will begin to see more clearly what is marked usage by Matthew (compared with broader use in the Hellenistic period) instead of just what is marked usage within Matthew (variations within the Gospel).

Although this is a desirable expansion of knowledge, a central question for discourse analysis—how an author develops a specific discourse and indicates prominence—can to a large extent be answered by examining patterns within the Gospel itself. The goal of the New Testament discourse analyst is not so much to know the full range of uses of a given form in Hellenistic Greek (that is, such knowledge is not an end in itself), as it is to use as much of that knowledge as is available to appreciate how a given biblical author constructs a text. While we are awaiting more detailed information, the quantitative analysis of one author's patterns of usage within one text is a significant, if preliminary, step forward in that understanding. And as there is no abstract language entity 'out there' that exists apart from the aggregate of usages in specific texts by individual authors, more detailed knowledge will come primarily as the sum of a number of smaller studies like this one.

Finally, the judicious use of numerical values in describing linguistic

77. As mentioned above, the Hellenistic Greek Text Annotation Project of the Centre for Advanced Theological Research, University of Surrey Roehampton, represents a potential way forward in such research.

phenomena in the New Testament has value, in spite of the fact that their appearance can sometimes suggest a level of precision that does not in fact exist. Areas of imprecision should be recognized and acknowledged by those who use statistics to describe linguistic phenomena. One such area is in the original 'parsing' of text—that is, the identification and labeling of lexical, grammatical and/or discourse features. While accuracy is always the goal, as Halliday notes no human (or mechanical) parser attains 100% accuracy in preparing a text for quantitative analysis, 'because some instances are inherently indeterminate and humans also make mistakes'.[78] It would be misleading to make statements like '33.35% of Matthew's independent clauses are found in expository sections', for example, when it has sometimes been a judgment call on the part of the parser whether to place a certain independent clause under 'exposition' rather than 'speech' in the first place. A figure of 33% or even a phrase like 'about a third' tends to be more representative of the level of precision.

Similarly, researchers using statistics in linguistic analysis need to be clear about the difficulties encountered in reducing some sentences to 'standard' patterns. In these situations it is inevitable that a certain amount of Procrustean manipulation occurs to fit the data into categories recognized by the database. For example, in the database of Matthew's Gospel constructed for this study conditional clauses are included in the field for interpersonal theme and modulation. This follows Halliday's treatment of *if*-clauses in English, although in fact Greek has two forms corresponding to *if*, εἰ and ἐάν, which have different ranges of use. At the same time that both εἰ- and ἐάν-clauses are included in the field for interpersonal theme and modulation, only ἐάν is treated in the field for sentence mode as a modal element (since only sentences with ἄν and its compounds are designated as modulated declarative sentences), while εἰ is not. This decision represents a degree of indeterminacy in the handling of conditional clauses with εἰ in order to accommodate the categories of the database. However, there are only about 35 conditional clauses with εἰ in the database, and as none of the sentences in the narrative framework includes a conditional clause, these instances do not affect the analysis of narrative structure. In a large enough database a few occasions of indeterminacy are not likely to distort the results significantly, especially if, as in this case, they are not relevant to the main thrust of the analysis. In some cases, however, it may be better to omit questionable data as, for

78. Halliday, 'Probabilistic Grammar', p. 34.

example, I have excluded the aspectually vague εἰμί from analyses of verbal tense/aspect.

In any case, quantitative analysis benefits from transparency and consistency—being as explicit as possible about how categories are determined and as uniform as possible in one's approach to difficult examples—as well as a healthy dose of realism about the relationship between quantitative description and the real-life vagaries of human language. With these caveats a cautious use of corpus linguistics in analyzing the Greek of the New Testament can be of material use in discourse studies now, and, as data accumulate and methods evolve, can be expected to have a more powerful effect in the future.

Using the procedures and methodological considerations outlined here, the following chapters offer detailed analyses of καί, δέ, asyndeton, τότε, γάρ and οὖν in Matthew's narrative framework, followed by an integrative analysis of the function of sentence conjunctions as a linguistic system in Matthew's 'miracle chapters', 8.1–9.34.

Chapter 4

Καί: Unmarked Continuity

Καί	All sentences in Matthew	Narrative sentences	Exposition sentences	Speech sentences	Old Testament quotations
n =	2302	720	768	733	81
# καί	700	335	212	128	25
% καί	30%	47%	28%	17%	31%

Frequency of καί

My analysis of sentence conjunctions in Matthew's narrative framework begins with καί, the most common sentence conjunction in Matthew's Gospel, appearing 700 times in sentence-initial position.[1] About 30% of the independent clauses in Matthew are conjoined by καί, although its frequency varies with discourse type within the Gospel: almost half (335/720, 47%) of sentences in the narrative framework begin with καί, but less than a third (212/768, 28%) in exposition and less than 20% (128/733, 17%) in quoted speech.[2] The large number of sentences in narrative beginning with καί makes it by far the most common sentence-initial conjunction in Matthew's narrative framework, with δέ (36%) the next most frequent.

The high frequency of καί as a narrative sentence conjunction in the New Testament, especially in the Synoptic Gospels, has led more than one

---

1. This study addresses only the sentence-initial conjunctive function of καί, not its use to conjoin parallel elements within phrases, nor its uses within clauses and phrases which are usually glossed in English as 'even' or 'also'.

2. However, these figures are somewhat skewed by the fact that asyndeton or ὅτι normally introduces the first sentence in a sequence of exposition or speech. An examination of independent clauses *beyond* the first in each sequence reveals somewhat higher frequencies of καί in exposition and speech, 30% and 33% respectively, yet still lower than the 47% in narrative.

grammarian to label its use as 'excessive'. Blass, Debrunner and Funk claim, 'The excessive and monotonous use of καί to string sentences together makes the narrative style of some New Testament authors, especially Mk..., but also Lk. ...unpleasing and colloquial...'[3] In a similar vein Turner writes, 'Its excessive use in the narrative of many New Testament writers, esp. Mark, would appear vulgar to the normal reader...'[4] However, a more linguistically based understanding of the function of καί in New Testament narrative may go far in accounting for its prevalence in such texts.

'Semitic' καί

A number of scholars have suggested that the use of καί in the Gospels and Acts, especially in Mark, is 'Semitic', with καί standing in for Hebrew ן in the same manner that καί is routinely chosen to translate ן in the Septuagint.[5] While it may be true that the language of Mark and of Matthew reveals Semitic influence or may perhaps even hint at Aramaic or Hebrew originals, it has not been established that the frequency of καί in the Gospels is disproportionate to its wider use in Hellenistic vernacular. Mayser, for example, notes that καί is the most frequent particle in the Ptolemaic papyri, just prior to the New Testament period.[6] Reiser, comparing the frequency of paratactic καί in the Gospel of Mark with its frequency in other Hellenistic narrative texts (some probably later than Mark's Gospel), concludes that Mark's use of καί to conjoin sentences is not unusual and does not warrant the label 'Semitic'.[7]

---

3. BDF, §442.

4. N. Turner, *A Grammar of New Testament Greek. III. Syntax* (Edinburgh: T. & T. Clark, 1963), p. 334.

5. See, for example, Robertson, *Grammar*, pp. 393, 426; N. Turner, *A Grammar of New Testament Greek. IV. Style* (Edinburgh: T. & T. Clark, 1976), p. 17; Turner, *Syntax*, p. 334. Horrocks observes, 'Most of these [alleged Semitisms in the New Testament] can be paralleled in the Septuagint, and most could equally well reflect contemporary Hebrew or Aramaic ... But many can also be paralleled in low-level Koine documents from Egypt ... and so presumably reflect either more general tendencies of colloquial Greek which were reinforced by Jewish bilingualism in Palestine, or accidental correspondencies between Coptic and Hebrew/Aramaic' (G. Horrocks, *Greek: A History of the Language and Its Speakers* [Longman Linguistics Library; London and New York: Longman, 1997], p. 92).

6. Mayser, *Grammatik der Griechischen Papyri*, p. 140.

7. M. Reiser, *Syntax und Stil des Markusevangeliums im Licht der hellenistischen Volksliteratur* (Tübingen: J.C.B. Mohr [Paul Siebeck], 1984), p. 136.

Moreover, the analysis of καί as a Semitism reveals a fundamentally diachronic approach. Such an approach may attempt to explain how καί came into use by Gospel writers, but simply to say that occurrences of καί have possible Semitic antecedents does little to explain what role καί plays within the conjunctive system of the Gospels at this point. Conjunctions, like other words, do not function in isolation but in opposition to other possible choices. Even if καί in the Gospels could be shown to be 'ו in disguise', as it were, speakers and writers of 'Semitic' Greek would need to stake out a distinct range of usage for ו-καί in relation to the other components of the Greek conjunctive system.

Buth appears to be unique in attempting to draw out some implications of 'Semitic' καί for discourse analysis of the Gospels and Acts.[8] He argues that since Greek distinguishes between two words for 'and', καί and δέ, but Hebrew and Aramaic have only ו, there is a tendency to use καί consistently in Greek texts translated from Hebrew. As a result, 'δέ is very much a "marked" relator when Hebrew underlies a Greek document. It takes a clearer purpose or higher threshold to get δέ into translation Greek than into a natural, idiomatic document.' From this Buth draws the conclusion that, assuming that Jesus taught in Hebrew and/or Aramaic and that many of the sources used by the Evangelists were first compiled in Hebrew and/or Aramaic, καί probably appears more often in the Gospels and Acts than would be the usual practice in Greek discourse. 'Generally, the ו's would become καί's unless the author or translator felt a need to intervene.' In Buth's view this leads to two practical applications: first, where δέ does exist in Greek texts which go back to Semitic originals it reflects both the Evangelist's and previous translators' sensitivity to Greek idiom; secondly, 'where the rules predict δέ but καί is found, one does not need to speak of a marked, emphatic καί but he can invoke "Semitic καί"'.[9]

Buth's analysis of καί is not without its problems. Not only does it incorporate a certain degree of circularity, resting on an assumption of the very Semitic originals for whose existence the presence of 'Semitic' καί in the Gospels is sometimes cited as evidence, but Buth himself recognizes that 'this can provide too easy a solution, a solution where any contradiction to δέ rules can be glibly written off'.[10] Nevertheless, Buth is to be commended for recognizing the need to investigate the use of καί in its

---

8.   Buth, 'Semitic Καί and Greek Δέ', pp. 12-19.
9.   Buth, 'Semitic Καί and Greek Δέ', p. 13.
10. Buth, 'Semitic Καί and Greek Δέ', p. 13.

current context (and in particular how it alternates with δέ), and for his attempt to use the diachronic development of καί not as an end in itself but as data in synchronic investigation.

'*Meaning' of* καί

Traditional Approaches

There is a consensus among Greek grammarians that continuation is the basic feature of καί. Traditional grammarians sometimes use the terms 'addition' or 'additive' in their descriptions of καί, which has affinities with the understanding of καί as a signal of continuity presented in this study, although it represents a somewhat different theoretical approach.[11] For example, Denniston writes that in Classical Greek the 'primary force is, beyond all reasonable doubt, addition'.[12]

At the same time, grammarians struggle to come to terms with the fact that καί can appear in contexts with a variety of semantic relations between the sentences it conjoins, even at times an adversative relation. Robertson delineates three main uses of καί in the New Testament: adjunctive (*also*), ascensive (*even*) and the mere connective (*and*),[13] while acknowledging, 'The context gives other turns to καί that are sometimes rather startling. It is common to find καί where it has to bear the content "and yet".'[14] Dana and Mantey give these three (the first of which they call transitional or continuative) as 'generally accepted classifications and meanings', but they argue that there should be two additional classifications: adversative and emphatic. At the same time they take the seemingly contradictory route of saying that καί 'is often used as a mere mechanical connective (a copulative), and it is left for the reader to determine which possible translation best suits the context', thus obscuring the issue of whether καί itself can be adversative or whether this sense is a function of its use in context.[15] BDF maintains that καί has a 'properly copulative meaning', but list first among

11. The terms 'continuous' and 'continuity' are preferred in this study, both because this allows a contrast to be drawn with markers of discontinuity in discourse (with δέ in particular) and because it facilitates an understanding of discourse comprehension as an ongoing process which the writer or speaker attempts to guide.

12. Denniston, *Greek Particles*, p. 289.

13. Robertson, *Grammar*, pp. 1179-82. However, Robertson recognizes that the ascensive sense 'depends wholly on the context' rather than on καί itself (Robertson, *Grammar*, p. 1181).

14. Robertson, *Grammar*, p. 1182.

15. Dana and Mantey, *Grammar*, p. 250.

its various uses that καί 'can be used even where there is actual contrast', thus acknowledging some role for context.[16] Turner notes three nuances καί can assume: 'and yet', consecutive, and even final, thereby leaning toward καί itself carrying an adversative sense at times.[17]

The categorizations offered by these grammarians reflect a generally maximalist view of the meaning of καί—that is, positing a larger role for καί itself and a smaller role for context in determining the semantic relation between sentences καί conjoins. This approach tends to downplay the question of how the audience recognizes 'which' καί is being used in a given context. Clearly, an analysis of context is the determining factor in the *ex post facto* description of the use of καί at a particular point as 'continuative', 'adversative', 'ascensive' or as having some other meaning, although a maximalist might say that the audience recognizes that one of the possible meanings of καί is consistent with the current context. In contrast, I take a minimalist perspective acknowledging that καί has a consistent low-level semantic value that allows it to be used in a variety of semantic relationships between conjoined propositions in Matthew's narrative framework—relationships which are pragmatically worked out by the audience on the basis of linguistic content, context, and knowledge of the world—but that in fact the meaning conveyed by καί is procedural rather than conceptual or 'logical'. In Matthew's narrative framework καί functions as a signal of unmarked continuity.

Unmarked Continuity
Using the approach to sentence conjunctions developed in Chapter 2, καί, as the unmarked or default sentence conjunction in Matthew, is a procedural, non-truth-conditional signal of continuity, normally found in contexts where there is—or is presented as being—continuity of time, action, or (especially) actor. As I show below, Matthew commonly combines καί with an unmarked tense-form (aorist), and unmarked or less marked constituent order (monolectic verb, or verb before subject if an explicit subject appears) in multiply reinforcing syntactical structures which guide the audience to process the following element in the discourse as continuous with that which immediately precedes. As the unmarked discourse connective, καί signals continuity, the unmarked condition in discourse. In most cases καί relates the following sentence to a previous

16. BDF, §442.
17. Turner, *Syntax*, p. 334. For the nuance 'and yet', Turner cites Mt. 3.14—see discussion of this passage below.

sentence; in a smaller number of cases continuity extends to a larger discourse unit such as an episode within a narrative sequence.

Studies by others with an interest in New Testament discourse have found καί functioning in much the same way in the other Gospels. Levinsohn identifies καί as the unmarked connector in the Synoptics and Acts, but not in John, where asyndeton is more commonly found.[18] Buth agrees with Levinsohn on this basic distinction between John's Gospel and the Synoptics, yet Buth finds that even in John's Gospel καί is used where there is 'close connection and some continuity', joining sentences into a block or event complex, or used in background information.[19] He characterizes καί in John as a signal of 'coordinated sameness'.[20] Similarly, Poythress finds that in exposition in John καί connects 'two successive sentences expressing closely related ideas',[21] and that in narrative καί connects sentences where the agents or most prominent participants (usually the grammatical subjects) are the same. Poythress also maintains that although in John's narrative καί occasionally connects sentences following some shift in agent or prominent participant, 'By using καί's the effect is created of a single whole block of events following in simple fashion directly one after the other'.[22]

In Chapter 2, I introduced Dik's view that 'a word like *and* is a multiple-purpose tool of low semantic specificity, used to combine semantic aspects which, in their final interpretation, may be characterized by a variety of different relations'.[23] To say that continuity is the basic feature of καί in Matthew's narrative framework is to define continuity as the semantic value of καί in Matthew's discourse. The low level of semantic specificity in this definition allows for the use of καί in a number of discourse contexts where various kinds of semantic relations between sentences may exist—including an adversative semantic relationship—but where an underlying continuity is being portrayed. When the audience encounters καί they recognize it as a signal that what follows is to be integrated into the current mental representation of the discourse without significant adjustment to that representation, that new material is to be processed within the model they have currently constructed.

18. Levinsohn, *Discourse Features*, pp. 81-82.
19. Buth, 'Οὖν, Δέ, Καί, and Asyndeton', pp. 152-53.
20. Buth, 'Οὖν, Δέ, Καί, and Asyndeton', p. 157.
21. Poythress, 'Intersentence Conjunctions', p. 323.
22. Poythress, 'Intersentence Conjunctions', p. 331.
23. Dik, *Coordination*, p. 269.

I also discussed in Chapter 2 Schiffrin's statement that 'markers *select* a meaning relation from whatever potential meanings are provided through the content of talk, and then *display* that relation'.[24] Of course, it is the speaker or writer who chooses to use one conjunction over against another alternative to select a meaning. At times Matthew chooses καί where another conjunction, especially δέ, might also be suitable in the literary context, seemingly because his intent is to convey continuity rather than discontinuity at that point in the discourse.

Evidence from Matthew's Gospel

Syntactical Interactions
I have stated that in Matthew's narrative framework καί tends to collocate with other unmarked syntactical elements to indicate unmarked continuity in discourse. For example, καί is most often found with aorist tense-form finite verbs, which, as I show below, should be understood as the unmarked tense-form in past-referring narrative. Similarly, καί is most often found with monolectic verbs or verb–subject constituent order, which, as I address in the following section, constitute less marked constituent order in narrative. At the same time καί occurs less frequently with more marked tense-forms in narrative (in particular, the so-called 'historic present'), or with more marked constituent order such as an explicit subject followed by a verb, especially with the subject in first, or thematic, position. The collocations between καί and these other features, forming multiply reinforcing syntactical structures conveying discourse continuity, are described in some detail in this chapter and evaluated in terms of their statistical significance.

Καί *and verbal tense-form.* In Matthew's narrative framework, καί tends to be associated with aorist finite verbs. This can be seen in examples such as 8.14-15, the healing of Peter's mother-in-law:

8.14   καὶ ἐλθὼν ὁ Ἰησοῦς εἰς τὴν οἰκίαν Πέτρου εἶδεν τὴν πενθερὰν αὐτοῦ βεβλημένην καὶ πυρέσσουσαν·

8.15a   καὶ ἥψατο τῆς χειρὸς αὐτῆς,

8.15b   καὶ ἀφῆκεν αὐτὴν ὁ πυρετός,

8.15c   καὶ ἠγέρθη

8.15d   καὶ διηκόνει [imperfect tense-form] αὐτῷ.

24. Schiffrin, *Discourse Markers*, p. 318.

In exposition similar patterns can also be found, especially in narrative-type passages such as the following from the parable of the wise and foolish builders (7.25).[25]

7.25a	καὶ κατέβη ἡ βροχὴ
7.25b	καὶ ἦλθον οἱ ποταμοὶ
7.25c	καὶ ἔπνευσαν οἱ ἄνεμοι
7.25d	καὶ προσέπεσαν τῇ οἰκίᾳ ἐκείνῃ,
7.25e	καὶ οὐκ ἔπεσεν,
7.25f	τεθεμελίωτο [perfect tense-form] γὰρ ἐπὶ τὴν πέτραν.

At the same time, there is a statistically significant *lack* of use of καί with present tense-forms (a marked form in past-referring narrative). Examples such as 26.40, in which Jesus' disciples sleep while he prays, are found only rarely (see also 17.1):

26.40a	καὶ ἔρχεται πρὸς τοὺς μαθητὰς
26.40b	καὶ εὑρίσκει αὐτοὺς καθεύδοντας,
26.40c	καὶ λέγει τῷ Πέτρῳ· οὕτως οὐκ ἰσχύσατε μίαν ὥραν γρηγορῆσαι μετ᾽ ἐμοῦ;

This example occurs at an important juncture in the narrative—Jesus' prayer in the garden of Gethsemane—and as a marked combination it plays a part in indicating the prominence in the discourse of Jesus' interaction with his uncomprehending disciples.[26]

The following table indicates that in Matthew's narrative framework, where καί begins 47% of sentences overall, it appears in 50% of clauses with aorist finite verbs (276/553), but only 30% (24/81) of clauses with present finite verbs (the 'historic present'). That such a large majority of sentences in the narrative framework have aorist finite verbs (553/720, 77%) makes it somewhat difficult to distinguish the relative frequency of καί with aorist forms from its frequency in all narrative. However, a z-score of -2.88 for καί with present tense-form verbs (approaching the ± 3 value chosen in this study as indicating statistical significance) suggests that the disassociation between καί and present tense-forms in narrative may be statistically significant:

---

25. About three-quarters (105/144, 73%) of the aorist indicative forms in exposition in Matthew are found in parables. As parables constitute a narrative discourse type within exposition, this is consistent with the use of the aorist as the default tense-form in narrative discourse.

26. See S.L. Black, 'The Historic Present in Matthew: Beyond Speech Margins', in Porter and Reed (eds.), *Discourse Analysis*, pp. 135-39.

Table 4.1: Καί *and verbal tense-form (omitting* εἰμί*)*[27]

	All narrative sentences	Sentences with aorist finite verbs	Sentences with present finite verbs
n =	720	553	79
# καί	335	276	24
% καί	47%	50%	30%
z-score[28]		1.59	−2.88

Given that καί commonly appears with aorist tense-forms in narrative, it remains to be shown that the aorist is the unmarked choice of tense-form for narrative, and that <καί + aorist> normally represents the unmarked choice in Matthew's presentation of narrative. One line of argument is simply numerical. Three-quarters of the sentences in Matthew's narrative framework (553/720, 77%) have finite verbs with aorist tense-forms. As discussed in Chapter 2, an unmarked form tends also to be one that occurs with high frequency. Or to return to Lyons's classic formulation, 'The "meaningfulness" of utterances (and parts thereof) varies in inverse proportion to their degree of "expectancy" in context'.[29] With aorist tense-forms occurring in such a high percentage of narrative clauses, readers and hearers come to expect their use in this context and assign little significance or markedness to them. Similarly, because the combination of καί and aorist tense-forms is so frequent in narrative, appearing in more than a third of the sentences in Matthew's narrative framework (276/720, 38%), its expectancy in context leads the audience to process it as unmarked. No other tense-form is as numerous in the narrative framework, no other sentence conjunction is as common, and no other combination appears as frequently (although <δέ + aorist> is not far behind, with 213 of 720 sentences, or 30%—see below and Chapter 5 for other distinctions between Matthew's use of καί and of δέ).

On the other hand, as I have discussed with respect to markedness, the unmarked element in discourse structure is not necessarily the numerically

27. Εἰμί is omitted from consideration in this table and in other analyses of sentence conjunction and verbal tense-form because it does not evidence fully developed morphological distinctions among tense-forms, or, in Porter's terms, it is 'aspectually vague' (see Porter, *Verbal Aspect*, pp. 442-47).

28. As explained in Chapter 3, a z-score expresses a distance from a mean in terms of standard deviations. In this study z-scores equal to or greater than ±3—that is, indicating that a value falls three standard deviations or, more above or below a mean—are taken to demonstrate statistical significance.

29. Lyons, *Introduction*, p. 415.

most frequent. However, grammarians taking a less quantitative approach to the New Testament have long observed that the aorist is the normal, unremarkable tense-form in narrative in the New Testament, and that by comparison the use of present tense-forms in past-referring narrative (the 'historic present') is in some way a special use, although their theoretical approaches in characterizing the role of present tense-forms in narrative may differ.[30] Robertson asserts that the aorist 'is the tense in which a verb in ordinary narrative is put unless there is reason for using some other tense'.[31] Porter, one of the few to deal directly with verbal tense-forms as a system and their interaction in 'planes of discourse', writes, 'Items which are placed in the background tense (aorist) comprise either the backbone (in narrative) or supporting illustrative material (in exposition) against which more prominent items are set. The foreground (present) and front-ground (perfect) tense-forms are used to mark prominent features.'[32]

Aorist finite verbs are the unmarked tense-form in narrative, and the combination of καί and aorist tense-forms represents the unmarked choice in Matthew's portrayal of continuous narrative.

Καί *and constituent order.* So far much of what has been said about the use of καί in Matthew's narrative framework is also true to varying degrees of his use of δέ (see Chapter 5). Καί and δέ are both common sentence conjunctions in the narrative framework: καί occurs in 47% of narrative sentences; δέ in 36% (257/720). In fact, both show a strong tendency to collocate with aorist tense-form verbs: aorist finite verbs appear in 82% (276/335) of the sentences in which καί is the sentence conjunction, and in 83% (213/257) of those with δέ. Neither shows a tendency to collocate with the so-called 'historic present': only 30% of narrative sentences with present tense-forms have καί (24/79; z = −2.88); only 11% have δέ (8/79; z = −4.74).

---

30. On the 'historic present' see, for example, BDF, §321; Turner, *Syntax*, pp. 60-62; B.M. Fanning, *Verbal Aspect in New Testament Greek* (Oxford Theological Monographs; Oxford: Clarendon Press, 1990), pp. 226-39; Porter, *Verbal Aspect*, pp. 195-97; K.L. McKay, *A New Syntax of the Verb in New Testament Greek* (SBG, 5; New York: Peter Lang, 1993), p. 42.

31. Robertson, *Grammar*, pp. 835-36.

32. Porter, *Idioms*, p. 302. See, similarly, the 'salience scheme' proposed by Longacre for verbal forms in narrative in Mark's Gospel (R.E. Longacre, 'Mark 5.1-43: Generating the Complexity of a Narrative from its Most Basic Elements', in Porter and Reed [eds.], *Discourse Analysis*, pp. 177-79).

Καί, δέ and aorist tense-forms are among the basic tools Matthew uses in constructing the narrative framework of his discourse. However, in his hands these tools have distinct uses in that framework. Καί is used primarily in sentences with a constituent order which is unmarked (monolectic verb) or less marked (verb before subject if an explicit subject appears), while δέ tends to appear with more marked constituent order (explicit subject followed by verb, especially with the subject as topical theme). In this way καί is combined with other unmarked or less marked features in its function as the unmarked sentence conjunction in Matthew's Gospel, a procedural, non-truth-conditional signal of continuity used when the author is connecting independent clauses without calling attention to any discontinuity in the discourse, while δέ indicates some discontinuity, most often simply a change in actor.

The dynamics of constituent order in the Greek of the New Testament are not universally agreed. There is some consensus that writers of Classical Greek preferred the SV order, but that by the Hellenistic period VS is the dominant structure.[33] Sentences with verb-first order or with monolectic verbs (that is, those with no grammaticalized subject) predominate in narrative in Matthew, but not overwhelmingly (419/720, 58%). However, Porter points out the high frequency of monolectic clauses and questions whether it is reasonable to characterize monolectic clauses as either VS or SV, involving as it does the need 'to hypothesize about the phantom presence of various syntactical phenomena'.[34] In fact, as Porter observes, when an explicit subject does occur with a verb it is more likely to appear before the verb than after it: '[I]n Greek, including that of the New Testament, the subject—when and if it is explicitly grammaticalized (this is an important caveat)—has a distinct tendency to precede its predicate and/or its complement…'[35] This is exemplified in Matthew's narrative framework. Of the narrative sentences with both an explicit subject and a verb, fully two-thirds (294/443, 66%) have the subject before the verb.

---

33. See K.J. Dover, *Greek Word Order* (Cambridge: Cambridge University Press, 1960), pp. 25-31; Horrocks, *Greek*, pp. 59-60; Porter, 'Word Order', pp. 186-87. However, for a study arguing that notions of topic and focus are more productive in the analysis of word order in Classical Greek than is the grammatical notion of subject, see H. Dik, *Word Order in Ancient Greek: A Pragmatic Account of Word Order Variation in Herodotus* (ASCP, 5; Amsterdam: J.C. Gieben, 1995).

34. Porter, 'Word Order', p. 187.

35. Porter, 'Word Order', p. 188.

In this study the relative markedness of constituent orders in Matthew's narrative framework is understood as follows. Since an explicit subject is not necessary, and monolectic verbs are the most frequent sentence pattern, monolectic verbs are considered the most unmarked form. Any grammaticalization of the subject is seen as marked to some degree. Given that an explicit subject represents a marked choice, it is not surprising that the tendency is to place it earlier in the sentence for further emphasis, with the first, or thematic, position seen as most marked. As I explained in Chapter 3, in this simplified analysis of constituent order only two elements are considered: the main verb (if any), and the grammaticalized subject (if any), in relation to each other. Other predicate or complement elements are not taken into account. In particular, the presence of any direct object is not considered even though most studies of language typology identify subject, verb and object as, for example, VSO, SOV, or SVO. (However, I treat thematic direct objects elsewhere in analyses of sentence conjunction and theme.)

A cline or scale of markedness was developed for the purpose of classifying constituent order in this study and its relation to sentence conjunctions. From less to more marked these are:

- monolectic verbs, or clauses where no subject is grammaticalized ('V'): e.g., Mt. 8.15, καὶ ἥψατο τῆς χειρὸς αὐτῆς; 12.9, καὶ μεταβὰς ἐκεῖθεν ἦλθεν εἰς τὴν συναγωγὴν αὐτῶν; 27.16, εἶχον δὲ τότε δέσμιον ...

- clauses with an explicit subject appearing after the verb ('VS'): e.g., Mt. 3.1, ἐν δὲ ταῖς ἡμέραις ἐκείναις παραγίνεται Ἰωάννης ὁ βαπτιστής...; 9.35, καὶ περιῆγεν ὁ Ἰησοῦς τὰς πόλεις πάσας...

- clauses with an explicit subject preceding the verb, but not in first, or thematic, position ('S₂V').[36] e.g., Mt. 8.14, καὶ ἐλθὼν ὁ Ἰησοῦς εἰς τὴν οἰκίαν Πέτρου εἶδεν τὴν πενθερὰν αὐτοῦ...; 9.8, ἰδόντες δὲ οἱ ὄχλοι ἐφοβήθησαν ...

- clauses with an explicit subject in thematic position ('S₁V'):[37]

---

36. By far the most common thematic element in this pattern is a nominative participle. Of the 99 sentences in Matthew's narrative framework with S_2V constituent order, 84 (85%) have a nominative participle as topical theme.

37. This refers to Halliday's 'topical theme' (see Halliday, *Introduction*, pp. 52-53). In this analysis of Matthew's constituent order the subject was considered thematic only if it preceded any participial phrase that might be present.

e.g., Mt. 8.2, καὶ ἰδοὺ λεπρὸς προσελθὼν προσεκύνει αὐτῷ λέγων ...; 13.2, καὶ πᾶς ὁ ὄχλος ἐπὶ τὸν αἰγιαλὸν εἰστήκει; 14.26, οἱ δὲ μαθηταὶ ἰδόντες αὐτὸν ἐπὶ τῆς θαλάσσης περιπατοῦντα ἐταράχθησαν...

Nominal sentences or clauses in which no main verb appears ('0') were also examined, but as only six examples were identified in Matthew's narrative framework, they are not included in the results reported below.[38]

Reversing the order in which the four most common constituent orders are presented, to portray more visually the movement of the grammatical subject (if any) from right to left within a written sentence, the cline can be represented as ranging from less marked constituent order (toward the right of the cline, with the subject in a later position in the sentence, or not grammaticalized at all) to more marked constituent order (toward the left of the cline, with the subject in an earlier position in the sentence):[39]

$$S_1V \Leftarrow S_2V \Leftarrow VS \Leftarrow V$$

The correspondence between καί and constituent order, with its implications for discourse continuity, can now be observed:

---

38. Mt. 1.1, 1.17, 3.17, 12.10, 15.36, 17.5. As explained in Chapter 3, there are also instances of independent clauses with a verb which seems to be so closely connected to the previous verb that the two could be understood as a single compound sentence ('+2'; seven examples were identified: Mt. 4.11, 14.3, 17.24, 20.32, 26.50, 27.30, 28.9; plus two verbless clauses with a similar relation to a preceding sentence, both in 1.17). Almost by definition, the conjunction in these is καί. Because the status of καί as a *sentence* conjunction is indeterminate in these examples—they have been designated as separate sentences, but could be classified as elements in longer sentences—they, too, are omitted from consideration in the analyses which follow.

39. Givón takes a similar approach in his attempt to define a cross-linguistic scale of word order reflecting topic continuity, although he places more continuous configurations toward the left rather than to the right as I have. His scale is:

COMMENT > COMMENT-TOPIC > TOPIC-COMMENT > TOPIC
(zero topic)   (zero comment)

The leftmost element on the scale ('comment [zero topic]', equivalent to a monolectic verb in Greek) is the most continuous, and the rightmost element ('topic [zero comment]', possibly equivalent to a hanging nominative construction in Greek), is the most discontinuous. In between, Givón's 'comment-topic' is roughly equivalent to my VS constituent order, and his 'topic-comment' is roughly equivalent to my SV (that is, S_1V or S_2V) constituent order. See Givón, 'Topic Continuity', pp. 19-20.

Table 4.2: Καί *and constituent order*

	All narrative sentences	*S₁V constituent order*	*S₂V constituent order*	*VS constituent order*	*V constituent order*
n =	720	195	99	149	262
# καί	335	23	40	69	191
% καί	47%	12%	40%	46%	73%
z-score		−9.73	−1.21	0.05	8.56

Not only does καί tend to appear with less marked constituent order, and not to appear with more marked constituent order, but the frequency of καί diminishes as the constituent order becomes progressively more marked. The earlier in the sentence the subject is placed, the progressively less likely καί is to appear; the later in the sentence the subject is placed (with no expressed subject at the far end of the cline), the progressively more likely καί is to appear. As I will show in the next chapter, the pattern is reversed for δέ: the earlier the subject is placed, the more likely δέ is to appear; the later the subject is placed, the less likely δέ is to appear.

The low z-scores of the two constituent orders in the center (S₂V and VS) warn that these may be random results in samples of this size. However, it is likely that the z-scores actually reflect the fact that the percentages found in these samples, while forming part of a meaningful pattern in the overall use of καί, are too close to the 47% 'καί in all narrative' figure for statistical significance to be apparent. The z-scores for the constituent orders at either end of the cline, S₁V and V, indicate a high degree of statistical significance. The incidence of καί with clauses with thematic subjects is extremely low. A strong association between καί and ἰδού (see on καὶ ἰδού, below) also affects this distribution. Omitting narrative sentences with ἰδού would show even less of a tendency to use καί with a subject as topical theme. In fact, there are only nine cases in Matthew's narrative framework in which καί is found with a thematic subject and in which ἰδού does not also appear.[40] At the opposite end of the cline, καί is so common with monolectic verbs that this pattern constitutes more than a quarter (191/720, 27%) of the sentences in Matthew's narrative framework.

40. Mt. 13.2, 14.36, 22.46, 26.63, 26.74, 27.51 (two examples), 27.52 (two examples); 27.51-52 is discussed below.

Καί *and subject switch*. In addition to the formal correlation between καί and aorist tense-forms and between καί and V(S) constituent order, there is a correlation between καί and continuity of notional subject between successive sentences in Matthew's narrative framework, or, in other words, there tends to be no 'subject switch' between narrative sentences conjoined by καί. For the purposes of this study, 'subject switch' as a variable for analysis is defined as a change in the notional subject from the previous independent coordinate clause in the narrative framework—a change in the grammaticalized subject if any, or in 'who or what the sentence is about' (that is, roughly 'who or what is the primary actor in the process or state described') as understood from surrounding text if there is no explicit subject.

Not surprisingly, καί is found most frequently in contexts where there is continuity of subject between sentences:

Table 4.3: Καί *and subject switch*

	All narrative sentences	*Subject switch*	*No subject switch*	*Title (1.1) and first sentence (1.2)*[41]
n =	720	516	202	2
# καί	335	183	152	0
% καί	47%	35%	75%	
z-score		−5.04	8.18	

Based on its distribution in the narrative framework as a whole, καί shows a significantly lower frequency of use in contexts where there is subject switch (183/516, 35%; z = −5.04) and a significantly higher frequency of use where there is continuity of subject (152/202, 75%; z = 8.18).

It is worth noting that although continuity is the unmarked condition in discourse, in this case the unmarked choice is not—at least in terms of the variable 'subject switch'—also the most frequent. As measured here, more than twice as many of the sentences in Matthew's narrative framework exhibit discontinuity of notional subject as exhibit continuity. Yet from the perspective of a psychologically based understanding of cognitive processing (see on continuity and discontinuity in discourse, Chapter 2), continuity can be understood to be the expected or unmarked condition in narrative.

41. Both the title and first sentence of Matthew's Gospel are asyndetic; see on asyndeton, Chapter 6.

Thus as a signal of unmarked continuity καί occurs in continuous discourse contexts such as those where there is continuity of actor from one sentence to another. This exemplifies the notion of 'markedness assimilation' introduced in Chapter 2, the idea that there is a correspondence between the markedness of forms and the markedness of the contexts in which they are used. As Battistella observes, 'Markedness assimilation ... provides a semiotic organization to the facts of language according to which units and contexts and expressions and meanings are patterned together in a single superstructure'.[42] Matthew's tendency to use καί, the unmarked sentence conjunction, in contexts of discourse continuity alongside an unmarked verbal tense-form (aorist) and with less marked constituent order (V or VS) represents one way components from various linguistic systems may interact to join form and meaning in 'a single superstructure'.

Summary. In this section the tendency of καί to collocate with other unmarked features in Matthew's discourse was examined. First it was shown that in Matthew's narrative framework καί is most often found with aorist main verbs, the unmarked tense-form in narrative, and rarely with present tense-forms, a marked form in past-referring narrative. Secondly, a cline for markedness in constituent order in Matthew's Gospel was introduced which revealed that the more marked the constituent order (the earlier in the sentence the subject is placed, with thematic subject as the most marked order) the less likely καί is to appear, and the less marked the constituent order (the later in the sentence the subject is placed, with monolectic verb as the least marked order), the more likely καί is to appear. Thirdly, the correspondence between καί and continuity of subject between sentences in Matthew's narrative framework (the unmarked condition) was demonstrated.

These findings support the contention that in Matthew's system of sentence conjunctions καί is the unmarked or default form. However, to this point Matthew's use of καί has been examined primarily at the sentence level. This may create a too simplistic impression that the use of καί is determined by features in the sentence that follows, when in reality Matthew's choices of sentence conjunction, verbal tense-form, and constituent order work together in the overall flow of discourse. To see how Matthew uses καί as a signal of continuity it is necessary to look also at larger blocks of text. This is the object of the following section.

---

42. Battistella, *Markedness*, p. 7.

Discourse Functions of καί

I have characterized καί as a procedural, non-truth-conditional signal of continuity in the Gospel of Matthew, normally found in contexts where there is—or is presented as being—continuity of time, action, or actor. In this section passages from the narrative framework are examined which illustrate ways Matthew tends to use καί in guiding the audience to process the following element in the discourse as continuous with their current mental representation of the discourse.

Clause complex with continuity of subject. Consistent with its high frequency with continuity of subject, perhaps the most straightforward use of καί by Matthew is to conjoin a series of actions by a single actor in a clause complex which may be larger than what would traditionally be understood as a single sentence, but smaller than what is traditionally understood as a paragraph (a *process chain* in Porter and O'Donnell's terminology[43]). In Matthew's narrative framework such a clause complex often begins with an independent clause in which a subject is explicitly grammaticalized, the subject usually appearing before the main verb (SV constituent order). In most cases this clause is introduced by a conjunction other than καί (often δέ). This is generally followed by a series of independent clauses joined by καί in which no explicit subject is given as long as the actor remains the same. Often these monolectic clauses also contain a nominative participle in thematic position.[44] The narrative clauses in the complex may be interspersed by reported speech. Theoretically the chain of clauses could extend indefinitely, but in practice the longest such complexes found in Matthew's narrative framework consist of four or five clauses, and most of only two or three clauses before some other conjunction and/or syntactical structure appears.

An example of this format, with a first clause with δέ and an explicit subject before the verb, followed by a complex of clauses with καί and monolectic verbs, may be seen in 1.24-25, where the actor is Joseph:

---

43. See S.E. Porter and M.B. O'Donnell, *Discourse Analysis and the New Testament* (in preparation).

44. The pattern <καί + nom ptc (thematic) + aorist (no explicit subject)> occurs 70 times in Matthew's narrative framework, representing almost a quarter (70/335, 23%) of the sentences in which καί is the sentence conjunction. Several of these have multiple participles at the beginning of the sentence: 4.13, 14.19 (three), 26.27, 26.44, 28.12.

1.24a ἐγερθεὶς δὲ ὁ Ἰωσὴφ ἀπὸ τοῦ ὕπνου ἐποίησεν ὡς προσέταξεν
αὐτῷ ὁ ἄγγελος κυρίου
1.24b καὶ παρέλαβεν τὴν γυναῖκα αὐτοῦ,
1.25a καὶ οὐκ ἐγίνωσκεν αὐτὴν ἕως οὗ ἔτεκεν υἱόν·
1.25b καὶ ἐκάλεσεν τὸ ὄνομα αὐτοῦ Ἰησοῦν.

In this sequence, in response to instructions he receives from an angel who appears to him in a dream, Joseph follows the angel's instructions, marries the pregnant Mary but does not consummate the marriage until after the birth of her child, and names the baby Jesus as he had been directed by the angel. Seen in this context, the dynamic behind the association of καί and monolectic verbs becomes apparent: the clauses introduced by καί represent a continuity of action by a previously introduced actor, Joseph, so that no additional explicit subject is needed. The context also clarifies the so-called adversative use of καί between 1.25a and 1.25b. The Evangelist has chosen to portray the continuity of this sequence of obedient actions by Joseph rather than any cultural discontinuity involved in Joseph's marrying Mary but postponing sexual relations with her after the marriage (see also below on 'adversative' καί).

But in fact, longer complexes like 1.24-25 with a single explicit subject and more than one or two subsequent clauses are not very common.[45] A number of variations appear. Sometimes a previously introduced actor or set of participants is taken up again in a clause complex after intervening material, as in 2.10-12, where the μάγοι earlier introduced in 2.1 are the unnamed actors in the complex, after Herod, 'all Jerusalem', chief priests and scribes, and the star appear in 2.3-9. The sentence in which the wise men again become the actors (2.10) begins with δέ but the subject is not grammaticalized. Subsequent sentences in the complex are conjoined by καί and feature monolectic verbs:

2.10 ἰδόντες δὲ τὸν ἀστέρα ἐχάρησαν χαρὰν μεγάλην σφόδρα.
2.11a καὶ ἐλθόντες εἰς τὴν οἰκίαν εἶδον τὸ παιδίον μετὰ Μαρίας τῆς
μητρὸς αὐτοῦ,
2.11b καὶ πεσόντες προσεκύνησαν αὐτῷ
2.11c καὶ ἀνοίξαντες τοὺς θησαυροὺς αὐτῶν προσήνεγκαν αὐτῷ
δῶρα, χρυσὸν καὶ λίβανον καὶ σμύρναν.
2.12 καὶ χρηματισθέντες κατ' ὄναρ μὴ ἀνακάμψαι πρὸς Ἡρώδην,
δι' ἄλλης ὁδοῦ ἀνεχώρησαν εἰς τὴν χώραν αὐτῶν.

45. One notably long 'chain' appears in 27.27-38, describing the soldiers' actions in crucifying Jesus—with the exception that in 27.34b Jesus is the actor (no grammaticalized subject), followed by δέ in the next clause, 27.35, when the soldiers again become the actors (δέ is common with change of subject, as I will show in Chapter 5).

Although Herod *et al.* are significant players in this pericope, the unit is syntactically structured to indicate that it is in some way 'about' the visit of the wise men. The use of καί with monolectic verbs in describing the subsequent actions of the previously introduced wise men helps to establish continuity within the unit.

Sometimes the intervention may be a discontinuity of time, as in 21.16-19, where there is a shift from one day to the next between Jesus' encounter with the chief priests and scribes following his clearing of the temple, and his cursing of the fig tree on the following morning. Here a sentence beginning with δέ and a time reference is found midway through a chain of clauses in which Jesus is the actor, shifting the action to the next morning and introducing a new unit in the narrative (21.18), but not breaking the continuity of actor:

21.16b   ὁ δὲ Ἰησοῦς λέγει αὐτοῖς·...
21.17a   καὶ καταλιπὼν αὐτοὺς ἐξῆλθεν ἔξω τῆς πόλεως εἰς Βηθανίαν
21.17b   καὶ ηὐλίσθη ἐκεῖ.
21.18   πρωὶ δὲ ἐπανάγων εἰς τὴν πόλιν ἐπείνασεν.
21.19a   καὶ ἰδὼν συκῆν μίαν ἐπὶ τῆς ὁδοῦ ἦλθεν ἐπ' αὐτὴν
21.19b   καὶ οὐδὲν εὗρεν ἐν αὐτῇ εἰ μὴ φύλλα μόνον,
21.19c   καὶ λέγει αὐτῇ· ...

Although a time shift from one day to the next morning is introduced with δέ, the repeated use of καί and (especially) the sequence of monolectic verbs in 21.19a-c ties the cursing of the fig tree to the previous interaction between Jesus and the chief priests and scribes, where Jesus has been named as the explicit subject (21.16b). Continuity is again reinforced at the beginning of the next unit, 21.23, where the combination of καί and a genitive absolute participial phrase describing Jesus' return to the temple, presumably later in the day (the day after he cleared it of buyers and sellers), begins a scene in which the chief priests and elders of the people question Jesus' authority: 21.23, καὶ ἐλθόντος αὐτοῦ εἰς τὸ ἱερὸν προσῆλθον αὐτῷ διδάσκοντι οἱ ἀρχιερεῖς καὶ οἱ πρεσβύτεροι τοῦ λαοῦ λέγοντες... The use of καί with a genitive absolute construction is relatively unusual, appearing in less than a third (11/39, 28%) of the uses of genitive absolutes at the beginning of sentences in Matthew's narrative framework.[46] In this case the continuity of the following unit concerning

---

46. Mt. 5.1, 8.28, 9.33, 14.32, 17.9, 17.14, 20.29, 21.10, 21.23, 26.21, 26.47. The use of a genitive absolute construction is a favorite 'scene shifting' technique of Matthew, and the most common conjunction with such constructions is δέ (23/39, 59%).

Jesus' authority with the one immediately preceding it, the cursing of the fig tree, is being signaled. The repeated use of καί helps to indicate that all three units—the clearing of the temple, the cursing of the fig tree, and the questioning of Jesus' authority—belong together in some way.

Discontinuity of subject presented as narrative continuity. Although καί is often used by Matthew in a clause complex where there is a sequence of actions by a single actor, there are also numerous cases in which καί connects clauses with more than one explicit subject. This again highlights the concept of authorial choice in the presentation of discourse. At times Matthew chooses to use καί to portray a section of discourse as part of a continuous 'chunk' (implying a continuous mental representation on the part of the hearer or reader) for rhetorical purposes, even if more than one actor is involved. One such example is found in 8.1-4, Jesus' healing of a leper immediately after the Sermon on the Mount (see also on 8.1–9.34, Chapter 9):

8.1 Καταβάντος δὲ αὐτοῦ ἀπὸ τοῦ ὄρους ἠκολούθησαν αὐτῷ
ὄχλοι πολλοί.
8.2 καὶ ἰδοὺ λεπρὸς προσελθὼν προσεκύνει αὐτῷ λέγων·...
8.3a καὶ ἐκτείνας τὴν χεῖρα ἥψατο αὐτοῦ λέγων·...
8.3b καὶ εὐθέως ἐκαθαρίσθη αὐτοῦ ἡ λέπρα.
8.4 καὶ λέγει αὐτῷ ὁ Ἰησοῦς·...

After the genitive absolute construction with δέ in 8.1—a common transitional or 'scene shifting' technique in Matthew's narrative framework—there follows a series of clauses conjoined by καί. As is often the case in Matthew's Gospel, in this passage sentence conjunction and constituent order work together in discourse structure. Four of the five clauses in this complex have explicit subjects: ὄχλοι πολλοί (8.1), λεπρός (8.2), ἡ λέπρα (8.3), ὁ Ἰησοῦς (8.4). In only one does the subject appear before the verb, καὶ ἰδοὺ λεπρός (8.2), and in this case the constituent order SV is virtually fixed by the presence of ἰδού, so should not be seen as a marked syntactical choice, although the use of ἰδού itself is a marked method of introducing or highlighting participants in the discourse (see below on καὶ ἰδού).[47] In the rest the less marked VS constituent order is found. Through a combination of sentence-initial καί and less marked constituent order, Matthew chooses to present continuity of action in this series of clauses rather than discontinuity of actor, in spite of the fact that

47. Of 33 appearances of ἰδού in Matthew's narrative framework, only 3 display VS constituent order, in Mt. 3.16, 8.32 and 17.3.

various subjects are grammaticalized and that the leper himself is marked by ἰδού. In other words, although several grammatical subjects appear, Matthew's syntactical choice to use καί and VS constituent order shows that this pericope is not 'about' the various grammatical subjects, but is in some sense 'about' Jesus, who is referred to, at least by pronoun, in four of the five clauses.

Matthew's description of Herod's birthday celebration, the actions of Herodias's daughter, and the subsequent beheading of John the Baptist in 14.6-12 is also told by means of a series of clauses conjoined with καί. The one exception, ἡ δέ … in 14.8, is (like καὶ ἰδού in 8.2) a fixed form and should not be considered marked.[48] Although various subjects are grammaticalized (some in SV order), by stringing together these sentences with καί Matthew portrays the circumstances of the party and beheading as one narrative 'chunk' or 'block', part of the embedded narrative which begins with γάρ in 14.3 and gives the background to Herod's reaction to Jesus in 14.1-2.[49]

A particularly striking example of a complex of sentences joined by καί in which every sentence has a different subject and each sentence has S₁V constituent order is found in 27.51-52:

27.51a   καὶ ἰδοὺ τὸ καταπέτασμα τοῦ ναοῦ ἐσχίσθη ἀπ᾽ ἄνωθεν ἕως
κάτω εἰς δύο

27.51b   καὶ ἡ γῆ ἐσείσθη

27.51c   καὶ αἱ πέτραι ἐσχίσθησαν,

27.52a   καὶ τὰ μνημεῖα ἀνεῴχθησαν

27.52b   καὶ πολλὰ σώματα τῶν κεκοιμημένων ἁγίων ἠγέρθησαν…

Following Jesus' death the curtain of the temple is torn in half, there is an earthquake, rocks split, tombs open up, and many dead saints arise. The use of καί with thematic subjects is very rare in Matthew's narrative, unless ἰδού also appears in the same clause (as in the first clause here; see on καὶ ἰδού below). This sequence of sentences includes four of only nine such clauses in the narrative framework and must be seen as highly marked.[50] It could be argued that the role of καί in this complex is simply to indicate a continuity of agent, with Matthew perhaps preferring a

---

48. With a pronominal article the sentence conjunction is invariably δέ and the combination <article + δέ> appears as the first element in the sentence.

49. See on γάρ and embedded narratives, Chapter 8.

50. Mark has only the first clause, also in SV order (Mk 15.38); Luke has a variation of the first clause, but in VS order (Lk. 23.45). Mark and Luke refer only to the rending of the temple curtain. The expanded clause complex is unique to Matthew.

passive construction due to some reluctance on his part to name God explicitly as the instigator of these events. However, this does not fully account for the unusual combination of καί and S₁V constituent order. By using this marked syntactical structure Matthew highlights each incident that takes place. At the same time, portraying the continuity of the clauses with καί signals the audience that the separate incidents form one significant event, an event of some prominence in Matthew's account of Jesus' death.

Episode-initial καί. So far I have dealt primarily with the use of καί within clause complexes. Most occurrences of καί in Matthew's narrative framework do appear within units of discourse in which other conjunctions and related features serve as boundary markers. However, it is not unknown for καί to appear at the beginning of what would traditionally be understood as a paragraph, as we have already seen in 21.23, the beginning of a scene in the temple in which the chief priests and elders of the people question Jesus' authority.[51] In Matthew's Gospel καί sometimes functions this way at the beginning of individual units which form part of a series of episodes.

When καί occurs at the beginning of a narrative episode in Matthew's Gospel, there is usually a geographic or spatial reference as well, moving the discourse on to a new setting. Less often there is also a genitive absolute construction with a verb of motion at the beginning of the sentence, reinforcing the movement of the discourse. Matthew makes repeated use of this structural technique in the narrative sections in 8.1–9.34 (a series of miracles stories—see on Mt. 8.1–9.34, Chapter 9), 14.1–17.27, and 19.1–21.17. By contrast καί appears only rarely at the beginning of units in the infancy narratives and the inauguration of Jesus' public ministry in 1.1–4.25 (its use in the summary statement of 4.23 is the only occurrence parallel to its usage in later narrative sections), in 11.1–12.50 (12.9 only, moving from a grainfield to a synagogue), or in the passion narrative (although 26.30, in which Jesus and his disciples sing a hymn and depart for the Mount of Olives, should be considered the beginning of the following series of events which occur outside Jerusalem, and thus an episode-initial use of καί). Examples of καί with spatial and/or geographic references beginning episodes in the narrative section 8.1–9.34 are found in 8.28 (genitive absolute of ἔρχομαι, and reference to the other

---

51. Horrocks reports similar uses of καί to begin paragraphs in Egyptian papyri (Horrocks, *Greek*, p. 92).

side of the sea and the country of the Gadarenes), 9.1 (reference to recrossing the sea to his own city) and 9.9 (reference simply to passing on 'from there').[52] In 14.1–17.27, the episode-initial combination of καί and a spatial or geographic reference at the beginning of episodes appears more frequently: 14.22 ('the other side'), 14.34 (Gennesaret), 15.21 (Tyre and Sidon), 15.29 (the Sea of Galilee), 15.39 (Magadan), 16.5 ('the other side'), 17.9 (genitive absolute of καταβαίνω, and 'down from the mountain') and 17.14 (genitive absolute of ἔρχομαι, but a spatial reference to coming 'to the crowd' rather than a specific geographic reference). In 19.1–21.17, more genitive absolute constructions appear with episode-initial καί and spatial/geographic references: 20.17 (Jerusalem), 20.29 (genitive absolute of ἐκπορεύομαι, and Jericho), 21.10 (genitive absolute of εἰσέρχομαι, and Jerusalem), 21.23 (genitive absolute of ἔρχομαι, and 'the temple').

The use of καί at the beginning of narrative episodes illustrates yet another of the discourse contexts in which καί may appear while retaining its 'low semantic specificity' as a marker of discourse continuity. At these points καί appears to function as a marker of continuity at a higher level of discourse than previously discussed, that is, to show continuity between discourse units rather than merely between sequential actions within the discourse. When καί is used to introduce episodes in a series it signals that the episode it introduces is continuous with its literary context and contributes to the picture of Jesus and his actions that Matthew is developing in that narrative section. However, this does not represent a different 'meaning' for καί itself than that previously described. Καί remains a signal of continuity in discourse processing. While the processing of discourse may have hierarchical elements as well as linear, the audience encounters καί during the linear processing of text.[53] The discourse level

---

52. In addition there are two unusual occurrences of καί with what might be described as a 'dative absolute' (Mt. 8.23, 9.27). See on 8.23 and 9.27, Chapter 9.

53. It is not to be assumed that the audience was visually reading Matthew's text. More likely, they were hearing it read aloud, in a group, and would have encountered the text as a stream of auditory signals. Even if reading alone, that reading was likely to be aloud and processed through auditory channels as well as visually. See P.J. Achtemeier, '*Omne verbum sonat*: The New Testament and the Oral Environment of Late Western Antiquity', *JBL* 109 (1990), pp. 3, 12, 18-20. Unfortunately Achtemeier overstates his case by arguing that writing and reading were exclusively oral. (See, for example, the critique by F.D. Gilliard, 'More Silent Reading in Antiquity: *Non omne verbum sonabat*', *JBL* 112 [1993], pp. 689-96.) Nevertheless, he makes the important point that literature of the time was largely experienced aurally by its audience—that

at which καί is to be applied—that is, the hierarchical level at which continuity is to be maintained in the mental representation of the discourse —is pragmatically worked out on the basis of surrounding text and other cues, such as the presence of geographical indicators.

As a final note on episode-initial καί, the combination found in 21.1 at the beginning of Jesus' entry into Jerusalem is unusual and should be considered a marked construction:

> 21.1 καὶ ὅτε ἤγγισαν εἰς Ἰεροσόλυμα καὶ ἦλθον εἰς Βηθφαγὴ εἰς τὸ ὄρος τῶν ἐλαιῶν, τότε Ἰησοῦς ἀπέστειλεν δύο μαθητὰς λέγων αὐτοῖς·

The pairing of καί with a geographic reference is present here (indeed there are three: Jerusalem, Bethany and the Mount of Olives), as well as a verb of motion similar to the genitive absolute constructions noted above (in this instance an aorist indicative, ἐγγίζω). However, in this example several variations appear: the genitive absolute is changed to an indicative construction with ὅτε, an additional conjunction is introduced (τότε), and SV constituent order is used (unusual with τότε, but when it does appear it usually occurs at the beginning of a paragraph or similar unit). There is no other example of this καὶ ὅτε ... τότε combination in the New Testament. The use of a rare conjunctive combination coincides with an

---

is, generally it was received through the ear rather than through the eye—and that the significance of such practice needs to be more broadly recognized by biblical scholars. See also P.J.J. Botha, 'Greco-Roman Literacy as Setting for New Testament Writings', *Neot* 26 (1992), p. 207; J. Dewey, 'Introduction', in *idem* (ed.), *Orality and Textuality in Early Christian Literature*, *Semeia* 65 (1995), p. 1. In this case the significance of an oral literary environment lies in the fact that Matthew's audience would encounter καί within a linear flow of aural signals, from which they might make inferences about any hierarchical organization of the text.

In addition, the Gospels, in common with other documents of the Greco-Roman period, were written in *scriptio continua* with no spaces left between words or sentences. Punctuation was used only rarely during this period. It was normally left to the reader to divide the stream of written letters into words and to divide word groups into meaningful units such as sentences. See B.M. Metzger, *The Text of the New Testament: Its Transmission, Corruption, and Restoration* (Oxford: Oxford University Press, 3rd edn, 1992), p. 13; also E.G. Turner, *Greek Papyri: An Introduction* (Oxford: Clarendon Press, 1968), p. 57. The practice of *scriptio continua* meant that in most cases even visual readers, like hearers, would encounter a procedural signal like καί as part of a linear flow of text rather than in combination with orthographic cues of discourse hierarchy such as the paragraphing that present-day readers largely take for granted.

important event in the discourse, Jesus' public entry into the city of Jerusalem, and should be understood as a marked choice indicating prominence.

Use of καί *in structural indicators (Bacon's formula).* Although I have argued that the meaning of καί in Matthew's narrative framework is to signal unmarked continuity, the instance in 21.1 just mentioned should serve as fair warning that as with any linguistic form, 'meaning is use'. An author can choose to use a word in any context, sometimes extending its conventional use in new and creative ways, or juxtaposing it in unusual combinations with other words to create new joint meanings. Matthew uses just such an inventive combination in his formulaic transitional statements in 7.28, 11.1, 13.53, 19.1 and 26.1, each of which begins with καὶ ἐγένετο ὅτε ἐτέλεσεν ὁ Ἰησοῦς ... and makes reference to Jesus completing a period of teaching. Since the publication of Bacon's *Studies in Matthew* (1930), this formula has been proposed as a structural indicator in Matthew, sometimes seen as dividing Matthew's Gospel into five 'books', possibly in a manner analogous to the Pentateuch.[54]

The introductory structure καὶ ἐγένετο ὅτε... is unique to these five instances in Matthew, appearing nowhere else in the New Testament. Even the shorter phrase καὶ ἐγένετο is not common in Matthew's narrative framework, appearing elsewhere only in 8.26 and 9.10, although it occurs 7 times in Mark's Gospel and is a favorite of Luke, who uses it 29 times. It does not appear in John's Gospel. Among the examples from the Synoptics, the incidences in which καὶ ἐγένετο introduces a subordinate clause which is then followed by a main clause with another indicative verb, as in these instances (e.g. Mt. 7.28, καὶ ἐγένετο ὅτε ἐτέλεσεν ὁ Ἰησοῦς...ἐξεπλήσσοντο οἱ ὄχλοι...), are fewer still. There is only one other example in Matthew (9.10) and only three in Mark (Mk 1.19, 2.23, 4.4). Simply put, this construction is rare in Matthew's narrative framework and as such is a marked and possibly prominent construction. As I have maintained, rarity alone does not make a lexical form or syntactical arrangement marked, but in this case unusual syntax coincides with what otherwise have been suggested as structural indicators of some type within the discourse.[55]

54. See B.W. Bacon, *Studies in Matthew* (London: Constable, 1930), p. 81.

55. This is not to say, of course, that this formula constitutes a single organizing principle for Matthew's Gospel. There is a long tradition of scholars attempting to discern an overarching structure in the Gospel of Matthew. Along with Bacon's now classic arrangement of five great discourses alternating with narrative passages,

Of relevance to this study is whether καί continues its common use as an unmarked indicator of continuity, or takes on some other meaning in this unusual context. In fact, καί appears to have very little meaning within this context because its use in combination with ἐγένετο seems to be fairly fixed in Matthew's Gospel. The combination ἐγένετο δέ occurs neither in Matthew nor in Mark, although it does occur 17 times in Luke.[56] If it is the case that it is Matthew's standard practice to pair ἐγένετο with καί, then Lyons's principle would again be relevant here, and the 'meaningfulness' of καί in this context would be low, in inverse proportion to its high degree of 'expectancy' in combination with ἐγένετο.[57] Unfortunately, the number of examples of either καὶ ἐγένετο or ἐγένετο δέ is too small to yield a definitive analysis. More research into the collocation of these forms in a larger corpus of Hellenistic Greek would be necessary to establish patterns of usage and their variations. In the meanwhile it is possible only to make the tentative suggestion that while the formula καὶ ἐγένετο ὅτε ἐτέλεσεν ὁ Ἰησοῦς *is* marked, the use of καί *within* this formula is not, and in fact contributes very little to the formula. In any case, the idea that any one of these formulae comes at the end of a teaching section (that is, is continuous with the preceding section) rather than forming the beginning of the following narrative section should not be promoted simply on the basis of the presence of καί, since the contribution of καί in this context may be negligible.

Kingsbury, among others, has suggested a threefold division (J.D. Kingsbury, *Matthew: Structure, Christology, Kingdom* [Philadelphia: Fortress Press, 1975]), and others have suggested various liturgical or chiastic arrangements. Gundry warns, 'We should avoid imposing an outline on Matthew. It is doubtful that the first evangelist thought in terms of one, for his favorite points keep reappearing' (R.H. Gundry, *Matthew: A Commentary on his Handbook for a Mixed Church under Persecution* [Grand Rapids: Eerdmans, 2nd edn, 1994], p. 10). Davies and Allison conclude, 'Matthew's gospel does feature five major discourses (so rightly Bacon). At the same time, Matthew's architectonic grandeur does not appear to derive from a clear blueprint (so rightly Gundry). We, in any case, cannot claim to have found the blue-print, and we cannot credit anyone else with the discovery' (Davies and Allison, *Matthew*, I, p. 61).

56. In Mt. 17.2 and 27.45, δέ and ἐγένετο appear together in a sentence, but in neither of these does the introductory formula ἐγένετο δέ (analogous to καὶ ἐγένετο) occur as it does in Luke. Hagner suggests that the presence of καὶ ἐγένετο in Matthew and Mark rather than ἐγένετο δέ is a Semiticism, influenced by ויהי (D.A. Hagner, personal communication).

57. See Lyons, *Introduction*, p. 415.

Other Lexical and Semantic Interactions

As shown in the discussion of καὶ ἐγένετο above, sentence conjunctions can occur in relatively predictable combinations with other lexical forms, in which case the meaning the individual conjunction contributes to that context becomes proportionately less.

Καί *with* ἰδού. One of the most common of the relatively fixed combinations in Matthew's Gospel—a pattern with high predictability—is the association of καί and ἰδού. In Halliday's understanding of the meta-functions of language and their related thematic elements, ἰδού functions as an interpersonal theme, but ἰδού can also be understood as a type of 'commentary pragmatic marker' in Fraser's terminology.[58] Ἰδού signals the audience, 'Hey, look! Something important or unexpected is happening here!', but does not add to or restrict the content of what is happening in the sentence. In the infancy narratives, for example, ἰδού draws attention to supernatural participants in the text (see Mt. 1.20, 2.1, 2.9, 2.13). In Matthew's miracle stories ἰδού may be used to introduce a suppliant, someone coming to Jesus for healing (see Mt. 8.2, 8.29, 9.18, 9.20, 9.32; see also on 8.1–9.34, Chapter 9).

In Matthew's narrative framework ἰδού is used 33 times, about three-quarters of these in the combination καὶ ἰδού (24/33, 73%).[59] Where ἰδού appears without καί, a genitive absolute construction is present and either the sentence conjunction is δέ (six times) or the sentence is asyndetic (three times).[60] In other words, the selection of a conjunction with ἰδού in narrative is highly predictable: if no genitive absolute appears, καί will be used; if a genitive absolute appears, δέ or asyndeton will be used—except in Mt. 26.47 (see below). In addition, ἰδού tends to be combined with SV constituent order, although on the whole V(S) is more common with καί in

58. Fraser, 'Approach', pp. 385-86.

59. See also A. Vargas-Machuca, '(Καὶ) ἰδού en estilo narrativo de Mateo', *Bib* 50 (1969), p. 233, who identifies 33 uses of ἰδού in Matthew's narrative framework and 16 in Luke's but none in the narrative frameworks of Mark or John. Hagner notes that as 'Matthew's favorite device for calling attention to something extraordinary that is about to occur', ἰδού appears a total of 62 times in Matthew's Gospel, 'thirty-four of which are insertions into parallel material and nine of which are in material unique to Matthew' (Hagner, *Matthew 1–13*, p. 18).

60. Buth observes that although the sequence ἰδού γάρ sometimes appears in the New Testament (Lk. 1.44, 1.48, 2.10, 6.23, 17.21; Acts 9.11; 2 Cor. 7.11), the sequence ἰδού δέ never occurs, even though the phonetic combination -*dou de* is not ruled out (R. Buth, personal communication).

the narrative framework. About 80% of all the uses of ἰδού in Matthew's narrative framework have SV constituent order (27/33, 82%), and similarly about 80% of the instances of the combination καὶ ἰδού have SV constituent order (19/24, 79%).

As a result, καί itself generally contributes little to discourse processing when καὶ ἰδού appears. While the use of the combination καὶ ἰδού is a marked choice, the use of καί within this idiom is not, because its presence in this context does not represent a meaningful option. An interpreter cannot build a case for discourse continuity on the presence of καί with ἰδού. Similarly, one cannot argue that καί with SV constituent order—as opposed to the V(S) order more frequently found with καί—is a marked combination if ἰδού is also present, since SV order is generally dictated by the use of ἰδού.

The single instance in which the predictive formula given above, καί with no genitive absolute but δέ or asyndeton with a genitive absolute, does not hold is in 26.47, describing Jesus' betrayal and arrest, where καί is combined with both a genitive absolute and ἰδού:

> 26.47 καὶ ἔτι αὐτοῦ λαλοῦντος ἰδοὺ Ἰούδας εἷς τῶν δώδεκα ἦλθεν
> καὶ μετ' αὐτοῦ ὄχλος πολὺς μετὰ μαχαιρῶν καὶ ξύλων ἀπὸ
> τῶν ἀρχιερέων καὶ πρεσβυτέρων τοῦ λαοῦ.

The phrase αὐτοῦ λαλοῦντος ἰδού appears with minor variations three other times in Matthew's narrative, in each of which it is asyndetic: in 9.18, when the ruler approaches Jesus to request help for his daughter who has died; in 12.46, when Jesus' mother and brothers arrive asking to speak with him; and in 17.5 at his transfiguration, when a bright cloud overshadows him and a voice speaks from the cloud.

Matthew's καὶ ἔτι αὐτοῦ λαλοῦντος ἰδού in 26.47 differs from parallel passages in the other two Synoptics, although the phrase ἔτι αὐτοῦ λαλοῦντος appears in each. Mark's Gospel has καὶ εὐθύς but not ἰδού (Mk 14.43, καὶ εὐθὺς ἔτι αὐτοῦ λαλοῦντος παραγίνεται Ἰούδας εἷς τῶν δώδεκα...),[61] while Luke has asyndeton and ἰδού (Lk. 22.47, ἔτι αὐτοῦ λαλοῦντος ἰδοὺ ὄχλος, καὶ ὁ λεγόμενος Ἰούδας εἷς τῶν

---

61. As Vargas-Machuca reports, there is no instance of ἰδού in the narrative framework of Mark's Gospel (Vargas-Machuca, '(Καὶ) ἰδού', p. 233), although it does appear within direct speech, including the Markan parallel to Mt. 27.45-46 immediately preceding (= Mk 14.41-42, ἦλθεν ἡ ὥρα, ἰδοὺ παραδίδοται ὁ υἱὸς τοῦ ἀνθρώπου εἰς τὰς χεῖρας τῶν ἁμαρτωλῶν. ἐγείρεσθε ἄγωμεν· ἰδοὺ ὁ παραδιδούς με ἤγγικεν).

δώδεκα προῆρχετο αὐτοὺς).⁶² Matthew's choice to use—or, possibly, retain Mark's use of—καί in 26.47, when asyndeton appears to be his usual or unmarked choice with αὐτοῦ λαλοῦντος ἰδού, should be understood as marked, and in this case the presence of καί, even with the presence of ἰδού, is significant. Matthew is making a close and explicit connection between Jesus' proclamation in 26.45-46 that the time for his arrest has arrived (ἰδοὺ ἤγγικεν ἡ ὥρα καὶ ὁ υἱὸς τοῦ ἀνθρώπου παραδίδοται εἰς χεῖρας ἁμαρτωλῶν. ἐγείρεσθε ἄγωμεν· ἰδοὺ ἤγγικεν ὁ παραδιδούς με) and the immediate arrival of Judas with the crowd. The threefold repetition of ἰδού and the parallelism between παραδίδοται, ὁ παραδιδούς and Ἰούδας in 26.45-47 (26.45, ἰδού... παραδίδοται; 26.46, ἰδού...ὁ παραδιδούς με; 26.47, καί...ἰδοὺ Ἰούδας) makes the association all the more explicit, giving prominence to Judas's betrayal and Jesus' resulting arrest.

Infrequence of καί *with* λέγω *speech margins.* Conjunctions can also show a tendency *not* to combine with certain lexical forms or syntactic constructions. The Evangelist uses καί less frequently as a sentence conjunction with speech margins with λέγω than he does with narrative sentences in general. Speech margins are defined as syntactical structures used to introduce reported speech, whether conversation or monologue, and to set it into the narrative framework. They can be grouped into two types: those which involve a verb of speaking, normally a finite form of λέγω, for example, Mt. 8.19, καὶ προσελθὼν εἷς γραμματεὺς εἶπεν αὐτῷ· διδάσκαλε...; and those which involve some other verb, generally not a verb of speaking, usually in combination with λέγων or λέγοντες (participles of λέγω are always present tense-form in Matthew's Gospel), such as Mt. 21.20, καὶ ἰδόντες οἱ μαθηταὶ ἐθαύμασαν λέγοντες· πῶς παραχρῆμα ἐξηράνθη ἡ συκῆ. In this study the first group—with finite verbs of speaking—will simply be called speech margins, and the second group—in which a λέγω participle is combined with another finite verb—will be referred to as 'compound' speech margins.

The two types of speech margins exhibit different patterns of use of sentence conjunctions. Compound speech margins follow the general pattern for narrative in terms of the frequency of καί: slightly less than half of the sentences in Matthew's narrative framework have καί as the sentence conjunction (335/720, 47%), as do slightly less than half of the speech margins in which another verb is combined with λέγων or

---

62. NA²⁷ gives δέ as a textual variant for Lk. 22.47.

λέγοντες (42/92, 47%). At the same time, speech margins with a finite form of λέγω show significantly less use of καί. Καί appears as the sentence conjunction in only 29% (54/186; $z = -4.31$) of sentences with λέγω as the finite verb.[63] Corresponding to the decreased use of καί in these sentences is a significantly increased frequency of asyndeton with λέγω speech margins (see on asyndeton, Chapter 6). Matthew chooses in these speech margins from the same system of sentence conjunctions that he uses in narrative as a whole, but in this special case (or subtype) of narrative discourse the distribution of choices within the system differs.

'Adversative' καί? I have characterized καί as a sentence conjunction with low semantic specificity, signaling continuity in discourse and used in a number of discourse contexts with varying semantic relations between the sentences it conjoins. As I have stated, traditional grammarians have long discussed whether καί is merely additive or can be adversative as well.[64]

Certainly καί appears in sentences where the context seems to indicate contrast or denial of expectation, as in Joseph's actions in 1.24-25 mentioned earlier:

1.24b καὶ παρέλαβεν τὴν γυναῖκα αὐτοῦ,
1.25a καὶ οὐκ ἐγίνωσκεν αὐτὴν ἕως οὗ ἔτεκεν υἱόν;

as well as in the following example from Jesus' baptism by John:

3.14b ἐγὼ χρείαν ἔχω ὑπὸ σοῦ βαπτισθῆναι,
3.14c καὶ σὺ ἔρχῃ πρός με;

In the first example, 1.24-25, Joseph takes Mary as his wife but, contrary to what might be expected in terms of the usual order of marriage, does not have sexual relations with her until after her baby is born. In the second example, John the Baptist points out that although it is he who presumably should be baptized by Jesus, instead Jesus has come to him for baptism. (Although this second example is from conversational discourse rather than from the narrative framework, it is offered by Winer as an example of an adversative use of καί, and so is considered here.[65])

---

63. Similarly, while φημί appears 11 times in speech margins in Matthew's narrative framework only one occurrence, Mt. 8.8, has καί as the sentence conjunction (9%; $z = -2.49$), although the small sample size precludes any guarantee of statistical significance.

64. See, for example, the brief historical survey in Blomqvist, *Das Sogennante KAI Adversativum*, pp. 9-14.

65. See Winer, *Treatise*, p. 544.

Of the traditional New Testament grammarians, Winer has particular insight regarding 'adversative' καί. Winer describes καί as 'the simple copula',[66] which is 'never really adversative'.[67] For Winer, καί has 'only two meanings, *and*, *also*'.[68] Although a translator might be tempted to supply additional words to draw out more fully the nuances these two incorporate, in Winer's view this would contradict the intention of the author, who has chosen to use καί 'either in accordance with the simplicity of Biblico-oriental thought, or designedly—on rhetorical grounds: sometimes both these causes coincided'.[69] Winer suggests that the juxtaposition of the two clauses in John's statements about Jesus' baptism in Mt. 3.14 more eloquently expresses the astonishment or sorrow of John than would more explicit terms such as *however*, *nevertheless*, or *notwithstanding*.[70] Current scholarship might rightly hesitate to label 'Biblico-oriental thought' as 'simplistic' or to assume its homogeneity in any terms as readily as Winer did in the early nineteenth century. And it is clear he is thinking in terms of sentence conjunctions primarily as truth-conditional forms indicating the semantic relations between sentences, rather than of καί as procedural, signaling the audience to take these two sentences together in some way. Nevertheless, what is relevant to this study is his recognition of the role of Matthew's creative purpose in choosing a conjunction for its rhetorical or literary impact in his portrayal of Jesus and his contemporaries, and that the Evangelist allows the audience to make inferences about the semantic relationship between the two propositions.

In his study of 'so-called adversative καί' Blomqvist concludes that there is no evidence for an unambiguously adversative use of καί, that in fact ' "adversative καί" never existed'.[71] For Blomqvist, the general function of καί as an indicator of 'context-relevant parallelism' is adequate to explain its use even in contexts where that parallelism may include an element of semantic contrast.[72] He observes that in opposition to adversative particles καί is the neutral or unmarked conjunction, and as such can be used when a speaker chooses, for his or her own purposes, not to express semantic contrast present in a given context.[73] Blomqvist argues

---

66. Winer, *Treatise*, p. 543.
67. Winer, *Treatise*, p. 545.
68. Winer, *Treatise*, p. 543.
69. Winer, *Treatise*, p. 543.
70. See Winer, *Treatise*, p. 544.
71. Blomqvist, *Das Sogennante KAI Adversativum*, p. 25.
72. See Blomqvist, *Das Sogennante KAI Adversativum*, pp. 44, 61.
73. See Blomqvist, *Das Sogennante KAI Adversativum*, p. 61.

that the majority of examples of καί in Greek literature which are traditionally labeled 'adversative' are actually one of several cases: either an
adverbial or emphatic use of καί misdesignated as a sentence conjunction;
or instances in which there is in fact no meaningful contrast present in the
context; or instances in which whatever element of semantic contrast there
may be is of little or no relevance to the discourse from the point of view
of the speaker.[74] The remaining examples Blomqvist describes as involving 'relevant contrast'—that is, an element of semantic contrast which
does appear to be of interest to the speaker at that point in the discourse. In
these instances the speaker chooses (for any of a range of reasons) not to
portray that contrast linguistically through the use of an adversative particle, but to use the unmarked καί.[75] Like Winer, Blomqvist recognizes the
element of authorial choice in the portrayal of discourse and that sentence
conjunctions play a role in those choices.

In sum, Matthew could have inserted ἀλλά or πλήν or δέ or some other
connector instead of καί in passages such as Mt. 3.14, but does not.[76]
Instead, καί is used as a procedural indicator to portray these two clauses
as a continuity, guiding the audience to construct not two separate mental
'boxes' in their representation of this encounter, one in which John is in
need of baptism by Jesus and another one in which Jesus requests John's
baptism—two baptisms which on the basis of the supposed irreconcilabil-
ity between human activity (John's) and divine activity (Jesus') the
audience might naturally place in separate mental constructs—but a single
surprising 'box' in which John's need of Jesus' baptism and Jesus' intention to submit himself to John's baptism coexist. The strategy of leading
the audience to integrate the two into one continuous mental representation by the use of καί has rhetorical power at this point in Matthew's
portrayal of Jesus' identity and purpose.

Similarly, the use of καί in 1.25 makes Joseph's abstinence with respect
to Mary part of a continuous mental representation incorporating a series
of things that Joseph does in 1.24-25 in obedient response to the angel's

74. See Blomqvist, *Das Sogennante KAI Adversativum*, pp. 25-43.
75. See Blomqvist, *Das Sogennante KAI Adversativum*, pp. 44-54. Blomqvist
notes, however, that in the New Testament there may be Semitic influence behind such
uses of καί (Blomqvist, *Das Sogennante KAI Adversativum*, pp. 46-48).
76. Of course, the choice may have been made previously in whatever written or
oral source(s) Matthew may have used, or even by John himself, if one allows the
possibility that these represent *ipsissima verba*, but in any case Matthew has chosen to
retain καί in his version.

pronouncements in 1.20-23, with the result that a virgin gives birth, as predicted in Isa. 7.14 (LXX), cited in 1.23. As pointed out above, the last three—marrying, not knowing, and naming—are all of the structure <καί + monolectic verb>, signaling that the actions are to be processed as continuous with ὁ Ἰωσὴφ...ἐποίησεν ὡς προσέταξεν αὐτῷ ὁ ἄγγελος, part of one integrated mental representation.

The tendency on the part of some grammarians to characterize καί as adversative in passages like those above exemplifies Dik's concern that the analysis of various semantic relations not be confused with describing the conjunction itself.[77] What the conjunction καί contributes to these conjoined sentences is a portrayal of continuity; what the context contributes is the semantic relation of contrast or denial of expectation.

Summary and Conclusions

In summary, καί is not only the most common sentence conjunction in the Gospel of Matthew, it is the unmarked choice in Matthew's system of sentence conjunctions. In Matthew's narrative framework καί serves as a procedural, non-truth-conditional signal of continuity, normally found in contexts where there is—or is presented as being—an underlying continuity of time, action and/or actor. To say that continuity is the basic feature of καί in Matthew is to define continuity as the (minimal and procedural) semantic value of καί in Matthew's discourse. The low level of semantic specificity conveyed by καί allows for its use in a number of discourse contexts where an underlying continuity is being displayed but where a variety of semantic relations may actually exist between propositions— including adversative or contrastive relations.

Matthew commonly combines καί with unmarked aorist tense-forms and unmarked or less marked constituent order (that is, monolectic verbs, or verb before subject if an explicit subject appears) in multiply reinforcing syntactical structures which facilitate the audience's construction of a continuous mental representation of the discourse. With respect to constituent order, not only does καί tend to appear with less marked order, but the frequency of καί diminishes in proportion to the markedness of the constituent order of the sentences it begins. The earlier in the sentence the subject is placed, the progressively less likely καί is to appear; the later in the sentence the subject is placed (with no expressed subject as the least marked structure), the progressively more likely καί is to appear.

77. See Dik, *Coordination*, p. 269.

This survey of καί as a narrative sentence conjunction in Matthew's Gospel, while not exhaustive, is intended to establish patterns of usage in the Gospel. In general, Matthew's choices of sentence conjunction, verbal tense-form, and constituent order work together to relate parts of the discourse to what has come before, helping to create texture, and to indicate (or in the case of καί, usually *not* to indicate) discourse prominence. An understanding of καί's specific role as a signal of continuity in Matthew's Gospel, a recognition of its frequent combination with aorist tense-forms and V or VS constituent order (particularly with continuity of actor), and an awareness of its varying patterns of usage—occurring more frequently, for example, with ἰδού than in Matthew's narrative framework overall, and less frequently with λέγω speech margins than in the narrative framework as a whole—constitute a background against which the interpreter can recognize more marked usage and begin to make meaningful evaluations of markedness and prominence within the narrative framework of Matthew's Gospel.

Chapter 5

Δέ: Low- to Mid-Level Discontinuity

Δέ	All sentences in Matthew	Narrative sentences	Exposition sentences	Speech sentences	Old Testament quotations
n =	2302	720	768	733	81
# δέ	470	257	159	50	4
% δέ	20%	36%	21%	7%	5%

What Does δέ 'Mean'?

Any first-year student of biblical Greek knows that δέ means *but*, except for the times it might just mean *and*, or—more often yet—when it means nothing at all and seems safely ignored. It is not just beginning students, however, who find it difficult to nail down the meaning of this conjunction. Robertson believes that δέ contains 'no essential notion of antithesis or contrast',[1] while Blass, Debrunner and Funk treat δέ as fundamentally adversative.[2] Zerwick states that it nearly always implies some sort of contrast.[3] Turner observes that at times δέ has a strong adversative force, although it is usually weaker and indistinguishable from καί,[4] and Dana and Mantey claim that δέ is commonly used as an adversative particle, but that it is also common as a transitional or continuative particle, and may at times have an explanatory usage.[5] Some, like Robertson, include δέ in a list of copulative conjunctions and again in a

---

1. Robertson, *Grammar*, p. 1184.
2. BDF, §447. They also note that δέ can introduce a parenthesis, explanation or intensification (BDF, §447[7]-[8]).
3. M. Zerwick, *Biblical Greek* (Rome: Scripta Pontificii Instituti Biblici, 1963), §467.
4. Turner, *Syntax*, p. 331.
5. Dana and Mantey, *Grammar*, p. 244.

second list of adversative conjunctions.[6] Others, like Dana and Mantey, handle separate adversative and continuative uses in a single treatment of δέ.[7] The only consensus seems to be that this form has a range of continuous and/or adversative senses which appear in a variety of contexts.[8]

The description of δέ as continuative appears to be little more than a recognition that δέ can be found as a narrative sentence connector at points where there is no obvious semantic contrast as well as at points where an adversative semantic relation is more apparent. This does little to identify what δέ itself contributes to the discourse at those points. As van Ophuijsen warns, all continuous discourse naturally exhibits coherence, and so 'it is presumably wise to appeal to the notions of connection and connectivity only sparingly in definitions of the values of particles...'[9]— unless, as with καί, continuity is the primary feature. Since continuative characterizations of δέ reflect little more than that discourse is connected and coherent, and adversative characterizations of δέ are subject to abundant counterexamples, the question of what δέ itself 'means' remains largely unanswered by traditional grammarians.

In Chapter 2, I stated that sentence conjunctions have a low level of semantic specificity, that is, a minimal semantic value allowing their use in a range of discourse contexts where there may be a variety of semantic relationships between propositions.[10] These forms encode procedural and non-truth-conditional meaning, indicating how the sentences they introduce are to be related to preceding text in the processing of discourse.[11] Speakers and writers use sentence conjunctions like καί and δέ to help guide the mental representations constructed by their audience.[12] These

---

6.   Robertson, *Grammar*, pp. 1183, 1186 (although Robertson clarifies that 'not all of these [adversative] conjunctions mean contrast...or opposition but the context makes the matter clear').

7.   Dana and Mantey, *Grammar*, p. 244.

8.   See, similarly, Kühner–Gerth: 'Bindewörten die Mitte, indem es sowohl kopulative als adversative Kraft in sich vereinigt ...' (R. Kühner and B. Gerth, *Ausführliche Grammatik der griechischen Sprache*. II. *Satzlehre* [Leipzig: Hahnsche, 1904], §526 [2]).

9.   Van Ophuijsen, 'OYN, APA, ΔH, TOINYN', p. 80.

10.   See Dik, *Coordination*, p. 269.

11.   See, for example, Blakemore, *Semantic Constraints*, p. 144; Blakemore, *Understanding Utterances*, p. 137; Wilson and Sperber, 'Linguistic Form and Relevance', pp. 12-16, 19; Givón, *Functionalism*, pp. 341-44; Hansen, *Discourse Particles*, pp. 73-75.

12.   On mental representations or mental models, see, for example, Minsky, 'Frame-

forms facilitate the audience's comprehension of discourse in two related ways: they guide hearers or readers to construct or modify the mental representations they make of discourse, and, at the same time, their presence reduces processing effort.[13]

Καί serves as a signal of unmarked continuity in Matthew's narrative framework (Chapter 4). Δέ, on the other hand, indicates low- to mid-level discontinuity. That is, the presence of δέ introducing a sentence cues the audience that some change is to be incorporated into their mental representation of the discourse. Such cues facilitate the processing of discourse because, as pointed out in the 'principle of continuity' introduced in Chapter 2, 'Unless specifically marked, the new meaning is incorporated into, and regarded as continuous with, the current ongoing construction'.[14] Or, as Bestgen explains, 'According to the Gricean maxims of communication, speakers and writers are expected to inform the addressees that continuity is not preserved, that there is a topic shift, and that specific action should be taken …'[15] The presence of δέ as a sentence conjunction serves as one such marker informing the audience that in some respect continuity is not maintained at this point in the discourse.

As with the other sentence conjunctions in Matthew's narrative framework, I take a minimalist approach to the semantics of δέ which recognizes that δέ functions as a signal of discourse discontinuity in a wide variety of contexts. The distinction between minimalist and maximalist perspectives helps to clarify what δέ contributes to the meaning of conjoined propositions in Matthew's Gospel, and what comes from the truth-conditional content of those sentences and from the semantic relations between them. Describing conjunctions as 'multiple-purpose tools' which can be used to combine propositions which may be characterized by a variety of semantic relations, Dik continues, 'These relational differences… [are] either inherent in the contents combined, or added to the total content of the coordinated expression on the basis of what may be called "interpretational probability"'. (Dik's reference to 'interpretational probability' anticipates later work on pragmatic principles of interpretation, such as Grice's Cooperative Principle or Sperber and Wilson's Relevance Theory.) Analyzing these various relations is,

work', pp. 211-77; Schank and Abelson, *Scripts*; Johnson-Laird, *Mental Models*; Givón, *Functionalism*, pp. 343-44.

13. See Blakemore, *Semantic Constraints*, p. 123.
14. Segal *et al*., 'Interclausal Connectives', p. 32.
15. Bestgen, 'Trace and Signal', p. 775.

according to Dik, necessary and rewarding, but is not to be confused with describing the conjunction itself.

> [T]o project them into the semantic values of a word like *and* as such is to confound…the semantic content conventionally laid down in the expression as such with the interpretational aspects added to the expressions when used in specific communicative situations.[16]

Two related errors need to be avoided. The first, in Dik's terms, is to over-differentiate a form's internal (semantic) properties, delineating for example a 'copulative δέ', a 'contrastive δέ', a 'resumptive δέ' and so on. As one of my colleagues has pointed out, a hammer can be used for a number of things besides hammering a nail: as a doorstop, as a paper-weight, or as a gavel. Should we then speak of a 'door-opening hammer', a 'paper-weighting hammer', or a 'table-banging hammer' as distinct entities? And more importantly, do any of these provide an adequate description of what a hammer *is*?[17] Securing doors, weighting paper, and banging on tables may be atypical functions of a hammer used to make a point, but the principle is valid: a single object would not normally be construed as several distinct entities according to its different uses, and describing its uses is not tantamount to describing the object. Similarly, differentiating different 'types' of δέ may reveal a range of contexts in which δέ is used, but does not necessarily bring us closer to understanding what kind of information δέ encodes and what it contributes to a discourse.

The second error, a variation on the first, is to describe a form like δέ on the basis of one or more of the contexts in which it is used to the exclusion of others, so that it appears that a single, 'basic' function of the form has been determined but in fact the description is still context-based. This last, I believe, is where Levinsohn's analysis of δέ in the Gospels and Acts as a 'developmental conjunction' runs into difficulty. At times Levinsohn seems to conflate his analysis of the minimal (but extant) meaning of the conjunction (what Dik calls 'the semantic value conventionally laid down') with that of the contexts in which it is employed.

Levinsohn
Levinsohn has long argued that while καί is the unmarked connector in the narrative sections of the Synoptics and Acts, δέ is a 'developmental' conjunction, by which he means that 'the information introduced by δέ represents a new step or development in the story or argument as far as the

---

16. Dik, *Coordination*, p. 269.
17. I am indebted to M.B. O'Donnell for this illustration (personal communication).

purpose of the author is concerned' and that 'this information *builds* on what has preceded it'.[18]

Although Levinsohn acknowledges that δέ occurs where an author adds 'distinctive' information (citing Winer's statement that δέ is often used to connect 'something new, different, and distinct'),[19] he argues that for δέ to be used, 'not only must the sentence contain something distinctive ... it must also represent *a new step or development in the author's story or argument*'.[20] He asserts that 'an analysis of δέ as a marker of distinctiveness is inadequate', offering as evidence a number of instances in Matthew's and Luke's Gospels in which καί is used rather than δέ, 'even when the sentences contain distinctive information'.[21] However, all that Levinsohn demonstrates here is that in these sentences whatever distinctive information may, in Levinsohn's determination, be present has not been *marked* as such by the author, at least in terms of the author's choice of sentence conjunction. Levinsohn himself writes that 'when the marker is absent, nothing is said about the presence or absence of the feature—the sentence is unmarked for that feature'.[22] That an Evangelist has chosen to use the unmarked conjunction καί in the instances Levinsohn cites says little about the adequacy of 'distinctiveness' as a description of δέ's function as a relatively marked sentence conjunction.

Seeking to explain the presence or absence of δέ in such sentences, Levinsohn rightly turns to 'the author's purpose in presenting his material',[23] but his attempt to characterize δέ as a marker of 'development' is unconvincing. Levinsohn presents several examples of καί and δέ in passages from Matthew's and Luke's Gospels, along with his assessment of whether each use of δέ represents a development in the narrative from the author's perspective.[24] The specific criteria by which the determination 'developmental' (as opposed to merely 'distinctive') is made in these examples remain unclear. Levinsohn appears to base his analysis of whether each incident is 'developmental' solely on his own reading of the ideational content of the passage, without reference either to other specifically 'developmental' markers or structures, or to ways in which other

18. Levinsohn, *Discourse Features*, p. 76 (his emphasis). See also, for example, Levinsohn, *Textual Connections*, p. 83.
    19. Winer, *Treatise*, p. 552.
    20. Levinsohn, *Discourse Features*, p. 72 (his emphasis).
    21. Levinsohn, *Discourse Features*, pp. 73-75.
    22. Levinsohn, *Discourse Features*, p. ix.
    23. Levinsohn, *Discourse Features*, p. 72.
    24. Levinsohn, *Discourse Features*, pp. 72-77.

New Testament commentators have understood the passage. Levinsohn expressly excludes 'points of departure' such as sentence-initial subjects or sentence-initial temporal phrases as formal indicators of 'development'. To illustrate this, he compares δέ in Lk. 4.1, in which Jesus is full of the Holy Spirit at his baptism (and which is, in Levinsohn's determination, 'developmental'), with καί in Lk. 1.67, in which Zacharias is filled with the Holy Spirit (and which in his view is not 'developmental'). 'In both examples, the subject is initial as a point of departure/prepositional topic.'[25] Levinsohn continues, 'I...want to emphasize that development and points of departure are *different* parameters'.[26] Levinsohn's argument would be strengthened by an explicit and consistent set of criteria for the determination of 'development' in Gospel narrative.

More significantly, Levinsohn himself finds instances in which sentences conjoined by δέ do not necessarily contribute to 'development' as he construes it. He writes,

> When δέ introduces background material, the sentence moves the narrative to something distinctive... Furthermore, this distinctive information is *often* significant for the further development of the story line that was being followed before the background material.[27]

He continues, 'Although the information contained in background material introduced by δέ is usually of significance for the further development of the story, it does not have to be. Sometimes, the material appears only to supply "information such as the number of people present".'[28] Elsewhere in the same volume Levinsohn writes, 'Δέ cannot be described as an exclusively developmental conjunction, since it also introduces background material, which can be viewed as a new *step* in a narrative, but scarcely as a new development'.[29] Unless 'development' can be shown unequivocally to be present in all uses of δέ in the Synoptic Gospels and Acts, Levinsohn's claim that 'development' is what δέ itself adds to discourse cannot be sustained. His lesser claim that δέ is associated with 'distinctive' information contributes more to an understanding of the use of δέ in the New Testament.

---

25. Levinsohn, *Discourse Features*, p. 76.
26. Levinsohn, *Discourse Features*, p. 77 (his emphasis).
27. Levinsohn, *Discourse Features*, p. 90 (my emphasis).
28. Levinsohn, *Discourse Features*, p. 90. Levinsohn cites here his *Textual Connections*, p. 91, with Acts 19.7 as an example of background material that simply enumerates those present.
29. Levinsohn, *Discourse Features*, p. 76 n. 4 (his emphasis).

In his earlier work on Acts, in discussing the role of δέ in introducing 'development units' in the discourse, Levinsohn observes, 'Two factors of distinctiveness account for more than 90% of the examples of *de*: a change of temporal setting…and a real change in the underlying subject'.[30] Other 'factors of distinctiveness' he enumerates in the use of δέ in Acts include a change in the participating cast, a switch back to the story line of the narrative (following a background comment), a switch to a background comment, a change of circumstances, and a change of spatial setting.[31] Levinsohn's perception that δέ is associated with a number of 'factors of distinctiveness' is probably more important than the extensive list he offers of what he believes those factors to be, as in this list he appears to be in danger of conflating the contexts in which δέ is found with what δέ itself adds to those contexts. Similarly, his characterization of δέ as a developmental conjunction appears to beg the question of whether the form δέ contributes the meaning 'development' or whether 'developmental' merely describes a type of literary context in which δέ may be found. Still, Levinsohn's recognition that καί is the unmarked connector in discourse while δέ appears to signal some distinctiveness or development (as opposed to contrast), and that either is chosen on the basis of the author's purpose, is significant.

Buth

In response to the work of Levinsohn and others, Buth proposes attributing 'a common feature of +DIFFERENT OR +CHANGE to δέ'.[32] Buth argues against using the term 'development' in describing δέ as a 'developmental conjunction' or in terms of 'development units' because the terminology suggests plot development and draws the discussion into an analysis of plot units or similar structures.

> Instead of 'units' or 'entities' it may be better to talk of quantum moves along a 'theme-line'… Narratives might…be related to a theme or plot line without necessitating special units. A label that might reflect the nature of such a Greek thematic relator system would be: 'thematic shift'.[33]

---

30. Levinsohn, *Textual Connections*, p. 87. More recently, Levinsohn speaks of δέ introducing 'event clusters' rather than 'development units'. He describes an 'event cluster' as 'a group of events that are linked by καί' (Levinsohn, *Discourse Features*, p. 74).

31. Levinsohn, *Textual Connections*, pp. 89-92.

32. Buth, 'Semitic Καί and Greek Δέ', p. 13.

33. Buth, 'On Levinsohn's "Development Units" ', p. 54.

Buth chooses 'shift' as a purposefully neutral term to reflect the fact that δέ can indicate a switch to or from background material as well as moving the narrative forward along a theme-line: ' "Shift"…could be forwards, backwards, or sideways.'[34] Some of the kinds of changes or differences δέ might signal (that is, the semantic contexts in which δέ may be found, rather than 'different types of δέ') 'could include change of participant, change of paragraph or episode unit, change of theme line…and a change of (reversal of) expectation (*in a limited binary frame this would be called contrast*)'.[35] To my knowledge Buth is the first to integrate the traditional understanding of δέ as contrastive or adversative with its function as a marker of discontinuity in discourse.[36]

Not only does Buth manage to separate the distinctive contribution of δέ from factors present in the contexts in which it appears, he also recognizes the role δέ plays as a signal in the ongoing process of discourse comprehension:

> The effect of marking 'thematic shifts' is to give a reader/listener an additional, partially redundant means of grouping and evaluating the narrative. Every time a 'thematic shift' is signaled the decoder (reader/listener) would understand that the micro-theme…of the previous clauses and/or sentences had been completed.[37]

Buth's analysis is very close to the view of δέ as a signal of discontinuity in the construction and manipulation of mental representations proposed here.[38]

---

34. Buth, 'On Levinsohn's "Development Units" ', p. 54.

35. Buth, 'Semitic Καί and Greek Δέ', p. 13 (my emphasis).

36. See also Titrud, 'Overlooked Καί', p. 20, who states that 'although δέ itself is not inherently adversative, yet due to its function of marking what follows as something new and distinct, it readily allows an adversative sense (dependent, of course, on the context)'.

37. Buth, 'On Levinsohn's "Development Units" ', p. 54.

38. In an introductory grammar, Black takes an approach similar to those of Levinsohn and Buth: 'καί is the basic or "unmarked" means of conjoining sentences and implies continuity with the preceding context. δέ marks the introduction of a new and significant development in the story or argument' (D.A. Black, *Learn to Read New Testament Greek* [Nashville: Broadman & Holman, expanded edn, 1994], p. 28; see, similarly, D.A. Black, 'The Article, Conjunctions and Greek Word Order [Greek for Bible Readers]', *BR* 9 [Oct. 1993], p. 23). Although Black has had some association with both Levinsohn and Buth (see, for example, Black *et al.* [eds.], *Linguistics*, in which Buth's article 'Οὖν, Δέ, Καί, and Asyndeton' appears [pp. 144-61]), it is unclear to what extent if at all Black's conclusions depend on the work of Levinsohn or

Bakker and Other Classicists

Although the functions of καί and δέ in Classical Greek have no necessary bearing on the nuances of their use in Greek of the Hellenistic era, given that conventions of use may change over time, the analysis of δέ in earlier periods suggests that δέ has a long history as a marker of discontinuity in Greek discourse.

In his study of δέ in pre-Classical and Classical Greek, Bakker describes δέ in terms of various types of 'boundary-marking', that is, as marking a number of kinds of shifts in discourse.[39] Bakker observes that '*de* forms tight combinations with topical [that is, thematic] elements (pronouns, participles, adverbs and adverbial subordinators etc.) which, by virtue of their creating discontinuity in the text, crucially contribute to the structure of discourse'.[40] In written discourse, δέ 'is used for a variety of functions: from local, intrasentential subject topic switch ("switch-reference") to the setting of "frames" in discourse and from the marking of boundaries that are "content-oriented" to rhetorically highly marked segmentation'.[41] On the other hand, while δέ is associated with various discontinuities in discourse,

> a speaker using *kai* as a connective, we may say, *extends* the discourse segment he is currently engaged in ... The result in discourse terms is that

Buth. Interestingly, in his more recent intermediate grammar Black returns to a more traditional treatment of δέ, stating under 'copulative conjunctions' that 'δέ may have a copulative use (*and*, *now*), though it frequently has an adversative sense (*but*)', and again under 'adversative conjunctions' that 'δέ is frequently adversative' (D.A. Black, *It's Still Greek to Me: An Easy-to-Understand Guide to Intermediate Greek* [Grand Rapids: Baker Book House, 1998], p. 131).

39. Bakker, 'Boundaries', pp. 275-311. Bakker is aware of Levinsohn's work, though apparently not of Buth's: 'Working outside the main stream of Greek linguistics, and dealing exclusively with New Testament Greek, Levinsohn reaches conclusions that are often close to mine' (Bakker, 'Boundaries', p. 277 n. 5).

Other classicists who have built on Bakker's work on the pragmatic function of δέ include Morpurgo Davies, who traces the function of δέ in Arcadian inscriptions; see A. Morpurgo Davies, 'Particles in Greek Epigraphical Texts. The Case of Arcadian', in Rijksbaron (ed.), *New Approaches*, pp. 49-73. She argues that the earliest, adversative, use of δέ gradually develops into the use of δέ as a transitive or continuative particle, so that in late Arcadian inscriptions 'at its simplest it marks a sectioning of the discourse indicating that a different piece of information is now introduced, in fact what Bakker calls a thematic break' (Morpurgo Davies, 'Greek Epigraphical Texts', p. 57). She sees this development as due to interdialectic borrowing.

40. Bakker, 'Boundaries', p. 305.

41. Bakker, 'Boundaries', p. 275.

kai in comparison with de is continuous, in that it does not imply any shift whatsoever in the presentation of the discourse.[42]

Again we see in this analysis not only the elements of continuity and discontinuity in καί and δέ respectively, but their function in discourse creation and processing (for example, the role of καί in 'extending the current discourse segment'), and a suggestion of the role of authorial selection in the presentation of discourse.

Similarly, Sicking argues that the distinction between καί and δέ in the material he analyzes from Lysias 1 and 12 can be described in terms of καί's 'including' a further item in the same context as the preceding text, while δέ 'opens' a new section of text. 'The use of δέ therefore results in a certain *discontinuity*, unlike that of καί, which establishes a *connection* between what precedes and what follows.'[43] Sicking identifies a number of thematic elements which combine with δέ to serve as boundaries structuring larger sections of discourse. In the 44 sentences he analyzes from Lysias 1, these include genitive absolute constructions and phrases such as καὶ πρότερον δέ, μετὰ δὲ ταῦτα, πρῶτον δέ, and ὅμως δέ.[44]

Traditional Grammarians

It is important not to overlook the intuitive grasp of discourse functions of sentence conjunctions that earlier grammarians have had in spite of the fact that their technical vocabulary differs from that of late twentieth-century linguists. Ruijgh notes that a scholiast commenting on Dionysius Thrax's *Grammatike* applies the term μεταβατικός to δέ, writing Καλεῖται δὲ καὶ μεταβατικός· ἀπὸ προσώπου γὰρ εἰς πρόσωπον ἢ ἀπὸ πράγματος εἰς πρᾶγμα μεταβαίνοντες αὐτῷ κέχρηνται πάντες.[45] This grammarian thus describes δέ as a particle used in 'step by step' advancement or thematic change from one person or one matter to another.[46]

With respect to the New Testament, both Winer in the nineteenth century and Robertson at the turn of the twentieth reveal an awareness of the

---

42. Bakker, 'Boundaries', p. 288.

43. Sicking, 'Devices for Text Articulation', pp. 11-12 (his emphasis).

44. Sicking, 'Devices for Text Articulation', pp. 12-13.

45. See Ruijgh, *'Te Épique'*, p. 135; also E.J. Bakker, *Poetry in Speech: Orality and Homeric Discourse* (Ithaca, NY: Cornell University Press, 1997), p. 62.

46. Bakker affirms this characterization of δέ as a 'step-over conjunction' (as Bakker translates μεταβατικός) as 'a felicitous choice, for steps are exactly what δέ marks, at least in Homeric discourse' (Bakker, *Poetry*, p. 62).

element of change or discontinuity signaled by δέ. Winer characterizes δέ as a particle which 'connects whilst it opposes', but, as mentioned above, he specifies that 'it adds something different, distinct, from that which precedes'. He concedes that δέ need not be adversative, as 'δέ is often used when the writer merely subjoins something new, different and distinct from what precedes, but on that account not sharply opposed to it'.[47] Robertson is even more to the point, claiming (as noted above) that 'there is in the word no essential notion of antithesis or contrast'. He continues, 'What is true is that the addition is something new and not so closely associated in thought as is true of τέ and καί'.[48] Similarly, Smyth writes that in Classical Greek δέ 'serves to mark that something is different from what precedes, but only to offset it, not to exclude or contradict it...'[49]

By contrast, Blass, Debrunner and Funk categorize δέ as fundamentally adversative and not as copulative, retaining to a high degree the treatment of δέ found in Blass's 1896 first edition.[50] Blass's approach is softened only slightly in Rehkopf's German revision of Blass and Debrunner, which maintains Blass's treatment of δέ as adversative but makes some mention that δέ is also used with a copulative sense.[51] Blass's original characterization of the distinction between ἀλλά and δέ as that between 'Gegentheil (ἀλλά) und Gegensatz (δέ)'—that is, between 'contradiction' (ἀλλά) and either 'antithesis' (Thackeray's translation) or 'general contrast' (Funk's)—is retained in current editions.[52] The widespread use of Blass, Debrunner and Funk in English and Blass, Debrunner and Rehkopf in

---

47. Winer, *Treatise*, pp. 551-52. See also G.B. Winer, *Grammatik des neutestamentlichen Sprachidioms* (Leipzig: F.C.W. Vogel, 7th edn, 1867), p. 412: 'δέ steht oft, wo nur etwas Neues, von dem Vorhergehenden Verschiedenes und Anderes ...'

48. Robertson, *Grammar*, pp. 1184. See, similarly, Schwyzer: 'Es bezeichnet, dass (gegenüber dem Vorhergehenden) etwas Anderes, Neues kommt...' (E. Schwyzer, *Griechische Grammatik auf der Grundlage von Karl Brugmanns Griechischer Grammatik. II. Syntax und Syntaktische Stilistik* (ed. A. Debrunner; Munich: C.H. Beck, 5th edn, 1988), p. 562.

49. H.W. Smyth, *Greek Grammar* (revd G. Messing; Cambridge, MA: Harvard University Press, 1956), p. 644.

50. See Blass, *Grammatik*, p. 261 (§77, 12); BDF, §447.

51. See F. Blass and A. Debrunner, *Grammatik des neutestamentliche Griechisch* (revd. F. Rehkopf; Göttingen: Vandenhoeck und Ruprecht, 15th edn, 1979), §447.

52. See Blass, *Grammatik*, p. 261 (§77, 12); F. Blass, *Grammar of New Testament Greek* (trans. H.StJ. Thackeray; London: Macmillan, 1898), p. 266 (§77.12); BDF, §447; F. Blass and A. Debrunner, *Grammatik des neutestamentlichen Griechisch* (revd F. Rehkopf; Göttingen: Vandenhoeck & Ruprecht, 15th edn, 1970), §447.

German as reference grammars for the New Testament may influence the adversative or contrastive understanding of δέ which appears to dominate among New Testament scholars.

Evidence from Matthew's Gospel

I have suggested that in terms of the procedural semantics of sentence conjunctions developed in Chapter 2, δέ functions in Matthew's narrative framework as a signal of low- to mid-level discontinuity.[53] It now remains to examine the text of the Gospel of Matthew for evidence supporting this claim. If δέ is found to collocate frequently with other features of discontinuity or change in the Evangelist's presentation of the narrative, one may argue that δέ and the related features serve as mutually redundant cues for discourse processing, mutually reinforcing that a low- to mid-level change is taking place in the flow of the discourse. I will demonstrate this by showing the tendency in Matthew's narrative framework for δέ to be combined with SV (especially S_1V) constituent order and with other non-verbal themes, as well as with a switch in notional subject from one sentence to the next.

Δέ and Verbal Tense-form

As a starting point, it is worth noting that in Matthew's narrative framework δέ, like καί, is most commonly combined with aorist tense-forms. As I have shown in the previous chapter, aorist finite verbs serve as the unmarked tense-form in narrative, with sentences with aorist verbs constituting the bulk of the narrative framework (553/720 narrative sentences, or 77%). Also like καί, δέ is used significantly less frequently with present tense-form finite verbs in past-referring narrative, the so-called 'historic present'. The relation between καί and δέ and verbal tense-form in Matthew's narrative framework is displayed in the following table:

---

53. This does not mean that δέ cannot be used as a signal of higher-level breaks elsewhere. Bakker comments, 'In Classical Greek, δέ does its work no matter how strong the discontinuity is. The very first sentence of Xenophon's *Hellenica* begins with δέ, as a continuation of Thucydides' *History*!' (Bakker, personal communication).

Table 5.1: *Sentence conjunction and verbal tense-form (omitting* εἰμί*)*[54]

	All narrative sentences	Sentences with aorist finite verbs	Sentences with present finite verbs
n =	720	553	79
# καί	335	276	24
% καί	47%	50%	30%
z-score[55]		1.59	−2.88
# δέ	257	213	8
% δέ	36%	39%	10%
z-score		1.39	−4.74

As the similar tendencies indicated above show, the distinctions in use between καί and δέ do not lie in the choice of verbal tense-form.

Formal Evidence of Discontinuity

Distinctions in use between καί and δέ appear both within sentences, in such features as constituent order, thematization and subject reference, and between sentences, reflected in the notion of subject switch.

Δέ and constituent order. There are statistically significant correlations in Matthew's narrative framework between δέ and constituent order. Δέ shows a strong tendency to appear with SV sentences, especially those with a grammatical subject as topical theme (what I have termed S_1V constituent order).[56] Conversely, there is a strong tendency for δέ not to

54. As mentioned in the preceding chapter, εἰμί is omitted from consideration in this table and in other analyses of sentence conjunction and verbal tense-form because it does not evidence fully developed morphological distinctions among tense-forms, or, in Porter's terms, it is 'aspectually vague' (see Porter, *Verbal Aspect*, pp. 442-47).

55. Again, a z-score expresses a distance from a mean in terms of standard deviations. In this study a z-score equal to or greater than ±3—that is, indicating that a value falls three standard deviations or more above or below a mean—is taken to demonstrate statistical significance.

56. As I outlined in previous chapters, this simplified analysis of constituent order incorporates only two elements: the main verb (if any), and the grammaticalized subject (if any), in relation to each other. Other predicate or complement elements are not taken into account. In particular, the presence of any direct or indirect object is not included in the description of constituent order, even though most studies of constituent order in language typology identify subject, verb and object. Participles which appear at the beginning of sentences are not considered as verbs in assessing constituent order, and genitive absolute constructions are treated in the same manner as other participial phrases.

appear with V(S) sentences. Assuming that in the Greek of the New Testament V(S) constituent order is the less marked order typically associated with continuous discourse while SV order is a more marked order—assumptions discussed in Chapter 4 with respect to καί—and that SV constituent order is generally associated with a shift in topic, as I argue below, the tendency of δέ to appear with SV sentences adds weight to the argument for its function as a signal of discontinuity.

As I explained in the previous chapter, I understand monolectic verbs to be the most unmarked form of constituent order in narrative (that is, the default sentence structure in terms of discourse continuity), with any grammaticalization of the subject seen as marked to some degree for change, often simply in terms of a shift in participant. Given that an explicit subject represents something of a marked choice, there is a tendency to place it earlier in the sentence for emphasis, with the first, or thematic, position seen as most marked. The cline introduced in Chapter 4 classifying constituent order can be represented as follows, with more marked constituent order to the left of the cline and less marked to the right:

$$S_1V \Leftarrow S_2V \Leftarrow VS \Leftarrow V$$

Using this cline, the correspondence between δέ and constituent order in the narrative framework of the Gospel of Matthew can be contrasted with the tendencies already demonstrated for καί:

Table 5.2: *Sentence conjunction and constituent order*

	All narrative sentences	*S_1V constituent order*	*S_2V constituent order*	*VS constituent order*	*V constituent order*
n =	720	195	99	149	262
# καί	335	23	40	69	191
% καί	47%	12%	40%	46%	73%
z-score		−9.73	−1.21	0.05	8.56
# δέ	257	155[57]	47	29	25
% δέ	36%	79%	47%	19%	10%
z-score		12.77	2.44	−4.13	−8.83

57. Sixty times with ὁ δέ/ἡ δέ/οἱ δέ/αἱ δέ. Even omitting sentences with the fixed combination of δέ with a pronominal article in thematic position, there is still a significant correlation between δέ and S_1V constituent order: of 135 remaining S_1V sentences, 95 sentences with δέ = 70%; $z = 10.30$.

The increased frequency of δέ with SV sentences (S_1V and S_2V), especially with the subject in thematic position (S_1V), is statistically significant. Taking S_1V and S_2V sentences together, in the 294 sentences with SV constituent order, δέ appears 202 times (69%; $z = 11.81$)—this accounts for more than three-quarters (202/257, 79%) of the uses of δέ in Matthew's narrative framework.

As the table above shows, not only does δέ tend to appear with the more marked SV order in narrative in Matthew's Gospel, but the frequency of δέ increases in proportion to the markedness of the constituent order of the sentences it begins. The earlier in the sentence the subject is placed (with S_1V the most marked constituent order), the more likely δέ is to appear; the later in the sentence the subject is placed (with no grammaticalized subject as the least marked choice) the less likely δέ is to appear. As before, the statistical significance of these figures was evaluated using z-scores. Z-scores greater than ±3 for δέ with constituent orders S_1V, VS and V suggest a high degree of statistical significance, while a z-score of 2.44 for δέ with S_2V constituent order approaches the ±3 threshold for statistical significance.

Using the data I compiled and selected from Matthew's Gospel, Allen's logistic regression analysis of constituent order as a factor in the choice of δέ rather than καί in the narrative framework indicates that when constituent order is S_1V, δέ is 51.49 times more likely to occur than is καί. Unadjusted odds ratios for other constituent orders are as follows: 8.98 times more likely to occur when constituent order is S_2V; 3.21 times when constituent order is VS; but only 0.64 (less likely to appear than καί) when constituent order is V.[58] Consistent with the results in the table above, the odds ratios associated with δέ are lower the further right one moves along the constituent order cline. Allen's odds ratios suggest that δέ is more likely to occur than καί in all constituent orders in which a subject is grammaticalized, and less likely to occur only in those cases where there is no explicit subject.

Allen's statistical analysis of these data underscores that in terms of discourse structure two syntactical issues representing choices made above the sentence level are involved: first, the presence of an explicit subject, if any; and secondly, thematization of the subject. As mentioned in Chapter 4, Porter and O'Donnell argue that when a subject is made explicit, it often represents a change from one participant to another as the actor in a

58. Allen, 'Greek Syntactical Analysis', p. 19; see also Allen and Farewell, this volume, §4.1(i).

process chain. They define 'process chain' as a string of monolectic verbal forms having the same actor (subject). These clusters of sentences 'chaining' from one explicit subject represent one way of structuring the flow of information in the discourse.[59] In Matthew's narrative framework this technique of grammaticalizing the subject to indicate changes in actor is apparent in sequences such as 14.26-31:[60]

14.26   οἱ δὲ μαθηταὶ ἰδόντες αὐτὸν ἐπὶ τῆς θαλάσσης περιπατοῦντα ἐταράχθησαν λέγοντες ὅτι ... καὶ ἀπὸ τοῦ φόβου ἔκραξαν.

14.27   εὐθὺς δὲ ἐλάλησεν [ὁ Ἰησοῦς] αὐτοῖς λέγων·...

14.28   ἀποκριθεὶς δὲ αὐτῷ ὁ Πέτρος εἶπεν ...

14.29   {Jesus speaks:} ὁ δὲ εἶπεν ... καὶ καταβὰς ἀπὸ τοῦ πλοίου [ὁ] Πέτρος περιεπάτησεν ἐπὶ τὰ ὕδατα καὶ ἦλθεν πρὸς τὸν Ἰησοῦν.

14.30   βλέπων δὲ τὸν ἄνεμον [ἰσχυρὸν] ἐφοβήθη, καὶ ἀρξάμενος καταποντίζεσθαι ἔκραξεν λέγων ...

14.31   εὐθέως δὲ ὁ Ἰησοῦς ἐκτείνας τὴν χεῖρα ἐπελάβετο αὐτοῦ καὶ λέγει αὐτῷ ...

In the verses above, the actor of each monolectic finite verb is the last grammaticalized subject, and each grammaticalized subject represents a change in actor.[61] In 14.26, the disciples are terrified to see Jesus walking on the water. An explicit subject is supplied with the disciples' first action in this sequence, οἱ δὲ μαθηταὶ...ἐταράχθησαν, followed by monolectic ἔκραξαν when they then cry out in fear. In 14.27, Jesus is again the actor, calming the disciples. Here the NA[27] editors have chosen a textual variant with a grammaticalized subject: εὐθὺς δὲ ἐλάλησεν [ὁ Ἰησοῦς] αὐτοῖς. Next Peter replies in 14.28, and again the subject (ὁ Πέτρος) is made explicit. In 14.29a, Jesus speaks again, inviting Peter to come to him, and again a grammaticalized subject is provided, although in the reduced form of a pronominal article, ὁ δὲ εἶπεν. When Peter gets out of the boat (14.29b) the subject Πέτρος is provided for his initial walking on the water, but his subsequent coming to Jesus, becoming afraid and crying out

59. See Porter and O'Donnell, *Discourse Analysis and the New Testament*.

60. Square brackets in Greek examples represent textual variants included in the NA[27] text.

61. See also I. Larsen, 'A Semantic Structure Analysis of Matthew 4:1-11', *Notes on Translation* 112 (1986), p. 35, where Larsen writes, 'If no explicit subject is given the use of *kai* normally includes a carry-over of the subject from the previous sentence (4.2, 5b, 6, 8b, 9), while the use of *de* signifies a new grammatical subject (4.4) and/or a new theme...'

are recounted with monolectic finite verbs (14.30). In 14.31, Jesus is the actor, reaching out his hand to Peter, and the subject is again grammaticalized, followed by a monolectic verb when he speaks to Peter.

It is not difficult, however, to find examples in Matthew's narrative framework in which a change of participant occurs without grammaticalizing the subject. One need look no further than the beginning of the pericope mentioned above, where the focus shifts back to Jesus from the five thousand who were fed, yet no explicit subject is supplied (14.22). There are instances as well where grammaticalized subjects do not correspond with a change in actor or participant, but these are far less common. (See, for example, 13.33-34 and 17.17-18.) As a general rule the Evangelist's choice of a grammaticalized subject implies a change of actor or participant, but not everywhere that there is a change in actor or participant does the Evangelist choose to represent that by providing an explicit subject. At these points as elsewhere the author may choose to portray discourse as continuous—the default condition in narrative— rather than grammaticalizing the more marked condition, discontinuity.

In terms of the theory of mental representations described in Chapter 2, the introduction of an explicit subject prompts a modification of the mental representation currently in operation to bring a different participant into focus (or back into focus, if previously introduced). The presence of δέ in more than half of the narrative sentences with a grammaticalized subject (231/442, 52%) serves as a partially redundant signal alerting the audience to this change. The most obvious example of this dynamic in Matthew's Gospel is the genealogy in 1.2-16, in which each clause after the first— that is, the naming of each subsequent progenitor—is connected to the preceding by δέ (see below on 1.2-16). At the same time, the presence of καί in almost three-quarters of the sentences in Matthew's narrative framework in which no subject is made explicit (191/263, 73%) serves as a partially redundant signal to continue without such a change.

But the presence or absence of a grammaticalized subject is not sufficient in itself to explain the distribution of δέ in the narrative framework of Matthew's Gospel. Although Greek is often described as a free word order language, grammarians recognize that writers of Greek do exploit linear organization in structuring information flow, often putting elements they wish to make more prominent before the verb.[62] In the Greek of the New Testament the first element in a clause or sentence is

---

62. See, for example, Moule, *Idiom Book*, p. 166; BDF, §472; Levinsohn, *Discourse Features*, p. 17.

understood to have a primary role in relating the sentence to previous discourse.[63] Porter writes, 'The expressed subject is often used as a form of topic marker or shifter…and is appropriately placed first to signal this semantic function'.[64] Making an explicit subject thematic brings the need to modify the mental representation currently in operation more overtly to the audience's attention. Δέ appears as the sentence conjunction in nearly 80% of the sentences in Matthew's narrative framework with a thematized subject (155/195, 79%), serving as a procedural signal reinforcing that the grammaticalized subject which is being processed is indeed to some degree discontinuous with discourse immediately previous. A grammaticalized subject placed later in the sentence may be understood as less discontinuous, or as not being the primary element of discontinuity in the sentence. Porter continues, 'When the subject is placed in the second or third position in the clause (i.e., after the predicate and/or complement), its markedness or emphasis apparently decreases'.[65] When the subject is placed later in the sentence presumably its role in the portrayal of discourse discontinuity likewise decreases, and the use of δέ as a mutually redundant procedural signal decreases proportionately.

Δέ *and article as pronoun.* While on the topic of grammaticalized subjects in Matthew's narrative framework, the fixed combination of ὁ δέ and its variations merits a brief comment. Throughout the New Testament, when the grammatical subject of a verb is an article functioning as a demonstrative pronoun, the conjunction is always δέ and the pronominal article is always thematic, that is, ὁ δέ, ἡ δέ, οἱ δέ, or αἱ δέ begins the sentence.[66] Of the 60 instances of this construction in Matthew's narrative framework, 47 (78%) appear in various types of speech margins, in which the discontinuity indicated by δέ is the alternation between or among speakers.[67] Of the remaining instances of the pronominal article, all but one introduce an action in response to a statement, question or command, for example,

---

63. See Porter, 'Word Order', p. 194; Porter, *Idioms*, pp. 295-96; Levinsohn, *Discourse Features*, pp. 7-13.

64. Porter, *Idioms*, p. 295.

65. Porter, *Idioms*, p. 296.

66. On this use of the article, see Winer, *Treatise*, pp. 129-31; Robertson, *Grammar*, p. 755, who decries the description 'substantive use of the article' in favor of 'plain substantival demonstrative'; Turner, *Syntax*, pp. 36-37 ('substantival article'); BDF, §§249-51.

67. See, for example, 15.21-28, 27.20-23.

2.9, οἱ δὲ ἀκούσαντες τοῦ βασιλέως ἐπορεύθησαν, where the magi depart after hearing Herod's instructions.[68] In other words, all but one of the instances of the pronominal article in Matthew's narrative framework occur in relation to speech or dialogue.[69] These instances all involve a switch in grammatical subject from the previous narrative sentence. In the entire Gospel of Matthew (not just the narrative framework) the only exception to the rule that δέ will occur where there is a pronominal article may be in 16.14, in the μέν component of a μέν–δέ–δέ sequence in the disciples' response to Jesus' question, 'Who do people say that I am?': οἱ μὲν Ἰωάννην τὸν βαπτιστήν, ἄλλοι δὲ Ἡλίαν, ἕτεροι δὲ Ἰερεμίαν ἢ ἕνα τῶν προφητῶν.[70]

The one occurrence in the narrative framework which is not in a context of speech or dialogue, 28.17, καὶ ἰδόντες αὐτὸν προσεκύνησαν, οἱ δὲ ἐδίστασαν, has engendered a great deal of discussion.[71] At issue is whether οἱ δέ refers to *all* the 11 disciples mentioned in 28.16, who both worshiped and doubted; *some* of the disciples, who doubted while all (or some of) the others worshiped; or *other* people, who doubted while the disciples worshiped. Although the idea that some of the disciples doubted is by far the most broadly accepted, Grayston takes a novel approach,

68. See also 2.14, 2.21, 4.20, 4.22, 8.32, 9.31, 22.19, 26.15, 27.66, 28.9, 28.15; see below on 28.17.

69. See K. Grayston, 'The Translation of Matthew 28.17', *JSNT* 21 (1984), pp. 105-109. Grayston cites 26.67, τότε ἐνέπτυσαν εἰς τὸ πρόσωπον αὐτοῦ καὶ ἐκολάφισαν αὐτόν, οἱ δὲ ἐράπισαν, as an additional instance in which ὁ δέ/οἱ δέ is not 'part of a conversational exchange'. I agree that the issues involved in 26.67 and 28.17 are quite similar—both can be understood as having a partitive sense (contra Grayston)—but because 26.67-68 continues, οἱ δὲ ἐράπισαν λέγοντες· προφήτευσον ἡμῖν, χριστέ, τίς ἐστιν ὁ παίσας σε; 26.67 has been treated in the database for this research as part of a speech margin.

70. BDF, however, note a textual variant in 22.5 in which this also occurs (BDF, §250). They observe that in the New Testament 'the relative forms [that is, relative pronouns] are more common' in such μέν–δέ constructions. This appears to be true in Matthew's narrative framework as well; see 13.4, 13.8, 13.23, 13.32, 21.35, 22.5, 23.27, 25.15.

71. See, for example, Grayston, 'Matthew 28.17'; K.L. McKay, 'The Use of *hoi de* in Matthew 28.17', *JSNT* 24 (1985), pp. 71-72; P. van der Horst, 'Once More: The Translation of οἱ δέ in Matthew 28.17', *JSNT* 27 (1986), pp. 27-30; D.A. Hagner, *Matthew 14–28* (WBC, 33B; Dallas: Word Books, 1995), pp. 884-85; W.D. Davies and D.C. Allison, *A Critical and Exegetical Commentary on the Gospel According to Saint Matthew*. III. *Commentary on Matthew XIX–XXVIII* (ICC; Edinburgh: T. & T. Clark, 1997), pp. 681-82.

arguing that a 'normal translation of *hoi de*' (by which he means not partitive, that is, not 'some') can be maintained with a fresh understanding of what it is that the disciples (all) doubted as they worshiped— specifically, that they all doubted the efficacy of their worship in saving them from condemnation for their earlier desertion of Jesus.[72] Hagner agrees with Grayston that all of the disciples are in view and that the resolution of the problem lies in the understanding of the verb διστάζω. He makes the more plausible proposal, however, that the disciples' doubt 'amounts to hesitation, indecision ... and perhaps uncertainty'.[73]

Contra Grayston, McKay counters—correctly, I believe—that the 'normal' use of οἱ δέ 'involves a change of subject, whether or not *hoi men* precedes it'. He cites two examples from Xenophon where οἱ δέ refers to a subgroup distinguished from a larger group.[74] Van der Horst reiterates McKay's point that the normal use of οἱ δέ involves a change of subject, and that the change of subject may be complete or partial.[75] He summarizes, 'All this implies that in Mt. 28.17 οἱ δέ *cannot* mean all of the disciples, *can* mean (from a strictly grammatical point of view) other persons than the disciples but, since no other persons are involved here at all, *must* be part of the disciples'.[76]

The understanding of οἱ δέ as necessarily involving a change (if only a partial change) of subject is consistent with the view expressed here of δέ as a signal of discontinuity, with a change in grammatical subject being the type of discontinuity most commonly associated with δέ (see also the discussion of δέ and subject switch below). The combination of δέ with a thematic subject—fixed in the idiom ὁ δέ/οἱ δέ—would be highly unlikely to occur if there were continuity of subject with the preceding sentence or clause. Grayston's argument that οἱ δὲ ἐδίστασαν in 28.17 indicates that precisely the same disciples mentioned in the previous clause are involved in the action that follows misinterprets both the customary use of οἱ δέ in particular and the broader issue of what δέ contributes to discourse processing, especially when combined with a thematic subject. Similarly, Hagner's claim that Matthew's use of οἱ δέ elsewhere in the Gospel can refer to all members of an already mentioned set of participants, while correct in that detail, overlooks the fact that in each of the examples he

72. Grayston, 'Matthew 28.17', pp. 107-108.
73. Hagner, *Matthew 14–28*, pp. 884-85.
74. McKay, 'Matthew 28.17', p. 71.
75. Van der Horst, 'Matthew 28.17', pp. 27-28.
76. Van der Horst, 'Matthew 28.17', p. 29 (his emphasis).

gives (with the exception of 26.67, τότε ἐνέπτυσαν εἰς τὸ πρόσωπον αὐτοῦ καὶ ἐκολάφισαν αὐτόν, οἱ δὲ ἐράπισαν, which I take, like 28.17, to be partitive) οἱ δέ occurs where there is a change in actor from the last narrative sentence in the discourse.[77] In none of Hagner's examples is the set of participants indicated by the οἱ δέ construction the same as the grammatical subject of the immediately previous narrative clause. The procedural function of δέ is to signal just such a discontinuity in the linear processing of discourse, exemplified in its use to indicate a change (in this case a partial change) between the disciples who worshiped Jesus in 28.17 and those who 'doubted'—whatever the nature of that doubt or hesitation may have been.

Δέ *and other thematized elements.* It is not just thematized subjects with which δέ collocates to signal change, although that is the combination most observable from the analysis of constituent order above. Similar to Bakker's observation that in pre-Classical and Classical Greek '*de* forms tight combinations with topical [that is, thematized] elements (pronouns, participles, adverbs and adverbial subordinators etc.)', in Matthew's narrative framework δέ is found with a variety of thematic elements which contribute to the portrayal of discontinuity in the discourse.[78] In contrast, καί is the sentence conjunction found most often in Matthew's narrative framework when thematization is least marked—that is, καί is used in two-thirds of the sentences with a finite verb as the topical theme (163/248, 66%; $z = 6.06$).

Besides grammaticalized subjects, thematic elements with which δέ tends to collocate include genitive absolute participial constructions (11.7, 14.23, 17.22, 17.26, 22.41, 26.26) and temporal indicators (21.18). Of the 22 instances in the narrative framework where δέ occurs with no switch in subject, some can be explained by the presence of one of these other thematic 'shifters'. In this section I examine the use of δέ with such elements, as well as the relatively rare use of δέ with thematic verbs.

Δέ *and genitive absolute participial constructions.* A strong association exists between δέ and genitive absolute participial constructions. Δέ is the sentence conjunction in 23 of the 39 sentences in Matthew's narrative framework in which a genitive absolute construction begins the sentence

77. Hagner, *Matthew 14–28*, p. 884. Hagner's examples are Mt. 2.5, 4.20, 4.22, 14.17, 14.33, 15.34, 16.7, 16.14, 20.5, 20.31, 21.25, 22.19, 26.15, 26.67, 27.4, 27.21, 27.23, 28.15.
78. Bakker, 'Boundaries', p. 305.

(59%). In her statistical analysis of my data on sentence conjunctions in Matthew's narrative framework, Allen states that 'features that have the most noticeable effect on choosing "de" as opposed to "kai" appear to be a constituent order of "subject before verb in first position"…and a topical theme of "genitive absolute participle"'.[79] In Allen's final model, after adjusting for all other variables and interactions the odds ratio of δέ rather than καί occurring in a sentence with a thematized genitive absolute is 49.53.[80] In other words, δέ is about 50 times more likely to be used as the sentence conjunction with a thematized genitive absolute construction than is καί.[81]

This association helps to account for the distribution of δέ with VS sentences. Almost half of the instances in which δέ is used with VS constituent order (13/29, 45%) include a genitive absolute construction before the finite verb, which as a way of grammaticalizing a shift from one set of actions to another may account for the presence of δέ more strongly than does constituent order.[82] The association between δέ and genitive absolute participial constructions even seems to override the collocation of καί with ἰδού. When ἰδού appears in narrative the conjunction is usually καί (24/33, 73%). However, in the six instances when δέ appears with ἰδού, there is also a genitive absolute before the main (finite) verb.[83] As mentioned in Chapter 4, there is only one case of καὶ ἰδού with a genitive absolute construction (26.47).

Δέ *and temporal shift.* Temporal indicators are another type of thematic element found in combination with δέ.[84] This can be a prepositional phrase (for example, 3.1, ἐν δὲ ταῖς ἡμέραις ἐκείναις; 27.46, περὶ δὲ τὴν ἐνάτην ὥραν), a dative construction (for example, 26.17, τῇ δὲ πρώτῃ τῶν ἀζύμων; 27.62, τῇ δὲ ἐπαύριον), or a temporal adverb (21.18, πρωῒ

79. Allen, 'Greek Syntactical Analysis', pp. 19-20; see also Allen and Farewell, this volume, §4.1(i).

80. Allen, 'Greek Syntactical Analysis', p. 26; see also Allen and Farewell, this volume, §4.1(iii).

81. Allen notes that a 95% confidence level incorporates a range from 14.82 to 165.59 for this odds ratio—that is, that δέ may actually be anywhere from 14.82 to 165.59 times more likely to appear with a thematized genitive absolute construction than is καί (Allen, 'Greek Syntactical Analysis', p. 26).

82. See, for example, 8.1, 11.7, 14.15.

83. Mt. 1.20, 2.1, 2.13, 2.19, 9.32, 28.11. In addition, asyndeton is found three times with ἰδού and a genitive absolute: 9.18, 12.46, 17.5.

84. See Mt. 1.12, 3.1, 9.25, 14.25, 21.18, 26.17, 26.73, 27.45, 27.46, 27.62, 28.1.

δέ). Several of these sentences have SV constituent order,[85] but the remainder are V(S). A change from one temporal setting to the next is simply
another of the discontinuities which δέ can signal in narrative discourse.
An element of temporal change can account for the presence of δέ with
V(S) constituent order in spite of the fact that δέ occurs relatively infrequently with V(S) constituent order in the narrative framework as a whole.
The temporal discontinuity in these sentences is apparently more important
to the Evangelist than whatever change there may be in participant, thus
the temporal element is thematized while the grammaticalized subject (if
any) follows the verb. The pairing of δέ with thematic temporal indicators
in Matthew's narrative framework is consistent with Levinsohn's observation mentioned above that either a change in subject or a change of temporal setting accounts for more than 90% of the uses of δέ in Acts.[86]

Δέ *and thematic finite verbs.* Only seven times in the narrative framework
does δέ appear with a thematized finite verb.[87] At least five of these can be
understood as background material or description which is 'off-line' with
respect to the unfolding action of the narrative. The discontinuity which δέ
signals in these instances is a discontinuity with the narrative line itself,
not in the action within the narrative.[88] As noted above, Buth comments
that the type of 'shift' δέ signals 'could be forwards, backwards, or sideways'.[89] Here we have a discontinuity that could be described as
'sideways', not back and forth between characters or settings within the
action of the narrative, but briefly standing aside from the narrative action
to provide additional information relevant to it.

In three instances, δέ combines with εἰμί in what Levinsohn terms a
'presentational' structure, comparable to English *there was/were.*[90]

---

85. Mt. 1.12, 27.45, 26.73.

86. See Levinsohn, *Textual Connections*, p. 87.

87. Mt. 8.30, 12.47, 26.5, 27.16, 27.55, 27.61, 28.3.

88. 'It is evidently a universal of narrative discourse that in any extended text an
overt distinction is made between the language of the actual story line and the language
of supportive material which does not itself narrate the main events' (P.J. Hopper,
'Aspect and Foregrounding in Discourse', in Givón [ed.], *Discourse and Syntax*, p.
213).

89. Buth, 'On Levinsohn's "Development Units"', p. 54.

90. See Levinsohn, *Discourse Features*, pp. 7, 90-91. Presentational structures
typically introduce a participant, although in 27.61 Mary and the other Mary are not
new to the narrative, having been mentioned in 27.55. On presentational articulation of
the sentence, see A. Andrews, 'The Major Functions of the Noun Phrase', in T. Shopen
(ed.), *Language Typology and Syntactic Description.* I. *Clause Structure* (Cambridge:

8.30   ἦν δὲ μακρὰν ἀπ' αὐτῶν ἀγέλη χοίρων πολλῶν βοσκομένη.
27.55   ἦσαν δὲ ἐκεῖ γυναῖκες πολλαὶ ἀπὸ μακρόθεν θεωροῦσαι...
27.61   ἦν δὲ ἐκεῖ Μαριὰμ ἡ Μαγδαληνὴ καὶ ἡ ἄλλη Μαρία...

Each of these can be understood as additional material off the narrative line—that is, not part of sequentially occurring events in the narrative, but providing information necessary to understand those events. In 8.30, the information that there is a herd of pigs nearby provides the context for the audience to make sense of the demons' request to be sent into the pigs. In 27.55, the Evangelist gives further information about participants in the narrative, reporting the presence of certain women as an aside to the main line of the narrative. In 27.61, two of these same women are mentioned again, still as an aside to the immediate sequence of events, but maintaining their presence 'on stage' in preparation for their important role in discovering and announcing Jesus' resurrection soon after. These are apparently the only occurrences of presentational sentences with thematic εἰμί in the narrative framework (but compare 22.25, in which the Sadducees explain, ἦσαν δὲ παρ' ἡμῖν ἑπτὰ ἀδελφοί...), and all have δέ as the sentence conjunction.

In one other instance δέ combines with thematic εἰμί in an equative, non-presentational sentence, describing the appearance of the angel at Jesus' tomb, again as material that is supplementary to the sequence of narrative events: 28.3, ἦν δὲ ἡ εἰδέα αὐτοῦ ὡς ἀστραπή...[91]

Another example of δέ with a thematic verb in off-line background material occurs in 27.16. In fact, the sequence 27.15-16 demonstrates two instances of δέ with off-line material:

27.15   κατὰ δὲ ἑορτὴν εἰώθει ὁ ἡγεμὼν ἀπολύειν ἕνα τῷ ὄχλῳ
        δέσμιον ὃν ἤθελον.
27.16   εἶχον δὲ τότε δέσμιον ἐπίσημον λεγόμενον ['Ιησοῦν]
        Βαραββᾶν.

In this sequence the first δέ (27.16) signals the movement from the narrative line to an explanation of Pilate's annual custom, while the second δέ signals the movement from a general statement (Pilate's customary action) to a specific circumstance (that a particular prisoner is being held), two

Cambridge University Press, 1985), p. 80.

91. In addition to these instances with thematic εἰμί, similar uses of εἰμί with δέ and S_1V constituent order are found in sentences providing description or background material, enumerating the five thousand who ate the fish and loaves in 14.21, and the four thousand in 15.38.

pieces of background information which help the audience make sense of Pilate's offer to let the crowd choose which prisoner will be released.

Summary. As a signal of low- to mid-level discontinuity, δέ is found to collocate frequently with other formal features of discontinuity or change in the Evangelist's presentation of the narrative, which serve as mutually redundant cues guiding the audience to modify the mental representation they construct of the discourse. Specifically, δέ tends to occur more frequently with SV constituent order than with V(S) constituent order, especially when a grammaticalized subject is thematic (S_1V constituent order), reflecting choices not only of constituent order but also of grammaticalization of the subject and of thematization. Δέ also occurs frequently with genitive absolute participial constructions and other thematic indicators of temporal shift. In addition, δέ can be found with another type of discontinuity, 'off-line' sentences providing information which helps clarify events in the main line of the narrative.

Ideational Evidence of Discontinuity: Δέ and Subject Switch
It appears that at least one function of supplying a grammaticalized subject is to signal a change in actor or participant. If this is so, we may expect the formal correlation between δέ and SV constituent order to be paralleled by a nonformal, ideational, correlation between δέ and a switch in grammatical subject, an association to which I have alluded in the discussion above. Statistical analysis shows this indeed to be the case.

To restate the definition given earlier, for the purposes of this study 'subject switch' is understood as a change in the notional subject from the previous independent coordinate clause in the narrative framework—a change in the grammaticalized subject if any, or in 'who or what the sentence is about' as understood from surrounding text if there is no explicit subject. Subject switch is no doubt only one of the issues involved in formal choices such as grammaticalization of the subject, thematization, and subject reference, but for the purpose at hand it is an obvious feature of discontinuity in the ideational content of discourse, making it particularly suitable as a test case for the role of δέ.

A statistical analysis of δέ and subject switch produces an outcome closely corresponding to the formal analysis of constituent order above. Moreover, this analysis reveals differences between καί and δέ with respect to subject switch. The results can be summarized as follows:

Table 5.3: *Sentence conjunction and subject switch*

	All narrative sentences	Subject switch	No subject switch	Title (1.1) and first sentence (1.2)[92]
n =	720	516	202	2
# καί	335	183	152	0
% καί	47%	35%	75%	
z-score		−5.04	8.18	
# δέ	257	235	22	0
% δέ	36%	46%	11%	
z-score		4.74	−7.36	

Compared with its distribution in the narrative framework as a whole, δέ shows a significantly higher frequency of use in contexts where there is subject switch and a significantly lower than expected frequency of use where there is continuity of subject. In fact, more than nine out of ten (235/257, 91%) of the occurrences of δέ in Matthew's narrative frame-work collocate with a switch in subject, although fewer than three-quarters of narrative sentences (514/720, 71%) involve such a switch. Z-scores in the table above suggest that the association between δέ and subject switch is statistically significant. At the same time καί is significantly less fre-quent where there is subject switch and significantly more frequent where there is continuity of subject.[93]

As I have said, the use of δέ in the Hellenistic era is not necessarily unchanged from its use in the Classical period, but it is worth noting that Ruijgh takes a similar approach and reaches similar conclusions with respect to δέ and subject switch in his analysis of 56 sentences from a narrative passage in Herodotus (1.6-22).[94] He plots the use of καί and δέ against whether the subject of the verb differs from the subject of the preceding verb, ignoring participial phrases, infinitives and verbless sen-tences. In Ruijgh's table, reproduced below, SC refers to 'sujet en

92. Both the title and first sentence of Matthew's Gospel are asyndetic; see on asyndeton, Chapter 6.

93. Similarly, in Givón's analysis of referential continuity across adjacent clauses joined by the English conjunctions *and, then, while, but, though* and *yet*—in which he quantifies 'referential continuity' in terms of subject switch—Givón concludes that a 'strong association exists between conjunctions that are thematically continuous ("and") and referential continuity, and between conjunctions that are thematically dis-ruptive or contrastive ("while", "but", "through", "yet") and referential discontinuity' (Givón, *Functionalism*, pp. 373-75).

94. See Ruijgh, *'Te Épique'*, pp. 131-32.

commun' (common subject, that is, no subject switch), and SD refers to 'sujets différents' (different subjects, that is, subject switch):[95]

Particule	SC	SD	Total
	[no subject switch]	*[subject switch]*	
δέ	9	34	43
καί	7	6	13
Total	16	40	56

From these data Ruijgh concludes that when a second action is introduced by δέ, most often the subject of the verb differs from the subject of the preceding action. He also concludes that when a second action is introduced by καί, the two verbs are about equally as likely to have the same subject as to have a different subject. Ruijgh characterizes δέ as marking the transition to another person or thing, or more generally as a coordinator of 'transition-opposition'.[96]

Ruijgh's findings raise the possibility that the correlation between δέ and a switch to a different subject in narrative discourse has a long history preceding its use in this way in Matthew's Gospel. Unfortunately, Ruijgh's analysis covers a sample of only 56 sentences and his results are not statistically significant. I calculate a z-score for δέ with 'sujets différents' of only 1.23, indicating that the frequency of δέ with subjects differing from the subject of the preceding finite verb (34/40, 85%) is not significantly higher for this sample size than its frequency overall (43/56, 77%).[97] This situation illustrates the need for more research into the role of sentence conjunctions in larger samples of Classical Greek, making use of quantitative techniques for linguistic analysis developed since the time Ruijgh wrote.

Multivariate Analysis
In her initial univariate analysis of my data from Matthew's Gospel, Allen observes that all fields (constituent order, subject switch, verbal tense-form, use as speech margin, topical theme, and subject reference) 'significantly affect the choice of conjunction "de" or "kai", however verbal tense form and speech margin are the least significant' in accounting for

---

95. Ruijgh, *'Te Épique'*, p. 132.
96. Ruijgh, *'Te Épique'*, p. 135.
97. A chi-square test of independence between the two variables in the table would be useful to test Ruijgh's conclusions, but the expected value for καί with 'sujet en commun' is less than five, making the use of a chi-square test problematic.

the choice of δέ rather than καί.[98] In her subsequent multivariate analysis the sentence's use as a speech margin loses any significance once all other variables are adjusted for, but all other fields remain significant.[99] Allen concludes:

> Having adjusted for all fields it can be seen that the features that have the most noticeable effect on choosing 'de' as opposed to 'kai' are all topical themes [that is, any choice other than a thematized verb], with the most marked effect caused by a topical theme of 'genitive absolute participle', a constituent order of 'subject before verb in first position' [S_1V constituent order] (with any subject reference), a subject reference 'proper noun' (with any constituent order) and having a topic switch [= subject switch].[100]

In addition, Allen finds several significant interactions between variables affecting the choice of δέ over καί, two of which are judged important enough to incorporate into her final model: first, an interaction between S_1V constituent order and a proper noun as the grammatical subject; and secondly, an interaction between subject switch and the 'less common forms of topical theme', that is, all topical themes besides verb, participle (genitive absolute or other), or subject, a set which includes prepositional phrases, temporal clauses, adverbs, genitive nouns, and hanging nominatives.[101]

S_1V constituent order and proper noun subject reference. The combination of S_1V constituent order and a proper noun strongly increases the likelihood of δέ occurring as a sentence conjunction. Based on her final model, Allen calculates an adjusted odds ratio for δέ occurring rather than καί when constituent order is S_1V and the grammaticalized subject is a proper noun of 1707.72 (compared to the 'default' choice of a thematic monolectic verb). She adds, 'It is worth noting that a 95% confidence interval for this odds ratio is [187.20,15578.56] indicating that the odds ratio of this combination (comparing it to the common default category) could be as large as 15578.56'.[102] Allen states that the combination of S_1V

---

98. Allen, 'Greek Syntactical Analysis', p. 18.

99. Allen, 'Greek Syntactical Analysis', p. 20.

100. Allen, 'Greek Syntactical Analysis', p. 21; see also Allen and Farewell, this volume, §4.1(ii).

101. See Allen, 'Greek Syntactical Analysis', pp. 21-26; see also Allen and Farewell, this volume, §4.1(iii).

102. Allen, 'Greek Syntactical Analysis', p. 26. A 95% confidence interval of [187.50,15578.56] suggests that δέ may actually be anywhere from 187.50 to 15,578.56 times more likely to appear with a combination of S_1V constituent order and a proper noun than is καί.

constituent order and a proper noun as the subject of a sentence is the feature with the largest effect on the choice of δέ rather than καί as a sentence conjunction in Matthew's narrative framework.

However, an examination of the database suggests some caution in drawing conclusions from this outcome regarding Matthew's Gospel, exemplifying the need for qualitative analysis to be combined with quantitative analysis. The first concern is that when the database was constructed subject reference was not considered a significant feature and so theoretical considerations regarding the 'parsing' of subject reference were not fully developed. The designation 'proper noun' was used for all personal names plus *Pharisees*, *Pharisees and scribes*, *Pharisees and Sadducees*, and *the devil* (ὁ διάβολος). At the same time, phrases such as *chief priests*, *chief priests and elders*, *chief priests and scribes*, *high priest*, *disciples*—items which could arguably be treated as proper nouns on the basis of their function as technical or quasi-technical titles in Matthew's Gospel—were given the designation 'noun phrase'. In addition, reinspection of the database shows that in ten instances personal names or references to the Pharisees were erroneously designated 'noun phrase' rather than 'proper noun'. Taken together, this suggests that while all of the subject references designated 'proper noun' in the data set used by Allen would, it appears, still be considered proper nouns after further analysis, there may be additional data that should also be included in Allen's data set. On the other hand, the ten misdesignated instances of subject reference (those parsed as 'noun phrase' rather than 'proper noun') reflect a collocation between δέ and S_1V constituent order consistent with what Allen finds elsewhere. Each of the three sentences in this group which have S_1V constituent order also has δέ as the sentence conjunction, and conversely, of the four instances of δέ as sentence conjunction in this set of ten sentences, three have S_1V constituent order—suggesting that the association Allen finds between δέ, a proper noun subject and S_1V constituent order would be strengthened rather than weakened by the inclusion of these additional data.

A more interesting question concerns the possible impact of the genealogy in 1.2-16 on the statistical frequency of δέ with S_1V constituent order and proper noun subjects. The genealogy consists of 39 sentences listing personal names in the line of descent from Abraham to Jesus. Of these 39 sentences, 38 (all but the first) have δέ as the sentence conjunction, and a different set of 38 (all but 1.12a) have S_1V constituent order. At issue is whether the use of δέ in 1.2-16 to introduce a succession of new participants reflects a general tendency on the part of the Evangelist, or whether this cluster of uses skews the statistical frequency of δέ with thematic proper nouns in the narrative framework overall.

Allen's analysis does not allow for sentences to be eliminated based on their location in Matthew's Gospel, so it is not possible to remove the genealogy in 1.2-16 from her model. Nevertheless, further examination of the database indicates that there is in fact a significant association of δέ, S_1V constituent order, and proper noun subjects even if the genealogy in 1.2-16 is eliminated, as Table 5.4 shows.

These results suggest that while the cluster of personal names in the genealogy in 1.2-16 may skew the association of δέ with proper nouns in Matthew's narrative framework (a question which the inclusion of the additional data may clarify), there is still a three-way association between δέ, S_1V constituent order, and proper nouns even if the sentences in 1.2-16 are omitted. In other words, in the narrative framework as a whole, when the Evangelist chooses a personal name or other proper noun as the subject of a sentence he reveals a strong tendency at the same time to thematize that subject and to use δέ as the sentence conjunction.

Table 5.4: *Sentence conjunction and constituent order with proper nouns*

	All narrative sentences	*Subject reference = 'proper noun'*	*Subject reference = 'proper noun' (omitting 1.2-16)*	*S_1V constituent order + 'proper noun'*	*S_1V constituent order + 'proper noun' (omitting 1.2-16)*
n =	720	182	143	69	31
# καί	335	42	42	1 (28.9)	1 (28.9)
% καί	47%	23%	29%	1%	3%
z-score		−6.34	−4.12	−7.51	−4.83
# δέ	257	95	57	60	23
% δέ	36%	52%	40%	87%	74%
z-score		4.65	1.04	8.89	4.47

The question of why this should be remains. So far I have treated all grammaticalized subjects alike in my analysis of constituent order, but variation in subject reference has been explored by other linguists in terms of its function in discourse processing. Givón, for example, suggests that differences in reference to topic—a functional notion he prefers to the more structural notion of 'subject'—may be represented by a cline of discourse continuity/discontinuity analogous to that developed in this study for constituent order.[103] Generally, Givón understands fuller references (noun phrases) and those occurring earlier in the clause to be more representative of 'inaccessible' information and more discontinuous, while reduced references (pronouns or zero reference) and those occurring later in the clause are understood to be more representative of 'accessible' information and more continuous.[104] From this perspective, selecting a personal name or other proper noun as subject (a form of noun phrase which represents a full and highly specific reference) and thematizing it may be mutually reinforcing choices in the introduction or reintroduction of a specific participant, presumably one who is important in terms of the discourse.[105] It is not surprising, then, that the Evangelist would also use δέ as the sentence conjunction in this context, resulting in δέ, the proper noun, and S_1V constituent order serving as mutually redundant procedural signals that the mental representation of the discourse is to be modified in terms of a new or resumed (and presumably important) participant.

As a final note, the single instance in which καί (in this case in combination with ἰδού) appears with a thematized personal name as subject occurs, as might be expected in terms of its distributional markedness, at a significant point in the narrative. In 28.9, Jesus meets Mary Magdalene and the other Mary in his first post-resurrection appearance. Instead of δέ the Evangelist chooses the more marked combination καί ἰδού to reintroduce Jesus as a participant in the narrative: 28.9, καὶ ἰδοὺ Ἰησοῦς ὑπήντησεν αὐταῖς λέγων· χαίρετε.

Subject switch and less common topical themes. The second multivariate interaction Allen includes in her final model is that between δέ, subject switch and the 'less common forms of topical theme'. In her model 'less

---

103. Givón offers one such possible cline, but acknowledges both that his proposal is too language-specific and that 'better and typologically more relevant predictions can be made by recognizing a number of scales each reflecting some specific syntactic *coding means*—be those word-order, morphology, intonation or phonological size— which alone or in various combinations make up the syntactic constructions that code our scalar domain' (Givón, 'Topic Continuity', p. 18).

104. See also Givón, *Functionalism*, pp. 51-52.

105. See also S. Wallace, 'Figure and Ground: The Interrelationships of Linguistic Categories', in P.J. Hopper (ed.), *Tense-Aspect: Between Semantics and Pragmatics* (Amsterdam: John Benjamins, 1982), pp. 211-12, where Wallace suggests that proper nouns may be 'more salient', that is, 'somehow more prominent or important with regard to certain properties of syntax or discourse', than common nouns.

common' topical themes are any elements in thematic position in the sentence other than finite verbs, participles (including genitive absolute constructions) or grammatical subjects. The set of such elements includes prepositional phrases, temporal clauses, adverbs, genitive nouns, accusative case direct objects, and hanging nominative constructions.

Only 57 of the 720 narrative sentences in the database have anything other than a finite verb, grammatical subject or participle as topical theme—that is, only 57 narrative sentences have a 'less common' topical theme. The sentence conjunctions in these 57 sentences are distributed approximately evenly among καί (22/57, 39%), δέ (18/57, 32%) and asyndeton (16/57, 28%). But when only those sentences in which there is also subject switch are considered, δέ predominates. Of 27 narrative sentences with both a 'less common' theme and subject switch, δέ is the sentence conjunction in 16 (59%). Again, this association can be accounted for by the role of δέ in narrative discontinuity. Levinsohn points out that a common reason for placing an element at the beginning of a sentence (that is, placing it before the verb, and especially in sentence-initial position) is to serve as the 'point of departure' at a point of discontinuity in the narrative, proving a basis for relating what follows to the context.[106] I have already discussed the tendency of δέ to collocate with thematic temporal indicators. The less common forms of theme in Matthew's narrative framework include a number of temporal indicators as well as other elements which are likely to signal various types of shift. The choice of one of these, combined with the ideational discontinuity of subject switch, makes it all the more likely that the Evangelist will also choose δέ as a reinforcing signal of discontinuity in the narrative.

Summary and Application

I have shown that in the narrative framework of Matthew's Gospel δέ collocates with formal systems such as constituent order and thematization, and with ideational factors such as subject switch, as mutually redundant signals of discontinuity in the Evangelist's presentation of the narrative. With respect to constituent order, δέ shows a significant tendency to appear with SV sentences, especially those with an explicit subject in thematic position (S_1V constituent order). The frequency of δέ increases in proportion to the markedness of the constituent order of the

106. Levinsohn, *Discourse Features*, pp. 7-13.

sentences it begins. The earlier in the sentence the subject is placed (with S_1V the most marked constituent order), the more likely δέ is to appear; the later in the sentence the subject is placed (with no grammaticalized subject as the least marked choice) the less likely δέ is to appear. Similarly, with respect to the ideational feature of subject switch δέ reveals a significantly higher frequency of use where there is a switch in subject and a significantly lower frequency of use where there is continuity of subject. Where a grammatical subject is not the topical theme, δέ may collocate with other thematic elements conveying temporal or spatial discontinuity, such as genitive absolute participial constructions and various temporal indicators.

The extent to which δέ is found with collocating features of discontinuity or change supports my argument that δέ functions alongside the related features as a procedural signal of discontinuity in narrative. The presence of δέ alerts the audience to introduce some aspect of discontinuity into their ongoing mental representation of the discourse. Semantic relations between sentences may involve a change in participant, a temporal or spatial shift, a move to or from the narrative line, or some other aspect of discontinuity, but these semantic relations are properties of the sentences conjoined by δέ and not of δέ itself. Καί, as the unmarked or default sentence conjunction, may be found where collocating features are consistent with the use of δέ, but δέ, the more marked choice, is less often found in unmarked contexts where καί is otherwise expected, that is, with VS constituent order, monolectic verbs, or where there is no change in notional subject.

Collocations of the sentence conjunctions καί and δέ with other features exemplify the manner in which different linguistic elements work together in Matthew's narrative. Lexico-grammatical choices (sentence conjunction), syntactical choices (constituent order), and nonformal features (subject switch)—no doubt alongside other as yet unidentified variables—form networks of systems in the structure of discourse.

Unfortunately, δέ is often mishandled by New Testament exegetes who, taking an 'adversative' sense as primary for δέ, either press that notion too far or find themselves baffled by its use in certain contexts. As an example I turn to Gundry's commentary on Matthew, not because I believe Gundry to be unique in this aspect, but because Gundry's otherwise laudable attention to syntactic detail clearly reveals his approach and illustrates some effects a misunderstanding of δέ as necessarily adversative or contrastive may have on exegesis.

Gundry states that 'Matthew normally uses δέ as an adversative'.[107] 'Probably', he suggests, 'δέ means "And" or "Now" in Mark and "But" in Matthew'.[108] Throughout the commentary, Gundry asserts that Matthew uses δέ to 'contrast' statements or actions,[109] to 'set opposite' or 'set in opposition' two statements or actions,[110] or to set one statement or action 'against' another.[111] However, at other points Gundry refers to the use of δέ to 'distinguish',[112] 'set off',[113] 'make stand out more distinctly',[114] or even to 'compare'[115] one statement or action with respect to another, suggesting that his understanding of δέ as an 'adversative' conjunction is somewhat broader than simply as an indicator of semantic contrast.

Just as there is necessarily a degree of connection between sentences in a discourse, there is also generally some element of 'contrast' or, more precisely, some degree of narrative discontinuity in terms of time, setting, action or participants that could be identified between most conjoined sentences. Thus it is not surprising that at most points where δέ is used Gundry can find some factor which can be labeled 'contrast' if that is what he is looking for. Notwithstanding, at times his claims of 'contrast' seem to require a manipulation of the context. For example, Gundry comments on 27.35, concerning the distribution of Jesus' clothes at the time of his crucifixion, 'The changing of [Mark's] καί to δέ produces a contrast between the soldiers' failure to make Jesus drink the galled wine and their parting Jesus' garments, about which Jesus does nothing because he is hanging on the cross'.[116] It is difficult to see from the context that Matthew is otherwise highlighting any distinction between Jesus' active resistance to the galled wine and his forced passivity in the distribution of his garments. On 27.39, when two thieves are crucified (27.38) and the bystanders blaspheme Jesus, Gundry writes, 'Mark's καί becomes δέ for a contrast

107. Gundry, *Matthew*, p. 550; see also, for example, pp. 477, 522, 538, 546.

108. Gundry, *Matthew*, p. 560; see also, for example, p. 573.

109. See, for example, Gundry, *Matthew*, pp. 288, 290, 295, 297, 300, 312, 325, 389, 415, 420, 450, 475, 476, 526, 527, 542, 548, 551, 560, 568, 569, 570, 572, 573, 579, 582-83, 585, 588, 592, 593.

110. See, for example, Gundry, *Matthew*, pp. 233, 255, 272, 312, 326, 343, 527.

111. See, for example, Gundry, *Matthew*, p. 405.

112. See, for example, Gundry, *Matthew*, pp. 352, 410.

113. See, for example, Gundry, *Matthew*, pp. 417, 524, 549, 573.

114. See, for example, Gundry, *Matthew*, p. 550 (although Gundry points to 'contrast' in this context as well).

115. See, for example, Gundry, *Matthew*, p. 409.

116. Gundry, *Matthew*, p. 569.

with being crucified'.[117] Here Gundry seems to argue that in effect Matthew is saying, 'The two thieves were crucified, but the bystanders, by contrast, deride Jesus'. It is difficult to understand in what sense this might be a meaningful contrast, beyond indicating the activities of two distinct sets of participants, especially when the thieves themselves subsequently join in reviling Jesus (27.44).

In a number of instances where Gundry argues that δέ points to a particular aspect of contrast he ignores indicators of temporal or spatial shift present in the text. With respect to 27.62, in which the chief priests and Pharisees petition Pilate that Jesus' tomb be sealed, Gundry writes that 'δέ contrasts the women's vigil at Jesus' tomb [27.61] with the chief priests' and Pharisees' request for a guard at the tomb. How different the two concerns!'[118] Different they may be, but, as Gundry himself notes, the chief priests and Pharisees' petition in 27.62-65 takes place the day following the vigil of Mary Magdalene and the other Mary—a temporal shift from one day to the next sufficient to account for the presence of δέ. Mt. 27.62 begins with τῇ δὲ ἐπαύριον, a type of temporal prepositional phrase which is typically combined with δέ. Similarly, on 28.1 at the beginning of the resurrection account Gundry comments, 'The exchange of [Mark's] καί for δέ makes a contrast between the securing of the tomb and the following account of Jesus' resurrection',[119] although the presence of the temporal phrase ὀψὲ σαββάτων at the beginning of 28.1 is sufficient justification for the use of δέ as a procedural signal of temporal discontinuity, indicating the shift to a time 'after the Sabbath'.[120]

In like manner, Gundry applies the label 'contrast' at a number of points at which δέ is combined with a genitive absolute construction in a typical Matthean 'scene shifting' technique. In 14.23, when evening comes and Jesus is alone before walking across the water to join his disciples, the sentence begins with ὀψίας δὲ γενομένης. Gundry writes, 'As often, Matthew exchanges Mark's καί for δέ in order to contrast the onset of evening with the daylight hours'.[121] Gundry is correct that the presence of δέ is related to the discontinuity of time (rather than, for instance, a

---

117. Gundry, *Matthew*, p. 570.

118. Gundry, *Matthew*, pp. 582-83. Gundry does not comment on the presence of δέ in 27.61 immediately preceding, which, as I have discussed above, is a presentational structure reintroducing the two women.

119. Gundry, *Matthew*, p. 585.

120. See also, for example, Gundry, *Matthew*, p. 573.

121. Gundry, *Matthew*, p. 297.

semantic contrast of Jesus being alone after being with the crowds), but to label this temporal progression as 'contrast' is difficult to justify without further evidence that the distinction between day and night is significant in Matthew's version of the story.[122]

More problematic than the failure to recognize indicators of narrative discontinuity that combine with δέ is the manner in which Gundry's 'adversative' understanding of δέ is allowed to serve as evidence for conflict in Matthew's Gospel. In 12.22-24, the crowds show amazement at Jesus' healing of a blind and mute demoniac while the Pharisees accuse Jesus of being in league with Beelzebub. Commenting on Jesus' response to the Pharisees in 12.25, Gundry writes that 'the replacement of Mark's καί with δέ (so also Luke) set[s] the Pharisees' statement and Jesus' sayings in sharper opposition. Such opposition accords with Matthew's overarching theme of conflict.'[123] There certainly appears to be conflict between the Pharisees and Jesus, and semantic contrast is, of course, one type of discontinuity with which the use of δέ is consistent (but not the most common or necessarily the one the audience would assume first), and the Evangelist has presumably made a choice to use δέ rather than καί at this point in the discourse. However, to argue that as an indicator of opposition δέ itself has a role in revealing the presence of conflict is to press the meaning of δέ too far. As Nida and Louw suggest, 'The meaning of a sign is the minimum of what that sign contributes to the context'.[124] The minimum of what δέ contributes to this context is a change in participant, first the Pharisees and then Jesus, in a manner typical of speech margins in Matthew's narrative framework. Perhaps tellingly, Gundry makes no comment on the presence of δέ in the genealogy of 1.2-16, where δέ conjoins each sentence and merely indicates the shift from one participant to the next.[125]

122. For other examples of Gundry labeling the use of δέ with a genitive absolute construction as indicative of contrast, see Gundry, *Matthew*, pp. 415, 450, 476, 526, 551, 579, 592.

123. Gundry, *Matthew*, p. 233.

124. E.A. Nida and J.P. Louw, *Lexical Semantics of the Greek New Testament: A Supplement to the Greek–English Lexicon of the New Testament Based on Semantic Domains* (SBLRBS, 25; Atlanta: Scholars Press, 1992), p. 18.

125. For other instances in which Gundry suggests that δέ serves as evidence of conflict, see, for example, his comments on 13.11, where he argues that δέ in Jesus' reply to his disciples' question about the purpose of parables 'sets Jesus' response opposite the disciples' question' (Gundry, *Matthew*, p. 255), and similarly on 13.37, where he writes that δέ in Jesus' response to the disciples' request for an interpretation

Again, it is not that I believe Gundry to be unique in his understanding of δέ as playing an adversarial role in Matthew's Gospel or indeed elsewhere in New Testament narrative. It is simply that Gundry is unusually explicit in his approach and offers more opportunity for discussion. The important point is that the results of linguistic research into sentence conjunctions offer New Testament scholars a more penetrating glimpse into the function of sentence conjunctions like δέ in Greek discourse and into the ways in which sentence conjunctions interact with other linguistic choices. A fuller awareness of the Evangelist's use of these small words promises a sounder linguistic basis for exegesis. In Matthew's narrative framework, δέ functions not as a logically 'adversative' conjunction, but as a procedural signal of discontinuity in the narrative.

of the parable of the weeds 'sets Jesus' reply opposite the disciples' request' (Gundry, *Matthew*, p. 272). The contrast which Gundry is developing here is between understanding—the mark of a true disciple—and the lack of understanding (see Gundry, *Matthew*, pp. 250-51).

Chapter 6

ASYNDETON: SPEECH MARGINS AND NARRATIVE BREAKS

	All sentences in Matthew	Narrative sentences	Exposition sentences	Speech sentences	Old Testament quotations
n =	2302	720	768	733	81
# asyndeton	721	57	201	419	44
% asyndeton	31%	8%	26%	57%	54%

Introduction

Καί and δέ, the sentence conjunctions considered in the two previous chapters, are by far the most common in Matthew's Gospel. Together they account for half of the sentences in Matthew's Gospel (1170/2302, 51%) and more than 80% of those in the narrative framework (592/720, 82%). But, in fact, asyndeton—the lack of a conjunction—occurs more frequently in Matthew's Gospel than does any single sentence conjunction (721/2302, 31%).

At the same time, in contrast to καί and δέ which proliferate in Matthew's narrative framework, even a cursory reading of the Gospel reveals that asyndeton is a relatively uncommon connective strategy in narrative. Only 57 of the 720 sentences in the narrative framework (8%) are asyndetic. Asyndeton occurs more frequently in other discourse types, largely because of the fact that the first sentence in any sequence of exposition or reported speech is either asyndetic or is introduced by ὅτι.[1] Speech and exposition sentences after the first in a sequence show less use of asyndeton. For example, although asyndeton appears in 57% of sentences identified in the database as reported speech (419/733), it occurs

---

1. If ὅτι is treated as an embedding particle in these contexts rather than as a conjunctive form, the first sentence in every continuous sequence of exposition or direct speech is asyndetic.

in only 30% of speech sentences after the first sentence in a continuous quotation (106/351), but still more frequently than in narrative.

As I stated in previous chapters, I understand the system of sentence conjunctions in Matthew's narrative framework to consist primarily of the set καί, δέ, τότε, γάρ and οὖν—plus asyndeton. Asyndeton is included in this system because it represents an option that alternates with other conjunctive choices. As the Evangelist joins succeeding sentences to construct his discourse he chooses from the relatively small set of sentence conjunctions listed here or he chooses instead to omit any grammatical conjunction.[2] Thus a systemic investigation of sentence conjunctions in the narrative framework also incorporates those instances in which no conjunction appears. On this basis I treat asyndeton as a structural element. In the discussion which follows I speak, for example, of the structure <asyndeton + thematic λέγει/λέγουσιν> although asyndeton is not represented by a visible element in the sentence.

Grammarians agree that asyndeton is relatively unusual in the Greek of the New Testament. Winer notes, 'In all continuous writing the connexion of sentences is the rule, the absence of connexion (asyndeton) the exception'.[3] Turner observes that asyndeton 'is contrary to the genius of Greek',[4] while Blass, Debrunner and Funk go as far as to pronounce that asyndeton in parataxis 'is repugnant by and large to the spirit of the Greek language'.[5] All concede that although asyndeton is relatively infrequent, it does occur regularly in the New Testament, particularly in Paul and Hebrews,[6] and, most notably, in John's Gospel where it seems to take over the role καί plays in the Synoptics as the unmarked form of connection.[7]

2.   Turner reports that Matthew has supplied a conjunction where Mark has asyndeton some 30 times, while using asyndeton in 21 other instances where Mark has a conjunction (Turner, *Style*, p. 31.)

3.   Winer, *Treatise*, p. 673.

4.   Turner, *Syntax*, p. 340.

5.   BDF, §458; see also Robertson, *Grammar*, p. 428.

6.   See Turner, *Syntax*, p. 340.

7.   See Winer, *Treatise*, p. 673; Robertson, *Grammar*, p. 444; Poythress, 'Intersentence Conjunctions', pp. 312-40; Buth, 'Οὖν, Δέ, Καί and Asyndeton', pp. 144-61. Abbott notes that 'John abounds in instances of asyndeton of the most varied and unexpected kind, too numerous to quote ... There is hardly any part of speech, or word, that might not come at the beginning of a Johannine sentence without a conjunction...' (Abbott, *Johannine Grammar*, p. 70). Suggestions for the apparent increase in asyndeton in the New Testament over against Classical literature include Semitic influence and/or the influence of non-literary Koine; see Turner, *Syntax*, p. 340; Buth, 'Οὖν, Δέ, Καί and Asyndeton', pp. 158-59.

However, Denniston, in his study of particles in Classical Greek, suggests that there are 'certain well-marked exceptions', that is, discourse contexts in which Greek tends to dispense with a connective particle in spite of the general principle of supplying a sentence conjunction. He characterizes the routine omission of a connective particle in certain specific contexts as 'formal', as distinct from 'stylistic', asyndeton.[8] Similarly, Winer distinguishes in the New Testament 'two kinds of asyndeton,—the grammatical and the rhetorical'.[9] Grammatical asyndeton as Winer describes it occurs, for example, in narrative contexts 'where the mere order of succession may of itself serve as a connexion in regard to time' (seen most frequently in John's Gospel), and also in didactic passages such as the book of James, discourses by Jesus in the Gospel of John, and the Sermon on the Mount in Matthew 5–7, where 'the writer is, so to speak, continually commencing anew'. The rhetorical use of asyndeton, on the other hand, occurs more frequently in Epistles where 'as the language receives from it terseness and swiftness of movement, it serves to render the style lively and forcible'.[10] If such a distinction can be maintained (and this is by no means certain), it is 'formal' or 'grammatical' asyndeton with which I am concerned here: not asyndeton used with an eye primarily toward stylistic or rhetorical effect—although all good storytelling exhibits something of this concern—but those contexts in narrative discourse in which asyndeton may be a natural or conventional connective strategy, as exemplified in Matthew's narrative framework.

The relative infrequency of asyndeton in narrative in Matthew's Gospel, vis-à-vis the more common sentence conjunctions καί and δέ, has two counterbalancing effects on an analysis of Matthew's use of asyndeton in narrative. On the one hand, significantly fewer examples (57 asyndetic narrative sentences, compared to 335 with καί and 257 with δέ) mean less data to work with, which suggests some caution in depending on quantitative analysis, although the existing data can certainly be quantified and described. On the other hand, fewer sentences allow the opportunity for more exhaustive qualitative analysis than is possible in practical terms for

8. Denniston, *Greek Particles*, p. xliii. See also Smyth, who writes, 'The absence of connectives in a language so rich in means of coördination as is Greek is more striking than in other languages' (Smyth, *Greek Grammar*, p. 484). Smyth, like Winer (below), distinguishes between 'grammatical' and 'rhetorical' asyndeton.

9. Winer, *Treatise*, p. 673.

10. Winer, *Treatise*, pp. 673-74. For a recent study of asyndeton in the Pauline epistles from a computational approach, see Güting and Mealand, *Asyndeton in Paul*.

καί or δέ. In this chapter I treat all the examples of asyndeton in Matthew's narrative framework.

I find two distinct tendencies among asyndetic narrative sentences in Matthew's Gospel, at what can be described as opposite ends of the continuity–discontinuity spectrum. On the one hand, asyndeton is used to link sentences with the closest of connections, specifically in speech margins, and especially in the margins of question–reply–response sequences. On the other hand, asyndeton also tends to be found where breaks in the flow of the narrative occur, often strong breaks: for example, between the title and first sentence, and at a number of breaks between episodes or between larger sections of the Gospel.

Grammarians recognize these two functions of asyndeton. Winer writes, 'Grammatically disconnected sentences are not merely such as begin a new division or section (of some length)… They also occur where the language flows on without interruption…'[11] Levinsohn observes that in non-narrative discourse, 'Asyndeton is found in two very different contexts… when there is a *close* connection between the information concerned…and when there is *no* direct connection between the information concerned…'[12] But as I show below, at opposing ends of this continuity–discontinuity spectrum asyndetic narrative sentences in Matthew's Gospel exhibit certain characteristic features.

Halliday writes, 'The speaker of a language, like a person engaging in any kind of culturally determined behaviour, can be regarded as carrying out simultaneously and successively, a number of distinct choices'.[13] These choices, while distinct, are not wholly independent of each other. Systems form networks within languages, and choices from various systems interact with one another. As I have demonstrated in the preceding chapters, the set of sentence conjunctions in Matthew's narrative framework interacts with other systems within the language such as constituent order, thematization and verbal tense-form. Or rather, it may be more to the point to say that the Evangelist tends to make use of mutually reinforcing elements from different systems in structuring his discourse.

I have shown, for example, the tendency for καί to be used with V(S) constituent order, especially with thematic verbs, and for δέ to be used with SV constituent order, especially with thematic subjects. In the same way, patterned collocations of elements can be observed with asyndeton,

---

11. Winer, *Treatise*, p. 673.
12. Levinsohn, *Discourse Features*, p. 118 (his emphasis).
13. Halliday, 'Systemic Grammar', p. 3.

and in fact vary between the 'continuous' and 'discontinuous' contexts in which asyndeton is found. In speech margins in tightly connected segments of narrated dialogue (what I term its continuous usage), asyndeton consistently appears with present tense-form λέγω in thematic position. On the other hand, when asyndeton occurs at what appear to be breaks in the narrative (its discontinuous usage), aorist (or occasionally imperfect, but never present) tense-forms are used. Either SV or V(S) constituent order may appear at these breaks, and yet the verb is never thematic.[14] Here again the Evangelist makes use of mutually reinforcing lexical and syntactic elements to help guide the audience through the discourse.[15]

As a conjunctive choice asyndeton signals either tight continuity in conversation or mid- to higher-level breaks in the narrative. The audience makes use of collocating features such as the presence of thematic present-tense λέγω or the presence of non-verbal thematic elements to disambiguate the function of asyndeton in context. Using these mutually reinforcing cues, the audience either continues a mental representation of conversation, or opens a new segment in their mental representation of the discourse.[16]

'Continuous' Use

Asyndeton with Speech Margins
The term 'speech margin' (or sometimes, 'speech orienter'[17]) refers to the syntactical structures used to introduce reported speech, whether conversation or monologue, and to set it into the narrative framework, the *he said...she said...*of the Greek of the New Testament.

---

14. Levinsohn notes that in John's Gospel asyndeton appears in contexts of continuity with thematic verbs, and at points of discontinuity with some other thematic element, what he terms 'points of departure' (Levinsohn, *Discourse Features*, p. 82). See also Poythress, 'Intersentence Conjunctions', p. 334.

15. Levinsohn observes that in the Epistles as well, 'the absence of a conjunction is significant only in connection with other potential boundary features' (Levinsohn, *Discourse Features*, p. 276).

16. I have found no research in cognitive linguistics which appears relevant to the function of asyndeton in discourse processing in the Greek of the New Testament. This is because asyndeton is generally assumed to be the 'default' connection in languages like English or French, rather than the less frequent, potentially more marked, narrative strategy that it is in the Greek of the New Testament. See, for example, Bestgen and Vonk, 'Temporal Segmentation Markers', p. 386.

17. See, for example, Levinsohn, *Discourse Features*, p. 216.

An overview of 'speech margins'. Speech margins play a large role in Matthew's narrative framework. Of the 720 narrative sentences in Matthew's Gospel, 299 (42%) function as speech margins, either with or without verbs of speaking like λέγω or φημί. Clearly the Evangelist is concerned with portraying oral communication via written text, both monologue by Jesus and dialogue between Jesus and others.

Not surprisingly, by far the most common lexical item used in speech margins in the narrative framework is λέγω. It appears in 282 of the 299 speech margins in Matthew's narrative framework (94%), as a finite verb 186 times and another 96 times as a present tense-form participle (or, rarely, a present tense-form infinitive) combined with various finite verbs which are not necessarily verbs of speaking.[18] Φημί occurs 11 times, always finite and never combined with a form of λέγω,[19] while there seem to be no more than 6 other instances where finite verbs appear in speech margins without some form of λέγω also present.[20] This accounts for all of the speech margins in Matthew's narrative framework identified in the database. The speech margins in which a finite verb combines with a non-finite form of λέγω—for example, 9.14, τότε προσέρχονται αὐτῷ οἱ μαθηταὶ Ἰωάννου λέγοντες..., or 14.33, οἱ δὲ ἐν τῷ πλοίῳ προσεκύνησαν αὐτῷ λέγοντες...—show syntactical patterns and collocations with sentence conjunctions which are nearly identical to those of narrative in general. However, speech margins which use finite forms of λέγω and φημί show distinct patterns and thus will be the focus of analysis here.

18. The infinitive appears in 4.17, 11.7, 13.54 and 26.22. Examples of λέγων/ λέγοντες with verbs of speaking include: ἐπερωτάω, 12.10, 17.10, 22.41, 27.11; ἐρωτάω, 15.23, 16.13, 22.23; κράζω, 8.29, 14.30, 15.22, 20.30, 20.31, 21.9, 27.23; λαλέω, 13.3, 14.27, 23.1, 28.18. Examples of λέγων/λέγοντες with verbs that are not verbs of speaking include: προσέρχομαι, 8.5, 9.14, 14.15, 18.1, 19.3, 21.23, 24.3, 26.17, 26.69; προσκυνέω, 8.2, 9.18, 14.33, 15.25; φαίνω, 1.20, 2.13, 2.19. In one instance the participle appears with a nominal (verbless) clause: 3.17, καὶ ἰδοὺ φωνὴ ἐκ τῶν οὐρανῶν λέγουσα... In one instance λέγω appears as an aorist participle, in a genitive absolute construction (17.26).

19. Mt. 4.7, 8.8, 14.8, 17.26, 19.21, 21.27, 22.37, 26.34, 27.11, 27.23, 27.65.

20. Mt. 13.33, λαλέω; 15.33, ἀποκρίνομαι (arguably not a speech margin, as no quotation follows); 22.35, ἐπερωτάω; 26.72, ἀρνέομαι; 26.74, ἄρχομαι with infinitives (τότε ἤρξατο καταθεματίζειν καὶ ὀμνύειν...); 27.37, ἐπιτίθημι with a participle (καὶ ἐπέθηκαν ἐπάνω τῆς κεφαλῆς αὐτοῦ τὴν αἰτίαν αὐτοῦ γεγραμμένην ...again arguably not a speech margin).

Asyndeton and thematic λέγει/λέγουσιν. Grammarians have long recognized the widespread use of asyndeton with speech margins in the Gospels, especially in John's Gospel.[21] Winer considers the combination of asyndeton and λέγω or ἀποκρίνομαι a characteristic feature of Johannine style.[22] Levinsohn notes that asyndeton in combination with the 'historic present' forms one of two principal strategies for connecting quoted speech in Matthew's Gospel (more on this below).[23] A statistical analysis of Matthew's narrative framework shows that asyndeton does in fact appear more frequently with λέγω and φημί speech margins than in narrative in general:

Table 6.1: *Asyndeton in speech margins*

	All narrative sentences	All speech margins	Speech margins with finite λέγω	Speech margins with finite φημί
n =	720	299	186	11
# asyndeton	57	41	29	5
% asyndeton	8%	14%	16%	45%
z-score[24]		3.73	3.89	4.64

Although asyndeton occurs in only 8% of sentences in the narrative framework, it appears in 14% of speech margins of all types, in 16% of speech margins with a finite form of λέγω, and in 45% of speech margins with φημί. Z-scores greater than ±3 indicate that the results for asyndeton with each classification of speech margin given here are statistically significant.[25]

Not only is the use of asyndeton with speech margins recognized by grammarians, but, as mentioned above, the tendency for asyndeton to be

21. See BDF, §462, who consider the use of asyndeton with λέγω and φημί 'good Greek' and note its appearance in *The Shepherd of Hermas*; see also Robertson, *Grammar*, p. 444; Turner, *Syntax*, pp. 340-41.

22. See Winer, *Treatise*, p. 673.

23. Levinsohn, *Discourse Features*, p. 217.

24. To reiterate, *z*-scores equal to or greater than ±3—that is, indicating that a value falls three standard deviations or more above or below a mean—are taken to demonstrate statistical significance.

25. The *z*-score of 4.64 for asyndeton with φημί may not be a reliable indicator because the sample size (n = 11) is less than 30. However, Allen finds a similar correlation in her analysis of my data, noting an unadjusted odds ratio of 72.79 for the use of asyndeton with φημί. That is, compared to sentences which are not speech margins, when φημί is used the sentence is 72.79 times as likely to be asyndetic as to have καί as a sentence conjunction (Allen, 'Greek Syntactical Analysis', pp. 29-30).

combined with the so-called 'historic present'—present tense-form finite verbs in past-referring narrative—is also noted.[26] This, too, is borne out by a quantitative analysis of Matthew's narrative framework:

Table 6.2: *Asyndeton and verbal tense-form (omitting* εἰμί *)*[27]

	All narrative sentences	Aorist	Present	Imperfect
n=	720	553	79	57
# asyndeton	57	24	26	3
% asyndeton	8%	4%	33%	5%
z-score		−3.12	8.23	−0.74

Although 8% of sentences in Matthew's narrative framework are asyndetic, a significantly higher percentage of the sentences with present finite verbs are asyndetic (26/79, 33%; $z = 8.23$), while a significantly smaller percentage of sentences with aorist finite verbs are asyndetic (24/553, 4%; $z = -3.12$).[28] Or, to put it another way, almost half of the instances of asyndeton in the narrative framework (26/57, 46%) occur with present tense-forms, in spite of the fact that only about one out of ten narrative sentences (79/720, 11%) have present tense-form finite verbs. In her statistical modeling of my data from Matthew's Gospel, Allen calculates an unadjusted odds ratio of 12.46 for the choice of asyndeton with present-tense finite verbs, indicating that where there is a present tense-form verb rather than an aorist form (the default category), asyndeton is 12.46 times more likely to occur than is καί.[29] This odds ratio increases to 138.35 when all other variables are adjusted for.[30] Allen notes a 95% confidence interval of [18.52,1033.29], which suggests that asyndeton could be as much as 1033.29 times more likely to occur than καί where there is a present tense-form finite verb rather than an aorist form.[31]

What the expanded table below (Table 6.3) indicates is that the affinity

26. See Winer, *Treatise*, p. 674; BDF, §462.

27. Again, εἰμί is omitted from consideration in this table and in other analyses of sentence conjunction and verbal tense-form because it does not evidence fully developed morphological distinctions among tense-forms, or, in Porter's terms, it is 'aspectually vague' (see Porter, *Verbal Aspect*, pp. 442-47).

28. There is no observable association between asyndeton and imperfect finite verbs.

29. Allen, 'Greek Syntactical Analysis', p. 29; see also Allen and Farewell, this volume, §4.2(i).

30. Allen, 'Greek Syntactical Analysis', p. 31; see also Allen and Farewell, this volume, §4.2(ii).

31. Allen, 'Greek Syntactical Analysis', p. 37.

between asyndeton and the so-called 'historic present' holds only with respect to λέγω as a finite verb in speech margins. In fact, in all 26 asyndetic sentences with present-tense finite verbs in Matthew's narrative framework the verb is λέγω.

I found no occurrence of asyndeton with the 'historic present' in Matthew's narrative framework outside of these uses with λέγω. A z-score of 10.31 indicates that the association between asyndeton and present tense-form λέγω is statistically significant for the given sample size. Allen, too, observes that because the data concerning asyndeton fall into two distinct structures—first those with thematic present-tense λέγω, and secondly non-speech margins with non-verbal topic themes—the odds ratio of 138.35 for asyndeton with present tense-forms can be seen to apply only to clauses of the first type.[32]

Similarly, as Table 6.4 demonstrates, patterns of constituent order differ between asyndetic sentences with and without λέγω.

Table 6.4 indicates that although the incidence of asyndeton in all narrative sentences with VS (verb–subject) constituent order appears to be significantly higher than would be expected based on its overall frequency in narrative (23/147, 16%; $z = 3.48$), it is actually only with finite forms of λέγω that asyndeton is significantly more frequent in VS sentences (9/26, 35%; $z = 5.04$), and not in other narrative sentences (14/121, 12%; $z = 1.49$).[33] And although the overall use of asyndeton with monolectic verbs (V constituent order) suggests no significant variation from what would be expected based on its frequency in the narrative framework as a whole (22/263, 8%; $z = 0.28$), a further breakdown indicates that its use with monolectic λέγω is significantly higher (17/55, 31%; $z = 6.33$), while its use in other narrative is lower (5/208, 2%; $z = -2.94$).

There are, then, several features which show a statistical tendency to collocate in speech margins with finite λέγω and not in other narrative: asyndeton, present tense-forms, and V(S) constituent order. Further inspection reveals two additional features in common: in each of the 26 sentences with present-tense finite λέγω the verb is thematic, and each sentence represents a switch in subject from the previous narrative sentence—presumably an alternation of speakers.[34]

32. Allen, 'Greek Syntactical Analysis', p. 37; see also Allen and Farewell, this volume, §4.2(iii).

33. The reliability of the z-score as an indicator of statistical significance for VS sentences with λέγω may be affected by a sample size of less than 30.

34. See Allen, 'Greek Syntactical Analysis', p. 36.

Table 6.3: *Asyndeton and verbal tense-form, λέγω vs. non-λέγω*

	All narrative	All narrative		Aorist		Present		Imperfect	
		non-λέγω	λέγω	non-λέγω	λέγω	non-λέγω	λέγω	non-λέγω	λέγω
n=	720	534	186	437	116	20	59	46	11
# asyndeton	57	28	29	22	2	0	26	2	1
% asyndeton	8%	5%	16%	5%	2%	0%	44%	4%	9%
z-score		-2.28	3.89	-2.22	-2.46	-1.31	10.31	-0.89	0.15

Table 6.4: *Asyndeton and V(S) constituent order, λέγω vs. non-λέγω*

	All narrative	VS constituent order			V constituent order		
		all VS	non-λέγω VS	λέγω VS	all V	non-λέγω V	λέγω V
n =	720	147	121	26	263	208	55
# asyndeton	57	23	14	9	22	5	17
% asyndeton	8%	16%	12%	35%	8%	2%	31%
z-score		3.48	1.49	5.04	0.28	-2.94	6.33

We might therefore expect to find a number of instances in Matthew's narrative framework where all these elements appear together, and this is indeed the case. The following example, 19.7-10, is taken from a conversation first between Jesus and a group of Pharisees and then between Jesus and his disciples.[35]

19.7 λέγουσιν αὐτῷ· τί οὖν Μωϋσῆς ἐνετείλατο δοῦναι βιβλίον ἀποστασίου καὶ ἀπολῦσαι [αὐτήν];

19.8 λέγει αὐτοῖς ὅτι Μωϋσῆς πρὸς τὴν σκληροκαρδίαν ὑμῶν ἐπέτρεψεν ὑμῖν ἀπολῦσαι τὰς γυναῖκας ὑμῶν, ἀπ' ἀρχῆς δὲ οὐ γέγονεν οὕτως...

19.10 λέγουσιν αὐτῷ οἱ μαθηταὶ [αὐτοῦ]· εἰ οὕτως ἐστὶν ἡ αἰτία τοῦ ἀνθρώπου μετὰ τῆς γυναικός, οὐ συμφέρει γαμῆσαι.

As Jesus leaves Galilee for Judea he is approached by a group of Pharisees who, in order to test him, question him about the legality of divorce (19.3, καὶ προσῆλθον αὐτῷ Φαρισαῖοι πειράζοντες αὐτὸν καὶ λέγοντες...). The speech margin introducing Jesus' first reply, in which he quotes the book of Genesis (19.4), is ὁ δὲ ἀποκριθεὶς εἶπεν, followed by καὶ εἶπεν as he continues to cite Genesis (19.5). The next three speech margins are each of the form <asyndeton + thematic λέγει/λέγουσιν>: the Pharisees ask a clarifying question (19.7), Jesus replies (19.8), and Jesus' disciples respond in amazement at his stern pronouncement limiting divorce (19.10). In Jesus' final statement to his disciples (19.11) the speech margin is ὁ δὲ εἶπεν.

In Matthew's narrative framework there are 17 instances like those in 19.7 and 19.8 above, in which asyndeton and λέγει/λέγουσιν appear with V constituent order, that is, with monolectic λέγω.[36] There are 9 additional instances like that in 19.10, in which asyndeton and λέγει/λέγουσιν appear with VS constituent order.[37] These 26 V(S) sentences account for all the occurrences of asyndeton with present-tense finite λέγω in Matthew's narrative framework.[38]

---

35. Square brackets in Greek examples represent textual variants included in the NA[27] text.

36. Mt. 9.28, 13.51, 16.15, 17.25, 19.7, 19.8, 19.18, 20.21, 20.22, 20.23, 20.33, 21.31, 21.41, 22.21, 22.42, 22.43, 26.25.

37. Mt. 18.22, 19.10, 19.20, 21.31, 21.42, 26.35, 26.64, 27.22, 27.22.

38. There are as well 33 other instances of λέγει/λέγουσιν in the narrative framework where καί, δέ, or τότε is found instead of asyndeton. Δέ appears in four instances (14.17, 17.20, 8.22, 21.16), in all of which the grammaticalized subject is thematic. Two of these, 14.17 and 17.20, have a pronominal article, for example, οἱ δὲ

On the strength of this evidence we may identify the structure <asyndeton + thematic λέγει/λέγουσιν + [grammaticalized subject]> as one of the formats the Evangelist favors for speech margins. Of the speech margins in the narrative framework, about one out of ten (26/299, 9%) exhibits the combination of asyndeton and thematic λέγει/λέγουσιν. The question then becomes whether there are recognizable discourse contexts in which the Evangelist chooses this combination over against other options. In other words, can one define the discourse 'slot' which the structure <asyndeton + thematic λέγει/λέγουσιν> fills as part of the system of speech margins in Matthew's narrative framework?

Asyndeton and λέγει/λέγουσιν: *A 'nondevelopmental' strategy?* Levinsohn has sought the answer to this question. He considers asyndeton, often combined with 'historic present' speech verbs, to be a 'nondevelopmental strategy' for presenting the non-initial speeches of a reported conversation, appearing only in Matthew's and John's Gospels.[39] He contrasts Matthew's use of asyndeton in speech margins with what he calls the 'default strategy' found in the Synoptic Gospels and Acts. Describing this 'default strategy', Levinsohn explains that in many cases individual speeches are treated by an author simply as intermediate steps toward the result of a conversation, a result 'which may be expressed either in the final speech or in an action that occurs in response to the conversation'. In such cases it is usual to begin with a reference to the speaker. 'Unless the speech is highlighted, this reference will be an articular pronoun', and the articular pronoun will be combined with δέ or μέν, that is, ὁ δέ, οἱ δέ, ἡ δέ and similar combinations.[40] Levinsohn attempts to delineate further the points at which Matthew chooses the 'nondevelopmental strategy' of asyndeton (and the 'historic present') rather than this 'default strategy'.

In the first edition of his *Discourse Features of New Testament Greek,*

λέγουσιν αὐτῷ, and so must be seen as a fixed combination with δέ. The association of δέ with thematic subjects is consistent with patterns of use of δέ in Matthew's narrative framework (see Chapter 5), but these four examples represent a significantly lower than expected frequency of δέ with present-tense λέγω than would be expected based on the use of δέ in narrative in general (7%, $z = -4.62$). Similarly, καί, although appearing 18 times, is found somewhat less frequently with present-tense λέγω than would be expected based on its use in the narrative framework as a whole (31%, $z = -2.46$; in each of these 18, λέγω is thematic). Only τότε, to a less dramatic extent than asyndeton, is found more frequently with λέγει/λέγουσιν than in narrative in general (11 instances: 19%, $z = 3.20$; λέγω is thematic in each occurrence but 15.12).

39. Levinsohn, *Discourse Features*, p. 217.
40. Levinsohn, *Discourse Features*, p. 218.

Levinsohn builds on Johnstone's proposal of a correlation between the 'historic present' and authority roles in speech margins in American English.[41] Levinsohn argues that where Matthew chooses to use the 'historic present', it is because one of the speakers in the exchange occupies an authority role:

> In the case of the developmental strategy (typically involving δέ and the articular pronoun), neither participant is credited with an authority role over against the other. However, when the nondevelopmental strategy is employed (typically involving the HP ['historic present'] and asyndeton), one participant is presented in an authority role over against the other.[42]

This early theory of Levinsohn's does not, however, stand up under a test case, an analysis of speech margins in Matthew's narrative framework in which Jesus himself is the speaker. It would be difficult to argue that the Evangelist is not presenting Jesus as an authority figure in his Gospel (see, for example, 7.28, 'For he was teaching them as one who had authority, and not as their scribes'). If the 'historic present' and asyndeton tend to be used where 'one participant is presented in an authority role over against the other', as Levinsohn contends, it is surprising that Jesus is the notional subject (grammaticalized or implied) less frequently in such sentences than in speech margins in general. Jesus is the explicit or implicit subject of the sentence, that is, the speaker, in about half (146/299, 49%) of the speech margins in Matthew's narrative framework, but in only about a third (9/26, 35%; $z = -1.45$) of the speech margins in which asyndeton and λέγει/λέγουσιν are used.[43] More tellingly, if in those instances where δέ and a pronominal article are used it is generally the case that 'neither

41. See B. Johnstone, ' "He Says ... So I Said": Verb Tense Alternation and Narrative Depictions of Authority in American English', *Linguistics* 25 (1987), pp. 33-52.

42. S.H. Levinsohn, *Discourse Features of New Testament Greek: A Coursebook* (Dallas: Summer Institute of Linguistics, 1992), pp. 148-49. Levinsohn goes beyond Johnstone's position by applying this distinction and the modifications of it that he identifies to each individual speech margin. Johnstone herself states that contrast between verbal tense-forms may not be used in all speech margins in a dialogue: 'For another thing, once a storyteller's audience gets a certain point, the teller does not need to keep making the point. It is possible, and I think it is sometimes the case, that a teller may mark status relations once or twice and then not keep marking them, once they are clear, until they change' (Johnstone, ' "He Says ... So I Said" ', p. 37).

43. Mt. 16.15, 18.22, 19.8, 20.23, 21.31, 21.42, 22.43, 26.25, 26.24. A sample size of less than 30 means that a z-score may not be a reliable indicator of statistical significance.

participant is credited with an authority role over against the other' it is difficult to explain why Jesus appears as the subject in such sentences more frequently than in speech margins in general. He is the speaker in nearly two-thirds (30/47, 64%; $z = 2.06$) of the speech margins in which δέ appears with a pronominal article.[44] His authority seems to be trans-parently on display in such contexts as his reply to the Pharisees who question the lawfulness of his actions on the Sabbath in 12.3-8 ('I tell you that one greater than the temple is here'), his rebuke of Peter in 16.23 ('Get behind me, Satan'), and his pronouncement of the greatest com-mandment in 22.37-40,[45] all of which have speech margins in which δέ and a pronominal article are used. Levinsohn's original solution appears to run counter to the data.

In the second edition of *Discourse Features*, Levinsohn turns from the notion of authority roles in Matthew's use of asyndeton and the 'historic present' to the suggestion that as 'a nondevelopmental way of conjoining sentences' asyndeton is 'used to conjoin reported speeches in Matthew's Gospel when the response to the speech concerned does not develop the conversation because it is *expected* or *predictable*'.[46] He adds that 'it is not unreasonable to consider that, when it is appropriate to begin a speech orienter with asyndeton, the HP ["historic present"] is automatically used as well'.[47] Unfortunately, Levinsohn's determination of what constitutes an 'expected' or 'predictable' response in these contexts suffers the same limitation that his notion of 'development' in Gospel narrative does (see on δέ, Chapter 5)—that is, Levinsohn offers no consistent criteria for 'expected' or 'predictable' responses, apparently basing each evaluation solely on his own reading of the passage, without reference to other formal markers or structures, or to ways in which other New Testament exegetes

44. Levinsohn offers several modifications of the so-called 'developmental strategy', one of which involves 'the inclusion of a participial form of ἀποκρίνομαι... indicating that the respondent to the previous speech has assumed an authority role or otherwise speaks with authority' (Levinsohn, *Discourse Features* [1992], p. 149). This would account for some of the instances in which Jesus is the speaker in a speech margin with δέ and a pronominal article. However, there are still 16 instances in which Jesus is the speaker and no participle of ἀποκρίνομαι appears: 9.12, 12.3, 12.11, 13.52, 14.16, 14.18, 14.29, 15.16 (but see textual variant), 15.23 (as noted above, arguably not a speech margin), 16.23, 17.20, 19.11, 19.17, 20.21, 22.37, 26.18.

45. Φημί is used here, in spite of the fact that Levinsohn says φημί shows less authority.

46. Levinsohn, *Discourse Features*, p. 235 (his emphasis).

47. Levinsohn, *Discourse Features*, p. 236.

have understood the passage.[48] For example, Levinsohn's first illustration is from Mt. 20.29-34, the healing of two blind men outside Jericho. In 20.33, the speech margin introducing the two men's response to Jesus' question 'What do you want me to do for you?' is asyndetic: λέγουσιν αὐτῷ· κύριε, ἵνα ἀνοιγῶσιν οἱ ὀφθαλμοὶ ἡμῶν. Levinsohn concludes that asyndeton occurs here because 'the response concerned is predictable and, therefore, *does not represent a new development in the conversation'*.[49] Yet in his commentary on Matthew's Gospel Hagner notes that Jesus' question 'is not for information but to provide an opportunity for the blind men to express their faith through their request'.[50] In a study of miracle story forms, Held observes that in Matthew's miracle stories, including this one, 'faith is expressed in the request; and Jesus acts in a way that corresponds to the suppliant's faith'.[51] Held suggests that Matthew uses conversational requests for healing, combined with other narrative features, 'to express that what faith desires is granted to it'.[52] The burden of proof lies with Levinsohn to show how such a request for healing is 'nondevelopmental' from the author's viewpoint. Until a more rigorous method of characterizing such discourse contexts is developed, Levinsohn's approach offers little as a way forward in characterizing Matthew's use of asyndeton and the 'historic present' in speech margins.

Further observations on asyndeton and λέγει/λέγουσιν. Nevertheless, Levinsohn is correct on at least two counts, the first being that <asyndeton + thematic λέγει/λέγουσιν> constitutes a speech-margin formula frequently used by the Evangelist which should be examined in opposition to δέ with a pronominal article—that is, that these two structures both belong to a system of speech margins in Matthew's narrative and have potentially differing discourse functions.

I have already shown that λέγω is the most frequently used verb in Matthew's narrative speech margins, and that the combination <asyndeton

---

48. An exception is Mt. 17.24-25, where Levinsohn notes that οὐ in the question in Mt. 17.24, ὁ διδάσκαλος ὑμῶν οὐ τελεῖ [τά] δίδραχμα;, anticipates a positive response in 17.25. More evidence of this type from other passages would strengthen Levinsohn's claim.

49. Levinsohn, *Discourse Features*, p. 236 (my emphasis).

50. Hagner, *Matthew 14–28*, p. 587.

51. H.J. Held, 'Matthew as Interpreter of the Miracle Stories', in G. Bornkamm, G. Barth and H.J. Held, *Tradition and Interpretation in Matthew* (trans. P. Scott; London: SCM, 1963), pp. 239-40.

52. Held, 'Miracle Stories', p. 240.

+ thematic λέγει/λέγουσιν> appears 26 times, or in nearly one out of ten speech margins in the narrative framework. By comparison, the combination <pronominal article + δέ + [ἀποκριθείς/ἀποκριθέντες] + εἶπεν/ εἶπον>, for example in 4.4, ὁ δὲ ἀποκριθεὶς εἶπεν· γέγραπται..., is a little more frequent, appearing 34 times, or in slightly more than one out of ten speech margins in the narrative framework (34/299, 11%). Δέ rarely occurs with present tense-form λέγω,[53] although overall δέ is the most frequent sentence conjunction when the Evangelist uses λέγω as a finite verb (83/186, 45%, $z = 2.57$), and is by far the most frequent when λέγω is used in an aorist tense-form (74/116, 64%, $z = 6.34$). In almost half of the instances in which δέ appears with εἶπεν/εἶπον a pronominal article is also present (34/74, 46%), as in 12.3, ὁ δὲ εἶπεν αὐτοῖς, Οὐκ ἀνέγνωτε τί ἐποίησεν Δαυὶδ ὅτε ἐπείνασεν καὶ οἱ μετ' αὐτοῦ... More than a third of these (14/34, 41%) include a participle of ἀποκρίνομαι, as in 13.11, ὁ δὲ ἀποκριθεὶς εἶπεν αὐτοῖς, Ὅτι ὑμῖν δέδοται γνῶναι τὰ μυστήρια τῆς βασιλείας τῶν οὐρανῶν... With or without an ἀποκρίνομαι particle, the speech-margin structure <pronominal article + δέ + [ἀποκριθείς/ἀποκριθέντες] + εἶπεν/εἶπον> is found in 34 sentences in Matthew's narrative framework.

There are also numerous instances of δέ with either a pronominal article or εἶπεν/εἶπον but not both (40 occurrences of δέ with εἶπεν in which the pronominal article is not used, and 13 other instances of δέ with a pronominal article in speech margins in which something other than εἶπεν appears), as well as 42 more examples in which εἶπεν/εἶπον appears with something other than δέ. Taken together the presence of δέ, the pronominal article and/or εἶπεν/εἶπον accounts for more than 40% (129/299) of all speech margins in Matthew's narrative framework and two-thirds (125/186) of those involving finite forms of λέγω.

At this point there is a danger of finding oneself awash in a sea of numbers. Nonetheless, the question remains—if the Evangelist tends to use narrative speech margins which consist of some variation on a combination of δέ, the pronominal article and/or εἶπεν/εἶπον, in what discourse contexts does he select instead the less common <asyndeton + thematic λέγει/λέγουσιν>, which displays none of these features?

Secondly, Levinsohn is correct in observing that asyndeton with the 'historic present', or rather, as we have seen, <asyndeton + thematic λέγει/ λέγουσιν>, occurs in what he calls 'tight-knit' conversation, and that it

---

53. There are only four instances in the narrative framework of δέ with present tense-form λέγω: 14.17, 17.20, 8.22, 21.16.

tends not to occur as the speech margin for the initial statement in a sequence.[54] That is to say, asyndeton and λέγει/λέγουσιν are found where there is close ongoing continuity within dialogue in the narrative framework. Although—given the flexibility of human language and the variety of semantic contexts within the narrative—it is not likely that strict rules for the Evangelist's use of asyndeton and present-tense finite λέγω can be delineated at anything near the level of detail Levinsohn attempts, I will add two further observations about the use of these speech margins in Matthew's narrative framework.

First, <asyndeton + thematic λέγει/λέγουσιν> is found in speech margins introducing replies to questions, as well as (to a lesser extent) those introducing questions and those introducing a final response in a question–reply–response sequence—in other words, asyndeton and λέγει/λέγουσιν are regularly found in relation to questions and answers. The example above, in which the Pharisees ask a clarifying question (19.7), Jesus replies (19.8), and Jesus' disciples respond in amazement at his pronouncement (19.10), illustrates this tendency. Uses of <asyndeton + thematic λέγει/λέγουσιν> in the narrative framework include:

- replying to a question (15 instances): 9.28, 13.51, 17.25, 18.22, 19.8, 20.21, 20.22, 20.33, 21.31, 21.41, 22.21, 22.42, 26.25, 26.64, 27.22;
- asking a question (6 instances): 16.15, 19.7, 19.18, 19.20, 21.42, 27.22;
- responding to a reply to a question (4 instances): 19.10, 20.23, 21.31, 22.43.

Along with one other occurrence (26.35, in which Peter replies to Jesus' prediction of his betrayal, with φημί in the speech margin of Jesus' prediction—see below on φημί), this accounts for all 26 uses of asyndeton with λέγει/λέγουσιν.

The crucial point is whether questions and answers are so common in Matthew's Gospel that the frequency of asyndeton in this discourse context has any statistical significance. This is difficult to establish quantitatively due to the complexity involved in creating a countable definition

---

54. Levinsohn defines a 'tight-knit' conversation as one in which 'each new speaker and addressee is drawn from the speakers and addressees of previous speeches of the conversation' and 'each successive speaker takes up the same topic as that of the previous speech and develops the conversation from the point at which the last speaker left off' (Levinsohn, *Discourse Features*, p. 215).

of what constitutes a question, what constitutes a reply, and how close a proximity of either to a speech margin would be required. (Should, for example, a question be counted which occurs as the third or fourth sentence in a sequence introduced by a single speech margin?[55]) Nevertheless, the Evangelist's tendency to reserve asyndeton and thematic λέγει/ λέγουσιν for use in the speech margins of question-and-answer sequences is readily apparent. This again is a context in which one would expect to find close continuity in the narrative framework.[56]

The second observation is that speech margins with asyndeton and λέγει/λέγουσιν appear predominantly in the second half of the Gospel (only 9.28 and 13.51 before ch. 16), with the largest cluster appearing in chs. 19–22.[57] These occur, alongside other speech-margin formats, in dialogues which tend to be characterized by conflict or confrontation, such as that in 20.20-23, where the mother of Zebedee's sons asks Jesus for special status for her sons:

20.21   ὁ δὲ εἶπεν αὐτῇ, τί θέλεις;
        λέγει αὐτῷ, εἰπὲ ἵνα καθίσωσιν οὗτοι οἱ δύο υἱοί μου εἷς ἐκ
        δεξιῶν σου καὶ εἷς ἐξ εὐωνύμων σου ἐν τῇ βασιλείᾳ σου.
20.22   ἀποκριθεὶς δὲ ὁ Ἰησοῦς εἶπεν, οὐκ οἴδατε τί αἰτεῖσθε. δύνασθε
        πιεῖν τὸ ποτήριον ὃ ἐγὼ μέλλω πίνειν;
        λέγουσιν αὐτῷ, Δυνάμεθα.
20.23   λέγει αὐτοῖς, Τὸ μὲν ποτήριόν μου πίεσθε...

In addition to the debate over divorce already cited above (19.3-12), see also Jesus' challenge to the rich young man (19.16-22); the aftermath of

---

55. This investigation is further hampered by the fact that the earliest manuscripts of the New Testament do not supply punctuation specifying when a sentence is a question, although the presence of an interrogative pronoun sometimes gives an indication. In this research I have followed the punctuation, that is, the designation of sentences as questions, of NA[27], but with the understanding that in some cases these editorial decisions may be open to debate.

56. BDF note that asyndeton occurs with λέγω and φημί in *The Shepherd of Hermas* as well as in the Gospels (BDF, §462). I observe that *Hermas* also offers examples of asyndeton and λέγει/λέγουσιν in question–reply–response sequences; see, for example, *Hermas, Vis* 1.3.3:

μετὰ τὸ παῆναι αὐτῆς τὰ ῥήματα ταῦτα λέγει μοι· Θέλεις ἀκοῦσαί μου
ἀναγινωσκούσης;
λέγω κἀγώ· Θέλω, κυρία.
λέγει μοι· Γενοῦ ἀκροατὴς καὶ ἄκουε τὰς δόξας τοῦ Θεοῦ.

57. Mt. 19.7, 19.8, 19.10, 19.18, 19.20, 20.21, 20.22, 20.23, 20.33, 21.31, 21.31, 21.41, 21.42, 22.21, 22.42, 22.43.

the parable of the vineyard and the tenants, which leads the Pharisees to plan Jesus' arrest (21.40-42); Jesus' deft avoidance of entrapment regarding the payment of taxes (22.15-22); and his challenge to the Pharisees concerning the identity of David's son (22.41-46). As above in the case of questions, it is nearly impossible to establish any statistical significance for <asyndeton + thematic λέγει/λέγουσιν> in situations of conflict or confrontation due to the complexity involved in creating countable definitions of the semantic features in such contexts. On the other hand, the nature of these dialogues and the clustering of asyndeton and λέγει/λέγουσιν in this portion of Matthew's narrative framework can be easily observed.

The Evangelist's increased use of asyndeton and λέγει/λέγουσιν at these points does not appear to be due to sources used in the composition of this part of the Gospel. Where there are parallels in the other Synoptic Gospels, asyndeton and λέγει/λέγουσιν do not appear. While 20.21-23 (above) has λέγουσιν αὐτῷ/λέγει αὐτοῖς, the Markan parallel, Mk 10.39, has οἱ δὲ εἶπαν αὐτῷ/ὁ δὲ Ἰησοῦς εἶπεν αὐτοῖς. For λέγουσιν αὐτῷ in 22.21, both Mk 12.16 and Lk. 20.24 have οἱ δὲ εἶπαν αὐτῷ.[58] In some instances the Evangelist adds speech margins to portray dialogue where the other Synoptic writers handle the section as running monologue.[59] <Asyndeton + thematic λέγει/λέγουσιν> in such contexts is a specifically Matthean feature.

Some narrative critics note that while the theme of conflict is present throughout the Gospel of Matthew, it is heightened as the Gospel progresses and Jesus' final appearance in Jerusalem nears.[60] It would not be surprising to find the Evangelist's manner of storytelling, that is, his lexical and syntactical choices whether intuitive or carefully selected, helping to portray the developing conflict within the narrative. <Asyndeton + thematic λέγει/λέγουσιν> in speech margins, making use of present

---

58. Similarly, for τότε with λέγει αὐτοῖς in Mt. 22.21, Mark has καὶ ἀποκριθεὶς ὁ Ἰησοῦς εἶπεν αὐτοῖς (Mk 12.17) and Luke has ὁ δὲ εἶπεν πρὸς αὐτούς (Lk. 20.25). But see καὶ λέγει in Mt. 22.12 = Mk 12.16.

59. See, for example, Mt. 19.18 = Mk 10.19 = Lk. 18.20; Mt. 21.41 = Mk 12.9 = Lk. 20.15-16; Mt. 22.42-43 = Mk 12.35-36 = Lk. 20.41-42.

60. See, for example, J.D. Kingsbury, *Matthew as Story* (Philadelphia: Fortress Press, 2nd edn, 1988), pp. 118-25, who describes the conflict between Jesus and the Jewish religious leaders as 'erupting' in 11.2–16.20, and being sustained at a high level in 16.21–28.20, with a direct confrontation in 19.3-9 and 'the last great confrontation' in 21.12–22.46.

tense-forms as a more marked form in narrative and the close continuity represented both by asyndeton and by the thematization of the verb, could be part of the means used to adjust the flow of the narrative (presumably to quicken its tempo) to reflect the underlying tension building to a climax.[61]

Asyndeton and thematic φημί. Although φημί occurs only 11 times in Matthew's narrative framework, the semantic contexts in which it is used are worth noting.[62] In the five instances where φημί is thematic, asyndeton occurs.[63] Δέ is used in another five instances when some other element is thematic, in line with its general patterns of use with non-verbal themes in the narrative framework. In four of these the thematic element is the subject (14.8, 22.37 and 27.23 with a pronominal article; 27.11 with ὁ Ἰησοῦς), and in one a genitive absolute participle (17.26, εἰπόντος δέ, the only time in the narrative framework λέγω appears as an aorist participle). Καί appears in the remaining example (8.8, καὶ ἀποκριθεὶς ὁ ἑκατόνταρχος ἔφη). All the occurrences of φημί, with the exception of the present tense-form in 14.8, are imperfect or aorist.[64]

---

61. On the use of present tense-forms in past referring narrative, see Robertson, *Grammar*, pp. 866-69; BDF, §321; Turner, *Syntax*, pp. 60-62; Porter, *Verbal Aspect*, p. 196; Porter, *Idioms*, p. 31; Fanning, *Verbal Aspect*, pp. 226-39; McKay, *Syntax of the Verb*, p. 42. On its use in Matthew specifically, see Luz, *Matthew 1–7*, p. 52; Black, 'Historic Present', pp. 120-39.

62. Mt. 4.7, 8.8, 14.8, 17.26, 19.21, 21.27, 22.37, 26.34, 27.11, 27.23, 27.65.

63. Mt. 4.7, 19.21, 21.27, 26.34, 27.65.

64. That is, as Robertson concedes, 'It is not always possible to decide' (Robertson, *Grammar*, pp. 310-11). See also BDF, §99. Porter argues, however, that φημί is not *ambiguous* with respect to aorist and imperfect forms, but (like εἰμί) is in fact 'vague'—that is, that φημί lacks the morphological distinctions which most verbs evidence because 'certain aspectual or tense differentiations were not developed, or at least were not developed fully by speakers' (Porter, *Verbal Aspect*, p. 446). Although εἰμί is omitted from my analyses of sentence conjunction and verbal tense-form, φημί is included, with the special handling described here. The finite forms in which it appears in Matthew's Gospel are treated as 'present tense-form' (unaugmented) or 'not present tense-form' (augmented). For the purposes of quantitative analysis, the ten augmented instances of φημί in Mt. 4.7, 8.8, 17.26, 19.21, 21.27, 22.37, 26.34, 27.11, 27.23 and 27.65 are classified in the field for verbal tense-form in the database as 'aorist'. This is simply a matter of methodological expediency, based on the assumption that ten indeterminate forms would have less statistical impact on the set of 553 aorist finite forms in Matthew's narrative framework than on the set of 57 imperfect forms, and is not meant as a determination of the morphological or aspectual status of φημί in any particular instance of its use in Matthew's Gospel.

These 11 speech margins all seem to introduce important statements or pronouncements, generally in response to a question or challenge. In seven of them Jesus is the subject of the verb, that is, the speaker; in two Pilate is the subject (27.23, asking 'What evil has he done?'; 27.65, ordering 'Take a guard... Go, make the tomb as secure as you know how'); in one it is the daughter of Herodias demanding John the Baptist's head on a platter (14.8, the only present tense-form, and unusual in that the speech margin comes in the middle of the direct speech); and in one it is the centurion confessing his understanding of Jesus' authority (8.8, the only occurrence with καί). The statements by Jesus include a reply to Satan during his temptation in the wilderness (4.7, 'Do not test the Lord your God'); his statement to Peter that the sons of kings are free from taxes (17.26, a reference to his own identity); his challenge to the rich young man to sell all he has and follow him (19.21); his refusal to tell the chief priests and elders by whose authority he acts (21.27); his pronouncement of the greatest commandment (22.37); his prediction of Peter's denial (26.34); and his response to Pilate's question, 'Are you the King of the Jews?' (27.11). Φημί should therefore be understood as a highly marked choice for a speech margin in comparison to λέγω.

In a pattern of use similar to that of asyndetic λέγει/λέγουσιν, speech margins with φημί appear with more frequency later in the Gospel (only 4.17 and 8.8 before ch. 14), alongside other speech-margin formats in dialogues which tend to be characterized by conflict or confrontation. Φημί, with and without asyndeton, can be found in combination with <asyndeton + thematic λέγει/λέγουσιν> interspersing the more common ὁ δέ...εἶπεν in several such dialogues, as in Jesus' challenge to the rich young man in 19.16-22, where λέγω is used in the young man's replies to Jesus' questions (19.18, 19.20) and φημί in Jesus' final pronouncement to him to sell all he has and follow Jesus (19.21):[65]

19.16 Καὶ ἰδοὺ εἷς προσελθὼν αὐτῷ εἶπεν, Διδάσκαλε, τί ἀγαθὸν ποιήσω ἵνα σχῶ ζωὴν αἰώνιον;

19.17 ὁ δὲ εἶπεν αὐτῷ, Τί με ἐρωτᾷς περὶ τοῦ ἀγαθοῦ; εἷς ἐστιν ὁ ἀγαθός· εἰ δὲ θέλεις εἰς τὴν ζωὴν εἰσελθεῖν, τήρησον τὰς ἐντολάς.

19.18 λέγει αὐτῷ, Ποίας;
ὁ δὲ Ἰησοῦς εἶπεν, Τὸ Οὐ φονεύσεις, Οὐ μοιχεύσεις, Οὐ κλέψεις, Οὐ ψευδομαρτυρήσεις,

---

65. See also 26.31-35 and 27.21-23; compare as well 26.64, λέγει αὐτῷ ὁ Ἰησοῦς, Σὺ εἶπας, and the subsequent 27.11, ὁ δὲ Ἰησοῦς ἔφη, Σὺ λέγεις.

19.19   Τίμα τὸν πατέρα καὶ τὴν ματέρα, καί, Ἀγαπήσεις τὸν
        πλησίον σου ὡς σεαυτόν.

19.20   λέγει αὐτῷ ὁ νεανίσκος, Πάντα ταῦτα ἐφύλαξα· τί ἔτι
        ὑστερῶ;

19.21   ἔφη αὐτῷ ὁ Ἰησοῦς, Εἰ θέλεις τέλειος εἶναι, ὕπαγε πώλησόν
        σου τὰ ὑπάρχοντα καὶ δὸς [τοῖς] πτωχοῖς, καὶ ἕξεις
        θησαυρὸν ἐν οὐρανοῖς, καὶ δεῦρο ἀκολούθει μοι.

19.20   ἀκούσας δὲ ὁ νεανίσκος τὸν λόγον ἀπῆλθεν λυπούμενος· ἦν
        γὰρ ἔχων κτήματα πολλά.

As with <asyndeton + thematic λέγει/λέγουσιν> in speech margins, the use of the more marked φημί, along with the close continuity signaled by asyndeton when it occurs, could be among the lexical and syntactical choices the Evangelist makes—not necessarily consciously, but as an intuitive aspect of good storytelling—to adjust the flow or tempo of the narrative and to highlight significant pronouncements as the element of conflict in the Gospel builds to a climax.

Asyndeton with repetition. A somewhat different context in which asyndeton occurs in speech margins in Matthew's narrative framework is alongside the repetition of similar words and/or syntactical structures. This usage is more common in other discourse types than in narrative, where it appears only infrequently. As mentioned above, Winer remarks on the occurrence of asyndeton in the Sermon on the Mount, where he notes its use to begin new subunits.[66] Its use with repeated elements in exposition is conspicuous, for example, in the Beatitudes (5.3-11), where μαχάριοι is repeated nine times without a conjunction (lexical repetition), and the Lord's Prayer (6.9-13), where the first four imperatives are juxtaposed without a conjunction (syntactical repetition). In Matthew's narrative framework there are two sets of examples which are similarly asyndetic, both of which can be broadly construed as speech margins: with the combination of ὁμοίως καί and λέγω in 26.35 and 27.41, and in the introduction of repeated parables in 13.24, 13.31, 13.33, 13.34.

Asyndeton + ὁμοίως καί + *subject* + λέγω. Alongside the more common use of asyndeton in speech margins with thematic present-tense λέγω, asyndeton also occurs twice with other tense-forms of λέγω, both times combined with ὁμοίως καί: an aorist form in 26.35, λέγει αὐτῷ ὁ Πέτρος... ὁμοίως καὶ πάντες οἱ μαθηταὶ εἶπαν, where the other disciples echo Peter's assurances that he will not deny Jesus; and an

66. See Winer, *Treatise*, p. 674.

imperfect form in 27.41, ὁμοίως καὶ οἱ ἀρχιερεῖς ἐμπαίζοντες μετὰ τῶν γραμματέων καὶ πρεσβυτέρων ἔλεγον..., where the chief priests, scribes and elders, like the other bystanders, deride Jesus on the cross (27.39-40, οἱ δὲ παραπορευόμενοι ἐβλασφήμουν αὐτὸν...καὶ λέγοντες...). These are the only appearances of ὁμοίως καί in the narrative framework, and both come at significant points in the passion narrative (but see 22.26 for a similar use in a reported narrative, the Sadducees' story of a woman married seven times). Both have close Markan parallels: Mt. 26.35 = Mk 14.31, ὡσαύτως δὲ καὶ πάντες ἔλεγον; Mt. 27.41 = Mk 15.31, ὁμοίως καὶ οἱ ἀρχιερεῖς ἐμπαίζοντες πρὸς ἀλλήλους μετὰ τῶν γραμματέων ἔλεγον...

In the two uses in Matthew's narrative framework the structure is <asyndeton + ὁμοίως καί + subject + [participle] + λέγω>. Not only does λέγω appear in a different tense-form than in the more frequent <asyndeton + thematic λέγει/λέγουσιν> (aorist in 26.35, and imperfect in 27.41), but the constituent order is reversed as well. These sentences are SV rather than VS, presumably due to the emphasis on who is speaking in the same manner as previous speakers.

It may be argued that ὁμοίως καί is itself the grammatical connector, and that this is not a true instance of asyndeton. There is some merit to this suggestion, especially given the presence of καί. However, ὁμοίως conveys conceptual, truth-conditional meaning, or, in other words, meaning which adds to the content of the proposition itself. In this context ὁμοίως conveys information about what was said—specifically, that the comments were similar in content and manner to those of previous speakers—rather than functioning primarily to join propositions as do sentence conjunctions and comparable discourse markers. Similarly, in these examples sentence-internal καί does not primarily serve to link together two propositions, signaling procedural meaning (continuity in the discourse) as does sentence-initial καί, but rather communicates the conceptual information that additional speakers ('all the disciples' in 26.32; 'the chief priests, scribes and elders' in 27.41) are participants in the action at this point. The additional presence of δέ as a sentence conjunction in the Markan parallel to 26.35 (Mk 14.31, ὡσαύτως δὲ καὶ πάντες) further suggests that καί itself is not understood as a sentence conjunction in this context.[67]

---

67. A similar and more difficult question arises with respect to πάλιν, which has been classified as a sentence conjunction for the purposes of this research. It occurs

Asyndeton + repeated forms. Asyndeton is also found at one point in the narrative framework where a feature in the discourse is repeated—specifically, structuring the collection of parables in ch. 13 and reiterating that Jesus used parables to speak to the crowds:

13.24   Ἄλλην παραβολὴν παρέθηκεν αὐτοῖς λέγων...
13.31   Ἄλλην παραβολὴν παρέθηκεν αὐτοῖς λέγων...
13.33   Ἄλλην παραβολὴν ἐλάλησεν αὐτοῖς·...
13.34   ταῦτα πάντα ἐλάλησεν ὁ Ἰησοῦς ἐν παραβολαῖς τοῖς ὄχλοις
        καὶ χωρὶς παραβολῆς οὐδὲν ἐλάλει αὐτοῖς...

In each instance the structure is <asyndeton + thematic direct object + aorist tense-form verb>, again differing from the more common <asyndeton + thematic λέγει/λέγουσιν>, but still serving as a type of speech margin (λέγω is used in 13.24 and 13.31, λαλέω in 13.33 and 13.34). Together, lexical repetition (παραβολή), syntactical repetition (thematic direct object and aorist tense-form verb) and asyndeton serve as mutually reinforcing linguistic elements conveying the close continuity in topic and structure of this portion of Matthew's Gospel.

Other Uses: Asyndeton with Thematic οὗτος

At four points in Matthew's narrative framework, asyndeton is used in a somewhat different manner in a continuous context—with a form of οὗτος as the first element in the clause:[68]

twice in Matthew's narrative framework, in 4.8 and again in 26.42. In clause-initial position, is it a discourse connective that has been derived from the class of adverbs in a manner analogous to τότε? That is, has it lost most of its adverbial (i.e. conceptual) force conveying that a specific *action* is being repeated, in favor of usage as a non-truth-conditional discourse connective signaling that *a structure or form within the discourse* is being repeated, specifically a temptation sequence in 4.8 and a prayer sequence in 26.42? Πάλιν also appears four times in parables, a narrative form within exposition. In 13.45 and 13.47 it appears to function as a discourse connective signaling that a structure or form within the discourse is being repeated, that is, a parable, but in 21.36 and 22.4 it appears to function adverbially, conveying the information that the action of sending servants is being repeated. Where πάλιν is understood as an adverb its use would be an example of <asyndeton + πάλιν> in the type of narrative repetition discussed in the following section.

68. Mt. 13.34, which has been treated under the topic of repetition, also has a form of οὗτος. Of the four instances here, only 10.5 functions as a speech margin. With respect to synoptic parallels, Mt. 27.46 is similar to Mk 15.34 (ὅ ἐστιν μεθερμηνευόμενον), and Mt. 27.58 = Lk. 23.52.

10.5   τούτους τοὺς δώδεκα ἀπέστειλεν ὁ Ἰησοῦς παραγγείλας
       αὐτοῖς λέγων· εἰς ὁδὸν ἐθνῶν μὴ ἀπέλθητε καὶ εἰς πόλιν
       Σαμαριτῶν μὴ εἰσέλθητε·
27.32 τοῦτον ἠγγάρευσαν ἵνα ἄρῃ τὸν σταυρὸν αὐτοῦ.
27.46 τοῦτ᾽ ἔστιν θεέ μου θεέ μου, ἱνατί με ἐγκατέλιπες;
27.58 οὗτος προσελθὼν τῷ Πιλάτῳ ᾐτήσατο τὸ σῶμα τοῦ Ἰησοῦ.

Blass, Debrunner and Funk observe, 'Those instances in which a new sentence is begun with a demonstrative pronoun or adverb referring to something preceding are not, strictly speaking, to be considered asyndeton'.[69] Nor, I might add, are the examples above, strictly speaking, to be considered new sentences. In particular, in the three uses in ch. 27 (27.32, where Simon of Cyrene is forced to carry Jesus' cross; 27.46, where a translation of Jesus' final cry is introduced by τοῦτ᾽ ἔστιν; and 27.58, where Joseph of Arimathea asks Pilate for Jesus' body) the tight connection between the clause introduced by asyndetic οὗτος and the preceding material suggests treating these clauses as extensions of a sentence, similar to a relative clause with οὗτος filling the slot of the relative pronoun.[70] The potential ambiguity is evidenced in the NA[27] editors' decision to punctuate 27.58 as a new sentence—possibly based on the fact that it is the only nominative form of the three—but 27.32 and 27.46 as continuations.

Particularly interesting is 10.5, which the UBS editors treat as the beginning of a new pericope under the title 'The Commissioning of the Twelve' but which arguably could be understood as the continuation of 10.2, the sense being, 'The names of the twelve apostles are…which twelve Jesus sent out…'[71] The anaphoric nature of οὗτος as a lexical choice in τούτους τοὺς δώδεκα ἀπέστειλεν, particularly as the phrase echoes the unusual thematic genitive phrase τῶν δὲ δώδεκα ἀποστόλων in 10.2, implies a certain degree of continuity, similar to the way the NA[27] editors treat 27.32. On the other hand, the choice of asyndeton and a non-verbal theme, the combination of οὗτος with a noun (its only attributive use among the four examples), and its discourse context as the speech margin for Jesus' 'commissioning speech' of ch. 10, suggest some measure of discontinuity. Of all the instances of asyndeton in Matthew's narrative framework, it is 10.5 that potentially bridges the polarity between continuous and discontinuous use in narrative.

69. BDF, §459.
70. See especially 27.58, where the οὗτος clause follows and parallels a relative clause, each giving information about Joseph of Arimathea.
71. The NA[27] editors similarly treat 10.5 as a new sentence beginning a new paragraph.

Summary
Although Matthew's choices of asyndeton with repetition and with οὗτος show that there is indeed variety in his use of asyndeton in continuous contexts, it is speech margins—especially those with thematic λέγει/ λέγουσιν—which constitute the most frequent type of asyndetic sentence in the narrative framework. These speech margins occur in closely connected dialogue, often forming the margins of question–reply–response sequences. Similarly, of the 11 times φημί is used in speech margins, asyndeton occurs whenever the verb is thematic. Φημί is used to introduce important statements or pronouncements, generally in response to a question or challenge, and should therefore be understood as a highly marked choice for a speech margin in comparison to λέγω. I have noted that asyndetic speech margins with thematic λέγει/λέγουσιν or φημί appear more frequently later in the Gospel. It may be that this combination of features helps to convey the conflict which some scholars see becoming stronger as the narrative progresses.

'Discontinuous' Use

At the opposite end of the continuity–discontinuity spectrum from the asyndetic speech margins considered above, asyndeton is also found where breaks in the flow of Matthew's narrative framework—sometimes major breaks—occur. This 'discontinuous' use of asyndeton is somewhat less frequent than its use to convey close continuity, accounting for a little more than a quarter of asyndetic sentences in Matthew's narrative framework (16/57, 28%). Here again one finds characteristic collocations with constituent order and verbal tense-form, this time differing sharply from thematic present tense-form λέγω or thematic φημί in speech margins. When asyndeton occurs at points of discontinuity in the narrative, aorist (or occasionally imperfect, but never present) tense-forms are used. Either SV or V(S) constituent order may appear at these breaks, but there is no instance of a thematic verb. Again the Evangelist supplies mutually reinforcing lexical and syntactic elements to help guide the audience in their mental representation of the discourse. In turn, the audience makes use of such mutually redundant cues to disambiguate the function of asyndeton in context.

Title and First Sentence
There is no conjunction beginning what is often arranged on the page as the first clause in the Gospel of Matthew: 1.1, Βίβλος γενέσεως' Ιησοῦ

Χριστοῦ υἱοῦ Δαυὶδ υἱοῦ Ἀβραάμ. This nominal construction functions as an introductory formula or title for the Gospel which follows, and is not linked to any previous discourse.[72]

Nor is there any conjunction beginning the next sentence linking it back to this first clause, further evidence that the previous clause is a title or introductory formula of some sort and that here in fact is the real beginning of the narrative: 1.2, Ἀβραὰμ ἐγέννησεν τὸν Ἰσαάκ... At this point of full discontinuity (that is, the opening of a new discourse at 1.2), asyndeton is the logical choice. Already we see differences in constituent order and verbal tense-form from those which characterize the close continuity of speech margins. The subject in 1.2 is thematic and the verbal tense-form is aorist. The remainder of the genealogy in 1.2-16 continues with a series of sentences with thematic subjects (except for the temporal indicator μετὰ τὴν μετοικεσίαν Βαβυλῶνος in 1.12, also thematic), each having δέ as the sentence conjunction. This is in keeping with the use of δέ with change of actor or temporal shift seen elsewhere in the narrative framework, and is the expected choice once past the first clause in the discourse.

Asyndeton at Narrative Breaks

Asyndeton, often in combination with a formulaic phrase or a genitive absolute participle, is found at a number of points within Matthew's Gospel which appear to be breaks in the flow of the narrative framework.

Asyndeton + ἐν ἐκείνῳ... Scholars have long noted that Matthew is fond of repetition and formulaic phrases. Von Dobschütz observes that 'when Matthew has once found a formula he sticks to it as much as possible, and uses it repeatedly'.[73] One of the most frequent of these is 'in that time/ day/hour', which appears with minor variations eight times in Matthew's narrative framework but in none of the Synoptic parallels:[74]

---

72. Kingsbury argues that 1.1 is not a title for the whole Gospel, but instead functions as a superscription for 1.1–4.16 (Kingsbury, *Matthew: Structure*, pp. 9-10). Even if Kingsbury is correct, because it lacks a link to any previous discourse the motivation for 1.1 to be asyndetic remains the same.

73. E. von Dobschütz, 'Matthew as Rabbi and Catechist (1928)', in Stanton (ed.), *Interpretation*, p. 28.

74. At one or two points Matthew uses a variation on this formula where the other Synoptic writers have a construction with ἐγένετο: see Mt. 12.1 = Mk 2.23 = Lk. 6.1; and possibly Mt. 13.1 = Lk. 5.1.

3.1   Ἐν δὲ ταῖς ἡμέραις ἐκείναις παραγίνεται Ἰωάννης ὁ
βαπτιστὴς κηρύσσων ἐν τῇ ἐρήμῳ τῆς Ἰουδαίας...

11.25 Ἐν ἐκείνῳ τῷ καιρῷ ἀποκριθεὶς ὁ Ἰησοῦς εἶπεν...

12.1   Ἐν ἐκείνῳ τῷ καιρῷ ἐπορεύθη ὁ Ἰησοῦς τοῖς σάββασιν διὰ
τῶν σπορίμων...

13.1   Ἐν τῇ ἡμέρᾳ ἐκείνῃ ἐξελθὼν ὁ Ἰησοῦς τῆς οἰκίας ἐκάθητο παρὰ
τὴν θάλασσαν...

14.1   Ἐν ἐκείνῳ τῷ καιρῷ ἤκουσεν Ἡρῴδης ὁ τετραάρχης τὴν
ἀκοὴν Ἰησοῦ...

18.1   Ἐν ἐκείνῃ τῇ ὥρᾳ προσῆλθον οἱ μαθηταὶ τῷ Ἰησοῦ λέγοντες...

22.23 Ἐν ἐκείνῃ τῇ ἡμέρᾳ προσῆλθον αὐτῷ Σαδδουκαῖοι, λέγοντες
μὴ εἶναι ἀνάστασιν, καὶ ἐπηρώτησαν αὐτόν...

26.55 Ἐν ἐκείνῃ τῇ ὥρᾳ εἶπεν ὁ Ἰησοῦς τοῖς ὄχλοις...

Some scholars assume Semitic influence in Matthew's variations on this phrase. Some note that the formula functions at points of transition in the narrative framework rather than designating a specific time. For example, von Dobschütz recognizes that Matthew uses ἐν ἐκείνῳ τῷ καιρῷ 'without chronological precision simply as a transition'.[75] Davies and Allison believe that in Matthew's use of the formula 'imitation of the LXX seems certain'.[76] In their comments on 12.1 they write, 'The phrase is not intended to supply chronological information but to serve as a thematic bridge...'[77] According to Luz, 'Phrases such as ἐν ἐκείνῳ τῷ καιρῷ and the like appear exactly where there is a new beginning in content and have the function of a bridge and of establishing the impression of a seamless run of the narrative (e.g. 3.1; 12.1; 14.1)'.[78] The image of ἐν ἐκείνῳ τῷ καιρῷ and its variants as a bridge, used both by Davies and Allison and by Luz, suggests that although there is at some level a new beginning in the events narrated, there is not a complete disjuncture in the structure of the narrative itself.

That these phrases tend to be found at points in the Gospel of Matthew

75. Von Dobschütz, 'Rabbi and Cathechist', p. 31.

76. Davies and Allison, *Matthew*, I, p. 82. They cite parallels in Exod. 32.28; Deut. 10.1, 8; Josh. 24.33.

77. W.D. Davies and D.C. Allison, *A Critical and Exegetical Commentary on the Gospel According to Saint Matthew*. II. *Commentary on Matthew VIII–XVIII* (ICC; Edinburgh: T. & T. Clark, 1991), p. 305.

78. Luz, *Matthew 1–7*, p. 37. 'Wendungen wie ἐν ἐκείνῳ τῷ καιρῷ u.ä. tauchen gerade dort auf, wo inhaltlich ein Neueinsatz vorliegt, und haben die Funkton, zu überbrücken und den Eindruck eines lückenlosen Erzählungsablaufs herzustellen ...' (U. Luz, *Das Evangelium nach Matthäus*. I. *Mt 1–7* [EKKNT, I.1; Zürich: Benziger Verlag, 1985], p. 19).

traditionally seen as significant breaks in the narrative is underscored by the fact that those who superimposed on the text the now standard chapter and verse divisions understood a number of such occurrences as marking the beginning of new chapters: 3.1 (the only use which is not asyndetic and the only one in which the time reference is plural), 12.1, 13.1, 14.1 and 18.1. In 3.1, the birth narrative ends and Jesus' public ministry is anticipated with the introduction of John the Baptist;[79] in 13.1, an important collection of parables on the kingdom of heaven begins; in 14.1, following the formula in 13.53, καὶ ἐγένετο ὅτε ἐτέλεσεν ὁ Ἰησοῦς τὰς παραβολὰς ταύτας...there is a transition from the parable collection to a long section of primarily narrative material in chs. 14–17; then in 18.1, there is a transition from that long narrative section to the so-called 'community discourse' of ch. 18. On the other hand, 12.1 occurs in the middle of what is often understood as one primarily narrative section comprising chs. 11 and 12—although Davies and Allison observe that in these chapters 'certain thematic units seem obvious enough'. They also note that ch. 11 appears to narrate the events of a single day, while ch. 12 contains six episodes with six transitional phrases (12.1, 9, 15, 22, 38, 46).[80]

The question remains whether the other three occurrences (11.25, 22.23, 26.55, with 11.25 and 26.55 also functioning as speech margins with εἶπεν) also represent some kind of break in the narrative. At 11.25, Jesus' recitation of woes against the cities who did not repent on the basis of his 'mighty works' ends and his address to the Father begins. The prayer's connection to the preceding series of woes is not completely clear, and although it is introduced by ἀποκριθεὶς ὁ Ἰησοῦς εἶπεν, it is by no means obvious to whom or to what question the prayer is understood as an answer. In the Lukan parallel (Lk. 10.13-24), in between the series of woes and Jesus' prayer Luke has inserted or retained the return of the seventy(-two?) disciples sent out by Jesus and his response to their joyful

---

79. Mt. 3.1 is distinct, not merely with respect to the presence of δέ nor because it contains the only plural referent ('days' rather than 'day/time/hour'), but in that it introduces 3.1-6, a unit in which only present and imperfect tense-form verbs appear in the narrative framework, in what must be considered a highly marked sequence. Kingsbury argues that the presence of δέ rather than asyndeton in 3.1 is important in linking the appearance of John and the baptism of Jesus to the preceding infancy narrative so that 1.1–4.16 forms a unified section of the Gospel (Kingsbury, *Matthew: Structure*, pp. 12-13).

80. Davies and Allison, *Matthew*, I, pp. 67-68. Of these six phrases, only 12.1 and 12.46 are asyndetic.

report. Lk. 10.21 (= Mt. 11.25) then begins with ἐν αὐτῇ ὥρᾳ, the closest parallel in the Synoptics of a phrase similar to Matthew's formula, and also asyndetic. This leads to two conjectures which, if correct, might help to explain the presence of Matthew's asyndetic ἐν ἐκείνῳ τῷ καιρῷ here. First, Matthew and Luke's common source may have placed the series of woes and Jesus' prayer at some distance from each other, as is evidenced both by Luke's retention (or insertion) of other material and by the awkwardness of ἀποκριθείς in Matthew's version. Secondly, the source may have had this formula or something similar introducing the prayer, accounting for the phrases used by Matthew and Luke. We can tentatively surmise both that Jesus' prayer is understood by Matthew as a unit discontinuous with the recitation of woes it follows, and that if there is not as strong a break as that generally represented by Matthew's use of ἐν ἐκείνῳ τῷ καιρῷ, the usage here is influenced by existing sources.

However, the occurrences in 22.23 and 26.55 cannot be quite so easily explained as significant breaks. In 22.23 asyndetic ἐν ἐκείνῃ τῇ ἡμέρᾳ begins the second in a series of attempts by Jewish leaders to entrap Jesus—first concerning taxes (22.15-22), now regarding resurrection (22.23-33), next concerning the greatest commandment (22.34-40)—followed by Jesus' question to them concerning the relationship between David and the Messiah (22.41-46). All three Synoptic Gospels have these four interactions (Mt. 22.15-46 = Mk 12.13-37 = Lk. 20.20-38, 10.25-28, 20.39-44), with Mark and Matthew showing the same order and Luke having one variation in their order,[81] which suggests that the material was understood to belong together. Matthew's use of asyndetic ἐν ἐκείνῃ τῇ ἡμέρᾳ in 22.23 may be said to introduce a new pericope within the larger unit, but not a major break in the narrative.

In 26.55 there appears to be even less discontinuity. Here asyndetic ἐν ἐκείνῃ τῇ ὥρᾳ appears in the speech margin of Jesus' rhetorical question to the crowd who comes to arrest him: ὡς ἐπὶ λῃστὴν ἐξήλθατε μετὰ μαχαιρῶν καὶ ξύλων συλλαβεῖν με; (Mt. 26.55 = Mk 14.48 = Lk. 22.52; neither of the other Synoptic speech margins is asyndetic). This saying of Jesus is identical in each of the Synoptics except that Luke omits συλλαβεῖν με. At this point in the narrative, after a brief insertion of material not found in the other Gospels (the elaboration in 26.52-54 of Jesus' command to Peter to put away his sword), Matthew returns to the common tradition, the point at which Jesus' pronouncement against the

---

81. The single exception is the question about the greatest commandment, which is placed elsewhere in Luke's Gospel.

mob and (in Matthew and Mark) his declaration of the fulfillment of the Scriptures begins. In this context ἐν ἐκείνῃ τῇ ὥρᾳ can at best be said to signal a new (and important) subunit within the pericope—still a point of discontinuity—but neither a new pericope nor a major break in the narrative.

The range of discourse contexts in which 'in that time/day/hour' functions in Matthew's narrative framework serves as warning against the desire to force a given discourse marker such as this asyndetic Matthean formula into service as a marker of a particular and consistent hierarchical level within the narrative. Certainly there is an observable tendency for 'in that time/day/hour' to mark higher-level breaks in the narrative. At the same time, however, the formula should be understood to have a range of usage in terms of discourse hierarchy: it generally marks higher-level breaks, but can range down to more local discontinuities in the narrative framework. More importantly, the sense of hierarchy itself may be relative rather than absolute. That is, the significance of higher and lower 'levels' of discourse may be seen by the Evangelist as holding primarily within the local context (however largely defined), rather than there being a global scheme of 'level A/level B/level C' and so forth imposed consistently on the Gospel as a whole.

Still, 'in that time/day/hour' invariably appears at points of some discontinuity, never within a continuous sequence of action or dialogue. And seven of the eight instances of this formula are asyndetic. Although VS constituent order predominates (SV order only in 11.25, and there a participle precedes the subject in the common construction ἀποκριθεὶς ὁ Ἰησοῦς εἶπεν), in none of them is the verb thematic, the formula phrase itself being the thematic element in the sentence. In the seven asyndetic occurrences, the verbal tense-form is aorist or imperfect, never present. Here again one can observe differences in constituent order and verbal tense-form from those which characterize asyndetic sentences in continuous discourse. As with the other sentence conjunctions I have examined, it is not just the choice of asyndeton, but the interrelated choices of asyndeton, the thematized formula 'in that time/day/hour', and verbal tense-form (and presumably other as yet unidentified features) which mutually signal mid- to higher-level discontinuity in Matthew's narrative framework and guide the audience to initiate a new segment in their mental representation of the discourse.

Asyndeton + ἀπὸ τότε... Another of the Evangelist's asyndetic formulae, ἀπὸ τότε ἤρξατο ὁ Ἰησοῦς... (4.17 and 16.21), has attracted a great deal of comment ever since Kingsbury, building on the suggestions of earlier scholars such as Lohmeyer, Stonehouse and Krentz, argued that its presence in these verses marks the division of Matthew into three major parts, 1.1–4.16, 4.17–16.20 and 16.21–28.20.[82]

Scholars disagree over whether the presence of ἀπὸ τότε ἤρξατο ὁ Ἰησοῦς in 4.17 and 16.21 reflects a tripartite scheme for the Gospel as a whole. One critique of Kingsbury's proposal has been that ἀπὸ τότε appears not only at these two points but also in 26.16, καὶ ἀπὸ τότε ἐζήτει εὐκαιρίαν ἵνα αὐτὸν παραδῷ, referring to Judas Iscariot's arrangement with the chief priests to betray Jesus to them, and that it should therefore not be understood as a structural feature which only signals major breaks in the narrative.[83] However, beyond noting the presence of καί in 26.16, critics by and large treat ἀπὸ τότε in isolation, rather than recognizing that features from different linguistic systems tend to reinforce continuity or discontinuity in the narrative. The occurrences in 4.17 and 16.21 are asyndetic and have SV constituent order, features which in combination with a non-verbal theme (ἀπὸ τότε as the first element in these sentences) tend to serve as mutually redundant signals of discontinuity in Matthew's narrative framework. On the other hand, in 26.16 one not only finds καί as the sentence conjunction but also a monolectic verb (that is, no grammaticalized subject), two features which tend to serve as mutually redundant signals of continuity in the narrative framework.[84] Although by virtue of lexical choice ἀπὸ τότε in 26.16 does indicate something happening from that point in time—specifically Judas

---

82. See Kingsbury, *Matthew: Structure*, especially pp. 7-25; also E. Lohmeyer, *Das Evangelium des Matthäus* (Göttingen: Vandenhoeck & Ruprecht, 1956), pp. 7*-10*; N.B. Stonehouse, *The Witness of Matthew and Mark to Christ* (London: Tyndale, 1944), pp. 129-31; E. Krentz, 'The Extent of Matthew's Prologue,' *JBL* 83 (1964), pp. 409-14. For a survey of critical responses to Kingsbury (albeit by an author sympathetic to Kingsbury's view), see D.R. Bauer, *The Structure of Matthew's Gospel: A Study in Literary Design* (JSNTSup, 31; Bible and Literature Series, 15; Sheffield: Almond Press, 1988), pp. 43-45.

83. See, for example, R.H. Fuller and P. Perkins, *Who Is This Christ? Gospel Christology and Contemporary Faith* (Philadelphia: Fortress Press, 1983), pp. 81-82; F. Neirynck, 'ΑΠΟ ΤΟΤΕ ΗΡΞΑΤΟ and the Structure of Matthew', in F. Van Segbroeck (ed.), *Evangelica II, 1982–1991. Collected Essays by Frans Neirynck* (Leuven: Leuven University Press, 1991), pp. 153-54.

84. The presence of a thematic prepositional phrase between καί and a monolectic verb, as here, is admittedly unusual but not unknown (see, for example, 14.26 and 20.17).

seeking an opportune time to hand Jesus over to the chief priests—by combining it with καί and a monolectic verb the Evangelist has chosen to portray Judas's actions as continuous with the immediate context of 26.14-16. While the rarity of ἀπὸ τότε in the Gospel of Matthew has understandably led to questions about its use in 26.16 vis-à-vis 4.17 and 16.21, any attempt to account for variations among the three needs to consider the interplay of syntactical features such as sentence conjunction and constituent order alongside the more standard treatment of the lexical and syntactical parallelism in 4.17 and 16.21. Without attempting to pronounce on the overall merit of Kingsbury's proposal, it is clear that 4.17 and 16.21, where asyndetic ἀπὸ τότε helps to signal a break in the narrative at whatever level, are syntactically distinct from 26.16.[85]

Asyndeton with Genitive Absolute Participial Constructions
As I have shown in Chapter 5 on Matthew's use of δέ, there is a strong association in Matthew's narrative framework between δέ and genitive absolute participial constructions.[86] I suggested that as a way of grammaticalizing a shift from one set of actions to another the presence of a genitive absolute may account for the presence of δέ even more strongly than does constituent order. Given the function of the genitive absolute as a 'scene shifter' signaling discontinuity in the narrative, it is not surprising that asyndetic genitive absolute constructions are found at four points in the narrative framework:

1.18 μνηστευθείσης τῆς μητρὸς αὐτοῦ Μαρίας τῷ Ἰωσήφ, πρὶν ἢ συνελθεῖν αὐτοὺς εὑρέθη ἐν γαστρὶ ἔχουσα ἐκ πνεύματος ἁγίου.

9.18 ταῦτα αὐτοῦ λαλοῦντος αὐτοῖς, ἰδοὺ ἄρχων εἷς ἐλθὼν προσεκύνει αὐτῷ λέγων ὅτι ἡ θυγάτηρ μου ἄρτι ἐτελεύτησεν· ἀλλὰ ἐλθὼν ἐπίθες τὴν χεῖρά σου ἐπ᾽ αὐτήν, καὶ ζήσεται.

12.46 ἔτι αὐτοῦ λαλοῦντος τοῖς ὄχλοις ἰδοὺ ἡ μήτηρ καὶ οἱ ἀδελφοὶ αὐτοῦ εἱστήκεισαν ἔξω ζητοῦντες αὐτῷ λαλῆσαι.

85. One could, however, make a case for all of 26.1-16 as a transitional pericope, beginning with the formulaic καὶ ἐγένετο ὅτε ἐτέλεσεν ὁ Ἰησοῦς πάντας τοὺς λόγους τούτους and ending with καὶ ἀπὸ τότε ἐζήτει εὐκαιρίαν ἵνα αὐτὸν παραδῷ. This treats ἀπὸ τότε in 26.16 as a modified repetition of the earlier uses of ἀπὸ τότε and recognizes that Matthew has inserted ἀπὸ τότε in 26.16 where the other Synoptics have no parallel element.

86. Δέ is the sentence conjunction in 23 of the 39 sentences in Matthew's narrative framework which have a genitive absolute construction before the main verb (59%).

17.5   ἔτι αὐτοῦ λαλοῦντος ἰδοὺ νεφέλη φωτεινὴ ἐπεσκίασεν
αὐτούς, καὶ ἰδοὺ φωνὴ ἐκ τῆς νεφέλης λέγουσα· οὗτός ἐστιν
υἱός μου ὁ ἀγαπητός, ἐν ᾧ εὐδόκησα· ἀκούετε αὐτοῦ.

The asyndetic genitive absolute construction in 1.18 follows a clause in the first half of the verse which displays highly unusual syntax: τοῦ δὲ Ἰησοῦ Χριστοῦ ἡ γένεσις οὕτως ἦν. The unusual feature is the thematic placement of the genitive τοῦ δὲ Ἰησοῦ Χριστοῦ,[87] the thematization of which makes it plain that in spite of the fact that the grammatical subjects of the next sentences are Mary (1.18), Joseph (1.19) and an angel (1.20), it is Jesus Christ and his origins (γένεσις) that are of interest. As Hagner observes, 'Indeed, the passage intends to explain in some detail the surprise encountered in v 16, namely that ἐγέννησεν, "he begat", gives way to ἐγεννήθη, "he was begotten"…'[88] While the first clause in 1.18 functions as a kind of title or formal introduction for what follows, the asyndetic μνηστευθείσης τῆς μητρὸς αὐτοῦ Μαρίας τῷ Ἰωσήφ is the actual beginning of the explanation of Jesus' origins, in a manner analogous to the asyndetic first sentence of the Gospel in 1.2 following the title in 1.1. Here again asyndeton combines with other thematic elements—in this case, the genitive absolute in 1.18—to signal the beginning of a new unit in Matthew's narrative framework.

The asyndetic sentences in 9.18, 12.46 and 17.5 all have λαλέω in the genitive absolute construction, ἰδού immediately before the main clause, and SV constituent order with the subject as the first element in the main clause.[89] Although the narrative breaks do not seem to be as strong or at as

87.   The only other example of a thematic genitive modifier in the narrative framework, apart from genitive absolute participles, is in 10.2.

88.   Hagner, *Matthew 1–13*, p. 14. Stendahl writes, 'The unusual word order indicates that Matthew consciously refers back to the constellation of the name Jesus and the title Christ in v. 16. Matthew is now to explain the details of this last point of the genealogy, a point where the nature of the case has caused a rather complicated formulation. He says: but as for this last link in the genealogy, "Jesus Christ", his origin was this wise. Thus, already the syntactical form of v. 18a indicates that vv. 18-25 are the enlarged footnote to the crucial point in the genealogy …' (K. Stendahl, 'Quis et Unde? An Analysis of Matthew 1–2 [1960]', in Stanton [ed.], *Interpretation*, p. 74).

89.   Ἔτι αὐτοῦ λαλοῦντος…ἰδού is another of Matthew's repetitions, appearing three times in the narrative framework. But in contrast to the two asyndetic usages here, which have no Synoptic parallels, see the third use, 26.47, καὶ ἔτι αὐτοῦ λαλοῦντος ἰδοὺ Ἰούδας εἷς τῶν δώδεκα ἦλθεν…, in which ἔτι αὐτοῦ λαλοῦντος appears in all three Synoptic Gospels (Mt. 26.47 = Mk 14.3 = Lk. 22.47).

high a level as some of those considered above, each does occur at a point of discontinuity within the narrative.[90] In both 9.18 and 12.46 the construction appears at the beginning of pericopes which are found in all three Synoptic Gospels but where Matthew's ordering of pericopes differs from that of the other Synoptic writers. In 9.18 it introduces a pericope recounting the healing of a ruler's daughter which includes an embedded account of the healing of a hemorrhaging woman (9.20-22; see also on 9.18-26, Chapter 9). Both Mark and Luke have this pair of incidents but Matthew's placement of it in the context of his Gospel differs from those of Mark and Luke (Mt. 9.18-26 = Mk 5.22-43 = Lk. 8.41-56). Similarly, 12.46 introduces the appearance of Jesus' mother and brothers, an incident which Mark and Luke place at different points in their Gospels (Mt. 12.46-50 = Mk 3.31-35 = Lk. 8.19-21). Neither of the other Synoptics includes similar introductory constructions. The use of an asyndetic genitive absolute in 9.18 and 12.46 represents a discontinuity in the action within the narrative; presumably, there is also a break in Matthew's arrangement of his sources at the same point.

In 17.5, the narrative discontinuity appears to be at an even lower or more local level. After Peter's seemingly foolish suggestion of building three shelters for Jesus, Elijah and Moses, a cloud appears, from which a voice speaks. All three Synoptics have this sequence (Mt. 17.5 = Mk 9.7 = Lk. 9.34), and Luke has a similar genitive absolute construction as well: Lk. 9.34, ταῦτα δὲ αὐτοῦ λέγοντος ἐγένετο νεφέλη. Rather than beginning a new pericope, this can be seen as nothing stronger than a new subunit within the pericope. The stronger breaks considered above, at 9.18 and 12.46, are also the points at which the introductory formula is unique to Matthew. Based on the parallel phrasing between Mt. 17.5 and Lk. 9.34, the use in 17.5 at a weaker break may be partially explained by the influence of a similar construction in one of Matthew's sources, in a manner analogous to his use of ἐν ἐκείνῳ τῷ καιρῷ in 11.25, discussed above.

'Off-line' Editorial Comment

One of the most striking discontinuities in Matthew's narrative framework occurs at 24.15, with the editorial comment, ὁ ἀναγινώσκων νοείτω, 'let the reader understand', referring to the coming 'abomination of desolation'.[91] At this point, to use the terminology of narrative criticism, one

90. For example, as I show in Chapter 9, most commentators understand 9.18 to begin a new section within the series of miracle stories in 8.1–9.34.

91. Matthew may have taken this over from Mark's Gospel; see Mk 13.14.

character (Jesus) is no longer speaking to other characters (his disciples), nor is the narrator speaking to the narratee. Instead the implied author suddenly addresses the implied reader directly.[92] This creates a startling discontinuity within the discourse. Indeed, it may be said to represent the beginning of a new and different discourse, between author and reader rather than narrator and audience or character and character, with this single clause representing the entirety of that discourse (although it indicates that the surrounding context is also of particular significance for the implied reader). Because a new discourse, or at least a new level of the current discourse, is initiated here, asyndeton is the logical choice. And again, asyndeton is combined with SV constituent order (rather than a thematic verb) to signal an important break in—or, in this case, break *from*—the narrative framework.

Summary

At the opposite end of the continuity–discontinuity spectrum from the asyndetic speech margins discussed at the beginning of this chapter, asyndeton is found in 16 instances where breaks in the flow of Matthew's narrative framework—sometimes major breaks—occur. Three examples may be described as fully discontinuous with surrounding narrative (the Gospel's title and first sentence in 1.1 and 1.2, and the aside to the reader in 24.15). A number of examples occur with characteristic Matthean phrases considered by some to be structural formulae: seven of the eight instances of the formula 'in that time/day/hour' are asyndetic, as are the two occurrences of the formula ἀπὸ τότε ἤρξατο ὁ Ἰησοῦς... There are also four instances of asyndeton with thematic genitive absolute constructions.

Here again one finds characteristic collocations with constituent order and verbal tense-form, this time differing sharply from thematic present tense-form λέγω or (more rarely) thematic φημί in speech margins. When asyndeton occurs at points of discontinuity in the narrative, aorist (or occasionally imperfect, but never present) tense-forms are used. Either SV or V(S) constituent order may appear at these breaks, but there is no instance of a thematic verb. Again the Evangelist supplies mutually reinforcing lexical and syntactic elements to help guide the audience in their mental representation of the discourse. In turn, the audience makes use of

---

92. For an introduction to this terminology, see M.A. Powell, *What is Narrative Criticism?* (Minneapolis: Fortress Press, 1990), especially pp. 23-34.

such mutually redundant cues to disambiguate the function of asyndeton in context.

Multivariate Analysis

Allen's multivariate analysis of my data on asyndeton in Matthew's narrative framework reflects the difficulty of distinguishing between continuous and discontinuous uses of asyndeton merely by quantitative means. Allen recognizes that 'clauses with "no conjunction" appear to fall into two quite distinct structures'. She explains, 'Firstly those with verbal tense form of "present" all have "lego" as speech margin, a topic switch [= subject switch], the default topical theme "verb" and constituent orders ["verb only"] or "verb followed by subject"'. The second set of sentences consists of those 'with the less common topical themes, predominately verbal tense form "aorist" and which are generally not used as a speech margin'.[93] Allen's models do not distinguish fully between these two clusters of features, and so results for some fields and variables may be skewed by a predominance of either of these two types of structure with respect to a particular feature. As in the multivariate analysis of δέ in the previous chapter, the need to combine qualitative analysis with quantitative analysis is apparent. Nevertheless, Allen's models do offer some additional insight into Matthew's use of asyndeton in narrative.

Allen's initial univariate analyses indicate that 'all fields significantly affect the choice of conjunction "asyndeton" or "kai", however verbal tense form, speech margin and topical theme are the most significant'. She observes that 'the effect of topical theme may be due to the fact that "asyndeton" never occurs with a topical theme "other participle"'—that is, any participle other than a genitive absolute construction.[94] For this reason, Allen removes narrative clauses with 'other participle' as topical theme from the data set before going on to construct a multivariate model for asyndeton.[95]

Allen reports that in a multivariate analysis subject reference and the sentence's use as a speech margin lose all significance once verbal tense-form, constituent order, topic switch (= subject switch) and topical theme are adjusted for.[96] Removing these two fields from the final model yields

---

93. Allen, 'Greek Syntactical Analysis', p. 36.

94. Allen, 'Greek Syntactical Analysis', p. 28; see also Allen and Farewell, this volume, §4.2(i).

95. Allen, 'Greek Syntactical Analysis', p. 30.

96. Allen, 'Greek Syntactical Analysis', p. 30; see also Allen and Farewell, this

adjusted odds ratios indicating the effects of constituent order, topic switch, verbal tense-form and topical theme on the choice of asyndeton rather than καί. Allen summarizes:

> Features that now most noticeably appear to affect the choice of having 'no conjunction' as opposed to conjunction 'kai' now appear to be: verbal tense forms 'present' and 'other' [tense-forms other than aorist, present, or imperfect, and including εἰμί], the less common topical themes [any thematic element other than subject, verb, or participle] and topical theme 'genitive absolute participle' and constituent order 'subject before verb in first position' [S₁V constituent order].[97]

Significant interactions identified by Allen include those between constituent order and topic switch (= subject switch), and between constituent order and topical theme. With respect to constituent order and topical theme, Allen considers the main feature of interest to be the fact that none of the sentences in Matthew's narrative framework with the combination of a thematic genitive absolute participle and VS constituent order is asyndetic. This occurs in spite of the fact that when all constituent orders are considered together the overall effect of a thematic genitive absolute is to increase the chance of a sentence being asyndetic rather than having καί as its sentence conjunction.[98]

Summary and Conclusions

I have shown that while there are a variety of points in the narrative framework at which the Evangelist chooses to omit a sentence conjunction between sentences, analysis of Matthew's narrative framework reveals two distinct tendencies in his use of asyndeton, at what can be described as opposite ends of the continuity–discontinuity spectrum. Asyndetic narrative sentences in Matthew's Gospel tend to exhibit characteristic features

---

volume, §4.2(ii). Although it may seem surprising that 'use as a speech margin' loses statistical significance, given the lengthy discussion of asyndetic λέγει/λέγουσιν above, it is likely that the variable 'verbal tense-form = present' adequately accounts for these speech margins in the data, as λέγω is present tense-form in each.

97. Allen, 'Greek Syntactical Analysis', p. 32; see also Allen and Farewell, this volume, §4.2(ii).

98. See Allen, 'Greek Syntactical Analysis', p. 33; see also Allen and Farewell, this volume, §4.2(iii). There are 23 sentences in Matthew's narrative framework with a thematic genitive absolute participle and VS constituent order: 13 have δέ as the sentence conjunction, 9 have καί (none with ἰδού), 1 has οὖν, and none is asyndetic.

in either 'continuous' or 'discontinuous' contexts in relation to other linguistic systems such as lexical choice, thematization, constituent order and verbal tense-form. Specifically, in speech margins in tightly connected segments of narrated dialogue (that is, 'continuous' usage), asyndeton consistently appears with present tense-form λέγω in thematic position. On the other hand, when asyndeton occurs at higher-level points of discontinuity in the narrative, including some major breaks, aorist (or occasionally imperfect, but never present) tense-forms are used. Either SV or V(S) constituent order may occur, but neither a finite verb nor a participle—other than a genitive absolute—is ever thematic.

Throughout this research on sentence conjunctions in Matthew's Gospel it is apparent that rarely, if ever, does a single linguistic element function independently to convey meaning in discourse. Instead, discourse is shaped by the use of mutually reinforcing elements from different linguistic systems. The patterns of use of asyndeton in Matthew's narrative framework further illustrate this dynamic. The audience makes use of collocating features such as the presence of thematic present-tense λέγω or, by contrast, the presence of thematic 'shifters' including genitive absolute constructions and formulaic phrases, to disambiguate the function of asyndeton in context, either continuing a mental model of conversation or opening a new segment in their mental representation of the discourse.

Chapter 7

Τότε: Marked Continuity

Τότε	All sentences in Matthew	Narrative sentences	Exposition sentences	Speech sentences	Old Testament quotations
n =	2302	720	768	733	81
# τότε	73	55	18	0	0
% τότε	3%	8%	2%	–	–

Introduction

Like asyndeton, the relative infrequence of τότε as a narrative sentence conjunction in the Gospel of Matthew, with only 55 uses in the narrative framework, has counterbalancing effects on an investigation of τότε's function in Matthew's Gospel. On one hand, fewer examples mean less data to work with, suggesting that the benefit of quantitative analysis may be limited. At the same time, fewer sentences allow more exhaustive qualitative analysis of τότε than is practical for the more common conjunctions καί and δέ.

A Distinctively Matthean Sentence Conjunction

Of the sentence conjunctions in Matthew's narrative framework, τότε is perhaps the most unusual—some would even say 'un-Greek' (see below). It is a distinct Mattheanism, with the Evangelist employing it as a discourse connective far more frequently than do any of the other New Testament authors. Τότε is used as a sentence conjunction 73 times in Matthew's Gospel: predominantly in narrative (55 times), less often in exposition (18 times, but 7 of these are in parables or other narrative forms within exposition),[1] and never in quoted speech.

---

1. Τότε occurs six times in parables in Matthew's Gospel: 13.26, 18.32, 22.8, 22.13, 25.1, 25.7. Of these only 13.26, in the parable of the weeds among the wheat,

By contrast, τότε appears far less frequently in the rest of the New Testament. Although Hawkins does not distinguish between sentence-initial conjunctive τότε and τότε following other conjunctions or elsewhere in the sentence, his statistics are illustrative. He finds 90 occurrences of τότε in Matthew's Gospel, but only 6 in Mark, 15 in Luke, 21 in Acts, 14 in the 13 Epistles attributed to Paul, 10 in John's Gospel, and 5 in the rest of the New Testament. He notes the relative frequency of τότε in narrative in particular, citing 60 occurrences in Matthew, but none in narrative discourse in Mark and only 2 in Luke.[2]

Where there are Synoptic parallels, there is no clear pattern by which Matthew's use of τότε corresponds to the use of καί, δέ, or asyndeton by another Evangelist. There is not, for example, a consistent use of τότε by Matthew where Mark has καί. As one would expect, there are indeed a number of instances where τότε appears in Matthew's Gospel while a parallel reading in Mark's Gospel has καί, but this may reflect the prevalence of καί in the Gospel of Mark more than any correspondence between Markan καί and Matthean τότε.[3] There are other examples in which Mark and Luke are both asyndetic while Matthew uses τότε,[4] or in which Mark and Luke have δέ while Matthew uses τότε.[5] In comparing passages in Matthew's Gospel with similar passages in the Gospel of Luke (that is, Matthew–Luke agreement with no Markan parallel), one finds instances of Matthean τότε where Luke has either καί or δέ.[6]

Recognizing that Matthew's use of τότε differs from its use elsewhere in the New Testament, scholars have sought to explain it as a Semitism or, more specifically, a borrowing from Aramaic, as I discuss below. This may well be the case, and some of the arguments for an Aramaic precursor to Matthew's use of τότε are summarized in the following section. However, few, if any, have sought to explain how τότε subsequently functions

---

should probably be taken as adverbial based on the presence of the ὅτε clause to which τότε refers (ὅτε δὲ ἐβλάστησεν ὁ χόρτος καὶ καρπὸν ἐποίησεν, τότε ἐφάνη καὶ τὰ ζιζάνια). The other five uses are instances of conjunctive τότε. There are two additional uses of conjunctive τότε in narrative-type discourse within exposition: 12.44 and 12.45, both in the pericope concerning the return of the unclean spirit.

2.   J.C. Hawkins, *Horae Synopticae* (Oxford: Clarendon Press, 1909), p. 8.

3.   See, for example, Mt. 26.31 = Mk 14.27; Mt. 26.38 = Mk 14.34; Mt. 27.38 = Mk 15.27.

4.   See, for example, Mt. 9.6 = Mk 2.10 = Lk. 5.24.

5.   See, for example, Mt. 26.74 = Mk 14.71 = Lk. 22.60.

6.   See, for example, Mt. 4.5 = Lk. 4.9; Mt. 4.10 = Lk. 4.8.

in Matthew's system of Greek sentence conjunctions. It is not enough merely to suspect that Matthew has incorporated τότε into his conjunctive system under Aramaic influence. Whatever linguistic influence may lie behind Matthew's use of τότε as a narrative conjunction, it is the systemic relationships among τότε and Matthew's other sentence conjunctions— that is, the choices the Evangelist makes among καί, δέ, τότε, οὖν, γάρ and asyndeton—that are of primary importance in understanding how τότε functions in Matthew's Gospel. Because Matthew's system of Greek conjunctions consists of a different set of forms than that found in an Aramaic conjunctive system, the meaning of τότε inevitably differs from the meaning of a similar Aramaic form. Simply put, the range or 'semantic space' it occupies within the system differs in contrast to other conjunctions. From the standpoint of systemic-functional linguistics, the meaning of τότε lies not just in the use of τότε in a particular context, but also in the contrast between τότε and the other sentence conjunctions which could have been chosen in that context but were not.

In spite of the relatively small sample size, Matthew's use of τότε reflects several general characteristics. First, τότε is used alone as a sentence conjunction only in narrative discourse, or narrative-type discourse in exposition (in particular in parables). Occurrences of τότε in other discourse types in the Gospel of Matthew are in combination with some other conjunction (for example, καὶ τότε appears in exposition but never in the narrative framework) and are generally adverbial rather than conjunctive.[7] Secondly, τότε is significantly more likely to appear with present-tense finite verbs in past-referring narrative (the so-called 'historic present') than would be expected based on its overall frequency in narrative. Thirdly, τότε is used primarily in sentences in which a finite verb is the topical theme, and in fact is found with only three types of thematic elements: a finite verb, an aorist nominative participle, or a nominative subject. In Matthew's narrative framework τότε is never found in sentences with, for example, a temporal prepositional phrase or a genitive absolute participial construction as the sentence's topical theme. Fourthly, the Evangelist seems to display a preference for combining τότε with verb–subject (VS) constituent order, although τότε with monolectic verbs and with subject–verb (SV) constituent order also occurs. When τότε is combined with SV constituent order it is often found at the beginning of a paragraph or similar unit. Fifthly, τότε appears seven times

---

7. For καὶ τότε see 5.24, 7.5, 7.23, 9.15, 12.29, 16.27, 24.10, 24.14, 24.30 (two occurrences).

with another distinctive Matthean feature, the lexical item προσέρχομαι, in both finite and participial forms. It is also used twice with passive forms of προσφέρω, forms which I will argue Matthew uses in a manner similar to προσέρχομαι. Each of these characteristics is described in more detail below, but none of them fully accounts for the discourse function of τότε in the Gospel of Matthew.

In terms of its discourse function in Matthew's narrative framework, scholars such as Levinsohn have observed that τότε is a marker of continuity.[8] My formal analysis of syntactical collocations with τότε bears this out. The tendency for τότε to be used with VS constituent order rather than SV constituent order is consistent with continuity in narrative, as is the fact that τότε, like καί, is overwhelmingly paired with thematic finite verbs. That τότε never appears with such signals of narrative discontinuity as temporal prepositional phrases or genitive absolute constructions is further evidence for its association with continuity rather than discontinuity in narrative. It may also be that τότε's sentence-initial position, again like καί, reflects its function as a marker of continuity, while conjunctions such as δέ, οὖν and γάρ which signal some kind of discontinuity tend to be postpositive.

However, at the same time that τότε is a marker of discourse continuity, it also appears to be a more marked choice relative to καί, signaling some measure of emphasis or prominence. Scholars have noted the tendency for τότε to begin paragraphs in Matthew's narrative framework (although it must be borne in mind that there is no general agreement regarding what constitutes or signals a paragraph, nor whether paragraphs actually exist as a formal hierarchical feature of discourse). Still, there is a strong intuitive recognition that τότε often appears where there is a shift to a new subunit within an episode. This usage retains an element of continuity, as τότε seems not to be used at higher-level breaks between episodes. Similarly, scholars have observed that τότε often introduces important statements within a paragraph, or the final, often climactic, sentence in a paragraph.[9]

In the following sections I examine these syntactical and lexical collocations and discourse functions in more detail, but first I summarize the discussion concerning possible Aramaic sources for Matthew's seemingly idiosyncratic use of τότε.

---

8. Levinsohn, *Discourse Features*, pp. 95-96.
9. See, e.g., Levinsohn, *Discourse Features*, p. 97; Buth, 'Perspective', p. 8.

Possible Aramaic Antecedents

McNeile's and more recently Buth are among those who have looked to Aramaic to explain Matthew's use of τότε as a narrative conjunction.

McNeile. McNeile's seminal article on the linguistic background of Matthew's use of τότε appeared in 1911.[10] In two brief pages he argues that 'St Matthew's usage is remarkably illustrated in Biblical Aramaic'.[11] The essence of his argument is that while there is little evidence of the use of a form corresponding to 'then' as a connective in Hebrew narrative, there is such precedent in Aramaic. As evidence he notes that the Hebrew word אז, 'then', is used only 20 times in the whole of the Hebrew Old Testament as a narrative connector, the so-called 'ו consecutive' being the usual connector denoting narrative continuity. 'The essence of the meaning of "*waw* consecutive"', McNeile writes, 'is that the event related is regarded as happening in due sequence to what has gone before'.[12] However, in the Aramaic portions of Daniel and Ezra two related Aramaic words אדין and בידין, which can both be translated 'then', are frequently used to carry on a narrative. In the majority of cases the LXX (and to a lesser extent Theodotian) renders these with τότε:

> In Dan. ii iii v vi אדין or בידין occurs 45 times, these instances being represented in the Greek as follows: τότε LXX 32, Theod. 22; καί LXX 8, Theod. 20. Five times the LXX has no word to correspond with it, and Theod. once. Moreover LXX has τότε 8 times, and Theod. 3 times, where the particle is absent from the present Aramaic text. In Ezr. iv v vi it occurs 11 times in the Aramaic, in 10 of which the LXX has τότε, and in the remaining passage no corresponding word.[13]

Positing an Aramaic original underlying the Greek Gospel of Matthew, McNeile concludes, 'It is probable that the Greek St Matthew, like the Greek of the LXX, represented the original by τότε in the large majority of cases'.[14] In this short article McNeile merely sketches the outlines of his argument. He does not, for example, contrast the use of τότε in Daniel and Ezra with its use elsewhere in the LXX. Nor does he justify the pairing of אדין and בידין or attempt to distinguish between the two in terms of their relationship to τότε. Still, for much of the twentieth century

10. A.H. McNeile, 'Τότε in St Matthew', *JTS* 12 (1911), pp. 127-28.
11. McNeile, 'Τότε in St Matthew', p. 127.
12. McNeile, 'Τότε in St Matthew', p. 127.
13. McNeile, 'Τότε in St Matthew', p. 127.
14. McNeile, 'Τότε in St Matthew', p. 128.

McNeile's article was considered a standard in the search for possible antecedents to Matthew's use of τότε as a narrative connector.[15]

Buth. More recently, Buth has taken up this subject again, using McNeile's work as a point of departure but attempting a more detailed analysis.[16] Buth believes that 'this simple word "then" is a significant touchstone for source criticism. It is like a fingerprint that distinguishes Aramaic from Hebrew.' He argues that ' "then" points toward a Hebrew background for Mark and Luke but demonstrates some kind of Aramaic connection for Matthew'.[17] Although source criticism is Buth's primary interest in this article, I will limit my summary to his discussion of τότε's distribution in LXX translation from Hebrew and Aramaic, in extra-biblical Greek texts, and in the four Gospels.

Buth analyzes the two Aramaic words, אֱדַיִן and בֵּאדַיִן, concluding that while both have the force of 'then' as a narrative connector, *bedayin* 'marks the clause as "more closely connected", either in the sense of being "more predictable, more expected", or in the sense of being a "more direct" result, response, or outcome of the previous event(s)'.[18] As Greek lacked conjunctions conveying this distinction, translators from Aramaic used τότε to represent both אֱדַיִן and בֵּאדַיִן.

Buth maintains that in contrast, '*tote* is virtually non-existent in LXX translation from Hebrew narrative'.[19] A check of Buth's claim against the tagged GRAMCORD LXX text indicates that while τότε does appear in the LXX outside Daniel and Ezra, it is relatively infrequent. Daniel, with 42 occurrences of τότε, has by far the highest frequency (3.36 per thousand words). All but four of the occurrences of τότε in Daniel are within the Aramaic portions, 2.4b–7.28. Ezra reveals the second highest frequency of τότε, with 1.79 occurrences per thousand words, all of them within the Aramaic portion in 4.8–6.18.[20] Other books in the LXX show a much lower

---

15. For scholars who make use of McNeile's work see, for example, Turner, *Syntax*, p. 341; BDF, §459(2); Davies and Allison, *Matthew*, I, p. 264. M.-J. Lagrange, *Évangile selon Saint Matthieu* (Paris: Librairie Lecoffre, 7th edn, 1948), p. cx, makes use of McNeile's 1938 commentary on Matthew (McNeile, *Matthew*), which includes the material from the earlier article.

16. Buth, 'ᵓEdayin/Tote', pp. 33-48.

17. Buth, 'ᵓEdayin/Tote', pp. 33-34.

18. Buth, 'ᵓEdayin/Tote', p. 39.

19. Buth, 'ᵓEdayin/Tote', p. 41.

20. None appears in the other Aramaic portion of Ezra, 7.12-26.

frequency of τότε, very few having more than one instance per thousand words, most having less than 0.5 per thousand words, and many having none.[21] While this brief survey does not distinguish between τότε as a sentence-initial narrative connector and τότε's other functions (for example, as a temporal adverb in future-referring narrative), the relative frequency between Aramaic and Hebrew texts is suggestive.

Buth goes on to argue that not only is τότε as a narrative connector non-Hebrew, it is also non-Greek. As examples of Greek texts 'reasonably close to the New Testament' he analyzes Josephus's *The Antiquities of the Jews* and *The Jewish War*, as well as *The Martyrdom of Polycarp*. Buth observes that while Josephus does use τότε, it does not function in his writing as a narrative connector.[22] In *The Martyrdom of Polycarp* he finds one occurrence of τότε, at 12.3, which he acknowledges 'is close to Matthew's use'. 'However', he argues, 'because this is the only example in the book it is better to view this as asyndeton plus *tote* co-occurring in an isolated example rather than any kind of Aramaic influence'. The fact that this instance is a singularity in *The Martyrdom of Polycarp*, Buth asserts, reveals 'just how un-Greek narrative *tote* is'.[23]

Similarly, in the other Gospels Buth finds little evidence of τότε as a narrative connector. Although Buth counts eight occurrences of τότε in the narrative framework of the Gospel of John, four of these are τότε οὖν and the other four follow other conjunctions, leading him to assert that 'John does not have one example of a narrative *tote* based strictly on an Aramaic paradigm'.[24] Buth finds no examples of τότε in the narrative framework of Mark and only two in the narrative framework of Luke's Gospel, in Lk. 21.10 and 24.45. With respect to the Gospel of Luke he writes, 'The gospel is quite long so that two occurrences of *tote* at the beginning of a clause are compatible with a Hebrew-based source' (that is,

---

21. The next highest frequency appears in 1 Esdras (15 occurrences, or 1.67 per thousand words). If Buth's theory is correct, this relatively high frequency of τότε may contribute to the discussion of a possible Semitic (specifically, Aramaic) antecedent to 1 Esdras. See R.H Charlesworth, *The Apocrypha and Pseudepigrapha of the Old Testament in English*. I. *Apocrypha* (Oxford: Clarendon Press, 1913), p. 3; R.J. Coggins and M.A. Knibb, *The First and Second Books of Esdras* (Cambridge Bible Commentary on the New English Bible; Cambridge: Cambridge University Press, 1979), p. 6.

22. Buth, 'ᵓEdayin/Tote', p. 43.

23. Buth, 'ᵓEdayin/Tote', p. 44.

24. Buth, 'ᵓEdayin/Tote', p. 44.

rather than a source influenced by Aramaic).[25] Buth notes that the scarcity of τότε in the narrative frameworks of the other Synoptic Gospels does not result from dislike or ignorance of the word, as each retains τότε in quoted speech, Mark 6 times and Luke 13.[26]

Set against these other Greek writings, Matthew's use of τότε is especially striking. Of 90 examples of τότε in the Gospel of Matthew, Buth identifies 52 as functioning as a sentence-initial narrative connector. Buth concludes, 'The obvious reason for such a frequency of narrative *tote* is Aramaic influence of some kind'.[27]

Although I find McNeile's and Buth's arguments for an Aramaic antecedent to Matthew's use of τότε at least plausible (but not necessarily implying Hebrew origins by contrast for Mark or Luke), nothing in their analyses explains why Matthew, having both καί and τότε at his disposal to conjoin narrative sentences, uses both. Nor does either McNeile or Buth suggest at what points Matthew selects τότε over the more frequent and supposedly more acceptable καί. In short, their diachronic approach may help to explain why Matthew's set of sentence conjunctions differs from that of the other Evangelists, but does not address the issue of how he subsequently uses that set in constructing his narrative. To address this question I turn to an analysis of τότε within Matthew's narrative framework.

Τότε *in Matthew's Narrative Framework*

Patterns of Use

Once a form like τότε has been incorporated into a system of sentence conjunctions, it begins to find its level, so to speak, within that system. Or, more precisely, an author begins to use the form in a more or less systematic way to fill certain syntactic and/or semantic 'slots' in the discourse. With καί, δέ and asyndeton, considered in Chapters 4 to 6, it is relatively straightforward to establish basic ranges of use as signals of continuity or discontinuity in Matthew's narrative framework along with the collocations that tend to mutually reinforce those procedural meanings: καί for unmarked continuity, most often with VS or monolectic constituent order; δέ for low- to mid-level discontinuity, usually with SV constituent order and especially with thematic subjects, genitive absolute constructions or other indicators of temporal shift; asyndeton at points of close continuity

25. Buth, 'ᵓEdayin/Tote', p. 45.
26. Buth, 'ᵓEdayin/Tote', pp. 44-45.
27. Buth, 'ᵓEdayin/Tote', p. 46.

(especially in speech margins with thematic present-tense λέγω) or at certain breaks in the narrative (usually with a non-verbal thematic element serving as a point of departure).

In the case of τότε, however, it is not possible to be as definitive in the description of Matthew's patterns of use. One reason for this is simply lack of data. The small sample size, only 55 instances of τότε as a narrative connector in Matthew's narrative framework, constrains empirical analysis. Although there is a similarly small sample size for narrative asyndeton, that asyndeton falls more or less neatly into two types of usage in Matthew's narrative framework makes its analysis more straightforward. In contrast, τότε appears in a greater range of discourse contexts, making the analysis of its basic discourse function or functions more problematic. No absolute statement about Matthew's use of τότε can be made on the basis of the limited data, although a cluster of characteristics of τότε in Matthew's narrative framework can be identified, and some tentative conclusions drawn.

It may also be the case that as a conjunction relatively confined to Matthew's own idiolect—that is, a form which apparently is not widely used by other authors—Matthew's use of τότε is not as consistently integrated within a network of linguistic systems in the grammar as a form might be which is more widely used and thus more 'well-worn' by linguistic convention. In her multivariate analysis of my data on sentence conjunctions in Matthew's narrative framework, Allen finds sentences with τότε to be 'less distinct' in structure as a group than the sentences found with other conjunctions.[28] That is, sentences with τότε do not show patterns of collocating linguistic features which are as distinctive as those with καί, δέ, or asyndeton.

It may be that the collocating features identified in previous chapters (including constituent order, thematization and verbal tense-form) do not fully account for Matthew's use of τότε and that additional features could be identified which would shed more light on τότε's role in Matthew's narrative framework. However, the limiting factor in exploring these possibilities further remains the small sample available for analysis.

Nevertheless, in spite of the small sample size several characteristics of Matthew's use of τότε as a narrative connector can be observed. The pairing of τότε with present tense-forms (the 'historic present'), for example, is easily discernible. With the caveat that much of this analysis is

28. See Allen, 'Greek Syntactical Analysis', p. 47; see also Allen and Farewell, this volume, §5.2.

suggestive rather than definitive, I first address the distinction between 'conjunctive' and 'adverbial' uses of τότε and how τότε is to be understood as part of the system of sentence conjunctions, and then offer an empirical analysis of features which tend to collocate with conjunctive τότε in narrative sentences. Following this, I discuss the discourse function of τότε as a signal of marked continuity in Matthew's narrative framework.

Τότε *in narrative: 'Conjunctive'* τότε *vs. 'adverbial'* τότε. As noted above, τότε appears 73 times in sentence-initial position in Matthew's Gospel, 55 times in the narrative framework and 7 more times in parables and other narrative discourse within exposition. Τότε appears only 11 additional times in sentence-initial position in Matthew's Gospel, all 11 in exposition and never in quoted speech.

A foundational question is whether sentence-initial τότε as Matthew uses it in narrative should be considered a sentence conjunction at all. Traditionally τότε has been classified as a temporal adverb, and certainly it continues to function as an adverb throughout the New Testament. Few if any grammarians include τότε in their discussion of coordinating conjunctions, except perhaps in passing reference to its unusual frequency in Matthew and its possible Aramaic antecedents.[29] However, with the surge of interest among contemporary linguists in sentence conjunctions, similar discourse connectives, and other discourse markers, has come a recognition that forms originally borrowed from a variety of speech categories may function as sentence connectors.

Fraser proposes that discourse markers be considered 'a well-defined pragmatic category within the grammar of a language'.[30] He defines discourse markers as 'expressions such as *now, well, so, however*, and *then*, which signal a sequential relationship between the current basic message and the previous discourse'.[31] Although in this article Fraser makes reference only to English, he intends his theoretical approach to be suggestive for the study of similar forms in other languages. The Greek sentence conjunctions I evaluate can be understood to be a subset of the discourse markers treated by Fraser. Matthew's use of τότε as a narrative connector exhibits properties Fraser describes as characteristic of such markers. Describing discourse markers as a 'pragmatic category', he writes that,

---

29. See, for example, Turner, *Syntax*, p. 341; Porter, *Idioms*, p. 217.
30. Fraser, 'Approach', pp. 383-95.
31. Fraser, 'Approach', p. 383.

> discourse markers…are not drawn from a single grammatical source, but reflect sources from throughout the lexical inventory: adverbials…literally used phrases…idiomatic phrases…verbs…interjections…coordinate conjunctions…subordinate conjunctions…as well as terms…which don't fall nicely into any of the usual grammatical slots.[32]

Of significance for Matthean τότε is Fraser's insistence that 'discourse markers are not adverbs, for example, masquerading as another category from time to time'. He adds, however, 'Of course, many expressions which function as a discourse marker are ambiguous [that is, they have multiple functions or meanings] and function as a different syntactic type on other occasions'. This is true of τότε, which is used as a temporal adverb elsewhere in the Gospel of Matthew.[33] Several of the properties of discourse markers Fraser lists help to disambiguate conjunctive τότε from adverbial τότε. One is the recognition that 'when an expression functions as a discourse marker, that is its exclusive function in the sentence'.[34] That is, if τότε can be shown to add temporal content to the meaning of the sentence itself (beyond mere sequentiality), it is adverbial rather than conjunctive; it will not be both simultaneously.[35] Another is that 'discourse markers typically occur only in utterance-initial position'.[36] This, too, is

---

32. Fraser, 'Approach', p. 388.

33. The occurrence in 27.16, εἶχον δὲ τότε δέσμιον ἐπίσημον λεγόμενον ['Ιησοῦν] Βαραββᾶν, may be the only example of adverbial τότε in the narrative framework, but see also 24.21, in which τότε refers back to a preceding ὅτε clause. (Square brackets in this and other Greek examples represent textual variants included in the NA[27] text.)

34. Fraser, 'Approach', p. 389.

35. One way of distinguishing between conjunctive and adverbial uses of τότε is that if τότε can be understood as answering the question 'when?', as opposed to introducing 'what happened next?', it is conveying conceptual information and is functioning adverbially. For example, in 9.15, ἐλεύσονται δὲ ἡμέραι ὅταν ἀπαρθῇ ἀπ' αὐτῶν ὁ νυμφίος, καὶ τότε νηστεύσουσιν, τότε can be understood as pointing to the answer to the question 'when will they fast?' See similarly 24.14, καὶ κηρυχθήσεται τοῦτο τὸ εὐαγγέλιον τῆς βασιλείας ἐν ὅλῃ τῇ οἰκουμένῃ … καὶ τότε ἥξει τὸ τέλος, in which τότε can be understood as indicating the answer to the question 'when will the end come?'

36. Fraser, 'Approach', p. 389. Fraser acknowledges the difficulty of defining the limits of a sentence when he adds, 'Actually, defining what constitutes an 'utterance' and hence what is utterance-initial/internal/final is problematic'. In addition, Fraser's characterization of discourse markers as 'utterance-initial' must be adapted when considering postpositive forms like δέ, γάρ and οὖν.

exemplified by conjunctive τότε, which occurs only as the first element in a sentence.[37]

An additional property of τότε, not found in Fraser's list, is that when τότε appears as a sentence-initial conjunction in Matthew's narrative framework, it does not combine with other sentence conjunctions, but instead displaces them. For example, the distribution of καί, δέ, τότε and asyndeton in the whole of the narrative framework is approximately 47% καί (that is, καί begins 47% of narrative sentences), 36% δέ, 8% asyndeton and 8% τότε, together accounting for 91% of the sentences in the narrative framework. In a more narrowly defined linguistic context such as 'narrative sentences with present-tense verbs which are not speech margins' (see discussion of τότε with the so-called 'historic present' below) the distribution becomes 30% καί, 20% δέ and 45% τότε, with no instances of asyndeton. Together these account for roughly the same proportion of sentences (95%) as in narrative in general. While the use of τότε increases in this context, the use of other sentence conjunctions decreases, with no examples of combined conjunctive forms. This suggests that for Matthew τότε has been incorporated into a system of sentence connectors which alternate with one another in various contexts.

Fraser argues further that discourse markers, while drawn from different lexical sources, should be understood as constituting a distinct category of forms with a shared function.

> On my analysis, discourse markers have a core pragmatic meaning, a meaning separate from any content meaning of the homophonous form, and a meaning which signals how the speaker intends the message following to relate to the foregoing discourse.[38]

Fraser's distinction between 'content meaning' and 'pragmatic meaning' is very close to the distinction between 'conceptual' and 'procedural' meaning I adopt in this research. As a discourse marker, conjunctive τότε serves to signal narrative continuity (conveying procedural information for discourse processing) rather than indicating a specific point in time (conceptual information adding to the proposition being processed).

Even though τότε is not drawn from the traditional lexical category of conjunctions, its function as a sentence-initial narrative connector and the fact that it alternates with other sentence conjunctions in Matthew's set

---

37. It may be that πάλιν has also made this shift from adverb to narrative connector. See note on asyndetic πάλιν in Chapter 6.

38. Fraser, 'Approach', p. 395.

justifies its inclusion with the sentence conjunctions in this study. The work of McNeile and Buth suggests that Matthew was not the first to incorporate τότε into a system of Greek sentence conjunctions, but that it is used similarly in LXX translation of Aramaic narrative. On their view, however, this type of use apparently is limited to linguistic contexts in which there is Aramaic influence of some kind.

Τότε *with present-tense verbs.* As I stated above, once a form like τότε has been incorporated into a system of sentence conjunctions the author begins to use the form in a more or less systematic way to fill certain syntactic and/or semantic 'slots' in the discourse. Patterns of use and collocations with other lexical or syntactical choices may be observable.

One strong association in Matthew's narrative framework is that between τότε and present-tense finite verbs (the so-called 'historic present'). The association between τότε and tense-forms of finite verbs is displayed in the following table:

Table 7.1: Τότε *and verbal tense-form (omitting* εἰμί*)*[39]

	All narrative sentences	Aorist	Present	Imperfect
# sentences	720	553	79	57
# τότε	55	34	20	1[41]
% τότε	8%	6%	25%	2%
z-score[40]		−1.32	5.92	−1.68

While τότε is the sentence conjunction in less than one out of ten narrative sentences (55/720, 8%), it is the sentence conjunction in one-quarter of the narrative sentences with present-tense finite verbs (20/79, 25%; $z = 5.92$). Or, expressed the other way around, more than a third of the occurrences of τότε in narrative appear with present tense-forms (20/55, 36%), although only about a tenth of sentences in the narrative framework have present tense-form finite verbs (79/720, 11%). In 19 of

39. As before, εἰμί is omitted from consideration in this table and in other analyses of sentence conjunction and verbal tense-form because it does not evidence fully developed morphological distinctions among tense-forms, or, in Porter's terms, it is 'aspectually vague' (see Porter, *Verbal Aspect*, pp. 442-47).

40. As before, z-scores equal to or greater than ±3 are taken to demonstrate statistical significance.

41. Mt. 3.5. There is no instance of τότε with εἰμί in Matthew's narrative framework.

these 20 sentences with τότε, the verb is also thematic (all but 15.12; see below on τότε and topical theme).

The tendency for τότε to be combined with present tense-forms holds both in speech margins (like asyndeton) and (unlike asyndeton) in other narrative. Present tense-forms in speech margins were discussed in Chapter 6 with respect to asyndetic λέγει/λέγουσιν. While 26 of the 59 sentences in Matthew's narrative framework with λέγει/λέγουσιν are asyndetic, another eleven have τότε as the sentence conjunction (11/59, 19%; $z =$ 3.18).[42] As with asyndetic speech margins, in these sentences (with the exception of 15.12) the verb λέγει/λέγουσιν is thematic.

The association between τότε and present tense-forms is all the more conspicuous in narrative sentences which are not speech margins. There are only 20 occurrences of the 'historic present' in Matthew's narrative framework which are not speech margins with λέγει/λέγουσιν. Of these 20 sentences, nearly half (9/20, 43%) have τότε as a sentence connector, and in all 9 of these the verb is thematic:[43]

3.13 τότε παραγίνεται ὁ Ἰησοῦς ἀπὸ τῆς Γαλιλαίας ἐπὶ τὸν
Ἰορδάνην πρὸς τὸν Ἰωάννην τοῦ βαπτισθῆναι ὑπ᾽ αὐτοῦ.

3.15 τότε ἀφίησιν αὐτόν.

4.5 τότε παραλαμβάνει αὐτὸν ὁ διάβολος εἰς τὴν ἁγίαν πόλιν ...

4.11 τότε ἀφίησιν αὐτὸν ὁ διάβολος ...

9.14 τότε προσέρχονται αὐτῷ οἱ μαθηταὶ Ἰωάννου λέγοντες ...

15.1 τότε προσέρχονται τῷ Ἰησοῦ ἀπὸ Ἱεροσολύμων Φαρισαῖοι καὶ
γραμματεῖς λέγοντες ...

26.36 τότε ἔρχεται μετ᾽ αὐτῶν ὁ Ἰησοῦς εἰς χωρίον λεγόμενον
Γεθσημανί

26.45 τότε ἔρχεται πρὸς τοὺς μαθητάς ...

27.38 τότε σταυροῦνται σὺν αὐτῷ δύο λῃσταί ...

By contrast, in the narrative framework there is no instance of asyndeton with a sentence having a present-tense finite verb other than λέγει/ λέγουσιν.

I have shown elsewhere that Matthew rarely uses present-tense finite

---

42. Mt. 4.10, 9.6, 9.37, 12.13, 15.12, 22.21, 26.31, 26.38, 26.52, 27.13, 28.10.

43. A sample size of less than 30 may affect the reliability of the z-score as a test of statistical significance. Of the examples listed, 9.14 and 15.1 function as speech margins in which a finite verb which is not a verb of speaking is combined with λέγοντες. These 'compound' speech margins are more difficult to categorize as either speech margin or non-speech margin, as they reflect features of both. In these two cases, however, the association of τότε with προσέρχομαι is an important feature of the sentence. See below on τότε with προσέρχομαι.

verbs in past-referring narrative other than in speech margins.[44] Outside
speech margins, the Evangelist uses the 'historic present' at points in the
Gospel which appear to have special importance in his portrayal of Jesus:
Jesus' baptism (3.13-17, with τότε in 3.13 and 3.15), his temptation in the
wilderness (4.1-11, with τότε in 4.5 and 4.11), his transfiguration (17.1-8,
but no use of τότε), his prayer in Gethsemane (26.36-46, with τότε in
26.36 and 26.45), and the crucifixion (27.32-44, with τότε in 27.38).[45]
These uses of the 'historic present' incorporate seven of the nine instances
with τότε listed above. Given that τότε is so closely associated with such
present-tense verbs—a relatively marked verbal choice in narrative—it is
likely that in the sentences above the narrative connector τότε and the
'historic present' serve as mutually reinforcing signals indicating the
prominence of these events in Matthew's Gospel. (The other two examples
above, 9.14 and 15.1, both have προσέρχομαι—see below on τότε and
προσέρχομαι.)

The Evangelist's tendency to use τότε with present tense-forms in narrative, both in speech margins and non-speech margins, is evident. However, these uses of τότε represent only about a third of its occurrences as a
sentence connector in Matthew's narrative framework. Thus its association
with present tense-forms does not fully account for τότε's role as a
narrative connector in Matthew's Gospel. Other features also need to be
considered in the attempt to understand Matthew's use of τότε.

Τότε *with only three thematic elements.* In Matthew's narrative framework a variety of items function as topical theme, including finite verbs,
participles (including genitive absolute constructions), grammatical subjects, direct objects, indirect objects, prepositional phrases (generally with
time or place reference), adverbs (also generally time or place reference),
temporal clauses with ὅτε, genitive modifiers, predicate nominative constructions in copulative or verbless clauses, and hanging nominative constructions. However, in narrative in Matthew's Gospel conjunctive τότε is
found in sentences with only three types of thematic elements: finite verbs,
aorist nominative participles, and grammaticalized subjects. Τότε is never
found as a sentence conjunction in sentences with, for example, a temporal
prepositional phrase or a genitive absolute participial construction as the
thematic element. Nor is τότε found with ἰδού, the only lexical item in
Matthew's narrative framework which functions within Halliday's notion

of interpersonal theme.[46] In the narrative framework, sentences with τότε as sentence conjunction (textual theme) contain no interpersonal theme and are combined only with a finite verb, an aorist nominative participle, or a nominative subject as topical theme.

Finite verb as theme. Finite verbs are by far the most common thematic element found in sentences in which τότε is the sentence conjunction. There are 35 such instances, representing almost two-thirds (35/55, 64%) of the uses of τότε in Matthew's narrative framework. In comparison, sentences with thematic finite verbs constitute only a third of those in the narrative framework (248/720, 34%). That is, τότε appears in 8% of all narrative sentences, but in 14% (35/248; $z = 3.85$) of those with finite verbal themes.

By far the most common connector in sentences with finite verbal themes is καί, which appears in two-thirds of such sentences in narrative (163/248, 66%; $z = 6.06$). Asyndeton is combined with thematic finite verbs almost as frequently as is τότε (31/248, 13%; $z = 2.68$), all of which are speech margins with thematic λέγει/λέγουσιν, as discussed in Chapter 6.[47] By contrast, δέ appears only eight times with a thematic finite verb (8/248, 3%; $z = -10.66$). Among the more common sentence conjunctions in Matthew's narrative framework (that is, καί, δέ, asyndeton and τότε), καί, τότε and asyndeton displace δέ in sentences with thematic finite verbs.[48] In other words, the frequency of τότε in this discourse context increases, as does that of καί and of asyndeton in speech margins, while the use of δέ decreases. This suggests that τότε and καί—and asyndeton in speech margins only—have some similarity in their function as sentence conjunctions. That common feature, that each signals continuity in the discourse, is discussed below.

Of the thematic finite verbs found with τότε, more than half are present tense-forms (19/35, 54%). This is consistent with the association between

46. See Halliday, *Introduction*, p. 53.

47. In fact, asyndeton and τότε show very similar increases in frequency of use with thematic λέγει/λέγουσιν. If the instances of thematic λέγω were distributed proportionally among the various tense-forms (present, imperfect and aorist) and the various sentence conjunctions (καί, δέ, τότε, γάρ and asyndeton) with which λέγω actually occurs as a topical theme in Matthew's narrative framework, the expected value for thematic present-tense λέγει/λέγουσιν with asyndeton would be about ten occurrences and the expected value with τότε would be about four occurrences. The observed values for asyndeton and τότε are each about 2.5 times the expected value (26 asyndetic sentences and 10 sentences with τότε).

48. But see on γάρ with thematic εἰμί in Chapter 8.

τότε and present tense-forms discussed in the previous section. In fact, all but one of the present-tense finite verbs found with τότε in the narrative framework are thematic (19/20, 95%). Thus τότε collocates not just with present tense-form finite verbs, but more specifically with *thematic* present tense-form finite verbs. The exception is 15.12, with προσελθόντες, S₂V constituent order and λέγουσιν: τότε προσελθόντες οἱ μαθηταὶ λέγουσιν αὐτῷ ... In this verse Jesus' disciples 'approach' him to say, 'Do you know that the Pharisees were offended (ἐσκανδαλίσθησαν) when they heard this?'—a significant interchange with respect to the growing conflict between Jesus and the religious leaders. The potential prominence of this exchange is displayed by means of relatively marked lexical and grammatical choices (see also on προσέρχομαι, below).

Participle as theme. The second largest set of thematic elements found with τότε in the narrative framework consists of aorist nominative participles. These appear in 11 sentences, or a fifth of the occurrences of τότε as a narrative connector (11/55, 20%).[49] No other type of participial construction is found as the topical theme in narrative sentences where τότε is the sentence conjunction—that is, there is no instance of a present nominative participle or a participle in another case (including genitive absolute constructions) in sentences beginning with τότε. However, while the combination of τότε and thematic participles indicates something about the limited range of thematic collocations with τότε, it reveals little about τότε's role in narrative discourse in Matthew. Τότε is the sentence conjunction in 8% of all sentences in Matthew's narrative framework and in 7% of sentences in the narrative framework with thematic participles other than genitive absolute constructions—a statistically insignificant difference in frequency.

Subject as theme. The third and smallest set of thematic elements in sentences with τότε in the narrative framework consists of grammaticalized subjects. These appear in nine sentences, less than a fifth of the occurrences of τότε as a narrative connector (9/55, 16%).[50] However, as is the case with τότε and thematic participles, the simple frequency of τότε with thematic subjects indicates more about the limited range of thematic collocations with τότε than it reveals about τότε's role in narrative dis-

49. Mt. 8.26, 13.36, 15.12, 15.28, 17.19, 18.21, 19.27, 22.15, 26.14, 26.50, 27.3.
50. Mt. 2.7, 2.16, 4.1, 16.24, 23.1, 26.56, 26.65, 27.27, 27.58. Davies and Allison observe, 'Matthew, as opposed to Mark and Luke, is fond of the sentence structure, τότε + subject (+ participial phrase) + verb ... The construction is common in the LXX only in 1 Esdras, 2 Esdras, and Daniel' (Davies and Allison, *Matthew*, I, p. 353).

course in Matthew. Τότε is the sentence conjunction in 8% of all sentences in Matthew's narrative framework and in 5% of sentences in the narrative framework with thematic subjects. Thus τότε appears somewhat less often with thematic subjects than might be expected based on its use in narrative in general, but the small sample size precludes any confidence that this difference is statistically significant.

On the other hand, a look at the discourse contexts in which τότε appears with thematic subjects is more suggestive. Two-thirds of the sentences in which τότε is combined with a thematic subject (6/9, 67%) coincide with the beginning of a paragraph in NA[27].[51] In addition, 26.56b, the only paragraph-final sentence in NA[27] with τότε and SV constituent order, could perhaps better be understood on semantic grounds as well as syntactical as the first sentence of the following paragraph. The substance of the first three sentences of that paragraph, which follows Jesus' betrayal and arrest in 26.47-56a, would then be, 'τότε all the disciples fled, Jesus' captors led him off to Caiaphas where the scribes and elders were gathered, and Peter followed at a distance', a transition from Jesus' arrest to the trial scenes, accounting for all the participants in the narrative at this point. Changing the paragraph division here to make 26.56b paragraph-initial would mean that more than three-quarters of the sentences in which τότε is combined with a thematic subject (7/9, 78%) occur at the beginning of a paragraph.

In fact, further analysis of the position of τότε-sentences in paragraphs in NA[27] suggests that constituent order plays a role in Matthew's use of τότε in discourse: the combination of τότε and SV constituent order is found in paragraph-initial position more often than would be expected based on its overall frequency in Matthew's narrative framework, whether or not the subject is thematic. The issue of paragraph-initial τότε leads to the more general question of τότε and constituent order in the following section.

Τότε *and constituent order.* There are two characteristic ways in which τότε collocates with constituent order in Matthew's narrative framework: first, Matthew tends to use τότε with V(S) constituent order, that is, verb–subject (VS) or verb only (V)—and especially VS order; and secondly, when τότε appears with subject–verb (SV) constituent order, it is likely to coincide with the beginning of a paragraph in NA[27].

51. Mt. 2.7, 2.16, 4.1, 16.24, 23.1, 27.27.

V(S) constituent order. In Matthew's narrative framework τότε appears with VS constituent order more frequently than it does with any other. More than a third of the narrative sentences in which τότε is the sentence conjunction (20/55, 36%) have VS constituent order with a grammaticalized subject following the verb. While τότε appears as the sentence conjunction in 8% of sentences in the narrative framework, it appears in 14% of sentences with VS constituent order (20/147; $z = 2.75$):

Table 7.2: Τότε *and constituent order*

	All narrative sentences	S_1V *constituent order*	S_2V *constituent order*	*VS constituent order*	*V constituent order*
# sentences	720	195	100	147	263
# τότε	55	9	8	20	18
% τότε	8%	5%	8%	14%	7%
z-score		−1.57	0.15	2.75	−0.46

Another third of the narrative sentences in which τότε is the sentence conjunction (18/55, 33%) have V (monolectic) constituent order, although τότε is found about as frequently in this context as it is in narrative in general. Together more than two-thirds of the uses of τότε in narrative sentences (38/55, 69%) have V(S) order. This is consistent with the association between τότε and thematic finite verbs discussed above.

SV constituent order. Only the remaining third of τότε-sentences in Matthew's narrative framework (17/55, 31%) have SV constituent order, in which a grammaticalized subject appears before the verb, whether or not the subject is thematic. Of these 17, three-quarters (13/17, 76%) coincide with the beginning of a paragraph in NA[27].[52]

In fact, of all 55 instances of τότε as a sentence conjunction in Matthew's narrative framework, half (27/55, 49%)—that is, the 13 just mentioned and an additional 14—coincide with the beginning of an NA[27] paragraph.[53] Scholars have recognized the tendency of τότε to occur at such transitional points.[54] Features with which τότε appears at the beginning of paragraphs

52. Mt. 2.7, 2.16, 4.1, 15.12, 16.24, 17.19, 18.21, 19.27, 22.15, 23.1, 26.14, 27.3, 27.27.

53. The additional 14 instances of paragraph-initial τότε are found in 3.13, 9.14, 11.20, 12.22, 12.38, 13.36, 15.1, 19.13, 20.20, 26.3, 26.31, 26.36, 26.67, 27.38.

54. Luz, for example, writes that 'the Matthean favorite word τότε (e.g. 3.13; 4.1; 11.20; 15.1; 18.21; 19.13; 20.20; 21.1; 27.3 etc.) or the phrase ἀπὸ τότε (4.17; 16.21; 26.16) often function as a transition between two pericopes', adding in a footnote,

or paragraph-like units include the syntactical collocation with SV constituent order just described, a morphological collocation with aorist tense-form finite verbs, and, to a lesser extent, a lexical collocation with the Matthean favorites προσέρχομαι and προσφέρω (see below on τότε with προσέρχομαι and passive forms of προσφέρω).

In actual practice it is difficult to state precisely where paragraphs begin and end in Matthew's Gospel, since features which consistently indicate paragraph breaks in Hellenistic Greek have not been identified, nor has the question of whether paragraphs in fact exist as a hierarchical level of discourse been definitively answered. There is no lexical form, syntactical property, or combination of the two that has been recognized as uniquely marking paragraph boundaries (that is, serving that function and none other), and various exegetes and editors differ in their intuitive placement of paragraph breaks. In fact, linguists debate whether there are unique features determining paragraph boundaries in any language. Some argue that a typology of paragraphs can be constructed which reflects how paragraphs function in larger discourse. Others question the existence of paragraphs altogether, arguing that discourse is a linear process of tighter or looser cohesion rather than a hierarchical system of which paragraphs form one level.[55] Halliday and Hasan suggest, 'Some writers in particular seem to achieve a sort of periodic rhythm in which there is a regular alternation between tight and loose texture. In this connection we see the importance of the paragraph. The paragraph is a device introduced into the written language to suggest this kind of periodicity.'[56] I suspect that their insight that orthographic paragraphs in English reflect tighter and looser topical cohesion rather than distinct hierarchical entities is applicable to the Greek of the New Testament as well.

Having said that, there are places in Matthew's narrative framework where stronger or weaker shifts of focus in the discourse are intuitively apparent, even if specific syntactical or semantic features associated with

'Neither at 4.17 nor at 16.21 does a new main part begin...' (Luz, *Matthew 1–7*, p. 37).

55. See, for example, R.E. Longacre, 'The Paragraph as a Grammatical Unit', in Givón (ed.), *Discourse and Syntax*, pp. 115-34, and J. Hinds, 'Organizational Patterns in Discourse', in Givón (ed.), *Discourse and Syntax*, pp. 135-57, who argue for the existence of the paragraph as a hierarchical level in discourse, and Unger, 'Scope', who argues that there is no evidence for hierarchical organization in discourse, but that intuitions underlying the notion of hierarchical discourse structure arise from cognitive processes in text comprehension.

56. Halliday and Hasan, *Cohesion*, p. 296.

such shifts are not yet fully recognized, and even if editors may sometimes disagree about assigning a transitional statement to a preceding unit or to a subsequent one. For want of a better term or a more precise definition, I will refer to stretches of tighter cohesion between shifts at various levels as paragraphs. The paragraph divisions supplied by the editors of NA[27] serve as the beginning point for this analysis, not because they are thought to be beyond debate, but because they serve as an ostensibly neutral witness for the present study.

As I have said, τότε appears 27 times in the first narrative sentence of an NA[27] paragraph. Τότε is also used 7 times in the last narrative sentence of a paragraph and 21 times in narrative sentences within a paragraph. Τότε-sentences with SV constituent order are paragraph-initial more frequently than are τότε-sentences overall: three-quarters (13/17, 76%) of the instances of τότε with SV constituent order coincide with paragraph breaks in NA[27].[57] As I proposed above, 26.56, the only one of the seven paragraph-final sentences with τότε in NA[27] which has SV constituent order, should also be understood as the first sentence of the following paragraph. This means that more than 80% of the instances of τότε with SV constituent order (14/17, 82%) coincide with paragraph breaks in NA[27].

In addition to SV constituent order as a paragraph-initial feature with τότε, sentences in which τότε is combined with an aorist tense-form finite verb also appear to be likely to coincide with the beginning of paragraphs in NA[27] (20/34, 59%), in spite of the strong association between τότε and present tense-forms. In contrast, only about a third of sentences with τότε and present tense-form verbs (7/20, 35%) are paragraph-initial in NA[27].

Simply put, τότε is often found at the beginning of an NA[27] paragraph. When τότε is combined with SV constituent order in Matthew's narrative framework it is even more likely to coincide with the beginning of a paragraph in NA[27] (14/17, 82%). Sentences with τότε and SV constituent order usually also have an aorist tense-form finite verb (16/17, 94%; the exception is 15.12, which has a present tense-form). Again, the small

---

57. Overall, sentences in which τότε is combined with a grammaticalized subject are more likely to coincide with the beginning of paragraphs in NA[27], regardless of constituent order. More than half of VS sentences with τότε (11/21, or 52%) are paragraph-initial, compared to less than one-fifth of sentences in which no subject is grammaticalized (3/17, or 18%). It is not surprising to find that a grammaticalized subject, as a formal feature associated with subject switch, is likely to occur at the beginning of a paragraph.

sample size limits conclusions based on these observations, but it appears that a combination of τότε, SV constituent order and finite aorist tense-forms serve as mutually reinforcing linguistic elements signaling the beginning of a paragraph or similar unit within Matthew's narrative framework. Given that τότε has a strong association in the narrative framework with VS constituent order and with present tense-form finite verbs, the combination of τότε with SV constituent order and an aorist tense-form finite verb represents a relatively marked use of τότε in narrative in terms of its distributional frequency, a use which tends to signal the beginning of a stretch of more tightly cohesive discourse traditionally understood as a paragraph.

Τότε *with* προσέρχομαι *and* προσηνέχθη/-θησαν. Not only do sentences in which τότε appears with SV constituent order tend to coincide with the beginning of paragraphs in NA[27], so also does the combination of τότε with either of two lexical items favored by Matthew, προσέρχομαι and προσφέρω (or, more specifically, passive forms of προσφέρω). The tendency for these two items to be thematic—whether as a finite verb or as a participle—appears to override Matthew's preference for SV constituent order in paragraph-initial uses of τότε.

Matthew uses προσέρχομαι far more frequently than do the other Evangelists. A search using GRAMCORD's Accordance program indicates that προσέρχομαι appears 51 times in Matthew's Gospel, either as a present or aorist finite form (23 times) or as an aorist participle (28 times), together representing a frequency of about 2.40 times per thousand words. By contrast, it appears only five times in Mark's Gospel (0.38 per thousand), ten times each in Luke's Gospel (0.45 per thousand) and in Acts (0.48 per thousand), but only once in John's Gospel (0.05 per thousand). Of Matthew's 51 uses of προσέρχομαι, 45 occur in the narrative framework. Seven of these 45 sentences (7/45, 16%; $z = 2.00$) have τότε as the sentence conjunction:[58]

9.14   τότε προσέρχονται αὐτῷ οἱ μαθηταὶ Ἰωάννου λέγοντες...
15.1   τότε προσέρχονται τῷ Ἰησοῦ ἀπὸ Ἱεροσολύμων Φαρισαῖοι
        καὶ γραμματεῖς λέγοντες...

58. See also Mt. 4.11, in which προσέρχομαι occurs in a clause following and closely related to one with τότε: τότε ἀφίησιν αὐτὸν ὁ διάβολος, καὶ ἰδοὺ ἄγγελοι προσῆλθον καὶ διηκόνουν αὐτῷ. Davies and Allison suggest, 'In our present passage, 4.1-11, presumably even the devil and the angels (vv. 3, 11) approach Jesus with some diffidence' (Davies and Allison, *Matthew*, I, p. 360).

15.12   τότε προσελθόντες οἱ μαθηταὶ λέγουσιν αὐτῷ...

17.19   τότε προσελθόντες οἱ μαθηταὶ τῷ Ἰησοῦ κατ' ἰδίαν εἶπον ...

18.21   τότε προσελθὼν ὁ Πέτρος εἶπεν αὐτῷ ...

20.20   τότε προσῆλθεν αὐτῷ ἡ μήτηρ τῶν υἱῶν Ζεβεδαίου μετὰ τῶν
        υἱῶν αὐτῆς προσκυνοῦσα καὶ αἰτοῦσά τι ἀπ' αὐτοῦ.

26.50   τότε προσελθόντες ἐπέβαλον τὰς χεῖρας ἐπὶ τὸν Ἰησοῦν καὶ
        ἐκράτησαν αὐτόν.

In each of these sentences προσέρχομαι is the thematic element, whether as a finite form or as a participle.[59] Both instances of προσέρχομαι as a present tense-form (9.14 and 15.1) occur with τότε. All but 26.50, the moment of Jesus' arrest, have a grammaticalized subject. All but 26.50 function as speech margins for questions asked of Jesus, five with forms of λέγω—finite where προσέρχομαι is a participle, and as a participle where προσέρχομαι is finite—and one with αἰτοῦσα. And all but 26.50 are the first sentence in a paragraph in NA[27].

Scholars have suggested that Matthew's use of προσέρχομαι has theological significance, that people 'approach' Jesus with reverence rather than merely coming to him. Davies and Allison write:

> Matthew's excessive use of προσέρχομαι (Mt: 52; Mk: 5; Lk: 10) may serve the function of emphasizing Jesus' majesty. Of its fifty-two occurrences, fifty involve people or spirits—friend and foe alike—making approach to Jesus. (In 28.18 the resurrected Jesus is the subject, in 17.7 the transfigured Jesus.) The linking with προσκυνέω (8.2; 9.18; 20.20; 28.9) and the use of the word in Judaism in connexion with the cult, with the worship of God, and with approaching kings and entering courts (e.g. Lev 9.5; Num 18.4; Deut 25.1; Jer 7.16; Heb 10.1; 1 Pet 2.4; Josephus, *Ant.* 12.19) should perhaps tell us that the verb implies reverence and circumspection.[60]

Gundry also comments on the association of προσέρχομαι with προσκυνέω in Matthew's Gospel and agrees that προσέρχομαι 'connotes the divine dignity of Jesus, who is to be approached only with reverence'.[61]

---

59. By contrast, when combined with other sentence conjunctions προσέρχομαι appears either thematically or with another topical theme.

60. Davies and Allison, *Matthew*, I, p. 360. (Davies and Allison's count of 52 occurrences as opposed to GRAMCORD's 51 may be due to textual variations.) See also, J.R. Edwards, 'The Use of ΠΡΟΣΕΡΧΕΣΘΑΙ in the Gospel of Matthew', *JBL* 106 (1987), pp. 65-74.

61. Gundry, *Matthew*, pp. 27, 55. An Accordance search indicates that Matthew and John use προσκυνέω more frequently than do the other Gospel writers (Mt.: 13 instances [0.61 per 1000 words]; Mk: 2 [0.15]; Lk.: 3 [0.13], and Acts: 4 [0.19]; Jn: 11 [0.60]), but that only Matthew combines προσέρχομαι and προσκυνέω: in a single

He adds, 'In Matthew, others approach Jesus; he does not need to approach them. There are only two exceptions, 17.7 and 28.18, where Jesus has to approach his disciples because his transfiguration and resurrection have incapacitated them.'[62]

Luz points out both the Evangelist's general tendency to replace Mark's simpler verbs with compound forms and his additional preference for another verb, προσφέρω, noting that 'Matthew with his inclination to formulaic phrases replaces in 17 of 22 cases a Markan *verbum simplex* with προσέρχομαι or προσφέρω...'[63] Although Matthew's use of προσφέρω is not as striking as his use of προσέρχομαι, like προσέρχομαι he uses it more frequently than do the other Evangelists. An Accordance search indicates that προσφέρω occurs 15 times in the Gospel of Matthew (0.71 times per thousand words), 10 of these in the narrative framework. It appears only three times in Mark's Gospel (0.23 per thousand), four times in Luke's Gospel (0.18 per thousand) and three times in Acts (0.14 per thousand), and twice in John's Gospel (0.11 per thousand). When people cannot 'approach' Jesus on their own (προσέρχομαι), others 'bring' them (προσφέρω).[64] See, for example, the catalog of those brought to Jesus for healing in 4.24.[65]

Matthew's Gospel is the only one of the four Gospels in which προσφέρω appears in a passive form.[66] He uses third-person aorist passive finite forms of προσφέρω three times: προσηνέχθη and προσηνέχθησαν once each in the narrative framework (12.22 and 19.13), and προσηνέχθη in one other instance, in a parable (18.24).[67] Both of the occurrences of προσηνέχθη/-θησαν in the narrative framework are

---

clause in 8.2 and 20.20, and in subsequent clauses in 28.9.

62. Gundry, *Matthew*, p. 148. There are, however, uses of προσέρχομαι in Matthew's narrative framework that do not involve others approaching Jesus. See, for example, 14.12, 26.60, 26.69, 26.73, 27.58 and 28.2.

63. Luz, *Matthew 1–7*, p. 52 n. 92.

64. 'Comparison with the Synoptic parallels shows that the word προσφέρειν is a stereotyped usage of Matthew's for the bringing of the sick to Jesus' (Held, 'Miracle Stories', p. 230). See also Edwards, 'ΠΡΟΣΕΡΧΕΣΘΑΙ', p. 72.

65. For similar uses of προσφέρω see Mt. 8.16, 9.2, 9.32, 14.35 and 17.16. But for προσφέρω with an inanimate object bought to Jesus, see Mt. 22.19.

66. But see one use of the passive form προσηνέχθη, in Acts 21.26, in the context of an offering (προσφορά) made in fulfillment of Paul's vow.

67. In the Parable of the Unforgiving Servant, the servant owing a thousand talents is 'brought' to the king for an ominous settling of accounts (18.24). Τότε is not used in this sentence.

combined with τότε in a manner similar to the combination of τότε and προσέρχομαι:

12.22 τότε προσηνέχθη αὐτῷ δαιμονιζόμενος τυφλὸς καὶ κωφός...
19.13 τότε προσηνέχθησαν αὐτῷ παιδία ἵνα τὰς χεῖρας ἐπιθῇ αὐτοῖς καὶ προσεύξηται·

Here we find two examples of those unable to approach (προσέρχομαι) Jesus on their own who are instead brought to him by others: first, the blind and mute man who no doubt required physical assistance (12.22), and secondly, children dependent on the initiative of adults (19.13). As is the case with the combination of τότε and προσέρχομαι, προσηνέχθη/-θησαν is the thematic element. As is the case with the combination of τότε and προσέρχομαι (except for 26.50, Jesus' arrest), there is a grammaticalized subject. And as is the case with the combination of τότε and προσέρχομαι (except for 26.50), both of these sentences are paragraph-initial in NA[27].

To summarize, τότε is found with προσέρχομαι and προσφέρω about twice as often as would be expected based on the overall frequency of these lexical items in Matthew's narrative framework. Τότε is used in about 16% of the occurrences of προσέρχομαι (7/45; $z = 2.00$) and 20% of the occurrences of προσφέρω in the narrative framework (2/10), although it appears as the sentence conjunction in only about 8% of narrative sentences. More specifically, it is found with both of the passive forms of προσφέρω in the narrative framework—a form unique to Matthew's Gospel—and none of the active forms. In each of these instances προσέρχομαι or προσηνέχθη/-θησαν is the thematic element in the sentence.

The combination of τότε and προσέρχομαι or προσηνέχθη/-θησαν appears in almost a third of the narrative sentences with τότε that begin paragraphs in NA[27] (8/27, 30%).[68] That is to say, not only does τότε appear more frequently with these forms than would be expected based on its overall frequency in narrative, but eight of the nine narrative sentences in which τότε occurs with προσέρχομαι or προσηνέχθη/-θησαν function as the first sentence in a paragraph in NA[27] (8/9, 89%).

Again an element of continuity is maintained in Matthew's use of τότε, in that each of these eight sentences at the beginning of NA[27] paragraphs introduces an incident within a block of narrative discourse—usually one in a series of related pericopes—rather than a higher-level break in the

---

68. Mt. 9.14, 12.22, 15.1, 15.12, 17.19, 18.21, 19.13 and 20.20.

narrative. The six with προσέρχομαι which function as speech margins introduce questions asked of Jesus which in some way arise from incidents or teaching in the same discourse context: questions asked by John's disciples in 9.14, by Pharisees and scribes from Jerusalem in 15.1, by Jesus' own disciples in 15.12 and 17.19, by Peter in 18.21, and by the mother of Zebedee's sons in 20.20. The two sentences in which προσηνέχθη/-θησαν appear (12.22 and 19.13) likewise introduce paragraphs which are tied to their immediate discourse context. The healing of the blind and dumb demoniac in 12.22 is linked both to the preceding general description of healings with an accompanying fulfillment statement (12.15-21), and to the following confrontation between Jesus and the Pharisees concerning his relationship to demons. Jesus' blessing of the children in 19.13-15 is less tied to the immediately preceding unit on divorce, but is part of a series of pericopes concerning teaching on the kingdom of heaven. Mt. 19.13-15, in which Jesus pronounces that the kingdom of heaven belongs to 'such as these', is preceded in this series by the interchange between Jesus and his disciples in 18.1-5 concerning greatness in the kingdom of heaven (18.4, 'Whoever becomes humble like this child is the greatest in the kingdom of heaven') and by a parable of the kingdom (the Parable of the Unforgiving Servant, 18.23-35), and followed by an account of a rich young man's difficulty entering the kingdom of heaven (19.19-26) and another kingdom parable (the parable of the laborers in the vineyard, 20.1-16).

The sample sizes for τότε with προσέρχομαι and προσφέρω are relatively small: only 55 occurrences of τότε, 45 of προσέρχομαι and 10 of προσφέρω among 720 sentences in Matthew's narrative framework. Thus conclusions drawn must be tentative. However, it does appear that in the Gospel of Matthew the combination of τότε and thematic προσέρχομαι or προσηνέχθη/-θησαν is used in the introduction of incidents within—but not higher-level breaks between—larger units. The marked status of προσέρχομαι and προσφέρω in Matthew's Gospel suggests that τότε is also in some sense a mutually redundant indicator of markedness in these discourse contexts.

Summary. I have identified four syntactical and lexical collocations which tend to be found with τότε in Matthew's narrative framework: present-tense finite verbs in past-referring narrative; thematic finite verbs; VS constituent order; and προσέρχομαι or προσηνέχθη/-θησαν. Of the 55 uses of τότε as a sentence conjunction in the narrative framework of

Matthew's Gospel, only 2 (9.14 and 13.36) share all four of these features, but one-third (18/55) share at least three of the four, more than half (30/55) share at least two of the features listed, and about 70% (39/55) are accounted for by at least one of these features. Of the remaining 16 uses of τότε as a sentence conjunction in the narrative framework, 11 are examples of paragraph-initial τότε with SV constituent order.

This leaves only five uses of τότε in Matthew's narrative framework unaccounted for by the present discussion of syntactical and lexical collocations:

8.26   τότε ἐγερθεὶς ἐπετίμησεν τοῖς ἀνέμοις καὶ τῇ θαλάσσῃ, καὶ ἐγένετο γαλήνη μεγάλη.

13.36   τότε ἀφεὶς τοὺς ὄχλους ἦλθεν εἰς τὴν οἰκίαν.

15.28   τότε ἀποκριθεὶς ὁ Ἰησοῦς εἶπεν αὐτῇ, ὦ γύναι, μεγάλη σου ἡ πίστις· γενηθήτω σοι ὡς θέλεις. καὶ ἰάθη ἡ θυγάτηρ αὐτῆς ἀπὸ τῆς ὥρας ἐκείνης.

26.65   τότε ὁ ἀρχιερεὺς διέρρηξεν τὰ ἱμάτια αὐτοῦ λέγων, ἐβλασφήμησεν· τί ἔτι χρείαν ἔχομεν μαρτύρων; ἴδε νῦν ἠκούσατε τὴν βλασφημίαν· (26.66) τί ὑμῖν δοκεῖ; οἱ δὲ ἀποκριθέντες εἶπαν, ἔνοχος θανάτου ἐστίν.

27.58   τότε ὁ Πιλᾶτος ἐκέλευσεν ἀποδοθῆναι.

Of these five, 13.36 is paragraph-initial, although it does not exhibit SV constituent order. Three others, 8.26, 15.28 and 26.65, may be considered climactic points in their respective pericopes—a possible discourse function of τότε which will be considered below, following a brief summary of Allen's multivariate analysis of my data on τότε in Matthew's narrative framework.

Multivariate Analysis

Allen's initial univariate analysis of the data I compiled and selected from Matthew's Gospel indicates that all fields (constituent order, topic switch [= subject switch], verbal tense-form, topical theme and subject reference)—with the exception of use as a speech margin—significantly affect the choice of τότε rather than καί.[69] She observes, however, that 'none of the effects are particularly large'.[70] The feature with the most notable effect is the verbal tense-form 'present'.[71] Allen calculates an odds ratio of 6.76

69. Allen, 'Greek Syntactical Analysis', p. 39.

70. Allen, 'Greek Syntactical Analysis', p. 41; see also Allen and Farewell, this volume, §4.3(i).

71. Allen, 'Greek Syntactical Analysis', p. 40; see also Allen and Farewell, this volume, §4.3(i).

for τότε with present tense-form verbs, indicating that τότε is 6.76 times more likely to appear with present tense-forms than is καί. Allen also finds that τότε is 5.88 times more likely to appear with proper nouns than is καί.

In her multivariate analysis, Allen identifies an interaction between τότε, proper noun subject reference and $S_1 V$ constituent order. However, in addition to being subject to the same concerns discussed in Chapter 5 regarding the parsing of 'proper nouns' in the database, this effect is based on only seven sentences in the data set for the model, six of which show the combination of τότε, proper noun subject reference and $S_1 V$ constituent order.[72]

Describing the logistic regression model she formulates for τότε in Matthew's narrative framework leads Allen to point out again that 'the effects are relatively small'.[73] In testing the model against the data, Allen finds that 'the average probability of assigning conjunction "tote" to a clause that did in fact have conjunction "tote" is 33.34%. The average probability of assigning conjunction 'tote' to a clause that in reality had conjunction "kai" is 12.55%.' Allen believes that the small difference between these two average probabilities 'reflects the less distinct structures associated with conjunction "tote"'.[74] As she explains

> It can be seen that clauses with conjunction 'de' and clauses with 'no conjunction' are very different in structure from each other and from clauses with conjunction 'kai'. The exception appears to be conjunction 'tote'; few variables have a noticeable effect on its choice over 'kai', and those that do also affect the choice of either using 'de' or having 'no conjunction'.[75]

These findings lead Allen to speculate, 'It could possibly be concluded that Matthew used "tote" as an option when variety was required'.[76]

Discourse Functions of τότε *in Matthew's Narrative Framework*

Allen may be correct that as a 'less distinct' sentence conjunction Matthew uses τότε simply for stylistic variety. However, combining qualitative

---

72. Mt. 2.7, 2.16, 4.1, 16.24, 23.1, 27.58 (all with aorist finite verbs). All but 27.58 are paragraph-initial in NA^{27}.

73. Allen, 'Greek Syntactical Analysis', p. 45.

74. Allen, 'Greek Syntactical Analysis', pp. 45-46; see also Allen and Farewell, this volume, §5.2.

75. Allen, 'Greek Syntactical Analysis', p. 47.

76. Allen, 'Greek Syntactical Analysis', p. 48; see also Allen and Farewell, this volume, §5.2.

analysis with quantitative analysis may help to give a more developed picture of the role of τότε in Matthew's narrative framework.

Each of the characteristic collocations identified above gives a piece of the picture, but none of them fully accounts for τότε's function at the level of discourse in Matthew's Gospel. Putting these pieces together, the evidence from Matthew's Gospel suggests that τότε is a signal of continuity in Matthew's narrative framework. However, at the same time that τότε is an indicator of discourse continuity, by its rarity and the contexts in which it is used it also appears to signal some measure of markedness or potential prominence. There are a number of discourse contexts in which τότε appears, but no single feature which it appears to mark. Instead it functions as a more general signal to the audience of 'marked continuity', that is, of something notable in the mental representation they are constructing of the discourse, whether on the level of discourse structure as a paragraph- or episode-initial signal, or within an episode.

Continuity

In some respects the discourse 'slots' τότε fills in Matthew's narrative framework are similar to those of καί, the unmarked signal of continuity, such as the Evangelist's tendency to use it with VS constituent order, and the fact that it is commonly paired with thematic finite verbs. It may also be that τότε's sentence-initial position, like that of καί, reflects its function as a marker of continuity, while conjunctions such as δέ, οὖν and γάρ which signal some kind of discontinuity are postpositive (see on οὖν and γάρ, Chapter 8). That τότε never appears with such signals of narrative discontinuity as temporal prepositional phrases or genitive absolute constructions is further evidence for a correlation between τότε and continuity rather than discontinuity in narrative discourse.[77]

Levinsohn concurs that τότε 'is used to indicate continuity of time and of other factors between subsections of an episode'.[78] He identifies several contexts in Matthew's narrative framework in which τότε serves as a

---

77. An analysis of τότε with subject switch is inconclusive in establishing an association between τότε and continuity in Matthew's narrative framework. While τότε appears in 8% of sentences in the narrative framework, it also appears in 8% of sentences in which there is a switch in subject from the previous narrative sentences ($43/516$; $z = 0.59$) and in 6% of sentences in which there is no subject switch ($12/202$; $z = -0.91$).

78. Levinsohn, *Discourse Features*, p. 96.

signal of continuity within discourse. Levinsohn's contexts of use and examples include the following:[79]

- between units that deal with the same topic but involve a modified cast—usually participants who featured earlier in the episode (2.16, 13.36, 13.43, 16.20)
- between sets of events that involve the same cast of participants (4.5, 26.31)
- between units in which the same major participant successively interacts with different participants (2.7, 11.20, 23.1)
- opening a narrative unit in which a presentational verb introduces new participants to an existing scene (3.13, 19.13)
- introducing a Scripture reference which was fulfilled at the time of and by the events that had just been described (2.17, 27.9)
- introducing the concluding event or speech to which an episode has been building up (8.26, 9.6, 9.29, 12.13, 15.28, 16.12, 26.74).

In each of these contexts τότε serves as a link between narrative units, statements or events rather than introducing a break in the narrative as does, for example, the asyndetic formula 'in that day/time/hour'. Levinsohn writes that ἐν ἐκείνῳ τῷ καιρῷ 'typically opens an episode that, while occurring in the same general time frame as the previous episode, is not otherwise associated together. Material linked by τότε, in contrast, is closely associated together.'[80]

Two comments on τότε's function as a signal of continuity in discourse can be added here. First, I am hesitant to describe τότε as a signal of 'narrative sequentiality' rather than 'discourse continuity', although the fact that conjunctive τότε is so evidently derived from the adverb τότε, 'then', and the observation that τότε has a more specialized use than does the more general continuous conjunction καί, might lead one in this direction. Temporal sequentiality is a semantic property of narrative discourse rather than of τότε as a sentence conjunction per se.[81] Καί could likewise be described as a signal of narrative sequentiality, in that temporal sequence is characteristic of the continuous narrative discourse in which καί is so frequently used (although of course καί is also used in different contexts of continuity, especially in non-narrative text). On the

79. Levinsohn, *Discourse Features*, pp. 96-97.
80. Levinsohn, *Discourse Features*, p. 95.
81. This excludes, of course, literary techniques such as flashbacks, which gain their power by contrast with the usual convention of temporal sequence.

other hand, that τότε is used as a sentence conjunction in Matthew's Gospel only in narrative or narrative-type discourse suggests that there is a very close correspondence between 'discourse continuity' as the procedural meaning conveyed by τότε and 'temporal sequentiality' as a semantic property of the narrative discourse in which τότε is used.

Secondly, Levinsohn observes that 'τότε both signals divisions of an episode into subsections and provides cohesion between them by indicating continuity of time and of other factors'.[82] The presence of some aspect of discontinuity—such as changes in cast or series of events that lead Levinsohn to identify divisions within episodes—raises the question why τότε rather than, for example, δέ would be chosen at these points. At this juncture the importance of authorial choice in the portrayal of discourse again becomes apparent. As narrative progresses there inevitably are aspects of both continuity (for example, continuing characters, temporal sequentiality, geographical settings which form the backdrop for a series of events) and discontinuity (for example, new characters being introduced, alternation between speakers, unreported gaps in time). At each step in the narrative the Evangelist determines whether continuity or discontinuity will be highlighted and then chooses from the system of sentence conjunctions the form which best conveys that preference. Or rather, a network of choices is made from different systems—sentence conjunction, constituent order, subject reference and so on. While καί, δέ, τότε or asyndeton may each be semantically compatible with a given set of circumstances in the narrative (that is, there are aspects of continuity or discontinuity that any one of these could be used to indicate), the author chooses which set of signals to use in the attempt to guide the audience toward a mental representation of the discourse which more closely corresponds to that intended by the author.

Markedness

At the same time that τότε is an indicator of continuity in the narrative, it is also a marked form in terms of its distributional frequency relative to καί and δέ, and thus appears to signal some degree of prominence in Matthew's narrative framework. While patterns of use of τότε and καί show certain similarities, τότε differs from καί in other respects. Not only is τότε considerably rarer in Matthew's narrative framework than is καί (335 occurrences of καί, but only 55 of τότε), τότε is also more sporadic

---

82. Levinsohn, *Discourse Features*, p. 96.

than καί. While a series of three or four sentences may have καί as the sentence conjunction, τότε is never found as the conjunction in even two subsequent narrative sentences. In terms of its distribution in Matthew's narrative, τότε is the marked form and καί the unmarked.

Τότε is also more likely to be found with a grammaticalized subject than is καί. Two-thirds (37/55, 67%) of sentences with τότε have grammaticalized subjects, while only 40% (135/335) of sentences with καί include a grammaticalized subject.[83] Since an explicit subject is not necessary in Greek, any grammaticalization of the subject can be seen as marked to some degree. Thus τότε is again more strongly associated with a marked syntactical feature, and καί with the unmarked form, that is, with monolectic verbs.

The use of τότε with present tense-forms in past-referring narrative (the 'historic present'), both in speech margins and in other narrative, is another example of τότε's association with a more marked feature. Such present tense-forms, in particular those outside speech margins, are used to establish prominence in the narrative.

In addition, τότε tends to be combined with lexical items which are significant in Matthean theology and which can be understood as marked lexical choices. I have described the use of τότε with προσέρχομαι and προσηνέχθη/-θησαν. Scholars have suggested that people 'approach' (προσέρχομαι) Jesus with reverence rather than merely coming toward him. Those who cannot 'approach' Jesus on their own are 'brought' (προσηνέχθη/-θησαν). Other lexical forms with which this may also be the case include συνῆκαν (with τότε in both its occurrences in Matthew's narrative framework, 16.12 and 17.13, when the disciples come to 'understand' something Jesus has said), and a Matthean fulfillment phrase variation, τότε ἐπληρώθη τὸ ῥηθὲν διὰ Ἰερεμίου τοῦ προφήτου λέγοντος (used in the only two references to Jeremiah by name in the narrative framework, 2.17 and 27.9).[84]

---

83. Overall, nearly two-thirds (448/720, 62%) of sentences in the narrative framework have a grammaticalized subject. In only a third of these does the subject follow the verb (VS constituent order: 147/448, 33%). However, the subject follows the verb in more than half of narrative sentences in which τότε occurs with a grammaticalized subject (20/37, 54%), exemplifying the Evangelist's tendency to use τότε with VS constituent order rather than SV.

84. Davies and Allison suggest two possible reasons why τότε occurs in these two formula quotations rather than the more common ἵνα: first, 2.17 and 27.9 both introduce citations which are related in the text to evils suffered as a result of

As important as syntactical and lexical collocations are the specific discourse contexts in which τότε-sentences tend to be found in Matthew's narrative framework. As discussed above, half of the occurrences of τότε in the narrative framework—and 80% of those with SV constituent order, especially with aorist finite verbs—coincide with the beginning of a paragraph in NA[27]. This may be described as a marked use of τότε in terms of discourse structure, the closest thing to a paragraph marker that one finds in Matthew's narrative framework. There is still an element of continuity in this use, in that τότε introduces units within an episode rather than serving as a signal of higher-level breaks between episodes.

Τότε also appears in Matthew's narrative framework in the speech margins of important statements within a paragraph, or as the sentence conjunction in a climactic, often final, sentence in a paragraph. Examples of τότε with climactic statements include Jesus' final refusal to succumb to the Devil's temptations (4.10, 'You shall worship the Lord your God and shall serve only him'); his command to the paralyzed man concerning his healing (9.6, 'Get up, pick up your bed and go home'); his statement to his disciples that 'the harvest is plentiful but the laborers are few' (9.37); his statement in response to the Canaanite woman, 'Great is your faith, woman. Let it be done for you as you desire' (15.28); and his admonition to 'render unto Caesar the things that are Caesar's' (22.21). Examples of τότε with actions or events which function as a climax of the pericope in which they are found (some of which can also be understood as indirect statements) include Jesus' rebuke of the winds and waves, calming the storm at sea (8.26); the disciples' eventual understanding concerning 'the yeast of the Pharisees and Sadducees' (16.12); Jesus' command to the disciples to keep his identity secret (16.20); Jesus' arrest (26.50); the high priest's judgment of blasphemy against Jesus (26.65); and Peter's third and final denial of Jesus (26.74). Again, this list of examples is illustrative rather than exhaustive, but it would be difficult to argue that the instances listed above do not represent important statements, actions or events in Matthew's portrayal of Jesus.

However, it should be noted that the use of τότε in the speech margins of 'climactic statements' in Matthew's Gospel does not equal a significantly increased use in 'pronouncements' or 'pronouncement stories' as traditionally understood by form critics—a form which has also variously

opposition to Jesus; secondly, in each case the Old Testament Scripture is fulfilled by human beings—presumably unintentionally—rather than by the direct action of God or Jesus. See Davies and Allison, *Matthew*, I, p. 266.

been labeled 'apophthegm',[85] 'paradigm',[86] 'anecdote' or, more recently under the influence of Greek rhetoric, 'chreia'.[87] Taylor, who coined the term 'pronouncement stories', states that their 'chief characteristic...is that they culminate in a saying of Jesus which expresses some ethical or religious precept'.[88] Tannehill describes a pronouncement story as 'a brief narrative in which the climactic (and often final) element is a pronouncement... This utterance must be the dominant element in the story as a whole.'[89]

Varying lists and systems of classification of pronouncement stories in the Gospels have been offered by scholars, but in Robbins's view there is a consensus that ten well-known stories in Mark's Gospel represent the form (plus an additional story, Lk. 14.1-6, which has no Matthean parallel): Eating with Tax Collectors and Sinners, Mk 2.15-17 = Mt. 9.10-13; the Question about Fasting, Mk 2.18-22 = Mt. 9.14-17; Plucking Grain on the Sabbath, Mk. 2.23-28 = Mt. 12.1-8; True Relatives of Jesus, Mk 3.31-34 = Mt. 12.46-50; Blessing the Children, Mk 10.13-16 = Mt. 19.13-15; the Rich Young Man, Mk 10.17-22 = Mt. 19.16-22; the Sons of Zebedee, Mk 10.35-40 = Mt. 20.20-23; Paying Taxes to Caesar, Mk 12.13-17 = Mt. 22.15-22; On the Resurrection, Mk 12.18-27 = Mt. 22.23-33; and the Anointing at Bethany, Mk 14.3-9 = Mt. 26.6-13.[90]

Although this is not an exhaustive list of pronouncement stories in Matthew, these ten may serve as the data set for a brief inquiry into τότε with 'pronouncements'. Of these ten, only four contain a use of τότε anywhere in the pericope (the Question about Fasting, 9.14-17; Blessing the Children, 19.13-15; the Sons of Zebedee, 20.20-23; Paying Taxes to Caesar, 22.15-22 [two occurrences]). In each of these four stories, τότε

85. See R. Bultmann, *The History of the Synoptic Tradition* (trans. J. Marsh; Oxford: Basil Blackwell, 1972), pp. 11-69.

86. See M. Dibelius, *From Tradition to Gospel* (trans. B.L. Woolf; London: Ivor Nicholson and Watson, 1934), pp. 37-69.

87. See, for example, V.K. Robbins, 'Chreia & Pronouncement Story in Synoptic Studies', in B.L. Mack and V.K. Robbins, *Patterns of Persuasion in the Gospels* (Sonoma, CA: Polebridge Press, 1989), pp. 1-29; see also V.K. Robbins, 'Apophthegm', in D.N. Freedman (ed.), *The Anchor Bible Dictionary. I. A–C* (New York: Doubleday, 1992), p. 307.

88. V. Taylor, *The Formation of the Gospel Tradition* (London: Macmillan, 1933), p. 63.

89. R.C. Tannehill, 'Introduction: The Pronouncement Story and Its Types', *Semeia* 20 (1981), pp. 1-2.

90. See Robbins, 'Apophthegm', p. 308.

occurs in the first sentence of the pericope—the paragraph-initial use of τότε discussed above. In only one case in the ten stories listed does Matthew use τότε in the speech margin of a concluding pronouncement: 22.21, τότε λέγει αὐτοῖς, Ἀπόδοτε οὖν τὰ Καίσαρος Καίσαρι καὶ τὰ τοῦ θεοῦ τῷ θεῷ. Thus while τότε is used with a number of 'climactic statements' in Matthew's Gospel, as in the examples above, it does not appear to be used systematically as a formal element in 'pronouncement stories'.[91]

In his discussion of τότε within paragraphs, Levinsohn observes that 'τότε is used also to introduce the concluding event or speech to which an incident has been building up'.[92] He argues that 'typically, conclusions introduced with τότε attain the goal sought or predicted in earlier events', offering Peter's denial in 26.74, predicted earlier by Jesus, as an example.[93] Even if this is true—and I suspect Levinsohn is overstating the case—any attempt to define 'attainment of goal' as a quantifiable discourse context in order to calculate whether τότε appears more frequently with goal attainment than do other sentence conjunctions would be problematic. Buth simply asserts, 'When Matthew uses *tote* in the middle or at the end of a paragraph, it usually marks a peak', offering a succinct statement of Matthew's tendency in using τότε within paragraphs.[94]

In summary, in Matthew's narrative framework τότε is relatively rare and tends to be used with a number of marked features (grammaticalized subject, present tense-form verbs, theologically important lexical choices) and in potentially marked discourse contexts (at the beginning of paragraphs, and in climactic statements, actions or events). Τότε is not used uniquely or consistently with any one of these features, but where it does

91. Reedy suggests that while Matthew uses προσέρχομαι in a number of contexts, 'the usage is most characteristic of Matthew's composition of pronouncement stories', offering 11 examples of προσέρχομαι in the introduction to pronouncement stories: 8.19, 9.14, 15.1, 16.1, 17.24, 18.1, 18.21, 19.3, 19.16, 21.23, 22.23-24a (C.J. Reedy, 'Rhetorical Concerns and Argumentative Techniques in Matthean Pronouncement Stories', in K.H. Richards [ed.], *Society of Biblical Literature 1983 Seminar Papers* [Chico, CA: Scholars Press, 1983], p. 221). Even here, however, the frequency of τότε is no higher than its general association with προσέρχομαι: τότε appears with 7 of the 45 uses of προσέρχομαι in the narrative framework, and with only 2 of the instances of προσέρχομαι in this set of 11 pronouncement stories (9.14, 15.1; 2/11, 18%).

92. Levinsohn, *Discourse Features*, p. 97.

93. Levinsohn, *Discourse Features*, p. 97.

94. See Buth, 'Perspective', p. 8.

occur it serves alongside such features as a mutually redundant signal of marked continuity in the narrative framework.

Summary and Conclusions

I have described a number of syntactical and lexical collocations characteristically found with τότε in Matthew's narrative framework: its combination with present-tense indicative verbs in past-referring narrative; its frequency with thematic finite verbs; the tendency for τότε to appear with VS constituent order (and with V[S] constituent order in general), but with SV constituent order when paragraph-initial; and the association between τότε and προσέρχομαι or προσηνέχθη/-θησαν. In some respects τότε shows patterns of use in Matthew's narrative framework similar to those of καί, the unmarked signal of continuity, and of asyndeton as a signal of close continuity in speech margins. On the other hand, τότε differs from καί in important respects such as its relative rarity and its tendency to be combined with a grammaticalized subject and present tense-forms. These characteristics, along with an examination of the discourse contexts in which τότε appears in Matthew's narrative framework, lead to its characterization as a signal of 'marked continuity'.

There are a number of discourse contexts in which τότε appears, but no single contextual feature which it appears to mark. Neither does τότε display collocations with other linguistic features as strongly as do καί and δέ—leading Allen to describe τότε-sentences as 'less distinct' than those with other sentence conjunctions. The small sample size (only 55 occurrences of τότε among 720 sentences in the narrative framework) means that any conclusions about its function as a narrative connector in Matthew's Gospel must be suggestive rather than definitive. Nevertheless, with those caveats, τότε can be described as a signal of 'marked continuity' in Matthew's narrative framework. Τότε may function either on the level of discourse structure, for example, marking paragraphs within an episode, or at a more local level, marking the use of a theologically significant lexical form or a climactic point within a pericope. As a signal of marked continuity, the presence of τότε—along with collocations such as constituent order, thematization, verbal tense-form and/or lexical choices—helps the audience identify potentially prominent features as they construct and modify their mental representation of Matthew's Gospel.

Chapter 8

Γάρ AND οὖν: 'Off-line' Inference

Γάρ & οὖν	All sentences in Matthew	Narrative sentences	Exposition sentences	Speech sentences	Old Testament quotations
n =	2302	720	768	733	81
# γάρ	124	10	61	51	2
% γάρ	5%	1%	8%	7%	2%
# οὖν	56	2	31	23	0
% οὖν	2%	–	4%	3%	–

Introduction: Γάρ and οὖν in Narrative

The two remaining narrative sentence conjunctions in Matthew's Gospel, γάρ and οὖν, are treated together in this chapter. I take this approach both because there are very few instances of either in Matthew's narrative framework (as opposed to expository discourse or speech where they are considerably more frequent), and because they have important similarities in their function in discourse processing.

Infrequent in Narrative

In comparison to καί, δέ, τότε and asyndeton, γάρ and οὖν are used as narrative connectors only a few times each in the Gospel of Matthew. Only 10 of the 124 uses of γάρ identified in the database (6%) appear in the narrative framework although narrative sentences account for about a third (720/2302, 31%) of all sentences in Matthew's Gospel. These ten instances are:[1]

4.18   ἦσαν γὰρ ἁλιεῖς.
7.29   ἦν γὰρ διδάσκων αὐτοὺς ὡς ἐξουσίαν ἔχων καὶ οὐχ ὡς οἱ γραμματεῖς αὐτῶν.

---

1.   Square brackets in Greek examples represent textual variants included in the NA[27] text.

9.21 ἔλεγεν γὰρ ἐν ἑαυτῇ ἐὰν μόνον ἅψωμαι τοῦ ἱματίου αὐτοῦ σωθήσομαι.

14.3 ὁ γὰρ Ἡρῴδης κρατήσας τὸν Ἰωάννην ἔδησεν [αὐτόν] …

14.4 ἔλεγεν γὰρ ὁ Ἰωάννης αὐτῷ· οὐκ ἔξεστίν σοι ἔχειν αὐτήν.

14.24 ἦν γὰρ ἐναντίος ὁ ἄνεμος.

19.22 ἦν γὰρ ἔχων κτήματα πολλά.

26.43 ἦσαν γὰρ αὐτῶν οἱ ὀφθαλμοὶ βεβαρημένοι.

27.18 ᾔδει γὰρ ὅτι διὰ φθόνον παρέδωκαν αὐτόν.

28.2 ἄγγελος γὰρ κυρίου καταβὰς ἐξ οὐρανοῦ καὶ προσελθὼν ἀπεκύλισεν τὸν λίθον

Nine of these also occur in parallel readings in Mark's Gospel—all, that is, except 28.2, which has no Markan parallel.[2]

In addition, Matthew uses γάρ at two other points, not paralleled in the other Gospels, which introduce Old Testament citations supporting narrative events:[3]

2.5 οὕτως γὰρ γέγραπται διὰ τοῦ προφήτου· (2.6) καὶ σὺ Βηθλέεμ, γῆ Ἰούδα …

3.3 οὗτος γάρ ἐστιν ὁ ῥηθεὶς διὰ Ἡσαΐου τοῦ προφήτου λέγοντος· φωνὴ βοῶντος ἐν τῇ ἐρήμῳ …

Οὖν is even rarer in Matthew's narrative framework than is γάρ. Only 2 of the 56 uses of οὖν identified in the database (4%) appear in the narrative framework:

1.17 πᾶσαι οὖν αἱ γενεαὶ ἀπὸ Ἀβραὰμ ἕως Δαυὶδ γενεαὶ δεκατέσσαρες, καὶ ἀπὸ Δαυὶδ ἕως τῆς μετοικεσίας Βαβυλῶνος γενεαὶ δεκατέσσαρες, καὶ ἀπὸ τῆς μετοικεσίας Βαβυλῶνος ἕως τοῦ Χριστοῦ γενεαὶ δεκατέσσαρες.

2. Mt. 4.18 = Mk 1.16; Mt. 7.29 = Mk 1.22; Mt. 9.21 = Mk 5.28; Mt. 14.3 = Mk 6.17; Mt. 14.4 = Mk 6.18; Mt. 14.24 = Mk 6.48; Mt. 19.22 = Mk 10.22 (= Lk. 18.23); Mt. 26.43 = Mk 14.40; Mt. 27.18 = Mk 15.10. Mt. 28.2 has no parallel in Mark's Gospel, in that Mark does not mention who removed the stone from the tomb.

3. These two instances were not originally identified in the database as part of the narrative framework, and so are not included in computations concerning γάρ in narrative in Matthew's Gospel. In 2.5, Matthew appears to place the Old Testament material on the lips of the chief priests and scribes, and thus the γάρ-sentence is probably not within the narrative framework as construed for this study. However, it also appears to function in a manner similar to Matthew's other fulfillment quotations, supporting and interpreting events in the narrative (see below). Mt. 3.3 was omitted from the original database, being taken, by analogy with 2.5, as part of John the Baptist's proclamation in 3.1-2. It is more likely, however, that it properly belongs to the narrative framework. Abbott includes both these instances in his count of 12 uses of γάρ in 'strict narrative' in Matthew's Gospel (Abbott, *Johannine Grammar*, p. 102).

27.17 συνηγμένων οὖν αὐτῶν εἶπεν αὐτοῖς ὁ Πιλᾶτος· τίνα θέλετε ἀπολύσω ὑμῖν ...;

Neither of these two verses has a parallel in the other Gospels.

Even more than is the case with τότε or asyndeton, one implication of there being so few uses of γάρ or οὖν in narrative in the Gospel of Matthew is that a study of γάρ and οὖν in Matthew's narrative framework must depend on qualitative analysis, with only a small role played by quantitative comparisons. A second implication is that any conclusions drawn about the function of these forms in narrative must be tentative, reflecting the very small sample size available for analysis. For this reason, in describing the semantics of γάρ and οὖν in the Gospel of Matthew I also look briefly later in this chapter at their use in exposition.[4]

Traditional Grammarians

Treatments of γάρ and οὖν by Greek grammarians have tended to classify these two forms according to the logical relations they are understood to indicate between propositions. Γάρ is generally understood to give a reason or explanation, and οὖν to introduce a logical inference. Winer calls γάρ 'the most common causal particle in cultivated prose', and in conformity with what he considers its 'primary meaning', that of expressing a reason, it is used 'first, and very naturally, to introduce explanatory clauses'.[5] Robertson emphasizes the explanatory use, observing that γάρ 'does not always give a reason. It may be merely explanatory.' He concludes, 'It is a mistake, therefore, to approach the study of γάρ with the theory that it is always or properly an illative [that is, logically inferential], not to say causal, particle. It is best, in fact, to note the explanatory use first.'[6] Alongside the primary uses of γάρ as introducing a reason (the grounds for what is said), and introducing an explanation or elaboration, some grammarians add confirmation or assurance (that is, an emphatic use of γάρ), and some note its frequent use in questions—as in 27.23, when Pilate asks the crowds demanding Jesus' crucifixion, τί γάρ κακὸν ἐποίησεν;—as well as in answers and rejoinders.[7]

---

4.   Although γάρ and οὖν are relatively rare in Matthew's narrative framework compared to exposition and speech, in John's Gospel οὖν is used much more frequently as a narrative connector. See below on οὖν in John's Gospel.

5.   Winer, *Treatise*, p. 558.

6.   Robertson, *Grammar*, p. 1190.

7.   See, for example, BDF, §452; Dana and Mantey, *Grammar*, pp. 242-43; Porter, *Idioms*, p. 207. Winer, however, believes that in its use in questions 'γάρ seems to

Although γάρ is usually described as introducing a reason or an explanation, traditional grammarians have, in fact, long recognized that γάρ is
used in a range of relationships between propositions, not merely as a
logically inferential causal connector. In his study of particles during the
Classical period, Denniston goes further in exploring the sometimes psychologically rather than logically based relations between propositions
connected by γάρ. He uses the two basic categories of 'confirmatory and
causal, giving the ground for belief, or the motive for action', and explanatory, which 'is nearly related to the confirmatory'.[8] But he goes on to
delineate what he labels as some 'peculiarities' in these two uses. One is
that γάρ sometimes gives the motive for saying something rather than
giving the grounds for what was said.[9] Another is that 'the connexion of
thought is sometimes lacking in logical precision'.[10] Denniston comments
that although one can sometimes assume an ellipse between sentences that
would supply what is lacking in the connection between two propositions,
'this, though a convenient method of exposition, is psychologically somewhat misleading'. That is, it does not accurately reflect the train of thought
underlying the text, where 'the use of γάρ is regulated by the substance of
the thought and not by its form'.[11] And finally, there are cases where 'the
γάρ clause explains the tone of the preceding words, rather than their
content'.[12] Although Denniston is describing the use of particles in the
Classical period, there is a consensus among grammarians that γάρ is used
in the New Testament in a manner consistent with its Classical usage.[13]
His insights into non-logical inferences in which γάρ is used suggest that
the function of γάρ in the Greek of the New Testament is something other
than simply giving reasons or explanations.

Bird takes a similar line in his study of γάρ in Mark's Gospel, suggesting that at some points where the use of γάρ does not seem to be directly
causal or explicative γάρ 'draws attention to a further fact which, without
directly explaining the preceding sentence, is extremely relevant to the

have wandered farthest from its primary meaning' (Winer, *Treatise*, p. 559). Matthew
also uses the combination καὶ γάρ three times (8.9, 15.27, 26.73), but never in the
narrative framework.

  8. Denniston, *Greek Particles*, p. 58.
  9. Denniston, *Greek Particles*, p. 60.
  10. Denniston, *Greek Particles*, p. 61.
  11. Denniston, *Greek Particles*, p. 61.
  12. Denniston, *Greek Particles*, p. 62.
  13. See, for example, Robertson, *Grammar*, p. 1190; Turner, *Syntax*, p. 331; BDF,
§452.

understanding of the context'.[14] Thrall insists, however, contra Bird, that the logical connection between the contents of the γάρ-sentence and the previous sentence may be seen more explicitly if the order of sentences is reversed. In Mk 1.16, for example, although ἦσαν γὰρ ἁλιεῖς may seem, in Bird's terms, 'tautologous and lame' as an explanation following ἀμφιβάλλοντας ἐν τῇ θαλάσσῃ,[15] Thrall asserts that,

> it is only the order in which these separate items of information occur which produces this effect. A more logical narrator might well have written: καὶ παράγων παρὰ τὴν θάλασσαν τῆς Γαλιλαίας εἶδεν ἁλιεῖς τινας, Σίμωνα καὶ Ἀνδρέαν τὸν ἀδελφὸν τοῦ Σίμωνος, ἀμφιβάλλοντας ἐν τῇ θαλάσσῃ.[16]

Thrall's insistence on a logical relation between sentences conjoined by γάρ leads her to rewrite Mark's Gospel rather than consider other types of relations.

The idea that οὖν, like γάρ, is not necessarily or even primarily an illative or logically inferential connector is also recognized by grammarians of biblical Greek. On the one hand, οὖν is sometimes described as a 'syllogistic particle', emphasizing its role in logical inference.[17] But Blass, Debrunner and Funk, for example, state that οὖν 'does not always furnish a strictly causal connection, but may be used more loosely as a temporal connective in the continuation or resumption of a narrative'.[18] Donaldson, in particular, expresses an understanding of οὖν that is similar to the approach that I adopt: while Winer describes οὖν as expressing consequence and as 'the proper syllogistic particle',[19] in his English edition of Winer's grammar Moulton includes Donaldson's view that in Classical Greek οὖν 'is indicative rather of continuation and retrospect than of inference: and, in general, it should be rendered rather "accordingly", "as was said", "to proceed", than "therefore"…'[20] This treatment of οὖν as

---

14. C.H. Bird, 'Some γάρ Clauses in St Mark's Gospel', *JTS* 4 (1953), p. 173. Bird's main argument is that a number of γάρ-clauses in Mark's Gospel function as Old Testament allusions. This concerns various contexts in which γάρ is used in Mark's Gospel rather than the meaning of γάρ itself.

15. See Bird, 'Some γάρ Clauses', pp. 174-76.

16. Thrall, *Greek Particles*, pp. 47-48.

17. See, for example, Winer, *Treatise*, p. 555. For treatments of οὖν as a 'syllogistic particle' in earlier periods, see, for example, Kühner and Gerth, *Grammatik*, §507, §544 (1); Mayser, *Grammatik der Griechischen Papyri*, p. 150.

18. BDF, §451.

19. Winer, *Treatise*, p. 555.

20. Winer, *Treatise*, p. 555; see also J.W. Donaldson, *A Complete Greek Grammar*

indicating 'continuation and retrospect', that is, progression in the discourse with an eye to that which precedes, is very close to a procedural semantics for οὖν along the lines of that developed for other sentence conjunctions in this study.

More recent work along similar lines on particles in Classical Greek has reached comparable conclusions regarding pragmatic functions of γάρ and οὖν. Sicking asserts that 'γάρ marks a section as containing information supposed to be necessary towards understanding *what* has been said, or *that* it has been—or will be—said...' Οὖν, on the other hand, 'conveys that what precedes served an introductory or explanatory purpose: the speaker proceeds from preliminaries to main substance, or continues his argument or narrative after an inserted explanation or digression'.[21]

Procedural Meaning of γάρ *and* οὖν

I have said in previous chapters that sentence conjunctions encode procedural and non-truth-conditional meaning, indicating the ways the sentences they introduce are to be related to preceding discourse. These forms have a low level of semantic specificity, that is, a minimal semantic value, allowing their use in a range of discourse contexts where there may be a variety of semantic relationships between propositions.[22] Sentence conjunctions help guide an audience in the process of constructing or modifying mental representations of discourse.

In their respective roles as procedural signals in Matthew's narrative framework, γάρ and οὖν share several characteristics. Both are postpositive in terms of their position in the sentence. When used in the narrative framework both involve 'off-line' information, or material outside the narrative's sequence of events. Most importantly, both γάρ and οὖν play a role in guiding pragmatic inferences those in the audience make as they process the narrative.

Postpositive
It may seem simplistic to observe that both γάρ and οὖν are postpositive forms—that is, that they never appear as the first element in the sen-

for the Use of Students (Cambridge: Deighton Bell, 3rd edn, 1862), pp. 596-97.

21. Sicking, 'Devices for Text Articulation', p. 48. Sicking's statement indicates that γάρ is not always backward-referring in Classical Greek, and may instead anticipate the proposition which it strengthens (see below).

22. See Dik, *Coordination*, p. 269.

tence—but I believe this position is not insignificant. Γάρ and οὖν are similar to δέ, the other postpositive form in Matthew's set of sentence conjunctions, in that all signal a type of discontinuity. This contrasts with the sentence-initial conjunctions καί and τότε which signal continuity in the discourse. While Matthew generally uses δέ to signal discontinuity within the narrated events themselves (but not always—see, for example, 27.15-16), γάρ and οὖν function with respect to material which is discontinuous with the sequential flow of the narrative.

Off the Narrative Line
As procedural signals, γάρ and οὖν guide the audience to integrate additional material into the narrative discourse, or rather, into the mental representations which they construct of the discourse. This supplementary information about (for example) states, actions, mental processes, or customary practices of participants in the narrative helps make sense of events in the narrative framework but may be said to be off-line in terms of the sequential flow of narrated events. As Hopper points out, 'It is evidently a universal of narrative discourse that in any extended text an overt distinction is made between the language of the actual story line and the language of supportive material which does not itself narrate the main events'.[23] Sentences introduced by γάρ are off-line with respect to narrative sequentiality, while sentences introduced by οὖν follow off-line material and represent a return to the narrative line, indicating that the discourse continues with the integration of that off-line material.

For example, in the context of the narrated events of 19.16-22, in which a young man asks Jesus how he might have eternal life, the audience might question why he goes away grieving after Jesus' challenge to sell his belongings, have treasure in heaven, and come follow him (19.21). The next sentence, 19.22, ἦν γὰρ ἔχων κτήματα πολλά, is not part of the sequence of events. Instead, it functions to confirm the preceding proposition that he left grieving (γάρ he had great wealth), although it still requires the audience to make a series of pragmatic inferences leading to the conclusion that a person with many possessions might find it especially difficult to respond to Jesus' challenge.

It is worth considering whether the notion 'off-line' should be understood as a semantic feature associated with the contexts in which γάρ and οὖν are found in narrative, rather than as part of the conventional semantic content of γάρ or οὖν themselves. However, as noted above, work along

23. Hopper, 'Aspect and Foregrounding', p. 213.

similar lines on Classical Greek has reached similar conclusions regarding the functions of γάρ and οὖν in discourse. Analyzing the use of particles in Lysias, Sicking observes that γάρ and οὖν 'share the characteristic of assigning to a section of the text a different status from the preceding section', similar to the notion of γάρ and οὖν functioning with respect to material that is off-line in narrative.[24] Sicking's insight that in Classical Greek γάρ and οὖν mark sections of text as having a 'different status' helps confirm that in some sense the feature of signaling a shift from the primary thread of the discourse is part of the procedural content of γάρ and οὖν as conventionally used.

Pragmatic Inferences

In indicating material that is off-line with respect to the sequence of narrative events, both γάρ and οὖν are used to guide inferences the audience makes in discourse processing. The term 'inference' does not refer here only to explicitly logical operations. Rather than indicating logical relations between the contents of propositions, γάρ and οὖν signal discourse relations between the sentences themselves—that is, how the sentences are to fit together in a mental representation of the discourse. By 'inferential' I mean that a mental representation is strengthened or otherwise enhanced by the integration of additional material, using pragmatic inferences in the Gricean sense rather than rules of inference from formal logic. As I explained in Chapter 2, Grice was one of the first to suggest that much of the process of making sense of conversation (and, by analogy, other discourse) relies on the hearer making a number of inferences not about the logical content of individual sentences, but about how the speaker intends a statement to be taken in the context of the unfolding conversation.[25]

In Matthew's narrative framework, γάρ and οὖν are concerned with inferential relationships in discourse processing rather than just the recounting of narrated events. While καί, δέ, τότε and asyndeton guide the audience in various ways through a sequence of events in the narrative framework, γάρ and οὖν serve to help the audience make connections

24. Sicking, 'Devices for Text Articulation', p. 48.

25. See Grice, 'Logic and Conversation'; also Brown and Yule, *Discourse Analysis*, pp. 31-35. As I noted in Chapter 2, Sperber and Wilson see an even richer role for inference in communication in general than does Grice, including the process of making sense of the conventional meanings of words (Sperber and Wilson, *Relevance*, pp. 161-63).

between additional information and the current thread of the narrative. Γάρ and οὖν are used to help the audience integrate material which is off-line with respect to the main narrative events, but which aids in comprehending the events in the narrative which are on-line. In terms of mental representations in discourse processing, γάρ and οὖν each signal the audience to modify the mental representations they construct of discourse: γάρ by introducing material which confirms and strengthens the preceding proposition (usually but not necessarily by giving either a reason or elaboration), and οὖν by signaling that the ongoing representation is dependent in some way on material which precedes. Winer's observation that etymologically γάρ is a compound of γε and ἄρα or ἄρ, and 'expresses generally an affirmation or assent (γε) which stands in relation to what precedes (ἄρα !)' appears—whatever the value of etymology per se—to capture the pragmatic function of γάρ quite well.[26]

Examples
To illustrate, in 4.18 (the Matthean parallel to Mk 1.16 discussed above), Jesus is walking by the sea and sees two brothers who are casting nets, ἦσαν γὰρ ἁλιεῖς. Why the sudden introduction of nets into the narrative? Γάρ they were fishermen. This information confirms that the casting of nets should be integrated into the mental representation being constructed of the discourse and not discarded as an extraneous detail. Similarly, when Jesus' disciples, in a storm-tossed boat, see him walking on the sea (14.22-33), the inclusion of 14.24, ἦν γὰρ ἐναντίος ὁ ἄνεμος, strengthens the previous proposition that the boat, already far from land, is being beaten by waves: γάρ the wind was against them. The γάρ-sentence gives information which enhances the mental representation of the disciples' boat as being far from the shore and subject to wind-driven waves. Referring to Jesus' resurrection, in 28.2, ἄγγελος γὰρ κυρίου καταβὰς ἐξ οὐρανοῦ καὶ προσελθὼν ἀπεκύλισεν τὸν λίθον, it is not clear from the context whether the great earthquake mentioned in the preceding sentence (καὶ ἰδοὺ σεισμὸς ἐγένετο μέγας) is triggered, directly or indirectly, by the angel's rolling away the stone, but information about an angel from heaven rolling away the stone from the tomb serves to confirm the integration of a great earthquake into the mental representation of the discourse: γάρ an angel of the Lord came down from heaven (associated, somehow, with the earthquake).

26. Winer, *Treatise*, p. 558.

Γάρ's function of drawing attention 'to a further fact which...is extremely relevant to the understanding of the context'—to use Bird's terms[27]—is on display, for example, when Matthew uses it to introduce the Old Testament citation in 3.3. Following the introduction of John the Baptist (3.1) and a brief synopsis of his preaching (which includes a separate instance of γάρ: 3.2, μετανοεῖτε· ἤγγικεν γὰρ ἡ βασιλεία τῶν οὐρανῶν), Matthew writes, οὗτος γάρ ἐστιν ὁ ῥηθεὶς διὰ Ἡσαΐου τοῦ προφήτου λέγοντος· φωνὴ βοῶντος ἐν τῇ ἐρήμῳ... The γάρ-sentence, with the quotation from Isaiah it introduces, does not so much offer a reason that John calls the people to repent or an explanation of the content of John's preaching as it does help the audience understand the significance of John's appearance and proclamation. The audience makes inferences concerning John's role as a precursor to eschatalogical events on the basis of the juxtaposition of the on-line narrated events (3.1-2) and the off-line Old Testament prophecy, making use also of the context of the discourse thus far (that is, Matthew's Gospel) and their wider knowledge of Old Testament concepts of salvation history.

Οὖν likewise signals the audience to integrate additional material into a mental representation of the discourse. For example, following the genealogy of 1.2-16, in 1.17 we find, πᾶσαι οὖν αἱ γενεαὶ ἀπὸ Ἀβραὰμ ἕως Δαυὶδ γενεαὶ δεκατέσσαρες, καὶ ἀπὸ Δαυὶδ ἕως τῆς μετοικεσίας Βαβυλῶνος γενεαὶ δεκατέσσαρες, καὶ ἀπὸ τῆς μετοικεσίας Βαβυλῶνος ἕως τοῦ Χριστοῦ γενεαὶ δεκατέσσαρες. This is not merely a summary statement of the material just presented, but a new conceptualization—a fourteen-generation schema—that takes up the information presented in 1.2-16 and guides the audience to construct a mental representation of the origins of 'Jesus Christ, son of David, son of Abraham' (1.1) which then becomes the context for the birth narrative beginning in 1.18.

Γάρ

Although there are similarities in the function of γάρ and οὖν in Matthew's Gospel, each has its own patterns of usage and makes its own contribution to discourse, and each is discussed in further detail below. Γάρ is used to direct the audience to strengthen and/or confirm a preceding proposition, more firmly establishing it as part of their ongoing mental

---

27. Bird, 'Some γάρ Clauses', p. 173.

representation of the discourse. In Matthew's narrative framework γάρ is frequently found with imperfect tense-forms and with εἰμί.

As I have said, the small number of instances of γάρ in the narrative framework makes the conclusions drawn here merely suggestive. In addition, the fact that nine of the uses of γάρ in Matthew's narrative framework are also found in parallel passages in Mark's Gospel may obscure any distinctive pattern of use by Matthew. Abbott believes that the use of γάρ in 'strict narrative' (by which he means something similar to my notion of 'narrative framework') is characteristic of Mark in contradistinction to the other Synoptic writers:

> Γάρ is used by Luke altogether about a hundred times, and by Matthew still more frequently, but always in Christ's words (and the words of other speakers)… Mark uses γάρ *altogether about seventy times, and, of these, as many as thirty or more are in strict narrative. The use of γάρ, therefore, in strict narrative, is characteristic of Mark (as distinct from Matthew and Luke)*, and the fact that Matthew and Luke agree with Mark in so large a proportion of the few instances in which they use 'strict narrative' γάρ indicates that they have copied these clauses from Mark.[28]

While Matthew's uses of γάρ as a narrative connector may in some way be influenced by Markan narrative, nevertheless Matthew demonstrates his willingness elsewhere to make changes in sentence conjunctions to suit his own style or narrative purposes. It can be assumed (if one presupposes Markan priority) that if Matthew uses γάρ in places where Mark also does it is because Mark's use of γάρ is consistent with his own at these points.

More on the 'Meaning' of γάρ

Dik warns against over-differentiating the internal (semantic) properties of forms like coordinating conjunctions.[29] The question at hand is whether there is some low-level semantic content conventionally conveyed by γάρ which is common to its use in the variety of contexts described by traditional grammarians. Sicking writes concerning γάρ in the Classical period that 'the received distinction in the description of γάρ between "explanatory" and "causal" (Denniston), or between "adverbial" and "kausal" or "begründend" (Kühner–Gerth) cannot do justice to the facts'.[30] In attempting to characterize γάρ in Matthew's narrative framework, I have found it productive to shift from a conceptual or logical under-

---

28. Abbott, *Johannine Grammar*, p. 102 (his emphasis).
29. See Dik, *Coordination*, p. 265.
30. Sicking, 'Devices for Text Articulation', p. 23.

standing to the procedural semantics described above. Rather than assigning γάρ several possible truth-conditional meanings that correspond to various logical relationships between the propositions it conjoins (and leave some of Denniston's 'peculiarities' unaccounted for), it is more likely that in these different contexts γάρ has a single pragmatic function signaling how the audience is to process the sentences it introduces in relation to preceding discourse.

In an unpublished paper on discourse connectives in the Pauline Epistles, Blass characterizes the function of γάρ as 'backward confirmation'. Blass is concerned with the structure of Paul's argument in Romans, a very different genre from Matthew's Gospel, but her claim that γάρ 'marks propositions which are meant to function as premises, backwards confirming and strengthening other propositions' is useful in understanding the procedural semantics of γάρ elsewhere.[31]

In Matthew's Gospel γάρ is used to guide the audience to take the following sentence as in some way confirming or strengthening what precedes. It is something of an artificial exercise to distinguish between causal and explanatory uses of γάρ in the narrative framework, as the distinction is not inherent in γάρ itself but is properly a function of semantic relations between propositions. Giving reasons, providing explanation or elaboration, emphasizing a point, giving the motive for saying something, explaining the tone of preceding words, and so on, can all be subsumed under the process of 'confirmation'. Sicking observes, 'The common factor of nearly all γάρ-clauses as to content is that they supply information in answer to a question which might be raised in the minds of the audience by what has just preceded or is about to follow'.[32] Sicking's statement that the material introduced by γάρ may relate to what 'has been—or will be—said' reflects the circumstance that γάρ is not always backward-referring in Classical Greek, and may instead anticipate the proposition which it strengthens.[33] In Matthew's narrative framework, however, the γάρ-sentence appears always to follow the proposition which it strengthens. Material introduced by γάρ brings additional information to bear on a preceding proposition, strengthening and/or confirming it, and thus more firmly establishing it as part of the audience's ongoing mental representation of the discourse.

In a very real sense this approach brings us back to Winer's understand-

---

31. Blass, 'Constraints on Relevance', pp. 6-8.
32. Sicking, 'Devices for Text Articulation', p. 20.
33. Sicking, 'Devices for Text Articulation', p. 48.

ing of γάρ as expressing 'affirmation or assent which stands in relation to what precedes', but without the intervening step of attempting to categorize γάρ variously as illative, explanatory and so on, or the necessity of accounting separately for each of Denniston's 'peculiarities' of use. Those nuances properly belong to the semantic relationships between the propositions which γάρ conjoins and not to the (minimal and procedural) semantic content of the conjunction itself. Or, in Dik's words, to project these differing relations onto γάρ itself would be to confound 'the semantic content conventionally laid down in the expression as such with the interpretational aspects added to the expressions when used in specific communicative situations'.[34]

Motivation for What Is Said

As noted above, Denniston observes that in Classical Greek γάρ sometimes gives the motive for saying something rather than giving the grounds for what was said.[35] Similarly, there are cases where 'the γάρ clause explains the tone of the preceding words, rather than their content'.[36] He comments that where the connection of thought between two sentences may be 'lacking in logical precision', an attempt to supply a logical connection between the two in order to fill an assumed ellipsis 'is psychologically somewhat misleading'.[37] In other words, it does not do justice to the

---

34. Dik, *Coordination*, p. 269. Edwards's argument that Matthew uses certain types of γάρ clauses in his narrative portrayal of Jesus is fundamentally a discussion of the contexts in which Matthew uses γάρ, rather than a statement on the meaning of γάρ itself (Edwards, '*Gar* in Matthew'). Edwards describes γάρ in the words of Jesus as either 'plot background γάρ' or 'ideological γάρ'. In Edwards's view, generally sentences with 'plot background γάρ' contain a reference to the past, while sentences with 'ideological γάρ' contain a present or future reference. Edwards's point is that the content of the 'ideological γάρ' sentences, with their present and future bases for argument, would be unlikely to be persuasive or to be perceived as authoritative if they came from anyone besides who Matthew is showing Jesus to be. Edwards is on solid ground methodologically as long as he is simply saying that Matthew is developing his characterization of Jesus in part by giving that character a distinctive style of speech, rather than implying that the linguistic function of γάρ differs in past-referring sentences and in present- and future-referring sentences or differs on the basis of who is speaking.

35. Denniston, *Greek Particles*, p. 60.

36. Denniston, *Greek Particles*, p. 62.

37. Denniston, *Greek Particles*, pp. 60, 61. Sicking likewise states that 'one should in general avoid a suggestion that the speaker is trying to substantiate a claim by rational argument; it should rather appear the explanation brings out the truth and in-

language actually used and to the flow of thought underlying the discourse.

As I have said, grammarians generally agree that the use of γάρ in the New Testament is similar to its range of use in Classical texts such as those addressed by Denniston. At least two of Matthew's uses of γάρ, in 14.3 and 27.18, are consistent with Denniston's idea that γάρ may give the motive for a preceding statement, in contrast to 2.5, for example, which in some sense connects the content of propositions. In 14.3 and 27.18 γάρ 'backwards confirms' a speech act rather than making a logical connection with the content of a proposition.

To illustrate, in 2.5, in reply to Herod's question demanding to know where the Christ would be born, Matthew places on the lips of the chief priests and scribes the response, ἐν Βηθλέεμ τῆς Ἰουδαίας. He then adds, presumably in the voice of the chief priests and scribes but possibly in the voice of the narrator, οὕτως γὰρ γέγραπται διὰ τοῦ προφήτου· (2.6) καὶ σὺ Βηθλέεμ, γῆ Ἰούδα... The immediate function of the γάρ-sentence, οὕτως γὰρ γέγραπται διὰ τοῦ προφήτου..., appears to be to connect the content of their statement that the Christ will be born in Bethlehem with the content of what was said by the prophet. Their point is that 'the birth will take place in Bethlehem, because through the prophet God announced that it would be Bethlehem'. In this sense γάρ relates facts concerning Bethlehem rather than simply giving a motive for what they say. Yet even in this instance it is not certain that γάρ is used merely as a logical connector. It seems to be the case (especially if 2.5b-6 is understood as being in the voice of the narrator), that in a manner similar to 3.1 discussed above, the prophecy from the Old Testament which Matthew introduces with γάρ does not simply offer an explanation of the content of the chief priests and scribes' response, but moreover is intended to help the audience recognize (or 'backwards confirm') the significance of their pronouncement of Bethlehem as the messianic birthplace vis-à-vis Matthew's narrative of Jesus' origins. The audience makes inferences concerning that significance on the basis of the off-line Old Testament quotation as well as their wider knowledge of messianic expectations.

In 14.3, ὁ γὰρ Ἡρῴδης κρατήσας τὸν Ἰωάννην ἔδησεν [αὐτόν], the information that Herod has had John arrested does not give a logical reason why he should infer that Jesus is John risen from the dead (14.1-2)—that is, there is not a logical and necessary progression from arrest and execution to resurrection or reincarnation—but rather helps to explain why

herent persuasiveness of the other statement' (Sicking, 'Devices for Text Articulation', p. 24).

Herod makes a statement of this kind. The added detail that Herod had John arrested (and subsequently killed) explains why John is very much on Herod's mind, and thereby gives the motivation for his statement in 14.2. Γάρ signals that the following information confirms the place of Herod's identifying Jesus with John in the audience's mental representation of the discourse.

Similarly, in 27.18, ᾔδει γὰρ ὅτι διὰ φθόνον παρέδωκαν αὐτόν, the γάρ-clause gives the motive for Pilate's question to the crowd in 27.17 rather than a logical basis for what Pilate actually says. There is no necessary logical relation between Pilate's knowledge of the Jewish leaders' envy of Jesus and a choice between two prisoners, but his knowledge of that envy motivates his offering the crowd a choice, that is, it motivates his speech act. He offers the crowd the possibility of Jesus' release γάρ he knows that Jesus had been handed over to the Romans 'out of envy'. This explanation of Pilate's action strengthens the integration of Pilate's question to the crowd into the mental representation of the discourse constructed by Matthew's audience.

Although Denniston describes such uses as peculiarities, he has in fact come across a more general distinction recognized by linguists. Van Dijk, for example, in an early work on discourse, distinguishes between what he calls 'semantic' and 'pragmatic' functions of sentence connectives. As van Dijk expresses it, 'The semantic function of connectives is to relate facts, whereas pragmatic connectives relate sentences (or propositions), as for instance in inferences'.[38] Van Dijk's distinction between 'semantic' and 'pragmatic' relations, groundbreaking in its time, has largely been super-seded by the understanding that pragmatic inferences are in play at all levels of language comprehension, even in the recognition of 'semantic' or logical relations. However, his insight that sentence connectives can relate a proposition to other text either on the basis of its truth-value or as an illocutionary act (as in the act of stating an inference or in asking a question) is useful in understanding how γάρ functions in Matthew's narrative framework.

It could be said that in 2.5 γάρ relates, at least on one level, facts concerning Bethlehem, while in 14.3 and 27.18 γάρ relates sentences to statements. However, this does not so much lead to a distinction among divergent functions of γάρ—based on a proposition's truth-value or its function as an illocutionary act—as it clarifies some differences in the

---

38. Van Dijk, *Text and Context*, p. 86.

contexts in which γάρ may be found. There are not two separate functions for γάρ, the 'semantic' and the 'pragmatic', to use van Dijk's terms, but a variety of contexts in which γάρ signals the audience that a previous proposition is being confirmed and/or strengthened in some way. Dik's characterization of sentence connectives as 'multiple-purpose tool[s] of low semantic specificity, used to combine semantic aspects which, in their final interpretation, may be characterized by a variety of different relations',[39] allows γάρ to be understood as conveying procedural information signaling 'backward confirmation' whether the preceding proposition is being strengthened in terms of its ideational content or as a speech act. That a single form, γάρ, is used in such a range of contexts suggests that the audience does not rely solely on the conjunction, but rather makes use of surrounding text, the context of situation, and/or knowledge of the world in the pragmatic inferences they make as they construct a mental representation of the discourse.

Embedded Narrative

The use of γάρ in 14.3, introducing the pericope describing John the Baptist's death, raises another issue, that of the forward scope of γάρ. While it appears that γάρ usually functions with respect to the sentence it immediately conjoins, de Jong observes in her study of γάρ in Herodotus that in Classical Greek γάρ may introduce a longer section which she describes as an 'embedded narrative'. She concludes that 'the use of γάρ to introduce narratives originated in a typical archaic (oral?) form of narration, viz. announcing an event and then going back in time and filling in the details as to how this event came about'. De Jong continues, 'When the narrator goes back in time step by step, γάρ hosts little pieces of narrative information; when he goes back in a single step, the particle hosts a continuous narrative, sometimes of considerable length'.[40] De Jong suggests that Denniston overlooks this function in his treatment of γάρ because he typically 'interprets particles largely at the level of the sentence rather than of the text'.[41]

In 14.3, γάρ introduces just such an embedded narrative, the events surrounding John's arrest and beheading (14.3-12). It is the entire narrative which explains why Herod has John on his mind when he makes the

---

39. Dik, *Coordination*, p. 269.

40. I.J.F. de Jong, 'Γάρ Introducing Embedded Narratives', in Rijksbaron (ed.), *New Approaches*, p. 179.

41. De Jong, 'Embedded Narratives', pp. 175-76.

inference in 14.2 that Jesus is John risen from the dead. Although in this instance the explanatory material introduced by γάρ extends to an extended narrative unit in 14.3-12, it appears that the recognition of this scope by the audience is properly an issue of the semantic relationship between 14.1-2 and 14.3-12 rather than a function of the conjunction itself—that is, that an embedded narrative is just one more type of semantic relation existing between units conjoined by γάρ. If the longer scope is understood to be part of the meaning of γάρ, one must ask how the audience recognizes that the off-line material extends to 14.12 before the content of 14.3-12 is itself processed. At minimum, γάρ serves as a procedural signal of off-line material at this point in the linear processing of the discourse, alerting the audience to supportive material that is usually brief but may extend to any length, while the structural relation between 14.3-12 and the rest of the narrative is outside the semantics of γάρ itself and is pragmatically worked out by the audience.

Formal Collocations with γάρ

As with the other sentence conjunctions I have analyzed, γάρ appears to have characteristic collocations with other linguistic features in Matthew's narrative framework. However, the fact that there are only ten uses of γάρ as a narrative connector in Matthew's Gospel makes statistical analysis problematic. One collocation, the use of γάρ with εἰμί, appears to have statistical significance in spite of the small sample size:

Table 8.1: Γάρ *and verbal tense-form*

	All narrative sentences	Aorist (omitting forms of εἰμί)	Present (omitting forms of εἰμί)	Imperfect (omitting forms of εἰμί)	εἰμί
n=	720	553	79	57	17
# γάρ	10	2	0	2	5
% γάρ	1%	–	–	4%	29%
z-score[42]				1.36	9.92

Although the database identifies only 17 occurrences of εἰμί as the finite verb in narrative sentences in Matthew's Gospel, either used alone or in a periphrastic construction with a participle, γάρ occurs in 5 of these (5/17,

---

42. Again, z-scores equal to or greater than ±3 are taken to demonstrate statistical significance, but especially in the case of γάρ and οὖν it is important to note that z-scores are less reliable as indicators of statistical significance when sample sizes are less than 30.

29%, z = 9.92).[43] By contrast γάρ occurs in only about 1% of all sentences in the narrative framework. Γάρ appears both with εἰμί as the main verb (4.18, ἦσαν γὰρ ἁλιεῖς; 14.24, ἦν γὰρ ἐναντίος ὁ ἄνεμος; 26.43, ἦσαν γὰρ αὐτῶν οἱ ὀφθαλμοὶ βεβαρημένοι), and with εἰμί in periphrastic constructions (7.29, ἦν γὰρ διδάσκων αὐτοὺς ὡς ἐξουσίαν ἔχων; 19.22, ἦν γὰρ ἔχων κτήματα πολλά).[44] These last two are the only periphrastic constructions in the narrative framework identified in the database. Even if the periphrastic uses in 7.29 and 19.22 are separated from the analysis of γάρ and εἰμί, by its use in 4.8, 14.24 and 26.43, γάρ remains the sentence conjunction in 3 out of 15 occurrences (20%) of εἰμί as the (non-periphrastic) main verb in sentences in the narrative frame-work, compared with its use in only 1% of all narrative sentences—but again, statistical significance is inconclusive in such small samples.

The use of γάρ in 4.18, 14.24 and 19.22 has been discussed above. In 7.29, ἦν γὰρ διδάσκων αὐτοὺς ὡς ἐξουσίαν ἔχων καὶ οὐχ ὡς οἱ γραμματεῖς αὐτῶν, the mental representation of the crowd's amazement at Jesus' teaching (7.28) is strengthened by supplying additional material—γάρ he was teaching as though he had authority—which could be under-stood as giving the reason for their amazement and/or explaining the con-tent of their amazement. In 26.43, ἦσαν γὰρ αὐτῶν οἱ ὀφθαλμοὶ βεβαρημένοι, γάρ introduces a relatively straightforward explanation, strengthening the mental representation of Jesus finding the disciples sleeping upon his return: γάρ their eyes were heavy (that is, the men were very tired).

In addition to its association with εἰμί, it also appears that γάρ and imperfect tense-forms tend to collocate, but several factors render it difficult to verify this statistically. Besides the issue of small sample size, the aspectual vagueness of εἰμί—that is, that it does not have distinct forms for aorist and imperfect tenses—means that examples with εἰμί must be left out of calculations of verbal tense-form even if εἰμί is under-stood to be used with an imperfective sense.

There are two remaining examples of γάρ with imperfect tense-forms,

43. As noted above, a sample size of less than 30 means that the z-score may not be a reliable indicator of statistical significance. The other use of γάρ in the narrative framework identified in the database, in addition to the 9 accounted for here, is with the pluperfect form ᾔδει in 27.18, ᾔδει γὰρ ὅτι διὰ φθόνον παρέδωκαν αὐτόν.

44. All three occurrences of <εἰμί + participle> in Matthew's narrative framework (7.29, 19.22, 26.43) have γάρ as the sentence conjunction. βεβαρημένοι in 26.43 is treated as a predicate nominative.

both with λέγω. When a woman with a 12-year flow of blood touches the hem of Jesus' garment (9.20), the narrator omnisciently details the reason for her action (9.21): ἔλεγεν γὰρ ἐν ἑαυτῇ ἐὰν μόνον ἅψωμαι τοῦ ἱματίου αὐτοῦ σωθήσομαι. This information helps to confirm the proposition that such a woman would approach Jesus in a public setting, and strengthens the integration of her action into the audience's mental representation of the discourse. It is worth noting that γάρ connects her on-line action as presented in the narrative framework with her off-line inner state ('she touched the hem of his garment γάρ she was saying to herself…'), rather than indicating more explicitly the logical connection the woman herself makes between her belief and her action ('If I only touch his garment I will be healed'). In other words, Matthew does not relate the fact that the woman touched Jesus to an objective truth that touching him would heal her. Instead, the narrator affirms that the woman believes this to be true and that this belief motivates her action. It is the faith behind her action to which Jesus responds in 9.22.

The use of γάρ in the second example, 14.4, ἔλεγεν γὰρ ὁ Ἰωάννης αὐτῷ· οὐκ ἔξεστίν σοι ἔχειν αὐτήν, seems to introduce the reason for John's actual arrest. In fact, more specifically it introduces a sentence giving more information about the preceding proposition, that Herodias, the wife of Herod's brother Philip, was in some sense the cause of John's arrest (14.3, ἐν φυλακῇ ἀπέθετο διὰ Ἡρῳδιάδα): *γάρ* John was saying that Herod should not have her. Thus the γάρ-sentence both helps the audience to make pragmatic inferences about the meaning of διὰ Ἡρῳδιάδα, and confirms the introduction of Herodias as an issue in the conflict and correspondingly into the audience's mental representation of the narrative. This prepares the audience for the embedded narrative material which follows concerning Herodias's daughter.

In these two examples γάρ appears with 2 of the 57 occurrences of imperfect tense-forms (other than εἰμί) in Matthew's narrative framework (4%), and at the same time in 2 of the 11 occurrences of λέγω in an imperfect tense-form (18%). However, while both these frequencies are higher than its use in 1% of sentences in the narrative framework, statistical significance is not conclusive for samples of this size.

Οὖν

Οὖν *in John's Gospel*

While οὖν appears only twice in Matthew's narrative framework, its high frequency as a narrative connector in John's Gospel means that in the New

Testament overall it is used more frequently in the Gospels and Acts than in Epistles.[45] Not surprisingly, grammatical discussion of οὖν in narrative overwhelmingly focuses on its use in the Gospel of John.[46] However, its proliferation as a narrative connector in John's Gospel suggests that John uses it in a somewhat different way than do Matthew or the other Synoptics, where it appears only rarely.

By Abbott's count, of about 195 occurrences of οὖν in John's Gospel only 8 appear in the words of Jesus, with the rest in the narrative portion.[47] Poythress, in his study of sentence conjunctions in the Gospel of John, refers to *therefore* as the 'ordinary sense' of οὖν, but notes that this use is relatively rare in John's narrative. Instead, the Fourth Evangelist tends to use οὖν more regularly in two contexts, either 'when the narrator returns to the main line of events after a digression, a parenthesis, or the supplying of background information', that is, resumptively in Poythress's terms, or else to continue the narrative 'whenever there is a shift to a new agent in the action described in the sentence immediately following' οὖν. Most importantly, in both contexts Poythress sees οὖν as the unmarked choice as sentence connector, used only where there is no specific reason to choose καί, δέ or asyndeton.[48]

More on the 'Meaning' of οὖν

By contrast, in Matthew's Gospel the extreme rarity of its use precludes any treatment of οὖν as simply an unmarked narrative connector. As I have affirmed, the precise discourse function οὖν fills in Matthew's narrative framework cannot be ascertained merely on the basis of two occurrences. Nevertheless, in a manner similar to its use in Classical Greek, in Matthew's narrative framework οὖν appears to serve as a procedural cue which directs the audience to continue on with the main line of the narrative, having more firmly established the mental representation they are currently constructing of the discourse by the inclusion of previous information. Οὖν in Matthew's narrative framework can be described as a signal, as Donaldson indicates, of continuation and retrospect. As with

45. See Robertson, *Grammar*, p. 1191.

46. See, for example, Robertson, *Grammar*, pp. 1191-92; Poythress, 'Intersentence Conjunctions', p. 313; Buth, 'Οὖν, Δέ, Καί, and Asyndeton'; Levinsohn, *Discourse Features*, pp. 81-90.

47. Abbott, *Johannine Grammar*, p. 165.

48. Poythress, 'Intersentence Conjunctions', pp. 327-28.

γάρ, the delineation of whether a particular context in which οὖν appears is resumptive,[49] transitional,[50] consecutive,[51] consequential,[52] logically inferential,[53] or something else properly belongs to an analysis of the semantic relationships between the propositions which οὖν conjoins and not to the (minimal and procedural) semantic content of the conjunction itself.

More recent work in Classical Greek has taken a similar approach. On οὖν in Lysias, Sicking writes that in using οὖν

> the speaker marks what precedes as relevant, and for the present purpose subsidiary, *to what follows*, and by extension to the story or argument as a whole. Often this takes the form of the speaker marking that which precedes the particle as somehow introductory, explanatory, or providing background.[54]

Van Ophuijsen, in his study of οὖν in Plato's *Phaedo*, states succinctly that 'what went before should from now on be considered in its bearing on some other proposition'.[55] As Sicking observes, 'This account does away with the need to assume a separate "resumptive" force as Denniston'—or Poythress—'does: returning from a digression is just one of the ways in which the general description here given may work out'.[56]

As with γάρ, there may not always be a logical relation between the content of the sentences conjoined by οὖν. Donaldson observes that οὖν 'does not imply a logical inference, like ἄρα, but merely recalls attention to something, which has been already said, in the way of confirmation or correction'.[57] Van Ophuijsen goes further, explaining, 'By using οὖν a speaker does not intimate that the truth of his present statement should be granted on the strength of his preceding statement; his is imposing an arbitrary relationship on his statements, indicating that what went before

---

49. See, for example, Turner, *Syntax*, p. 337; BDF, §451; Dana and Mantey, *Grammar*, p. 253; Levinsohn, *Discourse Features*, p. 85; Poythress, 'Intersentence Conjunctions', p. 328.

50. See, for example, Robertson, *Grammar*, p. 1191; Dana and Mantey, *Grammar*, p. 253.

51. See, for example, Turner, *Syntax*, p. 337; BDF, §451; Porter, *Idioms*, p. 214.

52. See, for example, Winer, *Treatise*, p. 555.

53. See, for example, Winer, *Treatise*, p. 555; Dana and Mantey, *Grammar*, p. 253; Porter, *Idioms*, p. 214; Levinsohn, *Discourse Features*, p. 85.

54. Sicking, 'Devices for Text Articulation', p. 27 (his emphasis).

55. Van Ophuijsen, 'ΟΥΝ, ΑΡΑ, ΔΗ, ΤΟΙΝΥΝ', p. 86.

56. Sicking, 'Devices for Text Articulation', p. 27.

57. Donaldson, *Grammar*, p. 571.

need occupy his listeners only in so far as it may assist them in grasping what follows'.[58]

Οὖν *in Combination with* γάρ

The use of οὖν in 1.17, introducing a fourteen-generation schema that takes up the information presented in 1.2-16 and becomes the context for the birth narrative beginning in 1.18, has been described above. In 27.17, συνηγμένων οὖν αὐτῶν εἶπεν αὐτοῖς ὁ Πιλᾶτος· τίνα θέλετε ἀπολύσω ὑμῖν...; οὖν similarly signals the audience to continue processing the discourse in light of the off-line material just given. In 27.15-16 Matthew explains the governor's custom of releasing one prisoner at the Feast, and also relays the information that Pilate has a prisoner named Barabbas. By using οὖν the Evangelist then signals the audience to integrate this material into their mental representation of Pilate's asking the crowd which prisoner they will have him release.

In addition, the context of 27.15-18 allows us to see the function of both γάρ and οὖν with respect to a single proposition:

27.15   Κατὰ δὲ ἑορτὴν εἰώθει ὁ ἡγεμὼν ἀπολύειν ἕνα τῷ ὄχλῳ δέσμιον ὃν ἤθελον.

27.16   εἶχον δὲ τότε δέσμιον ἐπίσημον λεγόμενον ['Ιησοῦν] Βαραββᾶν.

27.17   συνηγμένων οὖν αὐτῶν εἶπεν αὐτοῖς ὁ Πιλᾶτος· τίνα θέλετε ἀπολύσω ὑμῖν, ['Ιησοῦν τὸν] Βαραββᾶν ἢ 'Ιησοῦν τὸν λεγόμενον χριστόν;

27.18   ᾔδει γὰρ ὅτι διὰ φθόνον παρέδωκαν αὐτόν.

The central sentence, in 27.17, is the only one which is on-line with respect to the events recounted sequentially within Matthew's narrative framework. In 27.17 Pilate addresses the crowd, asking whether they prefer that he release Jesus or Barabbas. The sentence which describes Pilate's action is strengthened from two directions, both by preceding and subsequent material. Οὖν signals the audience to integrate into their mental representation of Pilate's question the preceding information that the governor has a custom of releasing one prisoner at the Feast and that he currently has a prisoner named Barabbas. Then in 27.18 γάρ introduces additional information about knowledge Pilate has which constitutes a motive for his question in 27.17. While the use of οὖν introduces an on-line narrative sentence (describing the choice Pilate offers the crowd) whose integration in the audience's ongoing mental representation of the narrative has already been motivated by the information in 27.15-16, the subsequent use of γάρ directs the audience to additional off-line material, further strengthening and confirming the place of the preceding proposition in the mental representation each hearer or reader constructs.

Similarly, van Ophuijsen finds instances of οὖν in combination with γάρ in his study of particles in Plato's *Phaedo*, although the order of the two forms is generally reversed, reflecting the sometimes forward scope of γάρ in Classical Greek (but not in Matthew's Gospel): 'Not seldom a sentence containing οὖν is preceded by one that is explicitly marked as subsidiary by the use of γάρ'.[59]

Γάρ *and* οὖν *in Exposition: Imperatives*

Because of the infrequency of γάρ and οὖν in Matthew's narrative framework, I turn briefly to their similar pragmatic functions in expository discourse, focusing on their use in relation to sentences with imperatival force.[60] As in narrative, in expository discourse in Matthew's Gospel γάρ and οὖν serve as markers with complementary functions. In exposition as well as in narrative, γάρ introduces sentences which strengthen and/or confirm a preceding proposition, while οὖν signals that the audience is to continue processing the discourse with a mental representation which now incorporates and is more firmly established by a preceding proposition.

This is particularly apparent in the use of γάρ and οὖν with respect to imperatives and other structures with imperatival force, such as the combination of οὐ μή and a subjunctive verb in prohibitions or future tense-forms functioning as imperatives. Οὖν is often used to introduce an imperative which rests upon a preceding proposition, and γάρ often appears following an imperative to introduce a proposition with an indicative verb (what is termed in the database a 'declarative' sentence) which 'backwards confirms' the imperative.[61] An analysis of the relative frequency of these uses appears in the following table:

59. Van Ophuijsen, 'OYN, APA, ΔH, TOINYN', p. 93.

60. The sections of Matthew's Gospel identified in the database as exposition consist of 5.3–7.27, 10.5-42, 11.7-30, 12.25-45, 13.3-52, 15.3-20, 18.3-35, 19.28–20.16, 21.28–22.14 and 23.2–25.46.

61. By Edwards's count, of the 124 uses of γάρ in Matthew's Gospel, 89 occur with Jesus as the speaker, 48 of these 'to support a command' (Edwards, '*Gar* in Matthew', p. 641).

Table 8.2: *Sentence conjunction and mode in exposition*

	All expository sentences, after the first sentence in a sequence	Declarative sentences[62]	Modulated declarative sentences[63]	Imperative sentences[64]	Interrogative sentences[65]
n=	702	488	31	125	39
# γάρ	61	57	1	0	3
% γάρ	9%	12%	3%	0%	8%
z-score		2.34	−1.08	−3.45	−0.22
# οὖν	30	10	3	15	2
% οὖν	4%	2%	10%	12%	5%
z-score		−2.42	1.49	4.26	0.26

In this analysis the first sentence in each passage of expository discourse or after a speech margin within exposition has been omitted because the first sentence almost invariably has ὅτι as a connector (or embedding particle) or is asyndetic. In the remaining sentences, there is a statistically significant increased frequency of use of οὖν with imperatives (15/125, 12%, $z = 4.26$) compared to the frequency of οὖν in all the expository sentences considered. Half of the occurrences of οὖν in exposition (15/30, 50%) are with imperatives. At the same time there is a statistically significant negative correlation between γάρ and imperatives (0/125, 0%, $z = -3.45$). In fact there is no instance of γάρ with an imperative in Matthew's Gospel. On the other hand, γάρ often appears following an imperative, usually with a declarative sentence (that is, generally one with an indicative verb). Although the relative frequency of this collocation is difficult to establish quantitatively due to the difficulty of determining how long a span to count as 'following' an imperative, examples like the following in 5.29-30 and 23.2-3 are readily observable:[66]

62. Sentences with indicative verbs, verbless sentences, and sentences with μή and a subjunctive used to express negation; see definition of 'mode' in Chapter 3.
63. Sentences with a modulating element containing ἄν or one of its compounds, whether having an indicative or subjunctive verb form or verbless; see definition of 'mode' in Chapter 3.
64. Sentences with imperative verbal forms, as well as some sentences with subjunctive (includes 15 examples of οὐ μή + subjunctive in prohibitions) or future tense-forms used with imperatival force (3 instances: 5.33, 5.43, 6.5); see definition of 'mode' in Chapter 3.
65. As punctuated in NA[27]; see definition of 'mode' in Chapter 3.
66. In the Sermon on the Mount, see also, for example, Mt. 5.12, 6.7, 6.16, 6.21,

5.29   εἰ δὲ ὁ ὀφθαλμός σου ὁ δεξιὸς σκανδαλίζει σε, ἔξελε αὐτὸν καὶ
βάλε ἀπὸ σοῦ·
συμφέρει γάρ σοι ἵνα ἀπόληται ἓν τῶν μελῶν σου καὶ μὴ ὅλον
τὸ σῶμά σου βληθῇ εἰς γέενναν.

5.30   καὶ εἰ ἡ δεξιά σου χεὶρ σκανδαλίζει σε, ἔκκοψον αὐτὴν καὶ βάλε
ἀπὸ σοῦ·
συμφέρει γάρ σοι ἵνα ἀπόληται ἓν τῶν μελῶν σου καὶ μὴ ὅλον
τὸ σῶμά σου εἰς γέενναν ἀπέλθῃ.

23.2   ἐπὶ τῆς Μωϋσέως καθέδρας ἐκάθισαν οἱ γραμματεῖς καὶ οἱ
Φαρισαῖοι.

23.3   πάντα οὖν ὅσα ἐὰν εἴπωσιν ὑμῖν ποιήσατε καὶ τηρεῖτε,
κατὰ δὲ τὰ ἔργα αὐτῶν μὴ ποιεῖτε·
λέγουσιν γὰρ καὶ οὐ ποιοῦσιν.

The second example above, Jesus' warning to the crowds and his disciples concerning the scribes and Pharisees (23.2-3), reveals the complementary functions of γάρ and οὖν with respect to the string of imperatives ποιήσατε, τηρεῖτε, μὴ ποιεῖτε. In a manner similar to the narrative example in 27.15-18, the central proposition (or complex of propositions) in 23.3—the essence of which is 'do what they say but don't do what they do'—is strengthened from two directions, both by preceding and subsequent propositions, involving the use of γάρ and οὖν. In 23.3 οὖν signals the audience to integrate into their mental representation of Jesus' command the preceding information that the Pharisees 'sit on Moses' seat', leading to the pragmatic inference that in some sense they share Moses' authority. Following the imperatives γάρ introduces the additional proposition that the Pharisees' speech does not match their actions. The use of γάρ directs the audience backward, strengthening and confirming the place of Jesus' double-edged command in their mental representation of the discourse. Other examples in which οὖν and γάρ work in tandem with respect to imperatives include 6.34, μὴ οὖν μεριμνήσητε εἰς τὴν αὔριον, ἡ γὰρ αὔριον μεριμνήσει ἑαυτῆς, and in 7.12, πάντα οὖν ὅσα ἐὰν θέλητε ἵνα ποιῶσιν ὑμῖν οἱ ἄνθρωποι, οὕτως καὶ ὑμεῖς ποιεῖτε αὐτοῖς· οὗτος γάρ ἐστιν ὁ νόμος καὶ οἱ προφῆται.

6.32 (where two occurrences of γάρ are found following a single imperative; see similarly 10.19-20), 7.2, 7.8. Occasionally ὅτι is found following an imperative in a 'slot' in which one might expect γάρ, suggesting ὅτι may be used with a similar 'backwards confirming' function in these contexts. See, for example, Mt. 5.45, 6.5, 7.13. On the tendency for ὅτι to follow rather than precede its main clause, including imperatives, see J.K. Elliott, 'The Position of Causal 'Οτι Clauses in the New Testament', *FN* 3 (1990), pp. 155-57.

Similarly, van Ophuijsen observes in his study of οὖν in Plato's *Phaedo*, 'Seven instances of οὖν form part of injunctions, six of them accompanying an imperative and one ... an adhortative subjunctive'.[67] He describes a γάρ–οὖν–γάρ sequence as 'somewhat more complicated rhetorically', but concludes that 'the purport is not in doubt: coming between two γάρ sentences conveying the necessary background information, οὖν points forward to the directive which this information is relevant to'.[68]

Mt. 23.2-3 raises the question of the backward scope of γάρ, that is, whether γάρ only functions in relation to an immediately preceding clause, or whether its scope can extend back over two or more imperatival clauses as, for example, to ποιήσατε in 23.2. While it appears that in most cases γάρ relates succeeding propositions in a linear fashion, there are examples where it appears to function over a slightly longer discourse span. Jesus' teaching on prayer in 6.7-15 is illustrative of both successive clauses and longer spans:

6.7 Προσευχόμενοι δὲ μὴ βατταλογήσητε ὥσπερ οἱ ἐθνικοί,
     δοκοῦσιν γὰρ ὅτι ἐν τῇ πολυλογίᾳ αὐτῶν εἰσακουσθήσονται.
6.8 μὴ οὖν ὁμοιωθῆτε αὐτοῖς·
     οἶδεν γὰρ ὁ πατὴρ ὑμῶν ὧν χρείαν ἔχετε πρὸ τοῦ ὑμᾶς
     αἰτῆσαι αὐτόν.
6.9 Οὕτως οὖν προσεύχεσθε ὑμεῖς·
     Πάτερ ἡμῶν ὁ ἐν τοῖς οὐρανοῖς·
     ἁγιασθήτω τὸ ὄνομά σου·
6.10 ἐλθέτω ἡ βασιλεία σου·
     γενηθήτω τὸ θέλημά σου,
     ὡς ἐν οὐρανῷ καὶ ἐπὶ γῆς·
6.11 τὸν ἄρτον ἡμῶν τὸν ἐπιούσιον δὸς ἡμῖν σήμερον·
6.12 καὶ ἄφες ἡμῖν τὰ ὀφειλήματα ἡμῶν,
     ὡς καὶ ἡμεῖς ἀφήκαμεν τοῖς ὀφειλέταις ἡμῶν·
6.13 καὶ μὴ εἰσενέγκῃς ἡμᾶς εἰς πειρασμόν,
     ἀλλὰ ῥῦσαι ἡμᾶς ἀπὸ τοῦ πονηροῦ.
6.14 Ἐὰν γὰρ ἀφῆτε τοῖς ἀνθρώποις τὰ παραπτώματα αὐτῶν,
     ἀφήσει καὶ ὑμῖν ὁ πατὴρ ὑμῶν ὁ οὐράνιος·
6.15 ἐὰν δὲ μὴ ἀφῆτε τοῖς ἀνθρώποις, οὐδὲ ὁ πατὴρ ὑμῶν ἀφήσει
     τὰ παραπτώματα ὑμῶν.

In 6.7 and 6.8, γάρ 'backward confirms' immediately preceding imperatives. However, in 6.14, γάρ either reaches back across the intervening content of the prayer itself to strengthen and confirm the instruction in 6.9a

67. Van Ophuijsen, 'ΟΥΝ, ΑΡΑ, ΔΗ, ΤΟΙΝΥΝ', p. 100.
68. Van Ophuijsen, 'ΟΥΝ, ΑΡΑ, ΔΗ, ΤΟΙΝΥΝ', p. 100.

to 'pray like this', that is, to include a request for forgiveness of sin based on the petitioner's own forgiveness of others, or it reaches back only to 6.12, confirming the need to link a request for divine forgiveness with interpersonal acts of forgiveness. The connection between 6.14 and 6.9a is syntactical, in that the second person imperative in each addresses the same audience, while the intervening imperatives are directed toward πάτερ ἡμῶν ὁ ἐν τοῖς οὐρανοῖς. The connection between 6.14 and 6.12 is lexical, based on the repetition of ἀφίημι. Neither possibility, however, involves a very distant connection. The connection from 6.14 to 6.12 has only two clauses between. Neither is the connection between 6.14 and 6.9a very distant in terms of discourse structure, when one considers that on the plane of Jesus' address to his audience they are subsequent clauses. That is, the intervening content of the prayer itself lies on what could be considered a separate level of the discourse, as is suggested by the NA[27] editors' orthographic convention of creating an inset paragraph.[69]

Overall, γάρ appears most often to 'backward confirm' an immediately preceding clause, but also at times to function over a slightly longer span in which there is a close syntactic or semantic link.

Summary and Conclusions

As sentence conjunctions in Matthew's narrative framework, γάρ and οὖν share several similar characteristics: both are postpositive in terms of their position in the sentence; both involve propositions which are off-line, or outside the main sequence of narrated events; and both are concerned with inferential relationships in discourse, the process by which a mental representation of a discourse is strengthened by the integration of additional propositions.

Γάρ is used to direct the audience to strengthen a preceding proposition, confirming it as part of the mental representation they construct of the discourse. In Matthew's narrative framework there is a tendency for γάρ to be used with εἰμί and imperfect tense-forms. While γάρ directs the audience backward to confirm a preceding proposition in the narrative, οὖν signals the audience to continue their processing of the discourse with a mental representation now strengthened by the inclusion of preceding information. Donaldson's characterization of οὖν as indicative of 'continuation and retrospect', and Winer's judgment that γάρ 'expresses gene-

---

69. For another example of γάρ in operation over a span of several clauses, see 5.43-48, in which a lexical semantic link is supplied by the repeated use of ἀγαπάω.

rally an affirmation or assent (γε) which stands in relation to what precedes (ἄρα !)' reveal that this approach to the semantics of γάρ and οὖν is consistent with the intuitions of earlier grammarians.

The conclusions drawn about the function of these forms in narrative are limited by the fact that there are so few uses of γάρ and (especially) of οὖν in Matthew's narrative framework. However, a brief examination of the use of γάρ and οὖν with imperatival sentences in exposition in Matthew's Gospel suggests that in exposition as well they serve as similar signals guiding inferences made by the audience in constructing a mental representation of the discourse.

Like καί, δέ, τότε and asyndeton, γάρ and οὖν are procedural signals which the Evangelist uses in his narrative framework to help guide the mental representations constructed by the audience—specifically, by signaling that an ongoing mental representation of the narrative is to be enhanced by the incorporation of additional off-line material.

Chapter 9

SENTENCE CONJUNCTIONS AS A LINGUISTIC SYSTEM:
COMMENTS ON MATTHEW 8.1–9.34

Sentence Conjunctions as a Linguistic System

In Chapters 4–8 I examined the use of καί, δέ, τότε, γάρ, οὖν and asyndeton as narrative connectors in Matthew's Gospel. For the purpose of discussion I have for the most part treated these sentence conjunctions and asyndeton individually (except for the pairing of γάρ and οὖν in Chapter 8). But as I have emphasized throughout, linguistically these forms constitute one conjunctive system from which the Evangelist makes choices in connecting sentences in his narrative framework. In actual use each form not only appears with its own characteristic syntactical, morphological and lexical collocations (features which themselves form parts of other linguistic systems), but is processed against the background of what might have been chosen but was not—that is, other conjunctions and other syntactical, morphological and lexical collocations. At this point it is appropriate to step back and take a broader look at the system of sentence conjunctions as a whole, examining how Matthew makes use of this system and collocating features from other systems in the narrative framework of his Gospel.

Halliday has observed that choices from a linguistic system are probabilistic.[1] One can describe what choices are likely to be made in certain contexts based on the conventional frequency with which various forms are used in similar contexts. Of course, given the flexibility of human language there are few if any rigidly prescriptive rules governing such choices. Instead, the discourse analyst attempts to recognize certain regularities of use, and on that basis propose what choices may be considered expected or unexpected in a given context.[2] With the focus on

---

1. See Halliday, 'Probabilistic Grammar', p. 31.
2. See Brown and Yule, *Discourse Analysis*, p. 22.

regularities rather than rules, the idea of probabilistic modeling can be applied to sentence conjunctions in Matthew's narrative framework. Based on the other linguistic features identified here—lexical and syntactical collocations that help define the linguistic context—one can develop models describing with varying levels of accuracy the distribution of sentence conjunctions in narrative in Matthew's Gospel. The models can then be used to suggest which sentence conjunction could be considered expected or unexpected in a particular context. The more knowledge one has about the interaction of multiple features, the more descriptively (and, it is to be assumed, predictively) powerful the model will be.

The logistic regression models Allen develops from my data on sentence conjunctions in Matthew's Gospel use sophisticated statistical techniques to describe collocations between conjunctions and related features in the narrative framework of Matthew's Gospel.[3] But the simplest model of sentence conjunctions in Matthew's narrative framework, not taking into account any other features, merely states that every narrative sentence has καί as the sentence conjunction. This is based on the fact that καί is both the most common sentence conjunction in Matthew's narrative framework and is understood to be the unmarked choice. Because καί appears in 47% of narrative sentences in Matthew's Gospel, this model will assign the correct sentence conjunction to 47% of the sentences in the narrative framework (but will incorrectly assign καί to the other 53% as well).

By adding δέ to the model as an alternative to καί and incorporating constituent order as a factor, the descriptive power can be increased significantly. In this model it is posited that καί occurs with V(S) constituent order while δέ occurs with SV constituent order. Adding δέ and constituent order to the model assigns the correct conjunction to 65% of the sentences in Matthew's narrative framework, in that 65% (469/720) of narrative sentences in Matthew's Gospel either consist of καί with V(S) constituent order (<καί + V(S)>, 267 sentences) or δέ with SV constituent order (<δέ + SV>, 202 sentences). This 'basic model', with its single collocating feature of constituent order, accounts for about eight out of every ten occurrences of καί (267/335, 80%) and of δέ (202/257, 79%) in Matthew's narrative framework.

A small refinement to the basic model above can be made by incorporating two other characteristic collocations of καί and δέ which override the

---

3.   See Allen, 'Greek Syntactical Analysis'; Allen and Farewell, this volume.

factor of constituent order. First, καί tends to be used in combination with ἰδού, regardless of constituent order, although in most cases it is accompanied by a thematic subject. Secondly, where there is a genitive absolute construction at the beginning of the sentence δέ can usually be expected, even if ἰδού is also present, and again regardless of constituent order.[4] Adding these two features to the model increases its descriptive power somewhat further, in that 69% (494/720) of the sentences in Matthew's narrative framework are of one of these types.[5] This 'working model' now accounts for more than eight out of every ten occurrences of both καί (275/335, 82%) and δέ (219/257, 85%) in the narrative framework, although the uses of asyndeton, τότε, γάρ and οὖν have yet to be addressed.

Developing the model beyond this point, with the goal of further increasing its descriptive power and incorporating the full set of sentence conjunctions which actually occur in Matthew's narrative framework, is a complex process well beyond the straightforward observations on which the model has been built thus far. In reality, simple binary choices such as SV versus V(S) constituent order may be few. Instead there can be gradations from which choices are made, such as those represented by the cline for constituent order introduced in Chapter 4, which shows that the subject may appear in thematic position (S_1V), before the verb but not in thematic position (S_2V), after the verb (VS), or not be grammaticalized at all (V). Towards either end of this cline differing frequencies of καί and δέ reveal a complex interaction between the system of sentence conjunctions and the system of constituent order, an interaction which also involves issues of thematization and the grammaticalization of the subject (see Table 5.2).

At the same time, the incorporation of additional conjunctive choices (asyndeton, τότε, γάρ and οὖν) and other collocating features such as

---

4.   Δέ occurs as the sentence conjunction in 59% (23/39) of the sentences in Matthew's narrative framework which begin with a genitive absolute construction. In the six instances when δέ appears with ἰδού, there is also a genitive absolute before the main (indicative) verb (1.20, 2.1, 2.13, 2.19, 9.32, 28.11). There is only one case of καί ἰδού with a genitive absolute (26.47).

5.   69% (494/720) of the sentences in Matthew's narrative framework are of one of the following four structures: καί with V(S) constituent order and no genitive absolute participle (<καί + V(S) + ~genitive absolute>, 257 sentences); καί with ἰδού and some other constituent order but no genitive absolute (<καί + ἰδού + ~V(S) + ~genitive absolute>, 18 sentences); δέ with SV constituent order (<δέ + SV>, 202 sentences); δέ with a genitive absolute participle and some other constituent order (<δέ + genitive absolute + ~SV>, 17 sentences).

thematization, verbal tense-form, or function as a speech margin greatly increases the number of variables involved. Allen's individual regression models, and her final polychotomous model in which καί, δέ, τότε and asyndeton are combined, indicate just how complex it is even making use of sophisticated computer programs to develop a model relating multiple conjunctive options to collocating features.[6]

Nevertheless, an outline of the ways sentence conjunctions function as a system in Matthew's narrative framework can be developed which accounts for most choices, simply by making use of the working model introduced above (which, of course, includes only καί and δέ) and then evaluating variations from those patterns by considering features characteristic of asyndeton, τότε, γάρ and οὖν. That is, where neither καί nor δέ is used, the alternative conjunction (or asyndeton) can usually be seen to reflect its own characteristic patterns of collocations. As explained in the preceding chapters, general patterns of use in Matthew's narrative framework are as follows:

Asyndeton can be expected:
- *either* in speech margins—especially question–response–reply sequences—with present tense-form λέγω in thematic position;
- *or* at higher-level narrative breaks with aorist or imperfect (but not present) tense-forms and non-verbal themes, often with a thematic 'shifter' such as a temporal prepositional phrase or a genitive absolute construction.

Τότε can be expected:
- with present-tense indicative verbs in past-referring narrative (the so-called 'historic present');
- with thematic finite verbs;
- with VS constituent order (but SV constituent order at the beginning of paragraphs within an episode);
- with forms of προσέρχομαι or passive forms of προσφέρω;
- at a climactic point within a pericope (especially a statement by Jesus).

Γάρ can be expected:
- with 'off-line' material which confirms and strengthens the preceding proposition (usually, but not necessarily, by giving either a reason or elaboration);

---

6. See Allen, 'Greek Syntactical Analysis', Appendix 5; Allen and Farewell, this volume, §5.2.

- with εἰμί and with imperfect tense-forms.

Οὖν, although very rare in narrative, occurs occasionally

- at a point at which preceding 'off-line' material is integrated into the narrative.

Together, the working model and these characteristics give an approximation of narrative syntax in Matthew's Gospel approached from the standpoint of the system of sentence conjunctions.

To test the descriptive power of this approach, in the following section I offer a sentence-by-sentence analysis of Mt. 8.1–9.34, sometimes referred to as Matthew's 'miracle chapters'. For each sentence I indicate whether καί or δέ is to be expected based on the working model, and then compare this with the actual conjunction in each sentence, evaluating variations on the basis of Matthew's characteristic patterns of use of asyndeton, τότε, γάρ and οὖν.

However, the real import of these patterns of narrative syntax is in fact not at the sentence level, but above the sentence level, at the level of discourse. An awareness of the relative expectedness of various combinations of sentence conjunctions and related features, with the contributions they make to discourse continuity/discontinuity and prominence, serves as a background against which to examine the structure and flow of discourse units. For each subunit in 8.1–9.34 I comment on the role of sentence conjunctions in the narrative. Then, in the final section of this analysis, I summarize the approaches various scholars have taken to the overall structure of Mt. 8.1–9.34 and suggest what a greater appreciation of the role of sentence conjunctions as discourse markers may contribute to that discussion.

Analysis of Matthew 8.1–9.34

Introduction
There is a wide consensus among biblical scholars that Mt. 8.1–9.34 forms a coherent and carefully constructed unit within Matthew's Gospel.[7] This

---

7.   See, for example, Held, 'Miracle Stories'; Thompson, 'Composition of Mt 8.1–9.34'; K. Gatzwieler, 'Les récits de miracles dans L'Évangile selon saint Matthieu', in M. Didier (ed.), *L'Évangile selon Matthieu: Rédaction et théologie* (BETL, 29; Gembloux: Duculot, 1972), pp. 209-20; C. Burger, 'Jesu Taten nach Matthäus 8 und 9', *ZTK* 70 (1973), pp. 272-87; J.P. Louw, 'The Structure of Mt 8.1–9.35', *Neot* 11 (1977), pp. 91-97; J.D. Kingsbury, 'Observations on the "Miracle Chapters" of Matthew 8–9', *CBQ* 40 (1978), pp. 559-73; J.P. Heil, 'Significant Aspects of the Heal-

collection of ten miracles, primarily healings, serves as a narrative complement to the Sermon on the Mount in chs. 5–7. An *inclusio* for the combined sections is formed by two summary statements, 4.23-25:

> And he went about all Galilee, teaching in their synagogues and preaching the gospel of the kingdom and healing every disease and every infirmity among the people. So his fame spread throughout all Syria, and they brought him all the sick, those afflicted with various diseases and pains, demoniacs, epileptics, and paralytics, and he healed them. And great crowds followed him from Galilee and the Decapolis and Jerusalem and Judea and from beyond the Jordan. [RSV]

and 9.35:

> And Jesus went about all the cities and villages, teaching in their synagogues and preaching the gospel of the kingdom, and healing every disease and every infirmity. [RSV]

In conjunction with chs. 5–7, chs. 8 and 9 play an important role in Matthew's portrayal of Jesus and his ministry. Between the two summary statements Matthew shows Jesus teaching and preaching (chs. 5–7) and healing (chs. 8–9), emphasizing both word and deed. At the end of each of the two extended sections Matthew indicates the response of the crowds, first in 7.28-29, 'And when Jesus finished these sayings, the crowds were astonished at his teaching, for he taught them as one who had authority, and not as their scribes', and then in 9.33b, '...the crowds marveled, saying, "Never was anything like this seen in Israel"'. The second section concludes, however, with a contrasting response, that of the Pharisees in 9.34, 'But the Pharisees said, "He casts out demons by the prince of demons".'

ing Miracles in Matthew', *CBQ* 41 (1979), pp. 274-87; H.J.B. Combrink, 'The Structure of the Gospel of Matthew as Narrative', *TynBul* 34 (1983), pp. 61-90; G. Theissen, *The Miracle Stories of the Early Christian Tradition* (Philadelphia: Fortress, 1983), pp. 209-11; France, *Matthew*, pp. 150-51; J. Moiser, 'The Structure of Matthew 8–9: A Suggestion', *ZNW* 76 (1985), pp. 117-18; U. Luz, 'Die Wundergeschichten von Mt 8–9', in G.F. Hawthorne and O. Betz (eds.), *Tradition and Interpretation in the New Testament* (Grand Rapids: Eerdmans, 1987), pp. 149-65; U. Luz, *Das Evangelium nach Matthäus*. II. *Mt 8–17* (EKKNT, 1.2; Zürich: Benziger Verlag, 1990), pp. 1-73; Davies and Allison, *Matthew*, II, pp. 1-142; Hagner, *Matthew 1–13*, pp. 195-96; U. Luz, *The Theology of the Gospel of Matthew* (trans. J.B. Robinson; Cambridge: Cambridge University Press, 1995), pp. 62-65; E.-J. Vledder, *Conflict in the Miracle Stories: A Socio-Exegetical Study of Matthew 8 and 9* (JSNTSup, 152; Sheffield: Sheffield Academic Press, 1997); G.H. Twelftree, *Miracle Worker* (Downers Grove, IL: InterVarsity Press, 1999), pp. 102-43.

Chapters 8 and 9 also have links with ch. 10. A number of scholars have suggested that the miracles in chs. 8–9, as well as the teaching in 5–7, serve as a foundation for the mission discourse in 10.[8] Davies and Allison maintain that 'one function of the miracle chapters is to set up an example: like master like disciples (cf. 10.24f.)'.[9] The two formula statements in 7.28 and 11.1 frame chs. 8–10 as the second of the five so-called 'books' of Matthew, beginning after 7.28, 'And when Jesus finished these sayings…', and ending with 11.1, 'And when Jesus had finished instructing his twelve disciples…'[10] While it is not likely that the five formulaic sayings in 7.28, 11.1, 13.53, 19.1, and 26.1 constitute a single organizing principle for Matthew's Gospel, the presence of this formula in 7.28 and 11.1 does suggest that the intervening chs. 8–10 are in some way to be taken together.[11]

At the same time, chs. 8 and 9, especially their culmination in the Pharisees' negative response to Jesus' miracles in 9.34, anticipate chs. 11–12, where the conflict between Jesus and Israel develops more fully.[12] Chapters 8 and 9 come at a pivotal point in Matthew's Gospel, following the birth and infancy narratives of chs. 1–4 and the first major discourse in chs. 5–7, portraying Jesus' authority to act as well as to speak, and anticipating the growing conflict that leads to Jesus' eventual arrest and crucifixion in the passion narrative of chs. 26–28.

The arrangement by which Matthew recounts the events in chs. 8 and 9 varies significantly from that of Mark. While some of the material in 8.1-22 is also found in Mk 1.29-45 (although the order is not the same), 8.23-34 corresponds to Mk 4.35–5.20, after which 9.1-26 parallels first Mk 2.1-22 and then Mk 5.21-43, before ending with material with no Markan

---

8.   See, for example, Davies and Allison, *Matthew*, II, p. 5; Gatzwieler, 'Les récits de miracles', p. 214; Held, 'Miracle Stories', p. 249; Kingsbury, ' "Miracle Chapters" ', p. 566; Twelftree, *Miracle Worker*, p. 104.

9.   Davies and Allison, *Matthew*, II, p. 5.

10.   For Bacon's division of Matthew's Gospel into five 'books' plus preamble and epilogue, see Bacon, *Studies in Matthew*, pp. 145-261.

11.   See Twelftree, *Miracle Worker*, pp. 104-105. Arguing against a five-book structure, Thompson observes that this section also concludes Jesus' Galilean ministry in 4.12–9.34 (Thompson, 'Composition of Mt 8.1–9.34', p. 367 n. 9).

12.   See, for example, Davies and Allison, *Matthew*, II, p. 5; J.D. Kingsbury, 'The Developing Conflict between Jesus and the Jewish Leaders in Matthew's Gospel: A Literary-Critical Study', *CBQ* 49 (1987), p. 67; Vledder, *Conflict*, pp. 43-56; and, especially, Luz's approach in, for example, 'Wundergeschichten', pp. 152-55, and *Theology*, pp. 62-65.

equivalent. Davies and Allison summarize the parallels between the two Gospels as follows:[13]

Mt.		Mk
8.1-4	A leper healed	1.40-45
8.5-13	The centurion	
8.14-15	Peter's mother-in-law	1.29-31
8.16	Summary report	1.32-34
8.17	Isa. 53.4 cited	
8.18-22	On discipleship	
8.(18,) 23-27	A storm calmed	4.35-41
8.28-34	The Gadarene demoniac(s)	5.1-20
9.1-8	Sins forgiven	2.1-12
9.9-13	Tax collectors and sinners	2.13-17
9.14-17	On fasting	2.18-22
9.18-26	Two healings	5.21-43
9.27-31	Two blind men healed	
9.32-34	A demoniac	

Likewise, some of the incidents in Mt. 8.1–9.34 also appear in Luke's Gospel, but it is clear that Matthew differs from Luke in compiling and arranging his account. Mt. 8.23-34 parallels Lk. 8.22-39; 9.1-15 parallels Lk. 5.17-39; and 9.18-26 parallels Lk. 8.40-56.

Together, these points make 8.1–9.34 an appropriate subject for an analysis of Matthew's narrative framework: the verses constitute an extended unit; it is primarily a narrative section;[14] the passage plays an

13. Davies and Allison, *Matthew*, I, p. 101.

14. But see Held, a primary focus of whose study is his claim that in the miracle stories Matthew greatly reduces the element of narrative description in comparison to Mark, and increases the focus on conversational interaction between Jesus and others, so that 'one cannot really speak of miracle "narratives"'... Rather, it has been shown that they exhibit the form of a conversation.' Held speaks of Matthew's miracle stories as approximating the form of 'controversy dialogues'. As a result, the 'formal and material' climax of Matthew's miracle stories lies in what Jesus says about faith, and the story is, 'as a whole, nothing other than an illustration of this saying' (Held, 'Miracle Stories', pp. 241-42). But Heil disputes Held's conclusions regarding the form of Matthew's healing stories in, for example, 9.1-8: 'Matthew has not eliminated or transformed the literary genre of the miraculous healing of the paralytic by his redactional activity. However "controversial" the story may be, it is nevertheless presented by Matthew as a miracle' (Heil, 'Healing Miracles', p. 278). See also Theissen, *Miracle Stories*, p. 202.

However the various stories may be categorized by form critics, Matthew integrates

important role in Matthew's portrayal of Jesus; and while comparisons can be made with Synoptic parallels, it represents a uniquely Matthean arrangement of materials.

Sentence Conjunctions in Matthew 8.1–9.34

The working model developed above, positing that καί occurs with V(S) constituent order or with ἰδού while δέ occurs with SV constituent order or with genitive absolute constructions, forms the starting point for the sentence-by-sentence analysis of Mt. 8.1–9.34 below. For each subunit the NA[27] text of the narrative clauses is reproduced, followed by a schematization which indicates relevant syntactical and lexical features, whether καί or δέ is to be expected in such a context ('expected' meaning here 'expected in terms of the working model', rather than in terms of the more finely nuanced expectations a native speaker might have), the actual conjunction found in the sentence, and a brief evaluative note. Subunit boundaries used for the initial analysis are those generally assumed by scholars and are consistent with the paragraphing of NA[27]. For each subunit I discuss any divergence from the working model, particularly in terms of whether the conjunction actually chosen and its related features reflect usual patterns in Matthew's narrative framework or whether this might be considered an example of markedness or prominence. Finally, for each subunit I comment on the role of sentence conjunctions in the structure and flow of the subunit, drawing in part from the work of Held and Theissen on miracle story forms.[15]

Following the initial analysis of sentences and subunits, I look at the overall structure of Mt. 8.1–9.34, briefly outlining the approaches of several scholars and suggesting what contribution a greater appreciation of the role of sentence conjunctions as discourse markers can make to the discussion.

them into the narrative framework of his Gospel, and it is that narrative framework which is of interest here. There is the same nearly even balance in 8.1–9.34 between the number of sentences designated as 'narrative' discourse type in the database and the number of sentences designated as 'speech' as there is in Matthew's Gospel as a whole: 720 narrative sentences to 733 speech sentences in the entire Gospel, and 86 narrative sentences to 84 speech sentences in 8.1–9.34.

15. See Held, 'Miracle Stories', pp. 211-46; Theissen, *Miracle Stories,* pp. 201-203.

Matthew 8.1-4: A Leper Healed

8.1 Καταβάντος δὲ αὐτοῦ ἀπὸ τοῦ ὄρους ἠκολούθησαν αὐτῷ ὄχλοι πολλοί.

8.2 καὶ ἰδοὺ λεπρὸς προσελθὼν προσεκύνει αὐτῷ λέγων·...

8.3 καὶ ἐκτείνας τὴν χεῖρα ἥψατο αὐτοῦ λέγων·...
καὶ εὐθέως ἐκαθαρίσθη αὐτοῦ ἡ λέπρα.

8.4 καὶ λέγει αὐτῷ ὁ Ἰησοῦς·...

Verse	Feature(s)	Expected conjunction	Actual conjunction	Comments
8.1	genitive absolute and VS constituent order	δέ	δέ	as expected
8.2	ἰδού and S₁V constituent order	καί	καί	as expected
8.3a	V constituent order	καί	καί	as expected
8.3b	VS constituent order	καί	καί	as expected
8.4	VS constituent order	καί	καί	as expected

The working model accounts for each of the sentence conjunctions in Mt. 8.1-4, in which Jesus descends from the mountain following the Sermon on the Mount and encounters a leper who asks for healing. In spite of VS constituent order, δέ appears with the genitive absolute construction καταβάντος ... αὐτοῦ ἀπὸ τοῦ ὄρους in 8.1. As expected, καί appears with ἰδού, along with S₁V constituent order, drawing attention to the leper in 8.2. In the three subsequent sentences καί occurs with V(S) constituent order.

However, more interesting than the syntactical combinations in individual sentences is their sequence in the pericope. Held identifies Matthew's tendency to use stereotyped introductions and conclusions in the miracle stories, but he primarily addresses the second element of the miracle stories, the suppliant's approach to Jesus.[16] It is Theissen who spells out in more detail the initial structures characteristic of Matthew's miracle stories. He describes three main variations on the formulaic phrases Matthew uses to introduce first Jesus and then his 'opposite number':

> i) Jesus' appearance is described in a participial construction while the main clause introduces his opposite number. If there is a change of subject between the participle and the main clause, we find a genitive absolute:
>
> a) εἰσελθόντος δὲ αὐτοῦ εἰς Καφαρναοὺμ
> b) προσῆλθεν αὐτῷ ἑκατόνταρχος (8.5)

16. Held, 'Miracle Stories', p. 226.

a) καὶ ἐλθὼν ὁ Ἰησοῦς εἰς τὴν οἰκίαν Πέτρου
b) εἶδεν τὴν πενθερὰν αὐτοῦ (8.14)

Cf. also 8.28; 9.27; 14.14; 17.14, 24.

ii) Jesus is introduced by a participial construction *a)*, the main verb gives a more detailed description of his coming *b)*, and the opposite number (or the storm on the lake) is introduced by καὶ ἰδού in a new independent sentence *c)*.

a) καταβάντος δὲ αὐτοῦ ἀπὸ τοῦ ὄρους
b) ἠκολούθησαν αὐτῷ ὄχλοι πολλοί
c) καὶ ἰδοὺ λεπρὸς προσελθών (8.1)

a) καὶ ἐμβάντι αὐτῷ εἰς τὸ πλοῖον
b) ἠκολούθησαν αὐτῷ οἱ μαθηταὶ αὐτοῦ
c) καὶ ἰδοὺ σεισμὸς μέγας (8.23)

Cf. 12.9; 15.21; 20.29a.

iii) The middle element of the introduction may be omitted and the ἰδού sentence comes immediately after the participial construction: in this case there is no καί before ἰδού.

a) ταῦτα αὐτοῦ λαλοῦντος αὐτοῖς
b) ἰδοὺ ἄρχων προσελθών (9.18).

Cf. 9.32.[17]

Matthew 8.1 exemplifies the second variation, in which Jesus is introduced by a participial construction, in this case a genitive absolute (καταβάντος... αὐτοῦ ἀπὸ τοῦ ὄρους) grammaticalizing a change in actor from Jesus in the participial construction to the crowds in the main verb; the main verb gives more details of his coming, specifically that the crowds followed him; and the 'opposite number', the leper, is introduced by καὶ ἰδού in the next sentence. The use of a form of προσέρχομαι as the leper 'approaches' Jesus is a characteristically Matthean feature.[18]

In terms of contributing to the discourse processing of the pericope, δέ and καί function in the roles I have identified as signals of discontinuity and continuity respectively. At the beginning of the new pericope (a point of narrative discontinuity between the Sermon on the Mount and an incident of healing) δέ is combined with a genitive absolute construction,

17. Theissen, *Miracle Stories*, pp. 201-202.
18. See, for example, Held, 'Miracle Stories', pp. 226-29; Edwards, 'ΠΡΟΣΕΡΧΕΣΘΑΙ', pp. 65-74; Davies and Allison, *Matthew*, I, p. 360; Gundry, *Matthew*, p. 55.

itself a discontinuous element which not only grammaticalizes a change in actor within the sentence, but is often used by Matthew as a 'scene shifter' in narrative, conveying a change in place or time between scenes. In this case the shift is one of place, indicating the movement down from the mountain where the preceding discourse was delivered (see Mt. 5.1). Then a marked variation of καί, the fixed combination καὶ ἰδού, is used with προσέρχομαι to introduce the suppliant, the leper. From that point, sentences with καί and V(S) constituent order continue the narrative in 8.3-4 (8.3a, καὶ...ἥψατο; 8.3b, καὶ ἐκαθαρίσθη...ἡ λέπρα; 8.4, καὶ λέγει... ὁ Ἰησοῦς). Even where there are subsequent grammaticalized subjects, specifically ἡ λέπρα in 8.3 and ὁ Ἰησοῦς in 8.4, Matthew chooses to convey continuity of action through the use of καί and by placing the subject after the verb once the two main participants, Jesus and the leper, have been established.

Matthew 8.5-13: A Centurion's Servant Healed[19]

8.5	Εἰσελθόντος δὲ αὐτοῦ εἰς Καφαρναοὺμ προσῆλθεν αὐτῷ ἑκατόνταρχος παρακαλῶν αὐτὸν (8.6) καὶ λέγων...
8.7	καὶ λέγει αὐτῷ....
8.8	καὶ ἀποκριθεὶς ὁ ἑκατόνταρχος ἔφη·...
8.10	ἀκούσας δὲ ὁ Ἰησοῦς ἐθαύμασεν καὶ εἶπεν τοῖς ἀκολουθοῦσιν·...
8.13	καὶ εἶπεν ὁ Ἰησοῦς τῷ ἑκατοντάρχῃ·... καὶ ἰάθη ὁ παῖς [αὐτοῦ] ἐν τῇ ὥρα ἐκείνῃ.

Verse	Feature(s)	Expected conjunction	Actual conjunction	Comments
8.5	genitive absolute and VS constituent order	δέ	δέ	as expected
8.7	V constituent order	καί	καί	as expected
8.8	S_2V constituent order	δέ	καί	*not as expected,* but καί default
8.10a	S_2V constituent order	δέ	δέ	as expected
8.10b	V constituent order	καί	καί	as expected
8.13a	VS constituent order	καί	καί	as expected
8.13b	VS constituent order	καί	καί	as expected

The working model adequately accounts for all but one of the sentence conjunctions in Mt. 8.5-13. As above, the pericope is introduced with a

---

19. Square brackets in Greek text represent textual variants included in the NA[27] text.

formulaic construction. Mt. 8.5 exemplifies Theissen's first variation, in which Jesus' appearance is described in a participial construction (εἰσελθόντος δὲ αὐτοῦ εἰς Καφαρναούμ) while the main clause of the sentence introduces his opposite number, the centurion. As in 8.1, δέ is combined with a genitive absolute 'scene shifter', here signaling the spatial movement to Capernaum. These two elements, δέ and the genitive absolute, serve as mutually reinforcing signals of discourse discontinuity as the new pericope begins.

In 8.8, containing the centurion's answer to Jesus, καί occurs with S_2V constituent order although δέ is predicted by the working model. As the unmarked or 'default' conjunction in Matthew's narrative framework καί not uncommonly appears in contexts where collocating features are consistent with some other conjunction. In fact, καί appears nearly as frequently as δέ does in S_2V sentences in Matthew's narrative framework (καί: 40/99; δέ: 47/99). In sentences in which there is a nominative participle in thematic position, as here, καί is slightly more frequent than δέ (καί: 37/80; δέ: 35/80). Although the association of καί with V(S) constituent order and δέ with SV constituent order is a productive generalization when applied to narrative in Matthew's Gospel, in fact Matthew appears to discriminate less between S_2V and VS constituent order when using καί as a sentence conjunction than he does when using δέ. Καί appears in 40% of S_2V sentences (40/99) and 46% of VS sentences (69/149), a difference which is not demonstrably significant.[20] Thus, in spite of the working model (and perhaps as an additional refinement to it), the appearance of καί with S_2V sentences should not be considered a particularly unexpected or necessarily marked use of καί. At the same time, it is notable that one-fourth of all the narrative sentences in which Matthew combines καί and S_2V constituent order (10/40, 25%) occur in the present extended unit 8.1–9.34, about twice as many as would be expected based on their frequency in the narrative framework as a whole.[21]

20. At the same time, δέ appears in 47% of S_2V sentences (47/99, $z = 2.44$) but in only 19% of VS sentences (29/149, $z = -4.13$), a highly significant difference. In terms of Matthew's use of καί, the more significant contrast lies between sentences at opposite ends of the cline developed in Chapter 4: καί appears in only 12% with thematic subjects (23/195, $z = -9.73$), more than half of which occurrences (14/23) are in combination with ἰδού, but in 73% of sentences with monolectic verbs (191/262, $z = 8.56$).

21. Mt. 8.8, 14, 19; 9.2, 4, 9, 11, 19, 23; see also 9.10, although the sentence structure is somewhat different. Frequency of sentences in the narrative framework

The sentences in 8.5-7 recount the initial action of the scene—Jesus' entrance into Capernaum, the centurion's approach and request, Jesus' affirmative reply, and the centurion's response—using a δέ–καί–καί sequence appropriate to the introduction of an element of discontinuity at the beginning of the scene and then the portrayal of continuity as the scene progresses. Mt. 8.8-9 recounts the centurion's statements revealing his understanding of Jesus' authority, made prominent by the use of φημί, a highly marked choice as a speech margin.[22] Δέ then occurs with Jesus' reaction in 8.10, introducing a low-level discontinuity in the flow of the pericope between actors, with the centurion speaking and Jesus responding in amazement. The use of δέ in indicating alternate participants in action or speakers in dialogue is not at all unusual in Matthew's Gospel. On the other hand, it represents only one of a broad range of lexical and syntactical options available to and used by Matthew, and so represents a choice—if possibly only a stylistic variation—made by Matthew at this point in the narrative. In the present context, where 8.10 is the only sentence with δέ in a series of καί sentences carrying the scene forward, δέ and the interruption of narrative continuity that it represents appear to highlight Jesus' amazement in the face of the surprising statements of the centurion. One imagines Matthew's audience thoughtfully turning their attention (actually, turning the focus of the mental representation they are constructing) from the centurion to Jesus in anticipation of his reaction. Together the marked use of φημί and the subsequent use of δέ make this exchange between the centurion and Jesus discontinuous with the smooth flow of the rest of the scene, so that their interaction becomes prominent in the pericope's narrative framework.

Following Jesus' amazed response and his statements in 8.10b-12, the narrative sentences in 8.13 continue with καί and V(S) constituent order, narrating the resolution that is expected in terms of Matthew's miracle story form: an affirmation of the suppliant's faith, and a successful and immediate healing of the servant.[23]

---

which are of the structure <καί + S_2V>: 40/720, 6%; frequency of narrative sentences in 8.1–9.34 of the structure <καί + S_2V>: 10/86, 12% ($z = 2.45$).

22. Φημί occurs only 11 times in Matthew's narrative framework (4.7, 8.8, 14.8, 17.26, 19.21, 21.27, 22.37, 26.34, 27.11, 23, 65), all of which introduce important statements or pronouncements, generally in response to a question or challenge. Seven usages introduce pronouncements by Jesus: 4.7, 17.26, 19.21, 21.27, 22.37, 26.34, 27.11. See on φημί in speech margins, Chapter 6.

23. See Held, 'Miracle Stories', pp. 230, 239-41.

Matthew 8.14-15: Peter's Mother-in-Law Healed

8.14   Καὶ ἐλθὼν ὁ Ἰησοῦς εἰς τὴν οἰκίαν Πέτρου εἶδεν τὴν
       πενθερὰν αὐτοῦ βεβλημένην καὶ πυρέσσουσαν·
8.15   καὶ ἥψατο τῆς χειρὸς αὐτῆς,
       καὶ ἀφῆκεν αὐτὴν ὁ πυρετός,
       καὶ ἠγέρθη
       καὶ διηκόνει αὐτῷ.

Verse	Feature(s)	Expected conjunction	Actual conjunction	Comments
8.14	S$_2$V constituent order	δέ	καί	*not as expected,* but καί default
8.15a	V constituent order	καί	καί	as expected
8.15b	VS constituent order	καί	καί	as expected
8.15c	V constituent order	καί	καί	as expected
8.15d	V constituent order	καί	καί	as expected

The working model adequately accounts for all but the first of the sentence conjunctions in Mt. 8.14-15, but this common exception, the use of καί in combination with S$_2$V constituent order, is addressed above.

While the pericope has the formulaic introduction of Theissen's first variation—Jesus' appearance is conveyed in a participial construction (ἐλθὼν ὁ Ἰησοῦς εἰς τὴν οἰκίαν Πέτρου) while the main clause of the sentence introduces his opposite number, Peter's mother-in-law—the lack of δέ setting the pericope off from preceding text is unexpected. The combination of καί with S$_2$V constituent order is not as notable at the sentence level as is the decision to use such a structure at the beginning of a pericope. This καί, along with the pared-down syntax of the following sequence of four sentences with καί and thematic finite verbs (καὶ ἥψατο..., καὶ ἀφῆκεν..., καὶ ἠγέρθη καὶ διηκόνει αὐτῷ...; three of these are monolectic), smoothly carries the narrative forward through 8.15. The sense of continuous narrative in Matthew's account is all the more palpable given that both Mark and Luke introduce Peter's mother-in-law in a separate sentence with δέ and S$_1$V constituent order: Mk 1.30, ἡ δὲ πενθερὰ Σίμωνος κατέκειτο πυρέσσουσα ...; Lk. 4.38, πενθερὰ δὲ τοῦ Σίμωνος ἦν συνεχομένη πυρετῷ μεγάλῳ ...[24] Matthew's lexico-gram-

24. Because of the widespread use of καί as a sentence conjunction in Markan narrative, where there are parallels between Matthew and Mark it tends to be the case that Matthew either agrees with Mark's use of καί or has δέ where Mark has καί. Contexts such as this one where Matthew has καί against Mark's δέ (although to be

matical choices, combined with the fact that there is no conversational exchange between Jesus and the suppliant nor an affirmation of her faith as in the preceding two scenes, gives this brief pericope a feel of swifter movement and the sense that it is more continuous with preceding text than was the case with the first two scenes.

Matthew 8.16-17: Many People Healed

8.16 Ὀψίας δὲ γενομένης προσήνεγκαν αὐτῷ δαιμονιζομένους
πολλούς
καὶ ἐξέβαλεν τὰ πνεύματα λογῷ
καὶ πάντας τοὺς κακῶς ἔχοντας ἐθεράπευσεν, (8.17) ὅπως
πληρωθῇ τὸ ῥηθὲν διὰ Ἡσαΐου τοῦ προφήτου λέγοντος·...

Verse	Feature(s)	Expected conjunction	Actual conjunction	Comments
8.16a	genitive absolute and V constituent order	δέ	δέ	as expected
8.16b	V constituent order	καί	καί	as expected
8.16c	V constituent order	καί	καί	as expected

After detailing the three previous healings, Matthew includes in 8.16-17 a statement summarizing a group of healings by Jesus. The sentence conjunctions in 8.16-17 are adequately accounted for by the working model. Again Matthew combines δέ and a genitive absolute construction at the beginning of a scene (ὀψίας δὲ γενομένης), introducing a temporal shift to evening. As the demon-possessed and sick are brought to Jesus in 8.16, the scene continues smoothly with καί and monolectic verbs (καὶ ἐξέβαλεν..., καὶ...ἐθεράπευσεν) culminating in the quotation from Isa. 53.4 which underscores Jesus' healing activity.

Matthew 8.18-22: Questions about Discipleship

8.18 Ἰδὼν δὲ ὁ Ἰησοῦς ὄχλον περὶ αὐτὸν ἐκέλευσεν ἀπελθεῖν εἰς
τὸ πέραν.
8.19 καὶ προσελθὼν εἷς γραμματεὺς εἶπεν αὐτῳ·...
8.20 καὶ λέγει αὐτῷ ὁ Ἰησοῦς....
8.21 ἕτερος δὲ τῶν μαθητῶν [αὐτοῦ] εἶπεν αὐτῷ·...
8.22 ὁ δὲ Ἰησοῦς λέγει αὐτῷ·...

precise, Matthew has no separate sentence here parallel to Mark's use of δέ to introduce Peter's mother-in-law) are more rare and as such are of greater interest in terms of Matthew's use of sentence conjunctions.

Verse	Feature(s)	Expected conjunction	Actual conjunction	Comments
8.18	S$_2$V constituent order	δέ	δέ	as expected
8.19	S$_2$V constituent order	δέ	καί	*not as expected,* but καί default
8.20	VS constituent order	καί	καί	as expected
8.21	S$_1$V constituent order	δέ	δέ	as expected
8.22	S$_1$V constituent order	δέ	δέ	as expected

As in 8.14-15, the working model adequately accounts for all the sentence conjunctions in Mt. 8.18-22, with the common exception of the use of καί with S$_2$V constituent order in 8.19.

The present scene recounts questions and answers between Jesus and two would-be followers rather than a healing. Nevertheless, there is a formulaic introduction similar to those described by Theissen. Mt. 8.18 begins with δέ and a participial construction which introduces Jesus in the scene (ἰδὼν δὲ ὁ Ἰησοῦς ὄχλον περὶ αὐτόν). The main verb, however, describes an action—the command to cross to the other side of the lake—that does not seem connected with the conversations which follow. As in the healing stories, Jesus is then approached (προσέρχομαι) by an opposite number, a scribe (καί but not ἰδού). The question-and-answer exchange is not about healing but concerns aspects of discipleship.

There is a repetition of this sequence when another opposite number, one of Jesus' disciples, approaches him. There is another question and Jesus makes another response. In each of two narrative sentences serving as speech margins for the interaction between Jesus and this second disciple the sentence conjunction is δέ and the subject is thematic. As I have said, the use of δέ to indicate alternate speakers in dialogue is not at all unusual, but given that καί or asyndeton and their related syntactical features are equally acceptable alternatives, where δέ does occur it represents a choice by Matthew in structuring the narrative that is marked to some degree (compare καί and VS constituent order in Jesus' first response, in 8.20). In a manner similar to Jesus' reply to the centurion in 8.10, Matthew uses the change in structure in 8.21-22—the shift to δέ and S$_1$V constituent order—to interrupt the continuity of the narrative framework, slowing down the flow of the narrative to a more deliberate pace to highlight first Jesus' disciple's request for a delay in following him (8.21) and then Jesus' response, 'Follow me, and leave the dead to bury their own dead' (8.22).

Matthew 8.23-27: A Great Storm Calmed

8.23   Καὶ ἐμβάντι αὐτῷ εἰς τὸ πλοῖον ἠκολούθησαν αὐτῷ οἱ
μαθηταὶ αὐτοῦ.

8.24   καὶ ἰδοὺ σεισμὸς μέγας ἐγένετο ἐν τῇ θαλάσσῃ, ὥστε τὸ
πλοῖον καλύπτεσθαι ὑπὸ τῶν κυμάτων,
αὐτὸς δὲ ἐκάθευδεν.

8.25   καὶ προσελθόντες ἤγειραν αὐτὸν λέγοντες....

8.26   καὶ λέγει αὐτοῖς·...
τότε ἐγερθεὶς ἐπετίμησεν τοῖς ἀνέμοις καὶ τῇ θαλάσσῃ,
καὶ ἐγένετο γαλήνη μεγάλη.

8.27   οἱ δὲ ἄνθρωποι ἐθαύμασαν λέγοντες·...

Verse	Feature(s)	Expected conjunction	Actual conjunction	Comments
8.23	VS constituent order	καί	καί	as expected
8.24a	ἰδού and S_1V constituent order	καί	καί	as expected
8.24b	S_1V constituent order	δέ	δέ	as expected
8.25	V constituent order	καί	καί	as expected
8.26a	V constituent order	καί	καί	as expected
8.26b	V constituent order	καί	τότε	*not as expected*
8.26c	VS constituent order	καί	καί	as expected
8.27	S_1V constituent order	δέ	δέ	as expected

The working model accounts for each of the sentence conjunctions in
8.23-27 except τότε in 8.26b. This pericope, like those which precede,
opens with a formulaic introduction in which Jesus' appearance is
described by a participial construction (ἐμβάντι αὐτῷ εἰς τὸ πλοῖον),
followed by a main verb giving a more detailed description of his coming,
specifically that his disciples followed him (8.23). As in 8.14, the sentence
conjunction in the introductory formula in 8.23 is καί rather than δέ,
suggesting some degree of continuity between this scene and preceding
text. Narrative continuity is also reflected in Matthew's choice not to use a
genitive absolute construction as a more explicit 'scene shifter' than the
dative case used here. Matthew's willingness to use a genitive absolute
construction with reference to a following dative noun at the beginning of
a pericope is evident in 8.1, 28 and 9.18, but in this instance he has not
done so.[25] Exemplifying Theissen's second variation, the opposite number

---

25. BDF consider the use of the genitive absolute with a following dative 'un-
classical', but observe that a popular tendency to make the genitive absolute independent of surrounding case relations is found in the LXX, papyri, and Hellenistic writers
as well as in the New Testament (BDF, §423).

(in this case the storm) is introduced by καὶ ἰδού in a new independent sentence (8.24).

Held describes Matthew's miracle story forms, especially the healing miracles, as encompassing four fundamental elements:

> 1. Formal introduction in which the suppliant is quite briefly introduced and an attitude of supplication is expressed (for example, *proskunein*, *parakalein*).
> 2. The request in direct speech in which faith is expressed and which can be carried on in a twofold exchange of conversation.
> 3. The reply of Jesus corresponding to the request, generally in the form of a healing saying, sometimes only in the form of a corresponding action, but occasionally both.
> 4. A brief formalistic notice that the miracle has taken place without a lengthy stay over it.[26]

While 8.23-27 does not recount a healing miracle, similar elements are present. There is a formal introduction of Jesus' opposite number (the storm) which, the audience might expect, is to be followed by a request for help expressing faith, and then Jesus' response. However, before proceeding further the expected story form is interrupted by an unexpected circumstance. Jesus is asleep. Δέ as the sentence conjunction, S_1V constituent order, and the supplying of αὐτός as a grammaticalized subject when one is not necessary (found in the nominative case only here in all of 8.1–9.34) all help draw attention to the incongruity of this state of affairs, both with respect to the interruption of the story form and in terms of the seeming impossibility that anyone could sleep through such a storm. The semantic relationship between the sentences conjoined by δέ—8.24a, in which there is a great storm causing waves that wash over the boat, and 8.24b, in which Jesus is asleep—may be described as a condition contrary to expectation. The present context is one of the few times in this extended unit that δέ approximates its traditionally understood role as an adversative or contrastive particle (see also 9.31, 34). However, δέ signals only that there is some low- to mid-level discontinuity in the narrative, a discontinuity which necessitates an adjustment in the audience's mental representation of the discourse. What is discontinuous is then pragmatically worked out by the audience on the basis of the semantic relationship between propositions, surrounding text, and their knowledge of the world (in this case, their recognition of the miracle story form and/or their knowledge of boats and storms).

---

26. Held, 'Miracle Stories', p. 241.

The expected form then resumes with a request by the disciples for help (προσέρχομαι, but with an expression of fear rather than faith), Jesus' rebuke of their little faith and, in spite of their lack of faith, Jesus' climactic act of quieting the storm. The sentences in this sequence of events in 8.25-26 have καί as the sentence conjunction—except for the climactic τότε in 8.26b (see below)—and V(S) constituent order. The sequence of καί and τότε sentences in 8.25-26 underlines the role of authorial choice in choosing to emphasize continuity over against discontinuity at this point in the narrative. Any of the changes in actor in 8.25 (from Jesus to the disciples), 8.26a (from the disciples to Jesus) or 8.26c (from Jesus to the impersonal ἐγένετο) could have been portrayed with δέ and a corresponding constituent order. For his own purposes Matthew has chosen to de-emphasize the changes in this sequence and instead to recount this sequence as relatively continuous narrative.

For the first time in this extended unit, in 8.26b Matthew chooses a sentence conjunction other than καί or δέ. I have described τότε as a signal of marked continuity, and as such it is not surprising to find it displacing καί, the unmarked signal of continuity and the conjunction predicted in 8.26b by the model. Although none of the lexical or syntactical features which tend to collocate with τότε occur in the present context—specifically, the so-called 'historic present', a thematic finite verb, VS constituent order, or the lexical choice of προσέρχομαι or a passive form of προσφέρω—τότε does appear to mark the climax of the pericope. As Buth points out, τότε may appear at 'peaks' within a narrative, especially climactic statements by Jesus.[27] In the present context it accompanies not Jesus' words to his disciples decrying their lack of faith, but his rebuke of the storm (a type of statement by Jesus, although the content of his words is not given).[28] Some exegetes, observing that Matthew's order is the reverse of Mark's, with Jesus' words to the disciples preceding the calming of the storm rather than following as in Mark's Gospel (Mk 4.39-40), argue that Matthew shows little interest in the miracle itself and directs his attention instead to the interchange between Jesus and the disciples.[29] However, the lexico-grammatical choices displayed here suggest otherwise. Matthew's interest in issues of discipleship is manifest

27. See Buth, 'Perspective', p. 8.
28. Regarding Matthew's omission of Jesus' comments in rebuking the storm, see Davies and Allison, *Matthew*, II, p. 74; Hagner, *Matthew 1–13*, p. 222.
29. See, for example, Held, 'Miracle Stories', pp. 203-204; Gundry, *Matthew*, p. 156.

in this pericope; nevertheless, it is not Matthew's habit to use τότε to downplay a statement or action in the middle of a paragraph, nor is it his habit to introduce a climactic statement with καί and monolectic λέγει, as in Jesus' rebuke of his disciples' lack of faith in 8.26a. The choices made by the Evangelist in recounting these events indicate that his primary focus is on Jesus' authority over the storm.

The phrase καὶ ἐγένετο, used in 8.26c with respect to the 'great calm' that occurred as a result of Jesus' words, is not common in Matthew's narrative framework. Outside the five formula statements in 7.28, 11.1, 13.53, 19.1 and 26.1, it is used only here and in 9.10. Thus this construction is rare in the narrative framework, and while rarity alone does not make a construction marked, as such it is potentially prominent. Here, in fact, it further highlights the phenomenon that even the storm responds to Jesus' authority. This is the only narrative sentence in Matthew's Gospel in which γίνομαι serves as the main verb of the sentence rather than functioning in a temporal clause followed by another finite verb.

Lastly, δέ and S₁V constituent order appear again in 8.27, shifting attention from the nature miracle to the astonished disciples, who wonder, 'What sort of man is this?'

Matthew 8.28-34: Two Demoniacs Healed

8.28   Καὶ ἐλθόντος αὐτοῦ εἰς τὸ πέραν εἰς τὴν χώραν τῶν Γαδαρηνῶν ὑπήντησαν αὐτῷ δύο δαιμονιζόμενοι ἐκ τῶν μνημείων ἐξερχόμενοι, χαλεποὶ λίαν, ὥστε μὴ ἰσχύειν τινὰ παρελθεῖν διὰ τῆς ὁδοῦ ἐκείνης.

8.29   καὶ ἰδοὺ ἔκραξαν λέγοντες·...

8.30   ἦν δὲ μακρὰν ἀπ’ αὐτῶν ἀγέλη χοίρων πολλῶν βοσκομένη.

8.31   οἱ δὲ δαίμονες παρεκάλουν αὐτὸν λέγοντες·...

8.32   καὶ εἶπεν αὐτοῖς·...
        οἱ δὲ ἐξελθόντες ἀπῆλθον εἰς τοὺς χοίρους·
        καὶ ἰδοὺ ὥρμησεν πᾶσα ἡ ἀγέλη κατὰ τοῦ κρημνοῦ εἰς τὴν θάλασσαν
        καὶ ἀπέθανον ἐν τοῖς ὕδασιν.

8.33   οἱ δὲ βόσκοντες ἔφυγον,
        καὶ ἀπελθόντες εἰς τὴν πόλιν ἀπήγγειλαν πάντα καὶ τὰ τῶν δαιμονιζομένων.

8.34   καὶ ἰδοὺ πᾶσα ἡ πόλις ἐξῆλθεν εἰς ὑπάντησιν τῷ Ἰησοῦ
        καὶ ἰδόντες αὐτὸν παρεκάλεσαν ὅπως μεταβῇ ἀπὸ τῶν ὁρίων αὐτῶν.

Verse	Feature(s)	Expected conjunction	Actual conjunction	Comments
8.28	genitive absolute and VS constituent order	δέ	καί	*not as expected,* but καί default
8.29	ἰδού and V constituent order	καί	καί	as expected
8.30	VS constituent order (εἰμί)	καί	δέ	*not as expected*
8.31	S₁V constituent order	δέ	δέ	as expected
8.32a	V constituent order	καί	καί	as expected
8.32b	S₁V constituent order	δέ	δέ	as expected
8.32c	ἰδού and VS constituent order	καί	καί	as expected
8.32d	V constituent order	καί	καί	as expected
8.33a	S₁V constituent order	δέ	δέ	as expected
8.33b	V constituent order	καί	καί	as expected
8.34a	ἰδού and S₁V constituent order	καί	καί	as expected
8.34b	V constituent order	καί	καί	as expected

The working model accounts for 10 of the 12 sentence conjunctions in 8.28-34, a story in which Jesus encounters two demon-possessed men. As in 8.1, 8.5 and 8.16, Matthew uses a genitive absolute construction in 8.28 as a 'scene shifter' at the beginning of the new pericope (ἐλθόντος αὐτοῦ εἰς τὸ πέραν), in this case indicating spatial movement to the other side of the lake. However, the sentence conjunction with the genitive absolute is καί rather than the expected δέ. Καί occurs with only 11 of the 39 thematic genitive absolute constructions in Matthew's narrative framework, 2 of which appear in these chapters: the present example, and 9.33, where the combination is manifestly within a continuous subunit rather than functioning as a unit boundary (9.33, καὶ ἐκβληθέντος τοῦ δαιμονίου ἐλάλησεν ὁ κωφός). As with the use of καί in 8.14 at the beginning of the pericope about the healing of Peter's mother-in-law, and in 8.23 at the beginning of the pericope in which Jesus calms the storm, Matthew appears to be signaling the audience to view the incident of the two demoniacs as more continuous than discontinuous with preceding text.

In fact, 8.28-34 represents the second in a series of four pericopes which have καί as the initial conjunction: 8.23-27, the calming of the storm; 8.28-34, two demoniacs healed; 9.1-8, a paralyzed man healed; and 9.9-13, the calling of Matthew—suggesting that together these four and the immediately preceding pericope in 8.18-22 concerning discipleship form a section within the extended unit 8.1–9.34. At these four points (8.23, 8.28, 9.1, 9.9) καί appears to function as a marker of continuity at a higher level of discourse than previously discussed, that is, to show continuity between discourse units rather than merely between sequential actions within the discourse. Nevertheless, this does not represent a different 'meaning' for καί than that previously described. Καί is a signal of continuity in discourse processing. The discourse level at which καί is to be applied—the hierarchical level at which continuity is to be maintained in the mental representation of the discourse—is pragmatically worked out on the basis of surrounding text and other cues, such as the presence of geographical indicators of a shift in setting.

After the formulaic introduction, which differs slightly from the three variations outlined by Theissen in that there is an extended description of the demoniacs and καὶ ἰδού does not occur until their challenge to Jesus rather than at their initial appearance, there is in 8.30 a use of δέ not accounted for by the working model: ἦν δὲ μακρὰν ἀπ' αὐτῶν ἀγέλη χοίρων πολλῶν βοσκομένη. The working model predicts καί with VS constituent order. Alternatively, γάρ might be expected, since as I have shown in Chapter 8 γάρ is found in combination with εἰμί (the finite verb here) more often than would be expected based on its overall frequency in Matthew's narrative framework. However, this is one of three instances in the narrative framework in which δέ is combined with εἰμί in a 'presentational' structure, comparable to English *there was/were* (see also 27.55, 27.61).[30] The discontinuity which δέ signals in these instances is a discontinuity with the narrative line itself, not in the action within the narrative, briefly standing aside from the narrative action to provide additional off-line information relevant to it. If the material contained in 8.30 strengthened or confirmed a preceding proposition, γάρ might be used, as in 9.21. However, as Matthew has not yet mentioned anything which might be supported by knowledge about the herd of pigs, and as γάρ is not used with forward scope in Matthew's Gospel, δέ introduces the off-line material. Correspondingly, δέ is also used in the return to the narrative line in 8.31 as the demoniacs continue addressing Jesus. There is no change in actor or speaker from 8.29 to 8.31 to account for the use of δέ; the discontinuity involved is a return from supplementary information to the sequential action of the narrative.[31]

---

30. See Levinsohn, *Discourse Features*, pp. 7, 90-91; Andrews, 'Noun Phrase', p. 80; and comments on δέ in presentational sentences in Chapter 5.

31. Οὖν could have been used here to underline that the demoniacs' request presupposes the presence of the herd. Authorial choice is the determining factor; nowhere in the extended unit 8.1–9.34 does Matthew use οὖν as a narrative connector.

The pericope continues as the demons invade the herd of pigs, the pigs run down the steep incline into the sea and drown in the water, the fleeing herdsmen tell what has happened, and the people beg Jesus to leave. Sentences with καί and V(S) constituent order carry much of the action (8.32a, καὶ εἶπεν αὐτοῖς; 32d, καὶ ἀπέθανον; 33b, καὶ ... ἀπήγγειλαν; 34b, καὶ ἰδόντες αὐτὸν παρεκάλεσαν). Δέ and S₁V constituent order are used at some, but not all, points where there is a change in actor: in 8.32b, a shift from Jesus to the demons, where δέ occurs as dictated by the choice of the pronominal article οἱ; and in 8.33a, a shift from the pigs to the herdsmen. Καὶ ἰδού is used more extensively than in previous pericopes, marking not just the initial appearance of the 'opposite number', the demon-possessed men (8.29), but also the death of the herd (8.32c) and the arrival of 'the whole city' to request Jesus' departure (8.34a).[32]

Matthew 9.1-8: A Paralyzed Man Healed

9.1   Καὶ ἐμβὰς εἰς πλοῖον διεπέρασεν
      καὶ ἦλθεν εἰς τὴν ἰδίαν πόλιν.
9.2   καὶ ἰδοὺ προσέφερον αὐτῷ παραλυτικὸν ἐπὶ κλίνης
      βεβλημένον.
      καὶ ἰδὼν ὁ Ἰησοῦς τὴν πίστιν αὐτῶν εἶπεν τῷ παραλυτικῷ...
9.3   καὶ ἰδού τινες τῶν γραμματέων εἶπαν ἐν ἑαυτοῖς·...
9.4   καὶ ἰδὼν ὁ Ἰησοῦς τὰς ἐνθυμήσεις αὐτῶν εἶπεν·...
9.6   τότε λέγει τῷ παραλυτικῷ·...
9.7   καὶ ἐγερθεὶς ἀπῆλθεν εἰς τὸν οἶκον αυτου.
9.8   ἰδόντες δὲ οἱ ὄχλοι ἐφοβήθησαν
      καὶ ἐδόξασαν τὸν θεὸν τὸν δόντα ἐξουσίαν τοιαύτην τοῖς
      ἀνθρώποις.

Verse	Feature(s)	Expected conjunction	Actual conjunction	Comments
9.1a	V constituent order	καί	καί	as expected
9.1b	V constituent order	καί	καί	as expected
9.2a	ἰδού and V constituent order	καί	καί	as expected
9.2b	S₂V constituent order	δέ	καί	*not as expected,* but καί default
9.3	ἰδού and S₁V constituent order	καί	καί	as expected
9.4	S₂V constituent order	δέ	καί	*not as expected,* but καί default

32. See Vargas-Machuca, '(Καὶ) ἰδού', pp. 233-44.

9.6	V constituent order	καί	τότε	*not as expected*
9.7	V constituent order	καί	καί	as expected
9.8a	S₂V constituent order	δέ	δέ	as expected
9.8b	V constituent order	καί	καί	as expected

The working model accounts for the sentence conjunctions in Mt. 9.1-8, with the exception of καί with S₂V constituent order (9.2b, 4), and τότε at a climactic point in 9.6.

There is a formulaic introduction, corresponding with Theissen's second variation, in which Jesus is introduced by a participial construction (ἐμβὰς εἰς πλοῖον), with the main verb giving the added detail that he returns to his own city (διεπέρασεν καὶ ἦλθεν εἰς τὴν ἰδίαν πόλιν). In fact, there are two main verbs and two sentences, allowing for movement both from the other side of the lake and to Jesus' own city to be described. The use of καί at the beginning of the pericope again suggests that the present episode is to be taken in continuity with the preceding narrative. The opposite number, the paralytic, is introduced in a new sentence (9.2a), using καὶ ἰδού and προσφέρω, the counterpart of προσέρχομαι when suppliants cannot approach under their own power.[33] Additional participants, scribes who function in the pericope as a set of antagonists, are also introduced with καὶ ἰδού (9.3).

As the story proceeds with Jesus' offer of forgiveness to the paralyzed man and the interaction between Jesus and the scribes, the pericope is narrated with καί connecting every sentence in 9.1-7 except Jesus' address to the paralytic himself in 9.6. There is a rhythm established in the alternation of καὶ ἰδού (9.2a)... καὶ ἰδών (9.2b)... καὶ ἰδού (9.3)... καὶ ἰδών (9.4)...[34] Matthew's choice of τότε in 9.6 in the speech margin of Jesus' pronouncement of healing to the paralytic—an addition which distinguishes Matthew's account from those of Mark and Luke—is typical of his patterns of use of τότε, combining a thematic verb and present tense-form with a climactic statement by Jesus.

Lastly, following a statement that the man's healing has been accomplished but 'without a lengthy stay over it',[35] δέ and S₁V constituent order are used in 9.8, shifting attention from the miracle event to the crowds' reaction, which mixes fear and the giving of glory to God. This final element in the pericope is similar in the use of δέ and S₁V constituent order in the disciples' response to Jesus' calming of the storm in 8.27.

33. See Held, 'Miracle Stories', p. 230.
34. See Davies and Allison, *Matthew*, II, p. 86.
35. See Held, 'Miracle Stories', p. 241.

Matthew 9.9-13: The Calling of Matthew

9.9 Καὶ παράγων ὁ Ἰησοῦς ἐκεῖθεν εἶδεν ἄνθρωπον καθήμενον
ἐπὶ τὸ τελώνιον, Μαθθαῖον λεγόμενον,
καὶ λέγει αὐτῷ·...
καὶ ἀναστὰς ἠκολούθησεν αὐτῷ.

9.10 καὶ ἐγένετο αὐτοῦ ἀνακειμένου ἐν τῇ οἰκίᾳ,
καὶ ἰδοὺ πολλοὶ τελῶναι καὶ ἁμαρτωλοὶ ἐλθόντες
συνανέκειντο τῷ Ἰησοῦ καὶ τοῖς μαθηταῖς αυτοῦ.

9.11 καὶ ἰδόντες οἱ Φαρισαῖοι ἔλεγον τοῖς μαθηταῖς αὐτοῦ·...

9.12 ὁ δὲ ἀκούσας εἶπεν...

Verse	Feature(s)	Expected conjunction	Actual conjunction	Comments
9.9a	S_2V constituent order	δέ	καί	*not as expected,* but καί default
9.9b	V constituent order	καί	καί	as expected
9.9c	V constituent order	καί	καί	as expected
9.10	ἰδού and S_1V constituent order	καί	καί	as expected
9.11	S_2V constituent order	δέ	καί	*not as expected,* but καί default
9.12	S_1V constituent order	δέ	δέ	as expected

Again, the working model accounts for the sentence conjunctions in Mt. 9.9-12, in which Matthew's calling as a disciple is recounted, with the exception of two instances of καί with S_2V constituent order (9.9a, 11).

This is not a healing miracle, and although there is a formulaic introduction in 9.9 establishing Jesus and his opposite number, the tax collector Matthew, in the scene, other elements of the miracle story form are not present. In a manner similar to the previous pericope, Jesus' calling of Matthew, his meal with the tax collectors and sinners, the interactions between the Pharisees and Jesus' disciples, and Jesus' final reply are narrated by a series of sentences connected with καί (9.9-11), until δέ and S_1V constituent order appear in the margin of Jesus' final pronouncement in 9.12, directed to the Pharisees.

That the sequence of καί sentences conveys continuity in the narrative does not mean that there cannot also be relative prominence within that continuity, as in the use of τότε in 9.6 in the previous pericope. The syntax of 9.10, καὶ ἐγένετο αὐτοῦ ἀνακειμένου ἐν τῇ οἰκίᾳ, καὶ ἰδού, is unique in Matthew's narrative framework, combining the phrase καὶ ἐγένετο with a genitive absolute construction and καὶ ἰδού. As mentioned above, outside the five formula statements in 7.28, 11.1, 13.53, 19.1 and

26.1, the phrase καὶ ἐγένετο appears in Matthew's narrative framework only here and in 8.26, and thus should be seen as potentially prominent. The genitive absolute (αὐτοῦ ἀνακειμένου ἐν τῇ οἰκίᾳ) serves to shift the action from Matthew's tax booth to the meal in the house. Καὶ ἰδού introduces new characters, 'many tax collectors and sinners'. Together the unusual combination of the three elements strongly marks Jesus' meal with the tax collectors and sinners and, one suspects, the juxtaposed reaction of the Pharisees.

As in Jesus' response when the centurion acknowledges his authority in 8.10 (of which the Pharisees' attitude expressed here is an inversion), Matthew's use of δέ with Jesus' statement to the Pharisees in 9.12 introduces a low-level discontinuity in the flow of the pericope between the Pharisees' accusation and Jesus' pointed reply. In a manner similar to 8.10 and to Jesus' reply to the would-be disciple in 8.21-22, δέ and the interruption of narrative continuity that it represents momentarily interrupt the flow of the narrative, highlighting Jesus' statement about righteousness.

Matthew 9.14-17: Questions about Fasting

9.14   Τότε προσέρχονται αὐτῷ οἱ μαθηταὶ Ἰωάννου λέγοντες·...
9.15   καὶ εἶπεν αὐτοῖς ὁ Ἰησοῦς....

Verse	Feature(s)	Expected conjunction	Actual conjunction	Comments
9.14	VS constituent order	καί	τότε	*not as expected*
9.15	VS constituent order	καί	καί	as expected

As before, the working model, incorporating as it does only καί and δέ, does not account for the presence of τότε in 9.14 where John's disciples approach Jesus with a question. However, this occurrence of τότε well represents Matthew's habits of use elsewhere in the Gospel. Combining several characteristic collocations, τότε appears with προσέρχομαι, which in this sentence is both present tense-form and thematic, and with VS constituent order. Six of the seven narrative sentences in which τότε occurs with προσέρχομαι in Matthew's narrative framework are, like this instance, paragraph-initial in NA[27]. Each of those six also introduces an incident within a block of narrative discourse—usually one in a series of related pericopes—rather than a major break in the narrative. The six narrative sentences with τότε and προσέρχομαι which function as speech margins all introduce questions asked of Jesus which stem from incidents or teaching in the same discourse context, as is the case here. John's disciples' question about fasting arises from Jesus' eating with tax collectors and sinners.[36] Matthew again signals the audience to process this scene as continuous with preceding discourse.

Matthew 9.18-26: A Ruler's Daughter and a Hemorrhaging Woman

9.18 Ταῦτα αὐτοῦ λαλοῦντος αὐτοῖς, ἰδοὺ ἄρχων εἷς ἐλθὼν προσεκύνει αὐτῷ λέγων...

9.19 καὶ ἐγερθεὶς ὁ Ἰησοῦς ἠκολούθησεν αὐτῷ καὶ οἱ μαθηταὶ αὐτοῦ.

9.20 Καὶ ἰδοὺ γυνὴ αἱμορροοῦσα δώδεκα ἔτη προσελθοῦσα ὄπισθεν ἥψατο τοῦ κρασπέδου τοῦ ἱματίου αὐτοῦ·

9.21 ἔλεγεν γὰρ ἐν ἑαυτῇ...

9.22 ὁ δὲ Ἰησοῦς στραφεὶς καὶ ἰδὼν αὐτὴν εἶπεν·... καὶ ἐσώθη ἡ γυνὴ ἀπὸ τῆς ὥρας ἐκείνης.

9.23 Καὶ ἐλθὼν ὁ Ἰησοῦς εἰς τὴν οἰκίαν τοῦ ἄρχοντος καὶ ἰδὼν τοὺς αὐλητὰς καὶ τὸν ὄχλον θορυβούμενον (9.24) ἔλεγεν...

9.24 καὶ κατεγέλων αὐτοῦ.

9.25 ὅτε δὲ ἐξεβλήθη ὁ ὄχλος εἰσελθὼν ἐκράτησεν τῆς χειρὸς αὐτῆς, καὶ ἠγέρθη τὸ κοράσιον.

9.26 καὶ ἐξῆλθεν ἡ φήμη αὕτη εἰς ὅλην τὴν γῆν ἐκείνην.

Verse	Feature(s)	Expected conjunction	Actual conjunction	Comments
9.18	genitive absolute, ἰδού and S₂V constituent order	δέ	asyndeton	*not as expected*
9.19	S₂V constituent order	δέ	καί	*not as expected, but* καί *default*
9.20	ἰδού and S₁V constituent order	καί	καί	as expected
9.21	V constituent order	καί	γάρ	*not as expected*
9.22a	S₁V constituent order	δέ	δέ	as expected
9.22b	VS constituent order	καί	καί	as expected
9.23	S₂V constituent order	δέ	καί	*not as expected, but* καί *default*
9.24	V constituent order	καί	καί	as expected
9.25a	V constituent order	καί	δέ	*not as expected*
9.25b	VS constituent order	καί	καί	as expected
9.26	VS constituent order	καί	καί	as expected

36. See Davies and Allison, *Matthew*, II, p. 107; Hagner, *Matthew 1–13*, pp. 241-42.

The working model accounts for only 6 of the 11 sentence conjunctions in 9.18-26, a pericope recounting healings of both a ruler's daughter and a hemorrhaging woman. Apart from the now familiar combination of καί with S₂V constituent order in 9.19 and 9.23, there are two instances of conjunctive choices not yet encountered in the extended unit 8.1–9.34— asyndeton in 9.18 and γάρ in 9.21—as well as one use of δέ in a context not yet addressed in the present discussion.

Following a series of subunits with καί as the initial conjunction (8.23-27, the calming of the storm at sea; 8.28-34, the two demon-possessed men; 9.1-8, the healing of the paralyzed man; and 9.9-13, the calling of Matthew), as well as the interchange about fasting in 9.14-17, which also follows closely upon its preceding episode, Matthew now signals a discontinuity between this pericope and the preceding series by the use of an asyndetic genitive absolute construction in 9.18 (ταῦτα αὐτοῦ λαλοῦντος αὐτοῖς). In Matthew's narrative framework, asyndeton either links sentences with the closest of connections, specifically in speech margins, or tends to be found at higher-level breaks in the narrative. This is one of only four examples in Matthew's narrative framework of an asyndetic genitive absolute (1.18, 9.18, 12.46, 17.5). Like the present instance, the occurrences in 12.46 and 17.5 have λαλέω in the genitive absolute construction, ἰδού immediately before the main clause, and SV constituent order, with the subject as the first element in the main clause. Each of the four occurs at a point of narrative discontinuity in Matthew's Gospel.[37] Although in 9.18 there is not a real break in the sequence of action—in fact Jesus is still in the same place, speaking to the same audience—the genitive absolute construction is used as a 'scene shifter' to portray the beginning of a new step in the narrative.

The formulaic introduction to this healing story exemplifies Theissen's third variation, in which the ἰδού sentence introducing the ruler as the 'opposite number' comes immediately after the participial construction and there is no καί before ἰδού. But 9.18-26 is atypical in that there are two miracles, the narration of one embedded within the narration of the other. The first narrative thread begins with the introduction of the ruler in 9.18 and continues until 9.20 when a second suppliant, the hemorrhaging woman, is introduced with καὶ ἰδού and προσέρχομαι. The interaction between Jesus and the woman proceeds according to expected miracle story forms: a request expressing faith in 9.20-21 (in this case expressed

---

37. See comments on asyndetic genitive absolute constructions in Chapter 6.

indirectly by the woman touching Jesus' garment and Matthew's report of her internal thoughts); a pronouncement of healing from Jesus in 9.22a; and a brief statement in 9.22b that the healing has taken place. The original narrative thread resumes in 9.23 with καί and a participial phrase indicating Jesus' movement to the ruler's house (καὶ ἐλθὼν ὁ Ἰησοῦς εἰς τὴν οἰκίαν τοῦ ἄρχοντος), and continues through 9.26. Matthew has not, however, chosen to mark the junctures between the two narrative threads as discontinuous, but treats the passage syntactically as a whole. There are, for example, no indicators of narrative discontinuity at 9.20 combining with the expected καὶ ἰδού introducing the woman. Formal markers when the first thread is resumed in 9.23 with καί and S_2V constituent order include only the participial phrase indicating movement, and the restating of Jesus' name as the grammaticalized subject rather than merely supplying a reduced form (pronoun) or omitting the subject.

Within the scene between Jesus and the woman, γάρ occurs as the sentence conjunction in 9.21. Here as elsewhere in Matthew's narrative framework γάρ functions as a signal of 'backwards confirmation', introducing off-line material which confirms and strengthens a preceding proposition. When the woman touches the hem of Jesus' garment (9.20), Matthew explains the mental state motivating her action: ' *γάρ* she was saying to herself…' (9.21). This information helps to strengthen the proposition that such a woman would approach Jesus in a public setting and confirms the integration of her unexpected action into the mental representation of the discourse. Characteristically, γάρ is combined with an imperfect tense form (ἔλεγεν).

In 9.22, when Jesus turns to speak to the woman, δέ and S_1V constituent order signal the return to the narrative line from Matthew's description of her internal state, as well as serving, as was the case in 8.10, 21-22 and 9.12, to interrupt the flow of the narrative momentarily, focusing attention on Jesus' response to what might have been seen as an affront.[38]

The story of the ruler's daughter continues from 9.23 to the expected result. Her healing, in 9.25, is narrated with VS sentences conjoined by καί, except for the appearance of δέ with a temporal clause in 9.25: ὅτε δὲ ἐξεβλήθη ὁ ὄχλος ... Matthew uses δέ with a variety of thematic indi-

---

38. In contrast to 8.31, οὖν would probably not have been an appropriate choice here in the return to the narrative line because the sentence in 9.22a is not dependent for its integration into the audience's mental representation on what precedes. Jesus' healing of the woman may be prompted by, but is not pragmatically inferred from, her touching his hem.

cators of time in his narrative framework, such as prepositional phrases, dative constructions, or temporal adverbs—temporal shift being simply another element of discontinuity signaled by δέ. Only a few such combinations have SV constituent order (1.12, 27.45, 26.73), while the remainder are V(S) as in 9.25. However, the present instance concerns not a specific time reference (not, for example, 'at that hour', or 'when evening came'), but time relative to an action: 'when the crowd had been put outside'. There are only two similar instances of ὅτε δέ in Matthew's narrative framework, both in parables (13.26, 21.34; both have V(S) constituent order). Although rarity is not itself a sufficient criterion to consider a construction marked, this use by Matthew is prominent relative to the immediate context, interrupting the continuity of the narrative to call attention to Jesus' sending away the crowd.

Matthew 9.27-31: Two Blind Men Healed

9.27 Καὶ παράγοντι ἐκεῖθεν τῷ Ἰησοῦ ἠκολούθησαν [αὐτῷ] δύο
      τυφλοὶ κράζοντες καὶ λέγοντες·...
9.28 ἐλθόντι δὲ εἰς τὴν οἰκίαν προσῆλθον αὐτῷ οἱ τυφλοί,
      καὶ λέγει αὐτοῖς ὁ Ἰησοῦς·...
      λέγουσιν αὐτῷ·...
9.29 τότε ἥψατο τῶν ὀφθαλμῶν αὐτῶν λέγων·...
9.30 καὶ ἠνεῴχθησαν αὐτῶν οἱ ὀφθαλμοί.
      Καὶ ἐνεβριμήθη αὐτοῖς ὁ Ἰησοῦς λέγων·...
9.31 οἱ δὲ ἐξελθόντες διεφήμισαν αὐτὸν ἐν ὅλῃ τῇ γῇ ἐκείνῃ.

Verse	Feature(s)	Expected conjunction	Actual conjunction	Comments
9.27	VS constituent order	καί	καί	as expected
9.28a	VS constituent order	καί	δέ	*not as expected*
9.28b	VS constituent order	καί	καί	as expected
9.28c	V constituent order	καί	asyndeton	*not as expected*
9.29	V constituent order	καί	τότε	*not as expected*
9.30a	VS constituent order	καί	καί	as expected
9.30b	VS constituent order	καί	καί	as expected
9.31	S₁V constituent order	δέ	δέ	as expected

The working model accounts for five of the eight sentence conjunctions in 9.27-31, in which two blind men are healed. In addition to these five sentences, there is an instance of asyndeton with thematic present-tense λέγω in 9.28c, a use of τότε at the climax of the pericope in 9.29, and in 9.28a an occurrence of δέ with VS constituent order unaccounted for by the model.

The present pericope, like those preceding, is portrayed in terms of its continuity with preceding text. Καί is the initial conjunction in the introduction in 9.27, and, as in 8.23, Matthew opts for a dative participial construction here (παράγοντι ἐκεῖθεν) rather than the genitive absolute he uses with a following dative noun in 8.1, 8.28 and 9.18. The introduction to this story represents a variation on the formulaic introductions elsewhere. Jesus' appearance is described in a participial phrase depicting his moving on from the previous place, and the main verb adds the detail that the blind men follow him. Following the first mention of Jesus' 'opposite number', the blind men (9.27), there is what amounts to a re-introduction of the suppliants after a second spatial shift into the house (9.28). A form of προσέρχομαι is present, but there is no occurrence of (καὶ) ἰδού associated with the appearance of the two blind men.

The combination of δέ with a participle that is not a genitive absolute and with VS constituent order in 9.28, ἐλθόντι δὲ εἰς τὴν οἰκίαν προσῆλθον αὐτῷ οἱ τυφλοί, is rare in Matthew's narrative framework, occurring elsewhere only in 14.6 and 26.71. Again, rarity alone does not make a construction marked, but as an unexpected narrative strategy 9.28a seems to be marked relative to its immediate context. Matthew may be syntactically calling attention to the movement into the house, or to the fact that the expected story form has been interrupted by an unexpected change of setting before the usual form resumes.

The miracle story continues in 9.28b-30b, narrated with V(S) sentences and a variety of conjunctive structures consistent with narrative continuity as Jesus carries on a conversation with the blind men, their eyes are healed, and Jesus enjoins them to tell no one. There are three examples of καί with VS constituent order (9.28b, καὶ λέγει αὐτοῖς ὁ Ἰησοῦς; 9.30a, καὶ ἠνεῴχθησαν αὐτῶν οἱ ὀφθαλμοί; 9.30b, καὶ ἐνεβριμήθη αὐτοῖς ὁ Ἰησοῦς). In 9.28c, asyndeton is used with λέγουσιν, a characteristic Matthean speech margin pattern for closely continuous conversational exchanges, especially in relation to questions and answers as in the present example.[39] This is the first such use in Matthew's Gospel, however. There is only one other instance (13.51) before ch. 16, after which the structure becomes more frequent in the narrative framework.

In 9.29, τότε functions in its role as a signal of marked continuity, mak-

---

39. Almost half the asyndetic sentences in Matthew's narrative framework (26/57, 46%) have λέγει or λέγουσιν as the thematic element. Of all the speech margins in Matthew's narrative framework, nearly one out of ten (26/299, 9%) exhibits the combination of asyndeton and thematic λέγει/λέγουσιν.

ing Jesus' healing statement the climax of the episode (compare 8.26b, 9.6). But as in Jesus' rebuke of the great storm in 8.26b, features which often collocate with τότε elsewhere in Matthew's narrative framework—the 'historic present', thematic finite verbs, VS constituent order, and προσέρχομαι or προσηνέχθην—are absent in 9.29.

As in previous pericopes (compare 8.27, 9.8), following a narrative statement that the healing has been accomplished the final sentence has δέ and S₁V constituent order, shifting attention from the miracle event to the ensuing reaction. In spite of Jesus' stern charge to them not to tell anyone, the two blind men spread the report throughout the district. As in 8.24, the semantic relationship between the sentences conjoined by δέ—Jesus' injunction in 9.30b and the action of the men in 9.31—may be described as a condition contrary to expectation, with δέ approximating its tradition-ally understood role as an adversative participle. Here again, however, δέ signals only that there is some low- to mid-level discontinuity in the narrative, with the actual element of discontinuity being pragmatically worked out by the audience.

Matthew 9.32-34: A Mute Demoniac Healed

9.32	Αὐτῶν δὲ ἐξερχομένων ἰδοὺ προσήνεγκαν αὐτῷ ἄνθρωπον κωφὸν δαιμονιζόμενον.
9.33	καὶ ἐκβληθέντος τοῦ δαιμονίου ἐλάλησεν ὁ κωφός. καὶ ἐθαύμασαν οἱ ὄχλοι λέγοντες·....
9.34	οἱ δὲ Φαρισαῖοι ἔλεγον·...

Verse	Feature(s)	Expected conjunction	Actual conjunction	Comments
9.32	genitive absolute, ἰδού and V constituent order	δέ	δέ	as expected
9.33a	genitive absolute, and VS constituent order	δέ	καί	*not as expected*, but καί default
9.33b	VS constituent order	καί	καί	as expected
9.34	S₁V constituent order	δέ	δέ	as expected

Three of the four sentence conjunctions in 9.32-34, the healing of a mute demoniac which stands as the final pericope of the extended unit 8.1–9.34, are accounted for by the working model. Left unaccounted for is the use of καί with a genitive absolute in 9.33a.

Genitive absolute constructions appear in the first two narrative sentences in the pericope (9.32, 33a). Mt. 9.32 exemplifies Theissen's third variation on Matthew's formulaic introduction, in which the appearance of the suppliant, the mute demoniac, contains ἰδού and comes immediately after the participial construction (αὐτῶν ... ἐξερχομένων), and there is no καί before ἰδού. As in 9.2, a form of προσφέρω in 9.32 is an alternative to προσέρχομαι, in that the mute demoniac presumably cannot 'approach' Jesus on his own so he is 'brought' by others. The combination of δέ and genitive absolute participial construction in 9.32 makes this the first pericope beginning with lexico-grammatical indicators of discontinuity since the asyndetic genitive absolute in 9.18.

The genitive absolute construction in 9.33 (ἐκβληθέντος τοῦ δαιμονίου) is unusual in its discourse function. Following the formulaic introduction the miracle story form sets up the expectation of a request for healing expressing faith, a response from Jesus probably including a healing pronouncement, and then a brief narrative statement that the healing has taken place. In 9.33 these elements are collapsed into the genitive absolute and main clause in 9.33a: 'And when the demon had been cast out, the dumb man spoke'. Held observes that Matthew has a tendency to abbreviate the descriptive aspects of healing miracles, relying on stereotypic formulae and omitting non-essential people and actions.[40] In 9.33, Matthew exhibits this tendency to an extreme. The use of καί and VS constituent order in 9.33a-b in combination with the genitive absolute in 9.33a may underline the uninterrupted continuity of expected elements—that the mute demoniac is healed and the crowd responds in wonder—however briefly they are dealt with.

In 9.33b the reaction of the crowds is given. There are examples in previous pericopes of a final reaction set off from the flow of the narrative by the use of δέ and $S_1 V$ constituent order (8.27, 9.8, 9.31). In the present pericope the reaction of the crowds is portrayed in terms of continuity within the narrative, with καί and VS constituent order. Instead it is the second response, the Pharisees' rejection of Jesus' miracle, in stark contrast to the response of the crowds in 9.33b, which is highlighted by the use of δέ and $S_1 V$ constituent order. As in some of its previous uses (see 8.24b, 9.31), there is an adversative or contrastive semantic relationship between the propositions δέ conjoins. But, as elsewhere, in 9.34 δέ merely signals the audience that there is some discontinuity in the narrative, helping guide the audience to work out pragmatically what that discontinuity is—in this case the difference between the crowds' response and that of the Pharisees.

---

40. Held, 'Miracle Stories', pp. 225-33.

Summary

Sentence-level analysis. The working model introduced above, positing that καί occurs with V(S) constituent order or ἰδού while δέ occurs with SV constituent order or genitive absolute constructions, accounts for 69% of the sentences in Matthew's narrative framework as a whole. When applied to the 86 narrative sentences in Mt. 8.1–9.34, the working model assigns the correct sentence conjunction—that is, the sentence conjunction which actually appears in the NA[27] text—to 76% (65/86) of the narrative sentences in the passage, a result which compares very favorably with its descriptive power in the narrative framework overall.[41] The working model accounts for 82% (58/79) of the occurrences of καί and δέ in 8.1–9.34 (consistent with results when applied to the whole narrative framework), but of course none of the instances of asyndeton, τότε, or γάρ. There are no instances of οὖν as a sentence conjunction in 8.1–9.34.

Occurrences of asyndeton, τότε and γάρ in 8.1–9.34 were evaluated on a sentence-by-sentence basis in comparison with characteristic features identified in this study. In most cases Matthew's choice of asyndeton, τότε or γάρ was found to be consistent with his habits of use elsewhere. Asyndeton is found either in speech margins, especially with thematic λέγει/λέγουσιν, or at narrative breaks with non-verbal themes (possibly a 'shifter' such as a temporal prepositional phrase or a genitive absolute construction). There is one example of each pattern in 8.1–9.34: in 9.18, at a narrative break with a genitive absolute; and in 9.28 with λέγουσιν as the thematic element. Τότε, which characteristically collocates with the so-called 'historic present', thematic finite verbs, VS constituent order, and/or προσέρχομαι or passive forms of προσφέρω, and can be found at

---

41. Because Matthew chooses καί as the sentence conjunction so frequently in 8.1–9.34—58 times in 86 narrative sentences (see below on the portrayal of continuity in 8.1–9.34)—the simplest model, which merely states that all sentences in the narrative framework have καί, would actually account for 67% (58/86) of the narrative sentences in 8.1–9.34.

Stating that καί occurs with V(S) constituent order while δέ occurs with SV constituent order accounts for 57 narrative sentences (66%) in 8.1–9.34. The result when this basic model is applied to 8.1–9.34 is consistent with its descriptive power of 66% when applied to Matthew's narrative framework as a whole

The working model, incorporating associations between καί and ἰδού, and δέ and genitive absolute constructions, assigns the correct sentence conjunction to ten additional sentences, but also produces two counterexamples (8.28, 9.33a), for a net gain of eight.

climactic points within pericopes (especially a statement by Jesus), occurs four times in 8.1–9.34 (8.26, 9.6, 9.14, 9.29). In only two of these does τότε occur with characteristic collocations: with a thematic, present tense-form finite verb in 9.6, and with προσέρχομαι in 9.14. In three instances, however, it marks a statement and/or action by Jesus which serves as a climax of a pericope: 8.26, 9.6, 9.29. When combined with προσέρχομαι in 9.14, τότε introduces, as is the case elsewhere, a question asked of Jesus which stems from a preceding incident or teaching. The one occurrence of γάρ, in 9.21, is consistent with its use elsewhere to introduce off-line material which confirms and strengthens a preceding proposition, often in combination with εἰμί or (as here) an imperfect tense-form.

In addition, two less common but not unknown patterns of use of καί and δέ appear in 8.1–9.34. In 8.30, δέ is combined with a form of εἰμί in thematic position in what has been described as a 'presentational' structure, comparable to English *there was/were* (compare 27.55, 27.61). In nine sentences καί is combined with S_2V constituent order, in spite of the fact that the working model predicts δέ with SV constituent order (that is, with both S_1V and S_2V constituent order) unless ἰδού is present.[42] As explained in the discussion of 8.5-13, although the association of καί with V(S) constituent order and δέ with SV constituent order is a productive 'rule of thumb' in terms of its descriptive power, in actuality καί appears nearly as frequently as does δέ in S_2V sentences in Matthew's narrative framework. Therefore, the appearance of καί with S_2V sentences should not be considered a particularly unexpected or necessarily marked use of καί. What is noteworthy in the present context is that one-fourth of the narrative sentences in which Matthew combines καί and S_2V constituent order occur in the extended unit 8.1–9.34, about twice as high a frequency as would be expected if they were spread proportionately throughout the narrative framework.

Sentences which were not accounted for by either the working model, characteristic features of asyndeton, τότε and γάρ, or the two patterns of use of καί and δέ just mentioned, include 8.28 (καί with genitive absolute), 9.25a (δέ with ὅτε clause), 9.28 (δέ with VS constituent order) and 9.33a (καί with genitive absolute). In addition, 9.10 was found to have a structure which is unique in Matthew's narrative framework. On the principle that where an unexpected use occurs one is free to explore the possibility that some degree of markedness is represented—and especially

---

42. Mt. 8.8, 14, 19; 9.2, 4, 9, 11, 19, 23.

in view of the fact that none of the instances of these combinations of elements have Synoptic parallels—the present analysis suggests that these sentences reflect marked choices made by Matthew in structuring the narrative framework of 8.1–9.34 and should be understood to indicate some measure of prominence. That does not mean that these sentences are necessarily the most prominent points within the discourse as a whole, but that they should be understood as relatively prominent at least within their immediate contexts.

Discourse functions. Given that sentence conjunctions and related features make their primary contribution to narrative not at the sentence level, but above the sentence level at the level of discourse, I commented on the role of sentence conjunctions in the structure and flow of each subunit or pericope. Although discourse functions appear to be even more difficult to model probabilistically than the intrasentential lexical and syntactical collocations which are incorporated in the working model, several generalizations can be made regarding the discourse functions of sentence conjunctions in 8.1–9.34. First, the role of καί as a signal of unmarked continuity is apparent. It functions both within pericopes, where it helps carry forward narrative action (especially expected elements of miracle story forms—see, for example, 8.2-4, 8.15a-d), and between pericopes, where it connects scenes which form parts of larger units (8.14-15, 8.23-27, 8.28-34, 9.1-8, 9.9-13, 9.23-26 [a subunit within a pericope], 9.27-31). At whatever level, καί is a signal that discourse is to be processed as continuous. The discourse level at which καί is to be applied—that is, the hierarchical level at which continuity is to be maintained in a mental representation of the discourse—is pragmatically worked out by the audience on the basis of surrounding text and other cues.

Secondly, δέ signals narrative discontinuity, although what is actually discontinuous may be any of a variety of elements or a combination thereof: a new discourse unit, a temporal or spatial shift, a change in speaker, a condition contrary to expectation, a departure from an expected miracle story form, and so on. As the unmarked or default conjunction καί may also appear in contexts where there are discontinuities in the narrative, but rarely the reverse—that is, δέ rarely appears where καί is expected. Thus any time Matthew chose to use δέ rather than καί it can be understood as marked to some degree. The interruption of narrative continuity that δέ and its related features represent often appears to be Matthew's way of guiding the audience to turn their attention to a particular participant or action in the discourse.

Thirdly, καί and δέ form the bulk of narrative sentence conjunctions in 8.1–9.34, as in Matthew's Gospel as a whole. Other conjunctive choices are used only intermittently, functioning in specific roles as procedural signals and markers as the discourse unfolds. Asyndeton is used with both the tightest and loosest of connections—in one speech margin in a question–answer sequence, and at a mid-level narrative break. At several points τότε marks a climactic statement or action. At one other point it is combined with προσέρχομαι in a speech margin which introduces a question asked of Jesus. That the working model consistently predicts καί where τότε in fact occurs highlights the role of τότε as a signal of marked continuity, alternating with καί, the signal of unmarked continuity. Finally, γάρ introduces material which is off the narrative line, 'backwards confirming' a preceding proposition.

As part of a system of sentence conjunctions, each conjunction and asyndeton not only exhibits its own characteristic syntactical, morphological and lexical collocations, but is processed against the background of what might have been chosen but was not. These sentence conjunctions and their related features contribute to discourse processing by functioning as signals of continuity and discontinuity in Matthew's portrayal of narrative events, guiding the audience to maintain or modify their ongoing mental representation of the discourse.

The Structure of Matthew 8.1–9.34

There may be a consensus among biblical scholars that Mt. 8.1–9.34 forms a coherent unit within Matthew's Gospel, but beyond that there is a wide range of scholarly opinion concerning the internal arrangement of the unit and its significance in the Gospel as a whole. The discussion, of which the approaches outlined below merely represent the main streams, involves several issues: the structure of the unit, especially its internal division into major sections; which themes, if any, characterize the resultant divisions; christology, or how Matthew presents Jesus in these chapters; and the relation of the unit to surrounding context and to the whole of Matthew's Gospel. In this brief assessment I address primarily the first issue, the division of the passage into major subsections.

To this point I have considered how sentence conjunctions function in smaller units or pericopes in 8.1–9.34, guiding the audience in their mental representations of the subunits of the discourse. Sentence conjunctions clearly have a local scope, signaling continuity and discontinuity in linear processing. The question remains whether such conjunctions can also have a larger scope, playing a role in linking units at higher levels of discourse. In 8.1–9.34 this appears to be the case, although, as I have said, the discourse level at which each instance of a sentence conjunction is relevant—that is, the hierarchical level at which continuity or discontinuity is to be incorporated into the mental representation of the discourse—must be pragmatically determined on the basis of other linguistic signals, surrounding text and knowledge of the world. The contribution of sentence conjunctions to the overall structure of 8.1–9.34 is considered below.

Schematic treatments of 8.1–9.34.
Proposals. In his classic study of the miracle stories in Matthew, Held argues that 8.1–9.34 comprises three major groups of miracles and a final section: 8.1-17, 8.18–9.17, 9.18-31 and 9.32-34. (The proposals of Held and other scholars are schematized at the end of this overview. The reader may wish to consult that outline while reading the following summaries of each approach.) In Held's view, the miracles in the first, clearly discernible, section in 8.1-17 function together 'as the fulfilment of the prophecy of the servant of God' (the theme of christology). Held acknowledges that the way Matthew has grouped the material following 8.1-17 is not as easily recognizable, but he sees the three healings in 9.18-31 as forming a section of their own, dealing with the theme of faith. In between is 8.18–9.17, where 'it is the most difficult to discover an ordering principle'. Nevertheless Held argues that the pericopes in 8.18–9.17 can be grouped together 'under the heading, "The Christ of the miracle stories is the Lord of his congregation"' (the theme of discipleship). The final section, the exorcism/healing in 9.32-34, 'forms the conclusion to the whole composition'.[43]

Thompson takes over Held's section divisions for 8.1–9.34.[44] But in contrast to Held's form critical approach, Thompson is interested in the redactional methods by which Matthew shapes his version of the miracle stories into a coherent narrative. Thompson gives detailed attention to the lexical and syntactical means by which Matthew structures his account. He agrees with Held that the three sets of miracle stories represent, respectively, the themes of the person of Jesus (christology), discipleship and faith, with 9.32-34 as the conclusion.[45]

43. Held, 'Miracle Stories', pp. 248-49.
44. Thompson, 'Composition of Mt. 8.1–9.34', pp. 365-66, 368. Gerhardsson also adopts Held's outline (B. Gerhardsson, *The Mighty Acts of Jesus According to Matthew* [Lund: C.W.K. Gleerup, 1979], p. 39).
45. Thompson, 'Composition of Mt. 8.1–9.34', pp. 368, 371, 380.

In contrast to Held and Thompson, Burger divides the long section 8.18–9.17 into two parts, and includes 9.32-34 in the final section, producing the following thematic arrangement: 8.1-17, with the theme of christology; 8.18-34, with the theme of discipleship; 9.1-17, which Burger sees as developing the theme of the separation of Jesus and his followers from Israel; and 9.18-34, with the theme of faith.[46] Burger further argues that the whole of chs. 8 and 9 are in fact directed to this issue of separation from Israel, and as such form 'the foundational legend of the Christian church'.[47]

Kingsbury, while claiming that Burger goes too far in his attempt to 'subsume the whole of these chapters under the single theme of the "church of Jesus Christ"', agrees with Burger's fourfold thematic schema.[48] In his approach to Matthew's miracle stories Kingsbury follows Held in the affirmation that 'the outstanding feature is the dialogue between Jesus and suppliant(s)' so that 'the emphasis is on the personal encounter, mediated as much or more by the dialogue as by the miraculous deed, between Jesus and the suppliant(s)'.[49]

Davies and Allison, taking a different line, contend that the series of healings and other material in 8.1–9.34 are arranged on the basis of the number three, taking as their 'point of departure Matthew's love of the triad, the number of miracle stories in 8–9 (nine), and the fact that the miracle stories appear in three different groups'.[50] In their view, the passage consists of three groups of three stories, interspersed by two units which serve as boundaries:[51]

1 – 2 – 3		1 – 2 – 3		1 – 2 – 3
miracles	8.16-22	miracles	9.9-17	miracles
8.1-15		8.23-9.8		9.18-34

They consider 9.35-38 a final summary section which follows 9.18-34, as 9.9-17 follows 8.23–9.8 and as 8.16-22 follows 8.1-15.[52] Davies and

---

46. Burger, 'Jesu Taten', pp. 284-87.

47. 'Die Kapitel 8 und 9 seines Evangeliums bieten den ἱερὸς λόγος, die Gründungslegende der christlichen Kirche' (Burger, 'Jesu Taten', p. 287).

48. Kingsbury, 'Miracle Chapters', p. 562.

49. Kingsbury, 'Miracle Chapters', p. 570.

50. Davies and Allison, *Matthew*, II, p. 3. For others who have emphasized a triadic arrangement see, for example, Allen, *Matthew*, p. 74; Gatzwieler, 'Les récits de miracles', p. 214; Twelftree, *Miracle Worker*, p. 122.

51. Davies and Allison, *Matthew*, II, p. 6.

52. Davies and Allison, *Matthew*, I, pp. 67, 102.

Allison see formal symmetry as more important than thematic unity in 8.1–9.34. 'The point to stress is that the key to unlocking structure cannot be found in topical interests (Christology, discipleship, faith). Not that there are no thematic threads… But the arrangement of the entire section is dictated by a formal consideration, the triad.'[53]

Although Louw's arrangement differs in a few details from that of Davies and Allison, he takes a similar triadic approach, with three sections on healing separated by 'narrations of incidents related to the teaching and preaching of Jesus, thus not only affording stylistic breaks in the series, but rather echoing the preceding section (5–7) leading on to 9.35'. The result is three sections of healing or miracle material, each composed of three scenes: healings, 8.1-17 (8.1-4, 5-13, 14-17); material on following Jesus, 8.18-22; a miracle and healings, 8.23–9.8 (8.23-27, 28-34; 9.1-8); material on Jesus and outcasts, 9.9-13, and on fasting, 9.14-17; healings, 9.18-34 (9.18-26, 27-31, 32-34).[54]

Thus there is little unanimity among scholars concerning the points at which 8.1–9.34 falls into three or four sections, with or without boundary units. The views of these scholars can be schematized as follows, with the sentence conjunction and related features for the first sentence in each pericope also indicated:

Proposed Divisions in Mt. 8.1–9.34

	Held/ Thompson	Burger/ Kingsbury	Davies & Allison	Louw
8.1-4 A Leper Healed δέ + gen abs	Section 1 (christology)	Section 1 (christology)	Section 1 (3 miracles)	Section 1 (3 scenes: healings)
8.5-13 A Centurion's Servant Healed δέ + gen abs	↓	↓	↓	↓
8.14-15 Peter's Mother-in-Law Healed καί + S₂V	↓	↓	↓	↓

53. Davies and Allison, *Matthew*, II, pp. 3-4.
54. Louw, 'Mt. 8:1–9:34', p. 91.

	Held/ Thompson	Burger/ Kingsbury	Davies & Allison	Louw
8.16-17 Many People Healed δέ + gen abs	↓	↓	Boundary unit	[combined with 8.14-15]
8.18-22 Questions about Discipleship δέ + S$_2$V	Section 2 (discipleship)	Section 2 (discipleship)	↓	On the teaching and preaching of Jesus (on following Jesus)
8.23-27 A Great Storm Calmed καί + VS	↓	↓	Section 2 (3 miracles)	Section 2 (3 scenes: a miracle and healings)
8.28-34 Two Demoniacs Healed καί + gen abs	↓	↓	↓	↓
9.1-8 A Paralyzed Man Healed καί + V	↓	Section 3 (separation from Israel)	↓	↓
9.9-13 The Calling of Matthew καί + S$_2$V	↓	↓	Boundary unit	On the teaching and preaching of Jesus (on Jesus and outcasts)
9.14-17 Questions about Fasting τότε + VS	↓	↓	↓	(on fasting)
9.18-26 A Ruler's Daughter and a Hemorrhaging Woman Healed ∅ + gen abs + ἰδού	Section 3 (faith)	Section 4 (faith)	Section 3 (3 miracles)	Section 3 (3 scenes: healings)

	Held/ Thompson	Burger/ Kingsbury	Davies & Allison	Louw
9.27-31 Two Blind Men Healed καί + VS	↓	↓	↓	↓
9.32-34 A Mute Demon-iac Healed δέ + gen abs + ἰδού	Conclusion	↓	↓	↓

While Held, Thompson, Burger, Kingsbury and Louw are at least agreed that the first section break occurs at 8.17, Davies and Allison's plan straddles this separation with a 'boundary unit' comprising 8.16-22. Held and Thompson's second section extends through 9.17, encompassing the second section and following material of Davies and Allison and Louw, while Burger and Kingsbury introduce a section break midway through this material, at 9.1. All begin a third section at 9.18, differing only in whether 9.32-34 constitute a separate concluding section (Held and Thompson) or are part of the previous section (Burger, Kingsbury, Davies and Allison, and Louw).

Discussion. A look at the sentence conjunctions and related features which Matthew incorporates into his narrative in 8.1–9.34 highlights relative strengths and weaknesses of the above proposals from a lexico-grammatical perspective. Regarding the first section, it seems justified to take together the series of units in 8.1-17 which begin with δέ and a genitive absolute 'scene shifter' (8.1, 8.5, 8.16)—setting aside for the moment the question of the place of 8.14-15. Such repetition in close succession suggests that these three constructions function at a similar level in the discourse, as indicators of subunits in the section. It must be recognized, however, that in another context δέ and a genitive absolute construction might be seen as an indicator of either higher- or lower-level discontinuity. This illustrates the principle that the audience's pragmatic working out of the hierarchical level at which an element of discontinuity is to be incorporated into their mental representation of discourse depends to a great extent on surrounding text. The general agreement by scholars on other bases that these pericopes belong together demonstrates that additional semantic relationships are in play which help to disambiguate the level at which δέ contributes to the narrative.

Regarding the scene in 8.14-15, it seems on the basis of the initial choice of καί and no genitive absolute to be more closely tied to 8.5-13 than to 8.16-17. If a triadic arrangement within the section is Matthew's intention, then 8.1-4, 8.5-15 and 8.16-17 fall neatly together. Otherwise, fewer indicators of discontinuity in 8.14 may simply reflect that the narrative is organized to follow the spatial movement down from the mountain (8.1) and into Capernaum (8.5; where Peter's house also is, 8.14), and then introduce a temporal shift to evening (8.16).[55]

Held, Thompson, Burger and Kingsbury see a section break at 8.18, while in the view of Davies and Allison and Louw the beginning of the next section is delayed until 8.23. The δέ which conjoins 8.18 suggests a discontinuity at some level from previous text at this point, and again, the agreement on other bases by Held, Thompson, Burger and Kingsbury that a new section begins here suggests that additional semantic relationships are in play which help to disambiguate the hierarchical level at which δέ functions at this point in the discourse. Contra Davies and Allison and Louw, a section break at 8.23 appears unjustified based on Matthew's choice of καί and a dative participle in 8.23 (less marked for discontinuity than a genitive absolute would be), particularly when Matthew has shown his willingness elsewhere to use a genitive absolute even with respect to a following dative noun (compare 9.18). While the content of the pericope that begins in 8.23, the calming of the storm, seems at first glance to be distinct from the exchanges regarding discipleship in 8.18-22, Matthew apparently intends for the two scenes to be taken as more continuous than discontinuous, that is, that the calming of the storm is to be integrated into a mental representation which also incorporates Jesus' statements on discipleship.[56] Exegetes also note the 'catchword' connections in the two scenes between ἀκολουθέω (8.19, 8.22, 8.23) and μαθηταί (8.21, 8.23), an example of additional cues in surrounding text which assist the audience in the attempt to disambiguate the hierarchical level at which continuity is to be maintained in their mental representation of the discourse.[57]

Similarly, contra Burger and Kingsbury, a section break at 9.1 appears unjustified based on Matthew's choice of καί with a monolectic verb in

---

55. 'The continuous movement reveals his intention to weave these episodes into a single unified composition' (Thompson, 'Composition of Mt. 8.1–9.34', p. 370).

56. See G. Bornkamm, 'The Stilling of the Storm in Matthew', in Bornkamm, Barth and Held, *Tradition and Interpretation*, pp. 54-55; Held, 'Miracle Stories', p. 202.

57. See Bornkamm, 'Stilling of the Storm', p. 54; Held, 'Miracle Stories', pp. 201-202.

the first (and second) sentence beginning the pericope. The series of scenes begins at 8.18 with δέ and is carried on with sentence conjunctions and related features that signal continuity: καί and V(S) constituent order in 8.23, 8.28 and 9.1; καί and S₂V constituent order in 9.9; τότε and VS constituent order in 9.14. This pattern continues until the asyndetic genitive absolute at 9.18. Based on these considerations 8.18–9.17 appears to be portrayed by Matthew as more continuous than discontinuous in terms of the relationship of units within the section. The structural continuity is matched by a continuity of movement, an uninterrupted sequence which begins on one side of the lake, crosses to the other side, returns, and enters the tax collector's house. Thompson observes, 'As in the first set of miracles, the continuous movement expressed in the narrative introduction'—that is, the narrative sentences in 8.18, 23, 28 and 9.1, 9, 10, 11, 14—'also contributes to a coherent sequence of thought'.[58]

All of the proposals posit a section break at 9.18, consistent with the asyndetic genitive absolute found there. The remaining question is whether there is an additional break at 9.32, as Held and Thompson claim, or whether 9.32-34 is to be seen, as by Burger, Kingsbury, Davies and Allison, and Louw, as part of the preceding section. Davies and Allison and Louw take 9.32-34 as the third story in the third set of stories, an approach which maintains their triadic arrangement but which does not do justice to the combination of δέ and genitive absolute in 9.32. This combination contrasts with Matthew's use of καί to conjoin the pericope immediately before to its predecessor (9.27) and suggests that he is portraying 9.23-34 as to some extent discontinuous from preceding text. Again the role of context comes into play in the disambiguation of the hierarchical level at which discontinuity is indicated. If there had been a series of pericopes beginning with δέ and other parallel features (as in 8.1, 5, 16), the audience might see this pericope as functioning at the same discourse level as others in the series. It is expectedness *in context* which makes the difference, with surrounding text forming one type of context used in discourse processing.

Held and Thompson see 9.32-34 as a conclusion to which the preceding sections lead, a final response to Jesus' miracles in which the wonder of the crowds and the derision of the Pharisees are contrasted. In this last section, in Thompson's view, Matthew is not so much interested in the cure itself (witness his 'matter-of-fact' treatment of it) as in introducing the double response of the crowds and the Pharisees 'in which the evan-

58. Thompson, 'Composition of Mt. 8.1–9.34', p. 378.

gelist lets each group speak for itself'.[59] This approach is supported both by the combination of δέ and a genitive absolute in 9.32, and by the collapsing of a number of the expected miracle story elements—a request for healing expressing faith, a response by Jesus usually including a healing pronouncement, and a brief statement that the healing has taken place—into one sentence composed of καί, a genitive absolute and VS constituent order (9.33a). This reduces the attention paid to the miracle itself and increases the focus on the double response, in particular on the rejection of Jesus' miracle(s) by the Pharisees, set off by δέ and S_1V constituent order in 9.34.

In sum, an analysis of the contribution that sentence conjunctions and related features make to the narrative framework of Mt. 8.1–9.34 favors the structural arrangement advocated by Held and Thompson over those of Burger, Kingsbury, Davies and Allison, and Louw. The unit can be divided into three main sections and a conclusion: 8.1-17; 8.18–9.17; 9.18-31; 9.32-34.

On the other hand, more recently Luz has taken a different line, arguing that 8.1–9.34 is a unitary composition arranged to convey a single theme. Luz's thesis and a brief assessment of it in the light of the sentence conjunctions in 8.1–9.34 form the topic of the next section.

Unitary treatment. Luz points out that there is a strong feel of continuous movement in the way Matthew recounts the events in 8.1–9.34. He observes that;

> events follow upon one another in quick succession: chapters 8 and 9 convey the impression that Jesus healed the sick without interruption. Each story emerges directly from its predecessor; Matthew offers a narrative thread without a single break in time or place.[60]

Luz argues that rather than merely a collection of miracle stories exemplifying Jesus' deeds or different facets of his teaching, or even Christian faith, Matthew constructs a single history (*Geschichte*).[61] In Luz's view, the organizing principle underlying the passage as a whole is Jesus' conflict with Israel:

59. Thompson, 'Composition of Mt. 8.1–9.34', p. 385.
60. Luz, *Theology*, p. 63.
61. 'Es geht Matthäus keineswegs um eine blosse Sammlung von Wundergeschichten, die beispielhaft die Taten des Messias oder gar verschiedene Aspekte seiner Lehre und des christlichen Glaubens erläuten, sondern es geht ihm um eine zusammenhängende *Geschichte*' (Luz, 'Wundergeschichten', p. 152).

Jesus began his ministry in Israel, among the people; he healed the sick among God's people; he summoned his first disciples from the people. At the same time, the first tensions begin to arise between him and the leaders of the people, above all the Pharisees. These form the contents of chapters 8 and 9.[62]

The narrative moves toward 9.33-34, where the crowds marvel even as the Pharisees reject. 'Matthew wishes to depict a historical progression culminating in the dual response of the people and Pharisees to Jesus' miracles.'[63]

While an analysis of sentence conjunctions may not determine whether Luz's claim for the thematic unity of 8.1–9.34 is justified, such an analysis can address his perception that 8.1–9.34 exhibits continuity of structure. In fact, καί appears as a sentence conjunction in 8.1–9.34 significantly more frequently than it does in Matthew's narrative frame–work overall, suggesting that in 8.1–9.34 as a whole Matthew is supplying more conjunctive signals of narrative continuity than is his wont elsewhere. Καί is the sentence conjunction in nearly half of the sentences in the narrative framework (335/720, 47%), but in two-thirds of the narrative sentences in 8.1–9.34 (58/86, 67%; $z = 3.89$). A z-score of 3.89 indicates that the high frequency of καί in 8.1–9.34 is not merely a chance occurrence.[64] At the same time, δέ, the signal of low- to mid-level discontinuity in narrative, is found less frequently in 8.1–9.34 than in the narrative framework overall. While it occurs as the sentence conjunction in slightly more than a third of sentences in Matthew's narrative framework (257/720, 36%), it appears in only about one-fourth of narrative sentences in 8.1–9.34 (21/86, 24%; $z = -2.18$). In sum, there are more uses of καί and fewer uses of δέ in 8.1–9.34 than Matthew tends to use in narrative in general.[65]

62. Luz, *Theology*, pp. 64-65. Luz agrees with Burger in his conviction that separation from Israel is central to Matthew's account in 8.1–9.34, but rejects Burger's fourfold division of the passage, as well as other thematic schemata (Luz, 'Wundergeschichten', p. 150).

63. Luz, *Theology*, p. 64. Vledder similarly sees conflict between Jesus and the Jewish leaders as the central issue in chs. 8 and 9. He addresses the dynamics of that conflict, seeking to explain the conflict between Jesus and the leaders of Israel from a sociological perspective. See Vledder, *Conflict*, pp. 12-13.

64. As I have stated in previous chapters, z-scores equal to or greater than ±3—that is, a value falling three standard deviations or more above or below a mean—are taken to indicate statistical significance.

65. The frequencies of τότε, γάρ and οὖν in 8.1–9.34 are consistent with the range that would be expected based on their distributions in Matthew's narrative framework

In terms of constituent order, in 8.1–9.34 there appears to be an increased use of VS constituent order, a constituent order associated with the portrayal of continuity in narrative, and a corresponding decrease in Matthew's use of S_1V constituent order, a constituent order associated with the portrayal of discontinuity in narrative, although z-scores do not guarantee statistical significance for this sample size. While VS constituent order is found in about two out of every ten sentences in Matthew's narrative framework (149/720, 21%), it appears in about three out of every ten narrative sentences in 8.1–9.34 (25/86, 29%; $z = 1.91$). And while S_1V constituent order is used in more than one-fourth of the sentences in Matthew's narrative framework (195/720, 27%), it appears in less than 20% of the narrative sentences in 8.1–9.34 (16/86, 19%; $z = -1.77$). In addition, as mentioned in the comments on 8.8 above, although καί and δέ are almost equally likely to be found with S_2V sentences in Matthew's narrative framework (καί: 40/99; δέ: 47/99), the frequency of καί with S_2V constituent order in 8.1–9.34 is almost twice as high as would be expected if the sentences with the combination of καί with S_2V constituent order were distributed evenly throughout the narrative framework.

Thus it is not surprising that Luz perceives the events in 8.1–9.34 as 'following upon one another in quick succession'. Matthew's storytelling portrays the sequence of narrative events as highly continuous compared to his habits in the Gospel as a whole, as is evidenced in the increased use of καί and related features associated with narrative continuity and the decreased use of δέ and related features associated with discontinuity. However, this does not mean that the extended unit cannot also have a measure of internal organization. In the context of the high frequency of signals of continuity, the breaks at 8.18, 9.18 and 9.32 are all the more noticeable. While the narrative moves forward at a rapid pace, and the pace seems to quicken as the passage unfolds—compare the three examples of δέ with genitive absolutes beginning pericopes in the first section with the use of καί to conjoin pericopes in succeeding sections, and the collapse of formal elements into one sentence in 9.33a in the final pericope—there are still points at which one momentarily catches one's breath

as a whole, each within two standard deviations of the mean for same-size samples. There is actually a lower than expected frequency of asyndeton (2% [2/86] as compared to 8% in the entire narrative framework, $z = -1.92$) but it is difficult to assess in terms of continuity in 8.1–9.34, not just because the z-score is inconclusive, but more importantly because asyndeton is found in both continuous and discontinuous contexts in narrative in Matthew's Gospel.

before the shift to a new series of pericopes. Held's internal arrangement
(8.1-17; 8.18–9.17; 9.18-31; 9.32-34) can be maintained, but only in light
of the overall portrayal of continuity perceived by Luz.

At the same time, Luz's contention that the entire unit is directed to the
imminent conflict between Jesus and leaders of Israel is consistent with the
fact that 9.32-34, with the contrasting responses of the crowds and the
Pharisees, comprises a section distinct from others in the extended unit.
Similarly, Luz's view is consistent with the manner in which Matthew
introduces elements of discontinuity (δέ with S_1V constituent order) at
8.27, 9.8 and 9.31 to focus the audience's attention on positive responses
which follow Jesus' miracles, but in the final pericope portrays the reaction of the crowds in terms of continuity while highlighting the Pharisees'
rejection of Jesus' miracle by the use of δέ and S_1V constituent order.

Summary and Conclusions

This analysis of 8.1–9.34 demonstrates the role of sentence conjunctions
as a linguistic system, forming networks with other systems in Matthew's
narrative framework. Each conjunction not only exhibits its own
characteristic syntactical, morphological and lexical collocations, but is
processed against other choices which might have been made but were
not. Sentence conjunctions and their related features contribute to discourse processing by functioning as signals of continuity and discontinuity
in Matthew's portrayal of narrative events, guiding those in the audience
to maintain or modify their ongoing mental representation of the discourse.

I introduced a working model positing that in narrative in Matthew's
Gospel καί occurs primarily with V(S) constituent order or with ἰδού
while δέ occurs primarily with SV constituent order or genitive absolute
constructions. Alongside that model I offered a summary of features
characteristic of asyndeton, τότε, γάρ and οὖν. The working model
accounts for three-quarters of the narrative sentences in 8.1–9.34 (65/86,
76%). Most occurrences of asyndeton, τότε and γάρ in 8.1–9.34,
evaluated by comparing their use with the characteristic features identified
for each form, were found to be consistent with Matthew's habits of use
elsewhere in the narrative framework.

More importantly, the role of καί and δέ in 8.1–9.34 as procedural
signals in discourse processing above the level of individual sentences has
been demonstrated. Καί functions as a signal of unmarked continuity, both
within pericopes, where it carries forward narrative action, and between

pericopes, where it connects pericopes which form larger units. Δέ functions as a signal of narrative discontinuity, although what is actually discontinuous may be any of a variety of elements or combination of elements, such as a new discourse unit, a temporal or spatial shift, a change in speaker, a condition contrary to expectation, or a departure from an expected miracle story form. The use of δέ represents a choice by Matthew that is marked to some degree, as there are a number of points of narrative discontinuity at which καί, as the unmarked or 'default' connector, appears rather than δέ. Καί and δέ are the sentence conjunctions found most frequently in narrative sentences in 8.1–9.34, as in Matthew's Gospel as a whole, while other conjunctive choices are used only intermittently, functioning in specific roles as procedural signals and markers.

Following the analysis of the role of sentence conjunctions in individual pericopes in 8.1–9.34, I examined the structure of the extended unit 8.1–9.34, further addressing the question of whether sentence conjunctions can have a larger scope, linking units at higher levels of discourse. In 8.1–9.34, καί, δέ and asyndeton each function at breaks between sections within the extended unit, but the hierarchical level at which continuity or discontinuity is to be incorporated into the mental representation of the discourse must be pragmatically determined by the audience on the basis of other factors each time they encounter a sentence conjunction.

The analysis of 8.1–9.34 presented in this chapter illustrates the benefits a greater appreciation of Matthew's use of sentence conjunctions and related features in narrative can have in the exegesis of Matthew's 'miracle chapters', and points to the importance of such lexico-grammatical concerns in the overall interpretation of Matthew's Gospel.

Chapter 10

CONCLUSIONS

Review of Sentence Conjunctions

I have shown that sentence conjunctions in the narrative framework of
Matthew's Gospel function as 'multiple-purpose tools with low semantic
content' (to use Dik's terms), joining sentences which may be characterized
by a variety of semantic relationships.[1] The content these forms convey is
procedural rather than conceptual, helping the audience to integrate the
content of the sentence which follows into the ongoing mental representation they construct as they process discourse. Using Halliday's
notions of system and choice, I describe sentence conjunctions and asyndeton in the Gospel of Matthew as constituting a conjunctive system. This
system forms networks of relationships with other linguistic systems such
as constituent order, verbal tense-form, and lexical choice. For example,
Matthew tends to use the unmarked sentence conjunction καί in contexts
of discourse continuity (the unmarked condition in narrative) alongside an
unmarked verbal tense-form (aorist) and with less marked constituent
order (V or VS). Correspondingly, he tends to use the more marked
sentence conjunction δέ—which I have characterized as a signal of low- to
mid-level discontinuity in narrative—in contexts where other signals of
discourse discontinuity such as SV constituent order (especially with a
thematic subject) or indicators of temporal shift are also present, and/or
where there is a switch in grammatical subject from the previous narrative
sentence. These collocations represent some of the ways components from
various linguistic systems may function together in what Battistella
describes as 'a single superstructure' incorporating form and meaning.[2]

Καί is the most frequent sentence conjunction in Matthew's narrative
framework (occurring in 335 of the 720 narrative sentences, or 47%),

---

1. See Dik, *Coordination*, p. 269.
2. See Battistella, *Markedness*, p. 7.

followed closely by δέ (257/720, 36%). Either καί or δέ occurs as the sentence conjunction in more than 80% of the sentences in the narrative framework. Another 8% (57/720) of narrative sentences are asyndetic, and a further 8% (55/720) have τότε as a sentence conjunction. In addition, there are ten occurrences of γάρ as a narrative connector in Matthew's Gospel and two of οὖν. Together these six choices account for 99% (716/720) of the sentences in the narrative framework.

I have said that καί, in addition to being the most common sentence conjunction in Matthew's narrative framework, is the unmarked connector, signaling discourse continuity. That is, καί signals to the audience that the proposition it conjoins is to be integrated into their mental representation of the discourse without significant change in that representation. When Matthew chooses sentence-initial καί in narrative he also reveals a strong tendency to use aorist tense-form finite verbs and unmarked or less marked constituent order (V or VS). In fact, the frequency of καί diminishes as constituent order becomes progressively more marked in terms of the cline developed in Chapter 4. The earlier in the sentence the subject is placed (with S_1V—that is, a grammaticalized subject in thematic position—considered the most marked constituent order), the less likely καί is to appear; the later in the sentence the subject is placed (with no expressed subject at the far end of the cline), the more likely καί is to appear. The exception to this tendency is the combination καὶ ἰδού, which usually appears with SV constituent order, especially with a thematic subject. Finally, as the unmarked or 'default' conjunction in Matthew's narrative framework, it is sometimes the case that καί appears in contexts where various features might lead one to expect δέ, but the more marked form δέ will rarely appear where contextual indicators of continuity are consistent with the use of καί.

While καί indicates unmarked continuity, δέ functions as a signal of low- to mid-level discontinuity. Far from being an adversative particle as it is often traditionally understood, its use signals those in the audience to make some adjustment in their current mental representation of the discourse. More often than not this discontinuity is simply a change of actor, but shifts in the time and, less frequently, the place of the action may also be indicated by the use of δέ, as well as a variety of other discontinuities, including contexts in which there is a contrastive or adversative semantic relationship between the δέ-sentence and preceding text. These, however, merely represent a number of semantic contexts in which δέ may be used, rather than different 'types' of δέ. Where Matthew chooses δέ he also tends to use SV constituent order (and especially S_1V constituent order) and aorist tense-form finite verbs. In contrast to καί, the frequency of δέ *increases* in proportion to the markedness of the constituent order of the sentences it begins. The earlier in the sentence the subject is placed, the more likely δέ is to appear; the later in the sentence the subject is placed (with no grammaticalized subject as the least marked choice), the less likely δέ is to appear. Other thematized elements which are frequently combined with δέ include genitive absolute participial constructions, temporal prepositional phrases, and other temporal indicators. Δέ invariably appears where a pronominal article serves as the subject of the sentence (ὁ δέ, οἱ δέ), usually in the context of alternating speakers in dialogue.

In principle, every instance in which δέ appears represents a marked choice by Matthew to use δέ and its related features over against καί and its related features. Throughout Matthew's Gospel there are narrative discontinuities—discontinuities of time, place, or actor, alternation between speakers, adversative or contrastive contexts, and so on—which have καί as the 'default' narrative connector rather than δέ. Where Matthew does choose δέ, the interruption of narrative continuity that it represents can be an attempt to guide the audience to turn their attention (or rather, the focus of the mental representation each is constructing) to a particular participant or action in the discourse.

Asyndeton appears in two quite different contexts in Matthew's narrative framework, with differing collocations. On the one hand, asyndeton links sentences with the closest of connections, specifically in speech margins, and especially in the margins of question–reply–response sequences. In this continuous usage asyndetic sentences usually have present tense-form λέγω in thematic position. On the other hand, asyndeton also tends to be found where higher-level breaks in the flow of the narrative occur, as for example between the title and first sentence, and at some (but not all) major breaks between episodes. At these points of discontinuity, aorist (or, less often, imperfect, but never present) tense-forms are used, and while either SV or V(S) constituent order may appear, a finite verb is never thematic.

Τότε is characteristically associated with several syntactical and lexical collocations in Matthew's narrative framework: present-tense finite verbs in past-referring narrative (the so-called 'historic present'); thematic finite verbs; VS constituent order; and/or προσέρχομαι or passive forms of προσφέρω. With the caveat that the small sample size and the wide range of contexts in which τότε is found limit firm conclusions about the function of τότε as a narrative connector in Matthew's Gospel, it appears that τότε is a signal of marked continuity. Discourse contexts in which τότε is commonly used include marking a climactic point within a pericope (especially a pronouncement by Jesus), marking the beginning of paragraphs within an episode (often collocating with SV constituent order and aorist finite verbs rather than the more common VS order or present tense-forms), and in combination with theologically marked lexical forms such as προσέρχομαι and passive forms of προσφέρω.

The last two sentence conjunctions considered in this study are γάρ and οὖν. In Matthew's narrative framework γάρ and οὖν guide pragmatic inferences, signaling the audience to strengthen or modify the mental representation they construct of discourse by integrating material that is 'off-line' in terms of sequential narrative: γάρ by introducing material which confirms and strengthens a preceding proposition (usually, but not necessarily, by giving either a reason or elaboration), and οὖν by signaling that the ongoing representation is dependent in some way on material which immediately precedes. Like δέ, these postpositive forms signal a type of discontinuity. However, while δέ usually signals discontinuity within the narrated events themselves, γάρ and οὖν signal moves from and to the narrative line. In spite of the small sample size, it can be shown that γάρ frequently collocates with forms of εἰμί, and apparently also combines with imperfect tense-forms.

Although for the purpose of discussion I treat the different sentence conjunctions and asyndeton in separate chapters, I emphasize throughout this study that from a linguistic standpoint καί, δέ, τότε, γάρ, οὖν and asyndeton constitute an integrated conjunctive system from which the Evangelist makes choices in connecting sentences in his narrative framework. In actual use each form not only appears with its own characteristic syntactical, morphological and lexical collocations, but is processed against the background of what might have been chosen but was not—that is, other conjunctions with other syntactical, morphological and lexical collocations. Matthew's choices of sentence conjunctions and their related features work together to signal continuity and discontinuity in his portrayal of narrative events, guiding the audience to maintain or modify the on-going mental representation they construct as they process the discourse.

Contributions of this Study

In detailing Matthew's use of καί, δέ, τότε, γάρ, οὖν and asyndeton in narrative, this study provides important linguistic data for the exegesis of

Matthew's Gospel. In addition, this research has value for the wider study of Hellenistic Greek, both in offering a theoretical framework for the linguistic function of sentence conjunctions, and in developing a quantitative methodology which can be applied to other lexico-grammatical analyses.

By outlining patterns of use of the sentence conjunctions καί, δέ, τότε, γάρ and οὖν, and showing how asyndeton also alternates with these forms as part of a conjunctive system, this research offers New Testament scholars a more informed understanding of ways Matthew constructs his narrative about Jesus. A number of specific applications are touched on in this study, such as a warning against allowing δέ to stand as evidence for conflict in the narrative (see Chapter 5); an awareness of the association between δέ and subject switch in contexts such as Mt. 28.17; a rethinking of the function of so-called 'adversative καί' in passages such as Mt. 1.24-25 and 3.14; a recognition of τότε's role as a marker of climactic statements by Jesus in, for example, the calming of the great storm in Mt. 8.23-27; and the identification of features such as sentence conjunction and constituent order which help to distinguish the use of ἀπὸ τότε as a potential structural element in Mt. 4.17 and 16.21 from its use in 26.16. However, the purpose of the present study is not so much to reach exegetical conclusions regarding the Gospel of Matthew, as to provide linguistic data to be used as evidence in the exegetical work of others. The analysis of Mt. 8.1–9.34 in Chapter 9 demonstrates a more extended application of this research to Matthew's 'miracle chapters', and underscores the need to incorporate such lexico-grammatical data into the study of Matthew's Gospel.

In terms of a linguistic framework for the semantics of sentence conjunctions in the Gospel of Matthew and beyond, the use of Halliday's notions of system and choice allows conjunctions to be identified as a system of forms which interact with each other and with other systems in the language. Halliday's concept of multiple themes gives sentence conjunctions a place in the grammar of the sentence as 'textual theme' and motivates the analysis of collocations between sentence conjunction and 'topical theme' (the first element in the transitivity structure of the sentence) or other sentence components. As I have shown, certain sentence conjunctions in Matthew's Gospel tend to combine with certain constituents as topical theme. Halliday's recognition that the textual metafunction of language concerns not just thematic choice, but the internal organization of the sentence as well, accounts for other collocations between sentence conjunctions and intrasentential features such as constituent order and verbal tense-form.

Other linguistic and cognitive notions incorporated in this study, such as the understanding of pragmatic inference offered by Grice, Blakemore's distinction between procedural and conceptual meaning, and a recognition of the role of mental representations in discourse processing, have implications not only for the study of sentence conjunctions but for the larger issue of how linguistic communication 'works', and therefore how biblical authors use language to convey meaning.

Finally, my ability in this study to identify and compare collocations between sentence conjunctions and other features in the sentence arises directly from the development of a syntactically coded database for the text under consideration, and points to the importance of corpus linguistic techniques in the study of Hellenistic Greek. Until clause- or discourse-level tags for machine-readable texts of documents from the Hellenistic period can be generated automatically—that is, until clause- or discourse-level parsing software is developed—a manually created database such as the one used here offers a viable alternative for relatively short texts like those of the New Testament. This technique has the value of being both empirical and exhaustive, and can easily be extended to the study of other lexical forms or syntactical features. The identification of relevant contextual variables to include in the database becomes a theoretical question specific to each investigation. The careful use of quantitative methods, including measures of statistical significance, is readily transferable to other investigations.

Suggestions for Further Research

As with all research, it seems that this study of sentence conjunctions in narrative in Matthew's Gospel raises as many questions as it answers. A number of avenues for further research present themselves. First and foremost is the need for comparable data from other Hellenistic texts— biblical and extra-biblical—in order to compare the results obtained here with the use of sentence conjunctions by other authors. In the development of such databases, a comparison of the use of narrative sentence conjunctions in the other Gospels and Acts with their use in Matthew's Gospel should perhaps be the next undertaking, as well as a comparison of sentence conjunctions in other discourse types with their use in narrative. Through broader studies it may be found that other contextual features show even stronger collocations with certain sentence conjunctions than do the features incorporated here.

The methodology developed in this research could also be applied to a variety of lexico-grammatical issues in the Greek of the New Testament. For example, broader questions of word order and constituent order, the role of pre-verbal participles in narrative structure (that is, participles which appear before a finite verb), or discourse functions of verbal tense-forms could be explored from this standpoint. Whatever the research program, this methodology encourages an approach which is empirical and exhaustive, and which takes seriously the use in context of the forms being studied, both at the sentence level and at the level of discourse. Perhaps more importantly, using a database or (when available) a syntactically tagged text to incorporate multiple variables into one study encourages the recognition that linguistic communication is rarely a matter of a single 'signal'—one lexical item or one syntactical structure—at a time. Instead, linguistic and contextual features interact in complex ways as human beings exploit them to convey meaning in discourse. As with any language in use, the Greek of the New Testament consists of networks of choices which not only transmit conceptual content, but which together reinforce elements of continuity or discontinuity, prominence or relative unimportance, tracing movements in topic, actor, action, setting and time.

Several years of study of sentence conjunctions in Matthew's Gospel have left me with a renewed commitment to the importance of the text in New Testament exegesis, the importance of the interpreter's taking seriously the ways an author puts together sentences and larger units in order to guide an audience through the discourse. A fuller appreciation of the multi-dimensional nature of biblical language begins with as thorough an awareness as possible of the ways authors use the linguistic elements available—including these sentence conjunctions and their related features—to convey meaning.

CROSS-TABULATION TABLES

Cross-Tabulation Table 1: *Sentence conjunction and discourse type in Matthew's Gospel*

	All sentences in Matthew	*Narrative sentences*	*Exposition sentences*	*Speech sentences*	*OT quotation sentences*
n =	2302	720	768	733	81
# asyndeton	721	57	201	419	44
% asyndeton	31%	8%	26%	57%	54%
# καί	700	335	212	128	25
% καί	30%	47%	28%	17%	31%
# δέ	470	257	159	50	4
% δέ	20%	36%	21%	7%	5%
# Sub-total	1891	649	572	597	73
% Sub-total	82%	90%	74%	81%	90%
# γάρ	124	10	61	51	2
% γάρ	5%	1%	8%	7%	2%
# τότε	73	55	18	0	0
% τότε	3%	8%	2%	–	–
# οὖν	56	2	31	3	0
% οὖν	2%	–	4%	3%	–
# Total	2144	716	682	671	75
% Total	93%	99%	89%	92%	93%

Cross-Tabulation Table 2: *Sentence conjunction and constituent order in Matthew's narrative framework*

	All narrative	Verbless	S_1V	S_2V	VS	V	+2[1]
n =	720	6	195	99	149	262	9
# καί	335	3[3]	23[4]	40	69	191	9
% καί	47%	–	12%	40%	46%	73%	100%
z-score[2]		2.79	−9.73	−1.21	0.05	8.56	
# δέ	257	1	155[5]	47	29	25	0
% δέ	36%	–	79%	47%	19%	10%	–
z-score		2.14	12.77	2.44	−4.13	−8.83	
# asyndeton	57	1	6	4	24	22	0
% asyndeton	8%	–	3%	4%	16%	8%	–
z-score		0.48	−2.50	−1.43	3.71	0.29	
# τότε	55	0	9	8	21	17	0
% τότε	8%	–	5%	8%	14%	6%	–
z-score			−1.59	0.17	2.98	−0.70	
# γάρ	10	0	2	0	3	5	0
% γάρ	1%	–	–	–	–	–	–
# οὖν	2	1	0	0	1	0	0
% οὖν	–	–	–	–	–	–	–
other	4				οὐδέ (22.46) πάλιν (4.8)	διό (27.8) πάλιν (26.42)	

1. Sentences in which a second (or third) clause has a finite verb so closely linked to the preceding clause that the two might best be described as forming one compound sentence.
2. A z-score expresses a distance from a mean in terms of standard deviations. In this study z-scores equal to or greater than ±3—that is, indicating that a value falls three standard deviations or more above or below a mean—are taken to demonstrate statistical significance.
3. All 3 times (100%) with ἰδού.
4. 14 times (61%) with ἰδού.
5. 60 times with article as pronoun (ὁ δέ/ἡ δέ/οἱ δέ). Without these, there is still a significant correlation between δέ and S_1V constituent order: 95 δέ of 135 S_1V constituent order = 70%; z = 10.30.

Cross-Tabulation Table 3: *Sentence conjunction and verbal tense-form in Matthew's narrative framework*[1]

	All narrative	Aorist	Present	Imperfect	εἰμί (augmented)	εἰμί (unaugmented/ 'present')	Verbless
n=	720	553	79	57	16	1	8
# καί	335	276	24	28	1 (2.15)	0	5
% καί	47%	50%	30%	49%	6%	–	–
z-score		1.59	-2.88	0.39	-3.22	–	–
# δέ	257	213	8	23	9	1 (10.2)	1 (15.36)
% δέ	36%	39%	10%	40%	56%	–	–
z-score		1.39	-4.74	0.73	1.71	–	–
# asyn	57	24	26	3	1(27.46)	0	1 (1.1)
% asyn	8%	4%	33%	5%	6%	–	–
z-score		-3.12	8.23	-0.74	-0.25	–	–
# τότε	55	34	20	1 (3.5)	0	0	0
% τότε	8%	6%	25%	2%	–	–	–
z-score		-1.32	5.92	-1.68	-1.15	–	–
# γάρ	10	2	0	2	5	0	0
% γάρ	1%	–	–	4%	31%	–	–
z-score				1.36	10.17	–	–
# οὖν	2	1 (27.17)	0	0	0	0	1 (1.17)
% οὖν	–	–	–	–	–	–	–
other	4	διό (27.8) οὐδέ (22.46) πάλιν (26.42)	πάλιν (4.8)	0	0	0	0

1. Omitting five perfect or pluperfect forms and one imperative form.

Cross-Tabulation Table 4: *Sentence conjunction and topical theme in Matthew's narrative framework*

	All narrative	Verb	Participle (not genitive absolute)	Genitive absolute participle	Subject	Prepositional phrase	Direct object	Other
n =	720	248	178	39	198	25	12	20
# καί	335	163	115	11	24	8	4	10
% καί	47%	66%	65%	28%	12%	32%	33%	50%
z-score		6.06	4.84	-2.30	-9.71	-1.46	-0.91	0.31
# δέ	257	8	52	23	156	8	2	8
% δέ	36%	3%	29%	59%	79%	32%	17%	40%
z-score		-10.66	-1.81	3.04	12.66	-0.38	-1.37	0.40
# asyn	57	31	0	4	6	9	6	1
% asyn	8%	13%	–	10%	3%	36%	50%	5%
z-score		2.68	-3.91	0.54	-2.55	5.20	5.43	-0.48
# τότε	55	35	11	0	9	0	0	0
% τότε	8%	14%	6%	–	5%	–	–	–
z-score		3.85	-0.73	-1.81	-1.64	-1.45	-1.00	-1.29
# γάρ	10	8	0	0	2	0	0	0
% γάρ	1%	–	–	–	–	–	–	–
# οὖν	2	0	0	1	1	0	0	0
% οὖν	–	–	–	–	–	–	–	–
other	4	0	0	0	0	0	0	πάλιν (26.42)
	διό (27.8) οὐδέ (22.46) πάλιν (4.8)							

Cross-Tabulation Table 5: *Sentence conjunction and subject switch in Matthew's narrative framework*

	All narrative	Switch = 'yes'	Switch = 'no'	Title, 1st sentence
n =	720	516	202	2
# καί	335	183	152	0
% καί	47%	35%	75%	–
z-score		−5.04	8.18	
# δέ	257	235	22	0
% δέ	36%	46%	11%	–
z-score		4.67	−7.36	
# asyndeton	57	44	11	2
% asyndeton	8%	9%	5%	100%
z-score		0.51	−1.30	
# τότε	55	43	12	0
% τότε	8%	8%	6%	–
z-score		0.59	−0.91	
# γάρ	10	6	4	0
% γάρ	1%	1%	2%	–
z-score		−0.44	0.71	
# οὖν	2	2	0	0
other	4	διό (27.8) ουδέ (22.46) πάλιν (4.8)	πάλιν (26.42)	0

Cross-Tabulation Table 6: Sentence conjunction and function as a speech margin in Matthew's narrative framework

	All narrative	Not a speech margin	Speech margins				
			All speech margins	λέγω as main verb	φημί as main verb	Other verb with λέγω participle	Other λέγω infinitive or other verb of speaking
n =	720	421	299	186	11	92	10
# καί	335	233	102	54	1 (8.8)	42	5
% καί	7%	55%	34%	29%	9%	47%	50%
z-score			-4.31	-4.79	-2.50	-0.17	0.22
# δέ	257	132	125[1]	83[2]	5[3]	35	2
% δέ	36%	31%	42%	45%	45%	38%	20%
z-score			2.21	2.54	0.67	0.47	-1.03
# asyn	57	16	41	29	5	5	2
% asyn	8%	4%	14%	16%	45%	5%	20%
z-score			3.72	3.88	4.64	-0.88	1.42
# τότε	55	28	27	17	0	9	1
% τότε	8%	7%	9%	9%	–	10%	10%
z-score			0.91	0.77	-0.95	0.78	0.76
other	16	12	4	γάρ (9.21, 14.4), οὖν (27.17)	0	πάλιν (26.42)	0

1. 46 times (37%) with article as pronoun.
2. 35 times (42%) with article as pronoun.
3. 3 times (60%) with article as pronoun.

STATISTICAL ANALYSIS OF THE CHOICE OF
CONJUNCTION IN THE GOSPEL OF MATTHEW

Elizabeth Allen and Vern Farewell

1. *Introduction*

In the emerging field of New Testament Greek linguistics there are many methodologies reflecting a variety of linguistic models. As has been described in the main body of this volume, the approach of Black's study is based primarily on Halliday's systemic-functional grammar. The work explores the possibility of applying Halliday's grammar to the use of intersentential conjunctions in the Gospel of Matthew.

The recognition that language is based on paradigmatic relations of either/or leads to the realization that overlaying such relations are relations of 'more likely'/'less likely'. It is in the description of these relations that probabilities enter grammatical description. The purpose of this section is to present a statistical analysis of the use of intersentential conjunctions in the Gospel of Matthew based on probabilistic models for the choice of conjunction.

To our knowledge, this is the first application to Greek linguistics of the particular statistical methodology used. The general form of the statistical models used is well known and the possible value of these and related methodologies is discussed by Oakes (*Statistics for Corpus Linguistics*). However, the nature of the data required the use of pragmatic, and relatively novel, selection criteria to determine particular models that reflect the grammatical features of the Gospel of Matthew. Further applications of the methodology will help to identify possible improvements to the approach that has been adopted.

2. *Statistical Methods*

In this section, a description is given of the statistical methodology used in the analyses presented in later sections. The description is not highly technical but does require some detail. Much of the material is not required in order to understand the main conclusions of the analysis. Therefore, a very brief non-technical summary of the key components of the analysis is given prior to the more detailed presentation of the methodology.

2.1 *A Brief Summary*

The aim of the statistical analyses presented in later sections is to examine the relationship between the choice of conjunction and various grammatical features of a sentence. The conjunction *kai* is taken as the default choice and three analyses are done which examine the grammatical features which influence the choice of *de, tote* and asyndeton (no conjunction) rather than *kai.*

Statistical tests are carried out to determine if there is evidence for a relationship between a number of grammatical features and the choice of conjunction, and the evidence is summarized as significance levels or p-values. A very small p-value is evidence for a relationship with a level of 0.05, or 5%, taken as providing reasonable evidence of some relationship being present. Simplistically a p-value can be thought of as the probability that one would observe the patterns seen in the available data if there was no relationship between a grammatical feature and the choice of conjunction. Thus a small p-value means that observing the available data is very unlikely if there is no relationship and this provides evidence for assuming that a relationship does in fact exist.

The magnitude of the relationship is measured numerically by odds ratios which have values greater than zero. An odds ratio of 1 corresponds to no relationship and the further the odds ratio is away from 1 in either direction, the stronger the relationship. Each grammatical feature examined has a number of classifications. For example, verbal tense-form has four categories, aorist, present, imperfect and other. One category is chosen as a baseline, for example aorist, and the odds ratios estimate how much sentences with another classification differ from those with the baseline classification with respect to choice of conjunction. In some cases, ranges of possible values, called confidence intervals, for the odds ratios are given, consisting of low and high values in brackets, separated by a comma. Thus an estimated odds ratio of 2 might have a range of possible values of [1.5, 3.0].

Two types of analyses are presented, unadjusted and adjusted. The unadjusted analyses examine the relationship of one grammatical feature with the choice of conjunction ignoring other features of a sentence. These are referred to as univariate analyses. The adjusted, or multivariate analyses, examine more than one feature and study relationships which exist between each feature and the choice of conjunction after making allowance for the influence of other aspects.

Within the multivariate analyses mention will be made of interactions. These are used when the influence of a grammatical feature on the choice of conjunction depends on the presence or absence of another feature in the sentence.

2.2 *Probability Models*

For simplicity, the analysis of Black's data is based on the development of probability models for pairs of conjunctions. This was done by defining *kai* as the 'default' conjunction as discussed earlier and modeling the probability of the other main conjunction classes, *de, tote* and asyndeton, in terms of the probability of observing these other conjunctions given that either that conjunction or *kai* is to be used. For example, the first analysis will look at all sentences which use either *de* or *kai* and, for that set of sentences, will model the probability of *de* being used, which shall be denoted pr(*de*). Since for these sentences either *de* or *kai* is used, then the probability of *kai* being used is [1–pr(*de*)]. For example, if the probability of using *de* were estimated to be 75% for a particular sentence, then the probability of using *kai* in that sentence would be 25%. The three separate models for *de, tote* and asyndeton can be combined to give a probability model for all the conjunctions in all types of sentences. This will be done in Section 5.2. In this section, the model for pr(*de*) will be used as an example to describe the methods being used.

The probability model, which is known under the technical term of logistic regression, is based on the concept of odds. For example, if pr(*de*)= 0.75 in some sentence in which either *de* or *kai* is used, then the odds of the use of *de* versus the use of *kai* is defined as pr(*de*)/pr(*kai*), or equivalently pr(*de*)/[1–pr(*de*)], which would be equal to 0.75/0.25 = 3. In common usage, this would be described as odds of 3 to 1 in favor of the use of *de*. If pr(*de*) = 0.60 then the odds would be 0.60/0.40 = 1.5 and this would be described as odds of 3 to 2 in favor of the use of *de*.

To relate probabilities of the use of conjunctions to other features of the sentence, it is necessary to define variables which code these aspects. For example, information on subject switch will be coded as 1, which represents no switch from the previous clause, or 2, which represents a switch from the previous clause (or no preceding clause). This will then be used to define a variable, denoted say as X_1, where

$X_1 = 1$ if subject switch is coded 2
and
$X_1 = 0$ otherwise (subject switch is coded 1).

A simple model for the odds of *de* versus *kai* can then be written as

$$\log\{\mathrm{pr}(de)/[1-\mathrm{pr}(de)]\} = a + b_1 X_1$$

where log stands for natural logarithm. The 'parameters' a and b_1 represent numbers which are to be estimated. Therefore an estimated model would look like

$$\log\{\mathrm{pr}(de)/[1-\mathrm{pr}(de)]\} = 0.5 + 0.7\, X_1$$

The important feature of this model is that if the true, but unknown, value of b_1 is equal to zero then subject switch is not related to the use of *de*. Thus the aim of the analysis will be to estimate quantities like b_1 and to test whether there is sufficient evidence to say that the true values must be different from zero thus establishing a relationship between the use of *de* and other grammatical features.

Mathematically, this model can also be written as

$$\mathrm{odds}(de) = \mathrm{pr}(de)/[1-\mathrm{pr}(de)] = \exp(a + b_1 X_1)$$

where exp stands for exponentiation, the opposite of a logarithm. For comparison purposes, a useful mathematical quantity is

$$\exp(b1)$$

which represents the ratio of the odds of *de* when subject switch is coded 2 and the odds when subject switch is coded 1. This is termed an odds ratio and provides a measure of the size of the effect of subject switch on the choice of *de* versus *kai*. If, for example, b_1 was estimated to be 0.69, then it would be estimated, since $\exp(0.69) = 2$, that the odds of the use of *de* would be twice as large if the sentence involved a subject switch than it would be if there was no subject switch. An odds ratio of 1, which corresponds to $b_1 = 0.0$, would represent no effect of subject switch.

Two more complicated forms of the model need to be described. Consider first a model which relates $\mathrm{pr}(de)$ to constituent order which is taken to have five possible classifications, 'verb only' coded 1, 'subject before verb, in first position' coded 2, 'subject before verb, not in first position' coded 3, 'verb followed by subject' coded 4, and 'other' coded 5. This would lead to a model which is written

$$\log\{\mathrm{pr}(de)/[1-\mathrm{pr}(de)]\} = a + b_1X_1 + b_2X_2 + b_3X_3 + b_4X_4$$

where

$X_1 = 1$ if constituent order is coded 2 [s_1v]
$X_1 = 0$ otherwise

$X_2 = 1$ if constituent order is coded 3 [s_2v]
$X_2 = 0$ otherwise

$X_3 = 1$ if constituent order is coded 4 [vs]
$X_3 = 0$ otherwise

and

$X_4 = 1$ if constituent order is coded 5 [other]
$X_4 = 0$ otherwise.

Note that there are five possible codes for constituent order and that this requires a model with four X variables. When dealing with subject switch there were two possible codes and the model only required one X variable. In general a classification with k possible codes will require $k-1$ X variables. The value $k-1$ corresponds to the 'degrees of freedom' associated with the classification. This is involved in tests of significance to be described later. It is sometimes a convenient shorthand to refer to a variable like X_1 as corresponding to or representing the feature for which it codes. In this example that would be a constituent order of subject before verb in first position. However, it must be remembered that, in fact, this means that X_1 has the value 1 when this feature is present and 0 otherwise.

Based on this model, it can be said that $\exp(b_1)$ is the odds ratio which compares the odds of the use of *de* versus *kai* in a clause with constituent order 'subject before verb in first position' to a clause with constituent order 'verb only'. Similarly $\exp(b_2)$ compares clauses with constituent order 'subject before verb, not in first position' to clauses with 'verb only'. Thus the b values compare each classification of constituent order with the same 'baseline' classification, constituent order = 1 or 'verb only'. The choice of the 'baseline' is mathematically arbitrary but it is always taken to be the category labeled 1 in the subsequent analyses. These categories typically represent the standard form. For a comparison of category 3 with category 2, say, it turns out that the relevant odds ratio is $\exp(b_2-b_1)$ and therefore this can be simply estimated from the model if the b's are estimated.

Both of the models discussed previously are used to provide 'unadjusted' analyses of the relationship between the choice of conjunction and some grammatical feature. This means that the relationship is examined without consideration of other features of grammar which might influence the choice of conjunction. To consider more than a single aspect, the model must be extended but this is simply done by adding all the variables which would be used in the separate 'unadjusted' analyses in a single model in order to provide a basis for an 'adjusted' analysis. This is usually termed a 'multivariate' analysis.

For example, a model which includes both subject switch and constituent order could be written as

$$\log\{\mathrm{pr}(de)/[1-\mathrm{pr}(de)]\} = a + b_1X_1 + b_2X_2 + b_3X_3 + b_4X_4 + b_5X_5$$

where (X_1, X_2, X_3, X_4) are used to represent the codings of constituent order as used in the previous model and X_5 is used to code subject switch as

$$X_5 = 1 \text{ if subject switch is coded 2}$$
$$X_5 = 0 \text{ otherwise.}$$

Thus X_5 is the same variable as the variable X_1 which was defined for the model which only included subject switch. Note that the numbering of the X variables is completely arbitrary but the model description used here is consistent with that used in most statistics books on this topic.

The difference between an 'adjusted' and an 'unadjusted' analysis is reflected in the interpretation of the b's. For example, in the model only involving constituent order, $\exp(b_2)$ was the odds ratio comparing a sentence with constituent order coded 3 with one with a code of 1. In the multivariate model, $\exp(b_2)$ is the odds ratio comparing two sentences with these different constituent orders IF both sentences have the same classification of subject switch, that is, have the same value of X_5. Similarly, in a symmetric fashion, $\exp(b_5)$ is the odds ratio comparing two sentences one with subject switch $= 2$ and the other with subject switch $= 1$, IF the two sentences have the same classification of constituent order, that is, have the same values for X_1, X_2, X_3 and X_4. Therefore, the b's in a multivariate model provide a measure of the effect of a grammatical feature on the choice of conjunction after allowing for any effect on the choice which is due to other features which are also represented in the model and might be related to the feature of interest.

Finally if having a subject switch was seen to influence the effect of one of the constituent orders (and vice versa) this would be called an inter-action between the two features and its inclusion would lead to a model of the form

$$\log\{\mathrm{pr}(de)/[1-\mathrm{pr}(de)]\} = a + b_1X_1 + b_2X_2 + b_3X_3 + b_4X_4 + b_5X_5 + b_6X_1X_5$$

The variable that represents the interaction will generally be referred to as a single variable, but is usually represented by the product of the two variables whose interaction is being considered. Essentially this variable codes for the presence of both features in the sentence since it has the value 1 only when this is true.

In this example the interaction included is between constituent order coded 2 ('subject before verb, in first position') and having a subject switch (coded 2). Here $\exp(b_1)$ is the odds ratio comparing a sentence with a constituent order coded 2 with one coded 1 as long as there is no subject switch. If, however, the two sentences being compared have a subject switch then the odds ratio becomes $\exp(b_1 + b_6)$.

Similarly $\exp(b_5)$ is the odds ratio comparing a sentence with a subject switch to one without, as long as the constituent order is not coded 2. If, however, the two sentences being compared have this constituent order the odds ratio becomes $\exp(b_5 + b_6)$.

Typically the discussion of models with interactions is somewhat com-plicated. In presenting the results, the main features will be highlighted with more complete details presented for the interested reader.

2.3 *Significance Tests*
Consider a specific b value associated with a particular X variable in a logistic regression model. As indicated earlier, a value of $b = 0$ is of particular importance because if $b = 0$ then there is no relationship between the X variable associated with b and the choice of conjunction. One aspect of logistic regression modeling is therefore to provide a test of the hypothesis that $b = 0$. This is done by the calculation of a probability called a significance level, or frequently a 'p-value', which represents the probability of observing the patterns seen in the data set available for analysis if, in fact, $b = 0$. If this probability is very small, then it is usually argued that there is evidence for a belief that b is not equal to zero and therefore that there is a relationship between the choice of construction and whatever grammatical feature is represented by the X variable.

Conversely, if the probability is reasonably large, which indicates that the observed data could have arisen if no relationship exists, then the conclusion is that the data provide no evidence for a relationship. This does not preclude the possibility that a relationship exists and that a larger data set might have provided evidence for it. A significance level of 5%, which corresponds to the probability of an event which only occurs 1 in 20 times, is conventionally taken as the level at which evidence against the hypothesis $b = 0$ is taken to be present. If the p-value is below 5%, the evidence for an effect is stronger and the strength of the evidence is reflected by how small the p-value is.

Sometimes it is not appropriate to examine only one b value. For example, if constituent order is in a model then four X variables, say X_1, X_2, X_3 and X_4, are used to represent the codings of constituent order. Thus, the model includes no relationship between constituent order and the choice of conjunction only if $b_1 = b_2 = b_3 = b_4 = 0$. Thus to test for a relationship, a significance level must be calculated which represents the probability of the observed data if all of b_1, b_2, b_3 and b_4 are equal to zero. If any of these are not equal to zero then there is some relationship present.

The technical details of the calculation of significance levels will not be discussed here. However, it can be noted that the usual approach to testing if a single b value is zero leads to the calculation of what is sometimes termed a 'z-score', which can be used to calculate a significance level based on the standard normal distribution. This would be appropriate to look at an aspect of grammar with only two codings. To examine an aspect with *k* possible codings, it is necessary to test that the *k–1* b values associated with the *k–1* X variables which represent these codings are all equal to zero. This will be based on the calculation of a chi-squared statistic which will be said to have *k–1* degrees of freedom and the calculation of the associated significance level will be based on a chi-squared distribution with *k–1* degrees of freedom.

It is possible to examine only one of a set of *k–1* b values, all of which relate to one aspect of grammar, but a cautious approach will only do this if there is evidence for a relationship based on a test involving all the values. This is related to a technical statistical issue which is termed 'multiple comparisons' and which will not be discussed in detail here. A sense of the potential difficulty can be gained by considering the examination of 20 b values. The logic of a significance test says that 1 in 20 tests, that is, 5% of tests, will be 'significant' if tested at the 5% level, even if there is no effect. Thus, if 20 tests are done for the 20 b values, one will be expected to lead to a 'significant' result even if none of the b values is actually different from zero. This problem is circumvented either by examining sets of variables jointly or by requiring much lower p-values to claim evidence of a relationship. The former approach is the one adopted here.

Note this issue is particularly relevant to the examination of interactions when the interaction between two types of grammatical features may involve the creation of large numbers of product variables. For example, the interaction between constituent order (with five categories) and subject reference (with five categories) requires the definition of $(5-1) \times (5-1) =$ 16 product variables. These are examined jointly for significance before individual terms are considered.

When a particular effect can be examined based on only a small number of sentences, it is sometimes necessary to use more accurate methods to calculate significance levels. A procedure called Fisher's exact test is used for this purpose at some points in the analyses. The interpretation of the significance levels remains the same and no technical details of the procedure will be given here.

2.4 *Estimation*

Significance tests represent only one component of the statistical analysis of logistic regression models. It is equally important to estimate the magnitude of any possible relationships and it has been shown above that, in these models, this is represented by odds ratios. In the analysis presented subsequently the estimated odds ratios are based on what is termed 'maximum likelihood estimation'. This means that the estimates are taken to be those values which would make the probability of seeing the observed data set as high as possible. They are, in this sense, the most likely values for the odds ratios.

Associated with any estimate of an odds ratio will be some indication of how close it is expected to be to the true value of the odds ratio. This leads to the calculation of what are termed 'confidence intervals'. Typically, 95% confidence intervals are presented. If an odds ratio is estimated to be 2 say, and a 95% confidence interval is given by the range of values [1.5, 3.0], then the meaning is that the best estimate of the odds ratio is 2 but that any value in the range [1.5, 3.0] can be regarded as a plausible value of the true odds ratio. It can be said that there is a 95% probability that the interval contains the true value.

Note that there is a specific link between significance tests and confidence intervals in that if the 95% confidence interval for an odds ratio, linked to some specific X variable, includes the value 1, which corresponds to the hypothesis of no association, then a test of significance of the odds ratio being 1, which corresponds to the associated b value being 0, would not lead to a rejection of this hypothesis. Therefore, it would be concluded that there is not sufficient evidence in the data set to conclude that a relationship between the relevant X variable and the choice of conjunction exists. Alternatively, if the confidence interval excludes 1 then the conclusion is that evidence for a relationship does exist.

2.5 *Overall Probability Model*

As mentioned earlier, the probability models for pairs of conjunctions can be used to define a single model for the choice of conjunction for any sentence. Based on the analysis of pairs of conjunctions, estimates will be available separately for the odds of choosing *de, tote* and asyndeton versus the 'default' conjunction *kai*. These odds are denoted odds(*de*), odds(*tote*) and odds(*asyndeton*).

For any sentence, then, some mathematical manipulations can establish that the probability of choosing the various conjunctions can be calculated using the formulae

pr(*kai*)	= 1/D
pr(*de*)	= odds(*de*)/D
pr(*tote*)	= odds(*tote*)/D
pr(asyndeton)	= odds(asyndeton)/D
where D	= 1 + odds(*de*) + odds(*tote*) + odds(*asyndeton*).

This is the formula used for the calculation of probabilities in Section 5.

It is possible to base an analysis on this comprehensive probability model directly but here models are all developed in terms of pairs of conjunctions for simplicity. It has been shown by Begg and Gray (1984) that, from a technical statistical point of view, little is lost by this simplification.

3. *General Methodology*

As discussed in Section 2, three analyses were initially undertaken: *de* vs. *kai, tote* vs. *kai,* and asyndeton (no conjunction) vs. *kai*. In each case univariate analyses, which examined each grammatical feature separately, were carried out initially. These were followed by multivariate analyses based on models which incorporated multiple grammatical features. This allowed not only an estimation of adjusted odds ratios, but also an investigation into possible interactions between grammatical features.

3.1 *Information Available*

The statistical analyses are based on the data collated by Black and described earlier in this volume. All the clauses identified by Black are considered in a final summary of the probabilistic model developed but some initial restrictions are required in order to develop the components of the model.

Given the consistent combination of subject reference 'pronominal article' (that is, the article functioning as a pronoun: *ho de*, *hoi de*) with intersentential conju
nction *de* all clauses with this subject reference were removed from the data set prior to analysis. (These 60 clauses also have a consistent combination of constituent order 'subject before verb, in first position' and topical theme[1] 'subject' and predominantly have a subject switch [58/60] and verbal tense-form 'aorist' [54/60]).

In the estimation of the probabilistic models, which proceeded (as previously mentioned) by the consideration of pairs of conjunctions, it is preferable to consider separately any identifiable type of clause with which only one or two uses of one of the pair of conjunctions is found. Therefore, clauses with constituent orders of 'verbless' and 'subsequent verb' were removed from any multivariate analyses as, of 15 clauses, 12 have conjunction *kai*.

Any clauses with *phemi* in speech margin were also removed prior to any of the multivariate analyses as, of 11 clauses, 5 have *no conjunction* (with a consistent combination of topical theme 'verb' and constituent order 'verb followed by subject', a subject switch, verbal tense-form 'aorist' and predominantly subject reference 'proper noun'), 5 have conjunction *de* (generally with constituent order 'subject before verb, in first position', topical theme 'subject' and verbal tense-form 'aorist'), and only 1 has conjunction *kai* (with topical theme 'other participle' with constituent order 'subject before verb, not in first position') with which the other conjunctions are paired in the model development.

Other clauses were removed from individual analyses, as certain combinations never occur. All clauses with topical theme 'other participle'

1. See Chapter 1, pp. 15-40.

were removed from the data for the multivariate analysis of asyndeton vs. *kai*, as clauses with that topical theme never have *no conjunction*. All clauses with the less common topical themes (anything besides a verb, a subject or participle as topical theme), topical theme 'genitive absolute participle' and the less frequent verbal tense-forms were removed from the data prior to the multivariate analysis of *tote* vs. *kai*, as those clauses never occur with conjunction *tote*.

3.2 *Coding the Variables*
The features 'constituent order', 'subject switch', 'verbal tense-form' and 'speech margin' were coded with the baseline value as one and with the classifications of small sample size grouped together. Constituent orders 'verbless' and 'subsequent verb' were grouped together. Clauses where a subject switch was not applicable as there was no preceding clause were grouped with clauses where there was a subject switch, and verbal tense-forms 'present tense of to be', 'imperfect tense of to be', any perfects, pluperfects, imperatives and verbless clauses were considered together.

Topical theme is linked to constituent order, because when the topical theme (the first element of the sentence proper) is 'subject', the constituent order will be 'subject before verb in first position'. Consequently for the purposes of any multivariate analysis clauses with a topical theme of 'subject', although coded separately, were grouped with clauses with the baseline topical theme 'verb'. This reflects the total confounding, or common identification, of topical theme 'subject' and constituent order 'subject before verb, in first position'. Thus the effect of constituent order 'subject before verb, in first position' can be interpreted as the effect of that constituent order with topical theme 'subject'. In addition, based on their low frequency, topical themes of 'prepositional phrase', 'direct object' and any others were grouped together for the purpose of analysis.

Subject reference also links with constituent order in that when subject reference is 'no explicit subject' constituent order will be 'verb only'. This confounding caused no particular problems as both variables are the baseline categories for their respective features. However, this means that it is not possible to estimate separate effects for all of the classifications in these features and that it is consequently necessary to consider combinations of constituent orders and subject references in the analyses, comparing the combinations to the single baseline category.

The codings used for analysis are given in the list of codings. These are used to define the variables which are used in the analysis, as is discussed in Section 2.

3.3 *Zeros*

One of the main problems that arises in the analysis of this language data is the relatively large number of what are commonly termed fixed and structural zeros. As discussed in the context of codings, some variables are totally confounded because certain combinations of grammatical features will never occur simultaneously. For example, it is never possible to have a clause with constituent order 'subject before verb, in first position' with any topical theme other than 'subject'. This is an example of structural (fixed) zeros. It is genuinely impossible to observe a clause with these combinations of features. There are many other combinations which do not occur and which lead to zeros in the data set, that is, combinations of coded variables for which no clauses are observed. It is not possible to ascertain whether these are further examples of combinations that cannot occur (i.e. fixed zeros) or are sampling zeros, which arise due to sampling variation and the relatively small size of the sample when compared with the large number of possible combinations.

It is important to note, however, that combinations, which appear to occur relatively infrequently when only two features are being considered, are often part of sets of consistent combinations of grammatical features that in the context of all features represent an appreciably large number of clauses. For example, in the analysis of *de* vs. *kai* there are six clauses with constituent order 'verb followed by subject' and the less common verbal tense-forms, all of which have conjunction *de*. Although six sentences are a relatively small number when sentences are only classified by these two features, these sentences also have a consistent combination of having a subject switch, not being used as a speech margin and having topical theme of either 'verb' or one of the less common forms. Thus they represent a set of six sentences with a clearly defined structure and six sentences are a reasonably large number when sentences are classified in such detail. Mention will be made of these special combinations and their effect on the choice of conjunction as they occur in the individual analyses.

It was decided that effects noticeable on cells with counts of less than ten would not generally be included in the model, but that their significance would be assessed using Fisher's exact test.

The specific structure of the data also led to problems in assessing some interactions; in some clauses the presence of a particular grammatical feature with a particular conjunction appears to lead to the automatic use of another feature and this can create a set of zeros. These cases are discussed in the results when they arise.

4. *Results*

Estimated odds ratios and significance levels are used to summarize the results of the statistical analysis as discussed in Section 2 with (as previously mentioned) a p-value of <0.05 being considered to indicate a significant association between the feature under consideration and the choice of conjunction. For simplicity, confidence intervals for the odds ratios will not generally be included but these will be given when the effect of a specific variable is of particular interest.

4.1 *Analysis of* de *vs.* kai

4.1(i) *Univariate analysis.* Initial analyses were carried out in order to assess the relationship of each grammatical feature to the choice of *de* as opposed to *kai.*

An example of a model used (for the feature constituent order) is,

$$\log\{\mathrm{pr}(de)/[1-\mathrm{pr}(de)]\} = -2.03 + 3.94X_1 + 2.19X_2 + 1.17X_3 - 0.45X_4,$$

where X_1 corresponds to constituent order 'subject before verb, in first position', X_2, to 'subject before verb, not in first position', X_3, to 'verb followed by subject' and X_4, to, 'other'.

Based on this model it can be seen that the odds ratio which compares the odds of the use of *de* vs. *kai*, when constituent order is 'subject before verb, in first position' ($X_1 = 1$) as opposed to the baseline constituent order 'verb only' is exp[3.94] = 51.42 (The slight difference between this result and that shown in Table 1 is due to the fact that 3.94 is the coefficient given to 3 significant figures.)

The unadjusted odds ratios are shown in Table 1 along with the frequency of *de* in the clauses with the same type of each of the grammatical features. Also given is the overall significance level, termed a p-value, associated with each feature.

It can be seen that features that have the most noticeable effect, as measured by the odds ratio, on choosing *de* as opposed to *kai* appear to be: a constituent order of 'subject before verb, in first position' (which corresponds to a topical theme of 'subject'), and a topical theme of 'genitive absolute participle'.

4.1(ii) *Multivariate analysis (adjusted effects).* A change in the effect of some variables is evident after adjustment for all other variables. Speech margin loses all significance as a feature, after adjustment for either constituent order, or subject reference. All other features remain significant. The results are summarized in Tables 2 and 3.

The effect of the less common verbal tense-forms changes from an odds ratio of 2.41 (Table 1) to an odds ratio of 73.73 (Table 2) after adjustment for subject switch, constituent order, subject reference and topical theme. This change in effect may be due to the fact that of 38 clauses with constituent order 'verb followed by subject', subject reference 'noun phrase' and topical theme 'verb', 34 have conjunction *kai*, none of which has any of the less common forms of verbal tense, and 4 have conjunction *de*, all of which have the less common verbal tense-forms.

Table 1: *Unadjusted odds ratios for all variables in the analysis of* de *vs.* kai

Feature	Unadjusted odds ratios	*de*/Total	P-value
Constituent order			<0.001
verb only*	1	25/216	
subject before verb, in first position	51.49	155/178	
subject before verb, (not in first position)	8.98	47/87	
verb followed by subject	3.21	29/98	
other	0.64	1/13	
Subject switch			<0.001
no subject switch*	1	22/174	
subject switch	8.86	235/418	
Verbal tense-form			0.036
aorist*	1	213/489	
present	0.43	8/32	
imperfect	1.10	23/51	
other	2.41	13/20	
Speech margin			<0.001
not used as speech margin*	1	132/365	
lego (finite)	2.71	83/137	
phemi	8.80	5/6	
lego (participle)	1.47	35/77	
other	0.71	2/7	
Topical theme			<0.001
verb*	1	8/171	
other participle	9.19	52/167	
genitive absolute participle	42.51	23/34	
subject	132.15	156/180	
other	16.63	18/40	
Subject reference			<0.001
no reference*	1	25/200	
pronominal article	ALL *de*	60/60	

noun phrase	6.34	69/156
proper noun	18.1	95/137
other	10.67	8/14

* Baseline category

Table 2: *Adjusted odds ratios calculated from the multivariate analysis of* de *vs.* kai

Feature	Adjusted odds ratio
Subject switch	
no subject switch*	1
subject switch	2.98
Verbal tense-form	
aorist*	1
present	0.76
imperfect	1.59
other	73.73
Topical theme	
verb*	1
other participle	8.39
genitive absolute participle	64.48
subject	NA
other	26.30

* Baseline category

Table 3: *Adjusted odds ratios for combinations of constituent orders and subject references (compared to the common baseline category) in the analysis of* de *vs.* kai

	Constituent Order			
Subject reference	verb only	subject before verb in first position	subject before verb, not in first position	verb followed by subject
no reference	1			
noun phrase		45.78	1.07	0.67
proper noun		181.22	4.25	2.63
other		100.19	2.35	1.46

The effects of the less common topical themes and topical theme 'genitive absolute participle' change noticeably when constituent order and subject reference are included in the model. These changes may be due to the structures shown in Table 4.

To understand Table 4, consider topical theme 'genitive absolute participle'; Table 1 shows that of 34 sentences with this topical theme, 23 have conjunction *de*. However, consider sentences with constituent order 'subject before verb, not in first position' and subject reference 'noun phrase'. Then having a topical theme 'genitive absolute participle' leads to 5 out of 5 sentences having conjunction *de*, whereas of 26 sentences with this combination of constituent order and subject reference but topical theme 'other participle' only 8 have conjunction *de*.

Table 4: *The numbers of clauses with various combinations of constituent order, subject reference and topical theme in the analysis of* de *vs.* kai

Constituent order and subject reference	Topical Theme			
	verb	other participle	genitive absolute participle	other
verb only & no reference	3/110	14/88	4/5	4/13
subject before verb, not in first position & noun phrase	0	8/26	5/5	5/6
verb followed by subject & noun phrase	4/38	2/4	8/16	6/7

After adjustment for all other features it can be seen that the categories of the features (relative to the respective baseline categories) that have the most noticeable effect on choosing *de* as opposed to *kai* are: all topical themes, with the most marked effect associated with the topical theme of 'genitive absolute participle', a constituent order of 'subject before verb, in first position' (with any subject reference), a subject reference 'proper noun' (with any constituent order) and a subject switch.

4.1(iii) *Interactions*. Significant interactions were found between constituent order and verbal tense-form, constituent order and subject reference, verbal tense-form and topical theme, and topical theme and subject reference. However, the interaction between verbal tense-form and topical theme loses significance when the interaction between constituent order and verbal tense-form is also included in the model and the interaction between topical theme and subject reference loses significance when the interaction between constituent order and subject reference is included in the model.

Further detailed investigation led to the decision to include only an interaction term which identified sentences with constituent order 'subject before verb, in first position' and subject reference 'proper noun'. The inclusion of this term led to the further decision to include an additional interaction term which identified sentences with a subject switch and one of the less common topical themes. The details are given subsequently.

Interactions between speech margin and other features were also looked at, however, none were significant and the significance of speech margin was in no way affected by any of the other interactions and consequently was again left out of the model.

Tables 5 and 6 show the actual numbers of sentences used for this analysis, with conjunction *de* classified by constituent order and subject reference and by constituent order and verbal tense-form respectively.

Table 5: *The number of clauses with conjunction* de *for combinations of constituent order and subject reference*

Subject reference	verb only	Constituent Order		
		subject before verb, in first position	subject before verb, not in first position	verb followed by subject
no reference	25/216			
noun phrase		30/50	18/37	20/65
proper noun		60/61	29/49	6/27
other		5/7	0/1	3/6[1]

Table 6: *The number of clauses with conjunction* de *for combinations of constituent order and verbal tense-form*

Verbal tense-form	verb only	Constituent Order		
		subject before verb, in first position	subject before verb, not in first position	verb followed by subject
aorist	20/175	75/95	42/76	22/83
present	0/18	2/2	2/2	1/7
imperfect	4/21	14/16[3]	2/8[2]	0/2
other	1/2	4/5	1/1	6/6[4]

On inspection it was decided to include only the single variable that coded the interaction between constituent order of 'subject before verb, in first position' and subject reference 'proper noun' in the model. Although there appear to be interactions between constituent order 'verb followed by subject' and the less common subject references, constituent order 'verb followed by subject' and the less common verbal tense-forms and constituent order 'subject before verb, not in first position' and verbal tense-form 'imperfect' the number of sentences involved in each case is small and consequently these interactions have not been included in the model.

It is worth noting that all six sentences with the less common verbal tense-forms and constituent order 'verb followed by subject' have conjunction *de*. These clauses also have a consistent combination of having a subject switch, not being used as a speech margin and having topical theme of either 'verb' or one of the less common topical themes.

Although, as has been said, effects noticeable on small numbers of sentences will not be included in the final model, as was mentioned in Section 2 their significance can be assessed by the use of Fisher's exact test. Using this, no evidence of any difference in the number of clauses with conjunction *de*, between clauses with constituent order 'verb followed by subject' and the less common subject references (Table 5[1]; [Table 5 entry labeled [1]]), and any other clauses with that constituent order or subject reference was found. No evidence of any difference between clauses with verbal tense-form 'imperfect' and constituent order 'subject before verb, not in first position' (Table 6[2]) and any other clauses with those features was found. A significant difference was found between these clauses and the clauses with verbal tense-form 'imperfect' and constituent order 'subject before verb, in first position' (Table 6[3]), however, that might well be expected due to the large effect of that particular constituent order. Finally, however, the number of clauses with conjunction *de* with the previously mentioned structure of the less common verbal tense-forms and constituent order 'verb followed by subject' (Table 6[4]) is significantly different from the number of clauses with conjunction *de* with that constituent order and any other verbal tense-form, but is not significantly different from the number involved in other clauses with those verbal tense-forms and any other constituent order.

When the interaction between constituent order 'subject before verb, in first position' and subject reference 'proper noun' is included in the model, the further addition of the interaction between subject switch and topical theme becomes significant. Looking at the number of sentences with conjunction *de* as shown in Table 7.

Table 7: *The number of clauses with conjunction* de *for combinations of topical theme and subject switch*

Subject switch	Topical Theme			
	verb	other participle	genitive absolute participle	other
no switch	3/79	9/62	6/8	2/14
switch	100/204	43/105	17/26	16/21

It was decided to include only the single variable representing the interaction between subject switch and the less common topical themes. This leads to the following model:

$$\log \{\text{pr(de)}/[1 - \text{pr(de)}]\} = -3.98 + 3.48X_1 + 0.71X_2 - 0.01X_3 +$$
$$0.62X_4 - 0.12X_5 + 0.50X_6 + 4.01X_7 + 2.15X_8 + 3.90X_9 + 1.95X_{10} +$$
$$0.67X_{11} + 0.92X_{12} + 3.92X_1X_{11} + 1.91X_4X_{10}$$

where $X_1 - X_{12}$ are respectively constituent orders 'subject before verb, in first position', 'subject before verb, not in first position' and 'verb followed by subject', a subject switch, verbal tense-forms 'present', 'imperfect' and 'other', topical themes 'genitive absolute participle' and 'other' and subject references 'proper noun' and 'other'.

It is necessary to remember that X_1, X_2 and X_3 should in fact be interpreted as the respective constituent orders with a subject reference 'noun phrase' (due to the total confounding or overlap of the two baseline categories).

Based on this model, it can be seen that the odds ratio which compares the odds of the use of *de* vs. *kai* when the constituent order is 'subject before verb, in first position' and the subject reference is 'proper noun' to the baseline category of constituent order 'verb only' and subject reference 'no reference' (with all other features having the same classification) is $\exp[3.48+0.67+3.29] = 1702.75$. Other estimates of effects, based on this model, are shown in Tables 8, 9 and 10.

Table 8: *Adjusted odds ratios for combinations of constituent orders and subject references (compared to the common baseline category) calculated from the final model in the analysis of* de *vs.* kai

	Constituent Order			
Subject reference	verb only	subject before verb, in first position	subject before verb, not in first position	verb followed by subject
no reference	1			
noun phrase		32.48	2.02	0.99
proper noun		1707.72	7.74	1.93
other		81.11	5.06	2.46

Table 8 reflects the effect of the interaction between constituent order 'subject before verb, in first position' and subject reference 'proper noun' while the effect of the interaction between the less common forms of topical theme and subject switch is reflected in the estimates shown in Table 9.

Table 9: *Adjusted odds ratios for combinations of the less common topical themes and subject switch*

no switch & verb	1
no switch & other	7.00
switch & verb	1.85
switch & other	87.52

The less common forms of topical theme ('other') modify the effect of subject switch changing the odds ratio from 1.85 (exp(0.62) = 1.85/1) to 12.50 (exp(0.62+1.91) = 87.52/7.00). The effect of the less common topical themes is modified by the presence of a subject switch changing the odds ratio from 7.00 (exp(1.95) = 7.00/1) to 47.31 (exp(1.95+1.91) = 87.52/1.85).

The effect of having a subject switch as opposed to not with topical themes 'genitive absolute participle' and 'subject' will be the same as for topical theme 'verb', that is to say it would have an odds ratio of 1.85.

Odds ratios for the features not involved in the interaction terms are shown in Table 10.

Table 10: *Adjusted odds ratios calculated from the final model in the analysis of* de *vs.* kai

Feature	Adjusted odds ratios
Topical theme	
verb*	1
other participle	8.62
genitive absolute participle	49.53
Verbal tense-form	
aorist*	1
present	0.90
imperfect	1.65
other	55.26

* Baseline category

The largest estimated effect on the choice of *de* is the combination of a constituent order 'subject before verb, in first position' and a subject reference 'proper noun' with an odds ratio of 1707.02 when compared to the common baseline category. This estimate, with an associated 95% confidence interval of [187.20,15578.56] should not be over-interpreted since it does depend critically on the particular form of the model but it clearly reflects the predominant choice of *de* over *kai* for clauses of this type.

Other features that significantly increase the chance of having conjunction *de* as opposed to *kai* are the less common verbal tense-forms with an odds ratio of 55.26 and a 95% confidence interval [7.78,392.58], and a topical theme 'genitive absolute participle' with an odds ratio of 49.53 and a 95% confidence interval [14.82,165.59].

4.2 *Analysis of asyndeton vs.* kai

4.2(i) *Univariate analysis.* Initial analyses were carried out in order to assess the relationship of each grammatical feature to the choice of asyndeton as opposed to *kai.*

An example of a model used (for the feature constituent order) is,

$$\log\{\text{pr}(asyndeton)/[1-\text{pr}(asyndeton)]\}$$
$$= -2.16 + 0.82X_1 - 0.41X_2 + 1.11X_3 - 0.32X_4,$$

where X_1 corresponds to constituent order 'subject before verb, in first position', X_2 to 'subject before verb, not in first position', X_3 to 'verb followed by subject' and X_4 to 'other'.

Based on this model it can be seen that the odds ratio which compares the odds of the use of asyndeton vs. *kai*, when constituent order is 'subject before verb, in first position' ($X_1 = 1$) as opposed to the baseline constituent order 'verb only' is $\exp[0.82] = 2.27$

The unadjusted odds ratios, proportion of clauses with asyndeton, and significance levels associated with each feature are shown in Table 11.

The significance of the feature topical theme may simply be due to the fact that, in this data set, asyndeton never occurs with topical theme 'other participle'.

The most noticeable other effect is due to *phemi* in the speech margin. However, the particular structure of these clauses has been mentioned before. Other features that have perceptible effects are verbal tense-form 'present', *lego* (finite) in the speech margin and the less common topical themes.

Table 11: *Unadjusted odds ratios for all variables in the analysis of asyndeton vs.* kai

Feature	Unadjusted odds ratios	Asyndeton/ Total	P-value
Constituent order			0.0076
verb only*	1	22/113	
subject before verb, in first position	2.26	6/29	
subject before verb, (not in first position)	0.87	4/44	

Feature	Unadjusted odds ratios	Asyndeton/ Total	P-value
verb followed by subject	3.02	24/93	
other	0.72	1/13	
Subject switch			<0.001
no subject switch*	1	12/164	
subject switch	3.11	45/228	
Verbal tense-form			<0.001
aorist*	1	24/300	
present	12.46	26/50	
imperfect	1.23	3/31	
other	6.57	4/11	
Speech margin			<0.001
not used as speech margin*	1	16/249	
lego (finite)	7.82	29/83	
phemi	72.79	5/6	
lego (participle)	1.58	5/47	
Other	5.82	2/7	
Topical theme			<0.001
verb*	1	31/194	
other participle	$-\infty$	0/115	
genitive absolute participle	1.91	4/15	
subject	1.73	6/30	
other	3.82	16/38	
Subject reference			<0.001
no reference*	1	22/222	
pronominal article	All *de*	0	
noun phrase	1.04	10/97	
proper noun	4.33	20/62	
other	7.58	5/11	

* Baseline category

4.2(ii) *Multivariate analysis (adjusted effects).* Clauses with a topical theme 'other participle' were removed from the data set.

The features speech margin and subject reference lose all significance after adjustment for verbal tense-form, constituent order, subject switch and topical theme. Consequently both features were removed from the model leading to the adjusted odds ratios shown in Table 12.

Table 12: *Adjusted odds ratios calculated from the multivariate analysis of asyndeton vs.* kai

Feature	Adjusted odds ratios
Constituent order	
verbless*	1
subject before verb, in first position	15.30
subject before verb, (not in first position)	1.75
verb followed by subject	0.94
Subject switch	
no subject switch*	1
subject switch	5.31
Verbal tense-form	
aorist*	1
present	138.35
imperfect	0.94
other	12.70
Topical theme	
verb*	1
genitive absolute participle	25.10
subject	NA
other	222.60

* Baseline category

The effects of the topical themes 'genitive absolute participle' and the less common topical themes change noticeably once verbal tense-form and subject switch are also included in a model. This could be due to the structures shown in Table 13.

Table 13: *Numbers of clauses with asyndeton for various combinations of topical theme, verbal tense-form and subject switch*

Subject switch & verbal tense-form	Topical Theme		
	verb	genitive absolute participle	other
no switch & aorist	1/55	0/2	10/20
switch & aorist	2/88	2/11	4/7

To understand the change in effect of the less common forms of topical theme (unadjusted odds ratio of 3.82 to an adjusted odds ratio of 222.60) consider the sentences with no subject switch and verbal tense-form 'aorist'. Of 55 sentences with this structure and the baseline topical theme 'verb', only 1 has *no conjunction*; whereas of 20 sentences with this verbal tense and no subject switch but the less common forms of topical theme, 10 have *no conjunction*. A similar pattern can be seen with topical theme 'genitive absolute participle'. For those clauses with a subject switch and aorist tense, 2 of 11 clauses with topical theme 'genitive absolute participle' have *no conjunction* whereas only 2 of 88 clauses with the baseline topical theme of 'verb' have *no conjunction*.

The effect of constituent order 'subject before verb, in first position' changes on adjustment for verbal tense-form and topical theme, this could be due to the structures shown in Table 14.

Table 14: *Numbers of clauses with asyndeton for various combinations of constituent order, verbal tense-form and topical theme*

Verbal tense-form & topical theme	Constituent Order			
	verb only	subject before verb, in first position	subject before verb, not in first position	verb followed by subject
aorist & verb	0/76	3/23	0	0/44
imperfect & verb	0/12	1/2	0	0/1
other & verb	0/1	2/3	0	0

The change can be understood by considering sentences with the verbal tense-forms and topical themes shown in Table 14. Of the sentences with those combinations, only those with constituent order 'subject before verb, in first position' have *no conjunction*.

Features that most noticeably affect the choice of having *no conjunction* as opposed to conjunction *kai* appear to be: verbal tense-forms 'present' and 'other', the less common topical themes and topical theme 'genitive absolute participle' and constituent order 'subject before verb, in first position'.

4.2(iii) *Interactions.* There are significant interactions between constituent order and subject switch, constituent order and topical theme and subject reference and subject switch. There are no significant interactions that involve speech margin, and the interaction between subject reference and subject switch loses its significance when the interaction between constituent order and subject switch is also included in the model. Consequently both the features speech margin and subject reference were still omitted from the model related to the choice of asyndeton vs. *kai*.

Further detailed investigation led to the inclusion of only one interaction term in the final model. This identified sentences with constituent order 'verb followed by subject' and a subject switch. The details are given subsequently, along with some additional tabulations based on the final model. One particular feature highlighted in these additional tabulations is that clauses with *no conjunction* appear to fall into two quite distinct structures: firstly, those with verbal tense-form of 'present' all have *lego* (finite) as speech margin, a subject switch, the baseline topical theme 'verb' and constituent orders 'subject before verb, in first position' or 'verb followed by subject'; secondly, clauses with the less common topical themes, predominantly verbal tense-form 'aorist', and which are generally not used as a speech margin. The effect of this on model interpretation is discussed.

The numbers of clauses of various types with no conjunction are shown in Tables 15 and 16.

Table 15: *Numbers of clauses with asyndeton for combinations of constituent order and subject switch*

	Constituent Order			
Subject switch	verb only	subject before verb, in first position	subject before verb, not in first position	verb followed by subject
no switch	4/87	1/1	1/1	6/13
switch	18/52	5/28	3/6	13/71

Table 16: *Numbers of clauses with asyndeton for combinations of constituent order and topical theme*

	Constituent Order			
Topical theme	verb only	subject before verb, in first position	subject before verb, not in first position	verb followed by subject
verb	17/124	6/29	0	9/59
genitive absolute participle	1/2	0	3/4	0/9[1]
other	4/13	0	1/3	10/16

Based on these tabulations it was decided to remove the two clauses with constituent orders 'subject before verb, in first position', 'subject before verb, not in first position' and no subject switch from the data set. Fisher's exact test provided no evidence of any difference between the distribution of conjunctions in these clauses and any other. The effect of these constituent orders may now be interpreted as always having a subject switch.

The interaction between constituent order 'verb followed by subject' and subject switch was then included in the model.

No interactions between topical theme and constituent order were included in the final model as the significant effect appears primarily to be caused by the interaction between constituent order and topical theme 'genitive absolute participle', and only 15 clauses in total are involved. The main feature of interest is that no clauses with a combination of constituent order 'verb followed by subject' and topical theme 'genitive absolute participle' have *no conjunction* despite the fact that the overall effect of that topical theme appears to be to increase the chance of having *no conjunction* as opposed to conjunction *kai*. Fisher's exact test shows that there is a significant difference between the number of clauses with *no conjunction* with this structure (Table 16[1]) and any other clauses with constituent order 'verb followed by subject' (with topical themes 'verb' or 'other') and clauses with constituent order 'subject before verb, not in first position' and topical theme 'genitive absolute participle' (that is to say, all the adjacent categories). This effect was not included in the final model as it only applies to 9 clauses and as has been previously mentioned effects on numbers this small are not included in the final model.

Including the interaction between constituent order 'verb followed by subject' and subject switch leads to the following model:

$$log\{pr(asyndeton)/[1-pr(asyndeton)]\}$$
$$= -7.01 + 1.79X_1 - 0.96X_2 + 1.65X_3 + 3.15X_4 + 5.04X_5$$
$$+ 0.21X_6 + 2.95X_7 + 3.69X_8 + 5.49X_9 - 2.78X_3X_4$$

where $X_1 - X_9$ are, respectively, constituent orders 'subject before verb, in first position', 'subject before verb, not in first position' and 'verb followed by subject', a subject switch, verbal tense-forms 'present', 'imperfect' and 'other' and topical themes 'genitive absolute participle' and 'other'.

Based on this model, the estimated odds ratio which compares the odds of the use of asyndeton vs. *kai* when the constituent order is 'verb followed by subject' and having a subject switch to the baseline categories of constituent order 'verb only' and 'no subject switch' (with all other features having the same classification) is $\exp[1.65+3.15-2.78] = 7.54$. Other estimated effects are shown in Tables 17 and 18.

Table 17: *Adjusted odds ratios calculated from the final model in the analysis of* asyndeton *vs.* kai

Feature	Adjusted odds ratios
Constituent order	
verb only*	1
subject before verb, in first position	0.26[a]
subject before verb, (not in first position)	0.02[a]
Verbal tense-form	
aorist*	1
present	154.96
imperfect	1.23
other	19.10
Topical theme	
verb*	1
genitive absolute participle	39.94
subject	NA
other	241.64

* Baseline category.

[a] Odds ratios comparing the effect of constituent orders 'subject before verb, in first position' and 'subject before verb, not in first position' to constituent order 'verb only' with a subject switch.

Table 18: *Adjusted odds ratios for combinations of constituent orders and subject switch*

Constituent order & Subject switch	
verb only & no switch	1
verb only & switch	23.43
verb followed by subject & no switch	5.22
verb followed by subject & switch	7.59

Table 18 shows that the effect of constituent order 'verb followed by subject' with a subject switch as opposed to without a subject switch gives an odds ratio of 0.32 (exp(1.65–2.78) = 7.59/23.43) as opposed to 5.22 (exp(1.65) = 5.22/1). Constituent order 'verb followed by subject' modifies the effect of having a subject switch giving an odds ratio of 1.45 (exp(3.15–2.78) = 7.59/5.22) as opposed to the odds ratio of 23.43 (exp(3.15) = 23.43/1) that applies only to a subject switch occurring with the baseline constituent order 'verb only'.

The effect of a subject switch with either a constituent order 'subject before verb, in first position' or 'subject before verb, not in first position' is the same as the effects for these constituent orders in Table 17. The only two clauses with these constituent orders and 'no subject switch' were removed from the data set, as previously mentioned.

Inspection of the data shows that clauses with *no conjunction* appear to fall into two quite distinct structures. Firstly, those with verbal tense-form of 'present' all have *lego* (finite) as speech margin, a subject switch, the baseline topical theme 'verb' and constituent orders 'subject before verb in first position' or 'verb followed by subject'. Of 35 clauses in the data set under consideration with this structure, 26 have *no conjunction*, 9 have conjunction *kai*. In the whole data set there are 41 clauses with this structure, the remaining 6 have conjunction *tote*.

Table 19: *The numbers of clauses with asyndeton for combinations of verbal tense-form and subject switch*

	Verbal Tense-Form			
Subject switch	aorist	present	imperfect	other
no switch	11/77	0/15	1/9	0/1
switch	8/106	26/35	2/12	3/4

There is clearly a significant difference in the number of clauses with *no conjunction* between the two highlighted cells in Table 19. (Fisher's exact test confirms this.) It is not possible to include interactions in the model between any of verbal tense-form, speech margin or subject switch to quantify the size of the effect because of the zeros or small numbers of clauses in some classifications.

Secondly, clauses with the less common topical themes, predominantly verbal tense-form 'aorist' and which are generally not used as a speech margin: of 27 sentences (in the data set under consideration) with verbal tense-form 'aorist' and the less common topical themes, 14 have *no conjunction*; of the 51 sentences with asyndeton, 26 have the first structure and 14 the second.

Table 20: *The numbers of clauses with asyndeton for combinations of verbal tense-form and topical theme*

	Verbal Tense-Form			
Topical theme	aorist	present	imperfect	other
verb	3/143	26/49	1/16	2/4
genitive absolute participle	2/13	0	1/1	1/1
other	14/27	0	1/4	0

It can be seen from Table 20 that only clauses of the first type have verbal tense-form 'present', and that consequently the odds ratios associated with verbal tense-form 'present' can be seen only to apply to clauses of that type. Similarly the odds ratios associated with the less common forms of topical themes, topical theme 'genitive absolute participle', and verbal tense-forms 'imperfect' and 'other', can be seen to apply only to clauses of the second type.

These findings are reflected in the estimated odds ratio associated with verbal tense-form 'present' which is 138.35, with a 95% confidence interval [18.52,1033.29], and the odds ratio associated with the less common topical themes which is 222.60 with a 95% confidence interval [26.41,1876.28].

4.3 *Analysis of* tote *vs.* kai

4.3(i) *Univariate analysis.* Initial analyses were carried out in order to assess the relationship between each grammatical feature and the choice of *tote* as opposed to *kai*.

An example of a model used (for the feature constituent order) is,

$$\log\{\mathrm{pr}(tote)/[1-\mathrm{pr}(tote)]\} = -2.42 + 1.48X_1 + 0.81X_2 + 1.23X_3 - 5.78X_4,$$

where X_1 corresponds to constituent order 'subject before verb, in first position', X_2 to 'subject before verb, not in first position', X_3 to 'verb followed by subject and X_4 to 'other'.

Based on this model it can be seen that the odds ratio which compares the odds of the use of *tote* vs. *kai*, when constituent order is 'subject before verb, in first position' ($X_1 = 1$) as opposed to the baseline constituent order 'verb only' is $\exp[1.48] = 4.39$.

Table 21: *Unadjusted odds ratios for all variables in the analysis of* tote *vs.* kai

Feature	Unadjusted odds ratios	*Tote*/total	P-value
Constituent order			<0.001
verb only*	1	17/208	
subject before verb, in first position	4.40	9/32	
subject before verb, (not in first position)	2.25	8/48	
verb followed by subject	3.42	21/90	
other	$-\infty$	0/12	

Subject switch			<0.001
no subject switch*	1	11/163	
subject switch	3.32	44/227	
Verbal tense-form			<0.001
aorist	1	34/310	
present	6.76	20/44	
imperfect	0.29	1/29	
other	$-\infty$	0/7	
Speech margin			0.081
not used as speech margin*	1	28/261	
lego (finite)	2.62	17/71	
phemi	$-\infty$	0/1	
lego (participle)	1.78	9/51	
other	1.66	1/6	
Topical theme			0.007
verb*	1	35/198	
other participle	0.45	11/126	
genitive absolute participle	$-\infty$	0/11	
subject	1.75	9/33	
other	$-\infty$	0/22	
Subject reference			<0.001
no reference*	1	17/217	
pronominal article	All *de*	0	
noun phrase	2.16	16/103	
proper noun	5.88	21/63	
other	1.96	1/7	

* Baseline category

It can be seen that the feature that has the most noticeable effect on the choice of *tote* is verbal tense-form 'present'. None of the effects are particularly large, with the exception of the less common constituent orders and topical themes, topical theme 'genitive absolute participle' and the less frequent verbal tense-forms, as in this data set they never occur with conjunction *tote*. All these represent categories with few clauses, however.

4.3(ii) *Multivariate analysis.* Clauses with the less common topical themes, topical theme 'genitive absolute participle' and the less frequent verbal tense-forms were removed from the data set. Speech margin remains insignificant after adjustment for all other features and was consequently removed from the model. Topical theme loses all significance as a feature once verbal tense-form is included in the model and consequently was removed. Subject switch loses all significance as a feature after adjustment for either constituent order or subject reference, and so was removed from the model. There are no apparent reasons for this, however, given the relatively small size of all the effects this is perhaps not surprising.

Finally, subject reference loses significance after adjustment for constituent order and verbal tense-form, but constituent order loses significance after adjustment for subject reference and verbal tense-form. However, removing both features simultaneously makes a significant difference.

Table 22: *The number of clauses with conjunction* tote *for combinations of constituent order and subject reference*

Subject reference	verb only	Constituent Order		
		subject before verb, in first position	subject before verb, not in first position	verb followed by subject
no reference	17/180			
noun phrase		3/22[2]	3/20	10/46
proper noun		6/7[1]	4/23	11/26
other		0/2	1/1	0/2

The only notable difference between the entries in Table 22 is between those labeled [1] and [2] (this interaction will be discussed later).

The numbers of clauses with conjunction *tote*, classified by categories of the two features separately, are shown in Tables 23 and 24.

Table 23: *The number of clauses with conjunction* tote *for all constituent orders*

	Constituent Order		
verb only	subject before verb, in first position	subject before verb, not in first position	verb followed by subject
17/197	9/31	8/44	21/75

Table 24: The number of clauses with conjunction *tote* for all subject references

	Subject reference		
no reference	noun phrase	proper noun	other
17/197	16/88	21/56	1/6

A model with constituent order and verbal tense-form was chosen, in order to avoid the possible problems caused by the small number of clauses with the less frequent subject references. This model leads to the adjusted odds ratios shown in Table 25.

Table 25: *Adjusted odds ratios calculated from the multivariate analysis of* tote *vs.* kai

Feature	Adjusted odds ratios
Constituent order	
verb only*	1
subject before verb, in first position	7.58
subject before verb, not in first posititon	3.96
verb followed by subject	3.73
Verbal tense-form	
aorist*	1
present	8.71
imperfect	0.32

* Baseline category

4.3(iii) *Interactions.* There are significant interactions between constituent order and subject reference, and subject reference and topical theme. However, the only interaction term included in the final model simply identified sentences with a subject reference 'proper noun' and constituent order 'subject before verb, in first position'. The details are given subsequently.

The numbers of clauses with conjunction *tote*, cross-classified by the features constituent order and subject reference, are shown in Tables 26 and 27.

Table 26: *The number of clauses with conjunction* tote *for combinations of constituent order and subject reference*

	Constituent Order			
Subject reference	verb only	subject before verb, in first position	subject before verb, not in first position	verb followed by subject
no reference	17/197			
noun phrase		3/22	3/20	10/46
proper noun		6/7	4/23	11/26
other		0/2	1/1	0/3

Table 27: *The number of clauses with conjunction* tote *for combinations of topical theme and subject reference*

	Topical Theme	
Subject reference	verb	other participle
no reference	14/120	3/77
noun phrase	13/66	3/22
proper noun	17/31[(2)]	4/25
other	0/5[(1)]	1/1

If the clauses with the less frequent subject references are removed from the data set the interaction between topical theme and subject reference loses significance. However, Fisher's exact test shows that there is evidence of a difference in the number of clauses with conjunction *tote*, between clauses with topical theme 'verb' and the less common forms of subject reference (Table 27[(1)]) and clauses with topical theme 'verb' and subject reference 'proper noun' (Table 27[(2)]). No other significant differences were found. The interaction between constituent order and subject reference remains significant, the most noticeable differences in effect being between subject reference 'proper noun' and constituent order 'subject before verb, in first position'. Although the number of sentences involved is small, given the fact that this effect was also noticeable in the analysis of *de* vs. *kai*,[2] it was decided to include this interaction in the final model, leading to

$$\log\{\text{pr(tote)}/[1\text{-pr(tote)}]\} = -2.67 + 0.97X_1 + 1.35X_2 + 1.30X_3 + 2.16X_4 - 0.96X_5 + 0.04X_6 + 0.15X_7 + 3.66X_1X_6$$

where $X_1 - X_7$ are, respectively, constituent orders 'subject before verb, in first position', 'subject before verb, not in first position' and 'verb followed by subject', verbal tense-forms 'present' and 'imperfect' and subject references 'proper noun' and 'other'.

It is necessary to remember that X_1, X_2 and X_3 should in fact be interpreted as the respective constituent orders with a subject reference 'noun phrase' due to the total confounding of the two baseline categories.

Based on this model, the estimated odds ratio which compares the odds of the use of *tote* vs. *kai* when the constituent order is 'subject before verb,

---

2.   In the complete data set there are 69 clauses with this combination; 60 have conjunction *de*, 6 conjunction *tote*, 1 *kai*, 1 asyndeton and 1 other.

in first position' and subject reference 'proper noun' to the baseline categories of constituent order 'verb only' and subject reference 'no reference' (with all other features having the same classification') is exp[0.97+ 0.04+3.66] = 106.70 (again the slight difference between this result and that shown in Table 28 is due to the rounding involved). In addition, the model leads to the estimates of effects shown in Tables 28 and 29.

Table 28: *Adjusted odds ratios for combinations of constituent orders and subject references (compared to the common baseline category) calculated from the final model in the analysis of* tote *vs.* kai

	Constituent Order			
Subject Reference	verb only	subject before verb, in first position	subject before verb, not in first position	verb followed by subject
no reference	1			
noun phrase		2.64	3.85	3.67
proper noun		105.59	1.38	3.80
other		3.07	4.49	4.27

Table 29: *Adjusted odds ratios calculated from the final model in the analysis of* tote *vs.* kai

Feature	Adjusted odds ratios
Verbal tense-form	
aorist*	1
present	8.70
imperfect	0.38

*Baseline category

As previously mentioned, the effects are relatively small. The only exception is the effect caused by a constituent order 'subject before verb, in first position' and subject reference 'proper noun'. This, however, is based on only seven clauses.

5. Conclusions

5.1 General Conclusions

It can be seen from the analysis already presented that the structures of clauses with different conjunctions are quite distinct. Variables that affect the choice of *de* over *kai* do not necessarily play any part in the choice of *no conjunction* or *tote*. There are, however, certain features that have a noticeable effect on the choice of more than one conjunction over the standard form *kai*.

To summarize: the variables that have the largest effects on the choice of *de* over *kai* are: all of the less common topical themes, a constituent order 'subject before verb, in first position', the less common verbal tense-forms and having a subject switch. There are noticeable interactions between constituent order 'subject before verb, in first position' and subject reference 'proper noun' and the less common forms of topical theme and subject switch. The variables that have the largest effect on the choice of asyndeton over *kai* are the less common topical themes and topical theme 'genitive absolute participle', the less common verbal tense-forms and verbal tense-form 'present', with an interaction between subject switch and constituent order 'verb followed by subject'. The variables that most noticeably affect the choice of *tote* over *kai* are constituent orders 'subject before verb, in first position' and 'verb followed by subject', subject reference 'proper noun', verbal tense-form 'present' with an interaction between constituent order 'subject before verb, in first position' and subject reference 'proper noun'.

It can be seen that the less common forms of topical theme, the less common verbal tense-forms and topical theme 'genitive absolute participle' affect the choice of both *de* and asyndeton over *kai*. A verbal tense-form 'present' noticeably affects the choice of both asyndeton and *tote* over *kai*. As previously mentioned the combination of constituent order 'subject before verb, in first position' and subject reference 'proper noun' significantly increases the chance of choosing both *de* and *tote* over *kai* (the effect is much larger for *de*).

There are some apparent differences in the structures of the clauses with the features mentioned above, which may indicate why one conjunction would be chosen over another.

Clauses with the less common topical themes and asyndeton differ from clauses with the less common topical themes and *de* in that those with asyndeton predominantly have no subject switch (11 out of 13 clauses do not have a subject switch), and those with *de* for the most part do (16 out of 20 have a subject switch). The particular structure of clauses with asyndeton and verbal tense-form 'present' has already been mentioned: of the 20 clauses with conjunction *tote* and verbal tense-form 'present', 6 have the same structure, whereas the others vary quite considerably.

There appear, however, to be no consistent differences between clauses with topical theme 'genitive absolute participle' and asyndeton and clauses with that topical theme but conjunction *de*. There also appear to be no consistent differences between clauses with the less common verbal tense-forms and asyndeton and clauses with those verbal tense-forms and conjunction *de*.

It can be seen that clauses with conjunction *de* and clauses with *no conjunction* are very different in structure from each other and from clauses with conjunction *kai*. The exception appears to be conjunction *tote*: few variables have a noticeable effect on its choice over *kai*, and those that do also affect the choice of either using *de* or having asyndeton.

5.2 Testing the Model and Prediction

An overall model was formed using the parameter estimates from the individualized regressions.

In order to examine the results further, it was decided to look at how accurately this model predicted the choice of conjunction. Each clause was systematically omitted from the data set, the parameters were estimated from the remaining clauses, and the probabilities of using *kai de*, *tote* and asyndeton in the omitted clause were then calculated. It transpires that the average probability of using *kai* in a clause that did in fact have conjunction *kai* is 69.65%, the average probability of using *de* in a clause that did in fact have conjunction *de* is 67.34%, the average probability of using asyndeton in a clause that did in fact have asyndeton is 41.35% and the average probability of using *tote* in a clause that did in fact have *tote* is 13.51%. The results are summarized in Table 30.

Table 30: *Average probabilities of using conjunctions in clauses*

Conjunction used in clause	pr(*kai*)%	pr(*de*)%	pr(*asyndeton*)%	pr(*tote*)%
kai	69.65	17.15	4.68	8.53
de	22.95	67.34	5.00	4.71
asyndeton	25.85	19.31	41.35	13.49
tote	38.50	22.71	25.29	13.51

These results would appear to indicate that the structures of clauses with conjunctions *kai* and *de* and asyndeton (no conjunction) are quite distinct. However, less distinct structures appear to be associated with *tote*.

Finally, as a summary of the model in terms of what it predicts about conjunction use, probabilities of using *kai*, *de*, *tote* and asyndeton for all possible sentence constructions[3] found in the data set were also calculated. The results are shown in Table 31. Note that of the 248 possible combinations of features that could occur only 74 actually occur.

The large number of structural and random zeros in the data set has already been mentioned. The possible combinations mentioned above do not include any combinations of variables that are known not to be able to occur, however, it is not possible to determine whether other structures that do not occur cannot (i.e. are structural zeros) or simply do not in the relatively small data set under consideration.

Looking at the probabilities of using all the conjunctions under consideration in all existing clauses it can be seen that there are high probabilities of using *kai*, *de* and asyndeton in various sentence structures; however, there is only one sentence structure where the highest probability corresponds to *tote* and only one clause is involved.

This bears out the previous conclusion that there are distinct structures associated with *kai*, *de* and asyndeton, but it could possibly be concluded that Matthew used *tote* as an option when variety was required.

List of Codings

Variable Names and Codes for Greek Syntactical Analysis

Intersentential Conjunction

1 *kai*		n = 335
2 *de*		n = 257
3 *tote*		n = 55
4 asyndeton		n = 57
5 other		n = 16
		total = 720

Constituent Order

1 verb only (V)	n = 262
2 subject before verb, in first position (S_1V)	n = 195
3 subject before verb, not in first position (S_2V)	n = 99
4 verb followed by subject (VS)	n = 149
5 other (verbless, subsequent verb) (0,+2)	n = 15
	total = 720

---

3.   The possible constructions are based on the features included in the final model.

Subject Switch

1 no switch from preceding clause   n = 202
2 switch from preceding clause   n = 518
(including clauses with no preceding clause)

                                                                        total = 720

Verbal Tense-Form

1 aorist   n = 553
2 present   n = 79
3 imperfect   n = 57
4 other (all the less common verbal tense-forms)   n = 31
                                                                        total = 720

Speech Margin

1 not used as speech margin   n = 421
2 *lego* (finite) in speech margin   n = 186
3 *phemi* in speech margin   n = 11
4 *lego* (participle) in speech margin   n = 92
5 other (*lego* infinitive in speech margin   n = 10
or other verb in speech margin)   total = 720

Topical Theme

1 verb   n = 248
2 other participle   n = 178
3 genitive absolute participle   n = 39
4 subject (= constituent order 'subject before verb,   n = 198
  in first position'*)
5 other (all the less common forms of topical theme)   n = 57
                                                                        total = 720

Subject Reference

1 no reference (= constituent order 'verb only'**)   n = 271
2 ap (conjunction always *de*,   n = 60
constituent order 'subject before verb, in first position')
3 noun phrase   n = 186
4 proper noun   n = 182
5 other (all the less common forms of subject reference)   n = 21
                                                                        total = 720

*195 constituent order 'subject before verb, in first position', 3 constituent order 'verbless'.

** 262 constituent order 'verb only', 9 constituent order 'subsequent verb'.

Table 31: Estimated probabilities of conjunction use for different sentence structures

Constituent Order	Verbal Tense Form	Topical Theme	Subject Reference	Subject Switch	PROB KAI %	PROB DE %	PROB ASYNDETON %	PROB TOTE %	KAI	DE	ASYNDETON	TOTE
verb only	aorist	verb or subject	no reference	no switch	92.91	1.73	0.08	5.28	52	0	0	3
verb only	aorist	verb or subject	no reference	switch	89.9	3.1	1.9	5.11	24	0	0	4
verb only	aorist	other participle	no reference	no switch	82.15	13.18	0	4.67	46	7	0	2
verb only	aorist	other participle	no reference	switch	73.85	21.95	0	4.2	24	7	0	1
verb only	aorist	genitive absolute participle	no reference	no switch	51.08	47.08	1.84	0	1	0	0	0
verb only	aorist	genitive absolute participle	no reference	switch	28.16	48.08	23.76	0	0	2	1	0
verb only	aorist	other	no reference	no switch	74.18	9.66	16.16	0	7	2	4	0
verb only	aorist	other	no reference	switch	12.93	21.06	66	0	1	2	0	0
verb only	present	verb or subject	no reference	no switch	60.57	1.01	8.46	29.96	14	0	0	5
verb only	present	verb or subject	no reference	switch	20.84	0.64	68.21	10.31	4	0	17	2

Constituent Order	Verbal Tense Form	Topical Theme	Subject Reference	Subject Switch	PROB KAI %	PROB DE %	PROB ASYNDETON %	PROB TOTE %	KAI	DE	ASYNDETON	TOTE
verb only	imperfect	verb or subject	no reference	no switch	94.92	2.92	0.11	2.06	7	2	0	0
verb only	imperfect	verb or subject	no reference	switch	90.54	5.15	2.35	1.96	5	1	0	0
verb only	imperfect	other	no reference	no switch	77.73	20.59	0	1.68	4	0	0	0
verb only	imperfect	genitive absolute participle	no reference	switch	20.6	58.04	21.35	0	0	1	0	0
verb only	imperfect	other	no reference	no switch	67.45	14.5	18.05	0	1	0	0	0
verb only	other	verb or subject	no reference	switch	48.89	50.27	0.84	0	1	0	0	0
verb only	other	genitive absolute participle	no reference	no switch	1.9	96.79	1.31	0	0	1	0	0
subject before verb in first position	aorist	verb or subject	noun phrase	switch	41.74	46.73	5.29	6.25	18	18	1	3

Constituent Order	Verbal Tense Form	Topical Theme	Subject Reference	Subject Switch	PROB KAI %	PROB DE %	PROB ASYNDETON %	PROB TOTE %	KAI	DE	ASYNDETON	TOTE
subject before verb, in first position	aorist	verb or subject	proper noun	no switch	2.58	81.94	0.01	15.47	0	0	0	1
subject before verb, in first position	aorist	verb or subject	other	no switch	37.18	56.13	0.2	6.49	0	0	1	0
subject before verb, in first position	aorist	verb or subject	other	switch	24.41	68.24	3.09	4.26	1	2	0	0
subject before verb, in first position	present	verb or subject	proper noun	switch	0.8	41.99	15.63	41.58	0	2	0	0
subject before verb, in first position	imperfect	verb or subject	noun phrase	switch	32.68	60.37	5.09	1.86	1	9	1	0

Constituent Order	Verbal Tense Form	Topical Theme	Subject Reference	Subject Switch	PROB KAI %	PROB DE %	PROB ASYNDETON %	PROB TOTE %	KAI	DE	ASYNDETON	TOTE
subject before verb, in first position	imperfect	verb or subject	proper noun	switch	0.99	96.58	0.15	2.27	0	3	0	0
subject before verb, in first position	imperfect	verb or subject	other	no switch	28.06	69.89	0.19	1.87	0	1	0	0
subject before verb, in first position	imperfect	verb or subject	other	switch	17.14	79.06	2.67	1.14	1	1	0	0
subject before verb, in first position	other	verb or subject	noun phrase	switch	1.53	94.76	3.71	0	1	3	1	0
subject before verb, in first position	other	verb or subject	other	switch	0.63	97.83	1.53	0	0	1	1	0

Constituent Order	Verbal Tense Form	Topical Theme	Subject Reference	Subject Switch	PROB KAI %	PROB DE %	PROB ASYNDETON %	PROB TOTE %	KAI	DE	ASYNDETON	TOTE
subject before verb, not in first position	aorist	other participle	noun phrase	switch	54.92	33.07	0	12.02	16	7	0	2
subject before verb, not in first position	aorist	other participle	proper noun	no switch	53.7	34.12	0	12.17	2	1	0	0
subject before verb, not in first position	aorist	other participle	proper noun	switch	41.61	48.96	0	9.43	14	26	0	4
subject before verb, not in first position	aorist	other participle	other	switch	36.25	54.51	0	9.24	0	0	0	1
subject before verb, not in first position	aorist	genitive absolute participle	noun phrase	switch	20.92	72.33	6.75	0	0	3	1	0

Constituent Order	Verbal Tense Form	Topical Theme	Subject Reference	Subject Switch	PROB KAI %	PROB DE %	PROB ASYNDETON %	PROB TOTE %	KAI	DE	ASYNDETON	TOTE
subject before verb, not in first position	aorist	genitive absolute participle	proper noun	no switch	21.44	78.26	0.3	0	0	1	0	0
subject before verb, not in first position	aorist	genitive absolute participle	other	switch	10.04	86.72	3.24	0	1	0	0	0
subject before verb, not in first position	aorist	other	noun phrase	switch	15.99	52.77	31.24	0	0	3	0	0
subject before verb, not in first position	aorist	other	proper noun	no switch	62.53	32.25	5.21	0	0	0	1	0
subject before verb, not in first position	aorist	other	proper noun	switch	10.64	68.59	20.78	0	1	1	0	0

Constituent Order	Verbal Tense Form	Topical Theme	Subject Reference	Subject Switch	PROB KAI %	PROB DE %	PROB ASYNDETON %	PROB TOTE %	KAI	DE	ASYNDETON	TOTE
subject before verb, not in first position	present	other participle	noun phrase	switch	29.03	15.67	0	55.3	0	0	0	1
subject before verb, not in first position	present	genitive absolute participle	noun phrase	switch	1.82	5.72	92.43	0	0	2	0	0
subject before verb, not in first position	imperfect	other participle	noun phrase	switch	48.15	47.84	0	4.02	2	1	0	0
subject before verb, not in first position	imperfect	other participle	proper noun	no switch	46.84	49.12	0	4.05	1	0	0	0
subject before verb, not in first position	imperfect	other participle	proper noun	switch	33.02	64.13	0	2.85	2	0	0	0

Constituent Order	Verbal Tense Form	Topical Theme	Subject Reference	Subject Switch	PROB KAI %	PROB DE %	PROB ASYNDETON %	PROB TOTE %	KAI	DE	ASYNDETON	TOTE
subject before verb, not in first position	imperfect	genitive absolute participle	noun phrase	switch	14.08	80.34	5.58	0	0	0	1	0
subject before verb, not in first position	imperfect	other	noun phrase	switch	11.31	61.56	27.14	0	1	1	0	0
subject before verb, not in first position	other	genitive absolute participle	noun phrase	switch	0.5	96.38	3.11	0	0	0	1	0
subject before verb, not in first position	other	other	noun phrase	switch	0.45	82.63	16.91	0	0	1	0	0
verb followed by subject	aorist	verb or subject	noun phrase	switch	73.93	2.51	8.15	15.41	33	0	0	8

Constituent Order	Verbal Tense Form	Topical Theme	Subject Reference	Subject Switch	PROB KAI %	PROB DE %	PROB ASYNDETON %	PROB TOTE %	KAI	DE	ASYNDETON	TOTE
verb followed by subject	aorist	verb or subject	proper noun	no switch	79.59	2.85	0.37	17.18	2	0	0	0
verb followed by subject	aorist	verb or subject	proper noun	switch	71.81	4.77	7.91	15.5	6	0	4	0
verb followed by subject	aorist	verb or subject	other	switch	69.55	5.9	7.66	16.88	3	1	1	0
verb followed by subject	aorist	other participle	noun phrase	no switch	73.17	11.58	0	15.25	0	1	0	0
verb followed by subject	aorist	other participle	noun phrase	switch	66.6	19.52	0	13.88	2	1	0	0
verb followed by subject	aorist	other participle	proper noun	switch	55.91	32.02	0	12.07	2	0	0	0

Constituent Order	Verbal Tense Form	Topical Theme	Subject Reference	Subject Switch	PROB KAI %	PROB DE %	PROB ASYNDETON %	PROB TOTE %	KAI	DE	ASYNDETON	TOTE
verb followed by subject	aorist	other participle	other	switch	50.64	37.07	0	12.29	0	1	0	0
verb followed by subject	aorist	genitive absolute participle	noun phrase	no switch	47.69	43.35	8.96	0	1	0	0	0
verb followed by subject	aorist	genitive absolute participle	noun phrase	switch	33.82	56.93	9.24	0	7	8	0	0
verb followed by subject	aorist	genitive absolute participle	proper noun	no switch	33.73	59.93	6.34	0	0	4	0	0
verb followed by subject	aorist	genitive absolute participle	proper noun	switch	21.91	72.1	5.99	0	1	0	0	0
verb followed by subject	aorist	genitive absolute participle	other	switch	18.26	76.75	4.99	0	0	1	0	0

Constituent Order	Verbal Tense Form	Topical Theme	Subject Reference	Subject Switch	PROB KAI %	PROB DE %	PROB ASYNDETON %	PROB TOTE %	KAI	DE	ASYNDETON	TOTE
verb followed by subject	aorist	other	noun phrase	switch	23.48	37.71	38.82	0	0	4	2	0
verb followed by subject	aorist	other	proper noun	no switch	41.88	10.52	47.6	0	3	0	5	0
verb followed by subject	aorist	other	proper noun	switch	17.26	54.19	28.54	0	1	1	2	0
verb followed by subject	present	verb or subject	noun phrase	switch	5.02	0.15	85.72	9.1	1	0	2	2
verb followed by subject	present	verb or subject	proper noun	switch	5	0.3	85.32	9.39	4	0	6	10
verb followed by subject	present	verb or subject	other	switch	4.93	0.38	84.27	10.43	0	0	1	0

Constituent Order	Verbal Tense Form	Topical Theme	Subject Reference	Subject Switch	PROB KAI %	PROB DE %	PROB ASYNDETON %	PROB TOTE %	KAI	DE	ASYNDETON	TOTE
verb followed by subject	present	other	proper noun	no switch	0.56	0.13	99.31	0	1	0	0	0
verb followed by subject	present	other	proper noun	switch	0.38	1.08	98.53	0	0	1	0	0
verb followed by subject	imperfect	verb or subject	proper noun	switch	75.34	8.26	10.2	6.2	1	0	0	1
verb followed by subject	imperfect	other	noun phrase	switch	17.6	46.65	35.75	0	1	0	0	0
verb followed by subject	imperfect	other	proper noun	no switch	35.58	14.74	49.68	0	0	0	1	0
verb followed by subject	other	verb or subject	noun phrase	switch	33.24	62.42	4.34	0	0	4	0	0
verb followed by subject	other	other	noun phrase	switch	0.82	73.15	26.03	0	0	2	0	0

BIBLIOGRAPHY

I. *General Linguistics*

A. *General Linguistics, Discourse Analysis, and Discourse Processing*

Andrews, A., 'The Major Functions of the Noun Phrase', in T. Shopen (ed.), *Language Typology and Syntactic Description*. I. *Clause Structure* (Cambridge: Cambridge University Press, 1985), pp. 62-154.

Andrews, E., *Markedness Theory: The Union of Asymmetry and Semiosis in Language* (Durham, NC: Duke University Press, 1990).

Battistella, E.L., *Markedness: The Evaluative Superstructure of Language* (Albany: State University of New York Press, 1990).

Blakemore, D., *Understanding Utterances* (Oxford: Basil Blackwell, 1992).

—'Relevance Theory', in J. Verschueren, J. Ostman and J. Blommaert (eds.), *Handbook of Pragmatics: Manual* (Amsterdam: John Benjamins, 1995).

Blass, R., *Relevance Relations in Discourse: A Study with Special Reference to Sissala* (Cambridge: Cambridge University Press, 1990).

Bloomfield, L., *Language* (London: George Allen & Unwin, 1935).

Bolinger, D., *Meaning and Form* (London: Longman, 1977).

Brown, G., and G. Yule, *Discourse Analysis* (CTL; Cambridge: Cambridge University Press, 1983).

Chafe, W., *Discourse, Consciousness, and Time: The Flow and Displacement of Conscious Experience in Speaking and Writing* (Chicago: University of Chicago Press, 1994).

Comrie, B., *Aspect: An Introduction to the Study of Verbal Aspect and Related Problems* (CTL; Cambridge: Cambridge University Press, 1976).

Crystal, D., *A Dictionary of Linguistics and Phonetics* (Oxford: Basil Blackwell, 4th edn, 1997).

De Saussure, F., *Course in General Linguistics* (trans. W. Baskin; London: Collins, 1974).

Dik, S.C., *Coordination: Its Implications for the Theory of General Linguistics* (Amsterdam: North-Holland Publishing Company, 1972).

—*Studies in Functional Grammar* (London: Academic Press, 1980).

Givón, T., 'From Discourse to Syntax: Grammar as a Processing Strategy', in *idem* (ed.), *Syntax and Semantics*. XII. *Discourse and Syntax* (New York: Academic Press, 1979), pp. 81-112.

—'Topic Continuity in Discourse: An Introduction', in *idem* (ed.), *Topic Continuity in Discourse: A Quantitative Cross-Language Study* (Amsterdam and Philadelphia: John Benjamins, 1983), pp. 1-42.

—*Functionalism and Grammar* (Amsterdam: John Benjamins, 1995).

Givón, T. (ed.), *Syntax and Semantics*. XII. *Discourse and Syntax* (New York: Academic Press, 1979).

Goldman, S.R., A.C. Graesser and P. van den Broek (eds.), *Narrative Comprehension, Causality, and Coherence: Essays in Honor of Tom Trabasso* (Hillsdale, NJ: Lawrence Erlbaum Associates, 1999).

Greenberg, J.H., *Language Universals: With Special Reference to Feature Hierarchies* (The Hague: Mouton, 1966).

Grice, H.P., 'Logic and Conversation', in P. Cole and J.L. Morgan (eds.), *Syntax and Semantics*. III. *Speech Acts* (New York: Academic Press, 1975), pp. 41-58.

—*Studies in the Way of Words* (Cambridge, MA: Harvard University Press, 1989).

Grimes, J.E., *The Thread of Discourse* (Janua Linguarum Series Minor, 207; The Hague: Mouton, 1975).

Halliday, M.A.K., *Explorations in the Functions of Language* (London: Edward Arnold, 1973).

—'A Brief Sketch of Systemic Grammar', in G.R. Kress (ed.), *Halliday: System and Function in Language* (Oxford: Oxford University Press, 1976), pp. 3-6.

—*Language as Social Semiotic* (London: Edward Arnold, 1978).

—'Dimensions of Discourse Analysis: Grammar', in T.A. van Dijk (ed.), *Handbook of Discourse Analysis*. II. *Dimensions of Discourse* (London: Academic Press, 1985), pp. 29-56.

—*An Introduction to Functional Grammar* (London: Edward Arnold, 2nd edn, 1994).

Halliday, M.A.K., and R. Hasan, *Cohesion in English* (London: Longman, 1976).

—*Language, Context, and Text: Aspects of Language in a Social-Semiotic Perspective* (Victoria, Australia: Deakin University, 1985).

Hinds, J., 'Organizational Patterns in Discourse', in T. Givón (ed.), *Syntax and Semantics*. XII. *Discourse and Syntax* (New York: Academic Press, 1979), pp. 135-57.

Hopper, P.J., 'Aspect and Foregrounding in Discourse', in T. Givón (ed.), *Syntax and Semantics*. XII. *Discourse and Syntax* (New York: Academic Press, 1979), pp. 213-41.

Johnson-Laird, P.N., *Mental Models: Toward a Cognitive Science of Language, Inference, and Consciousness* (Cambridge: Cambridge University Press, 1983).

Johnstone, B., ' "He Says … So I Said": Verb Tense Alternation and Narrative Depictions of Authority in American English', *Linguistics* 25 (1987), pp. 33-52.

Kempson, R.M. (ed.), *Mental Representations: The Interface between Language and Reality* (Cambridge: Cambridge University Press, 1988).

Kintsch, W., and T.A. van Dijk, 'Towards a Model of Text Comprehension and Production', *Psychological Review* 85 (1978), pp. 363-94.

Kress, G. (ed.), *Halliday: System and Function in Language* (Oxford: Oxford University Press, 1976).

Levinson, S.C., *Pragmatics* (CTL; Cambridge: Cambridge University Press, 1983).

Li, C.N. (ed.), *Subject and Topic* (New York: Academic Press, 1976).

Li, C.N., and S.A. Thompson, 'Subject and Topic: A New Typology of Language', in C.N. Li (ed.), *Subject and Topic* (New York: Academic Press, 1976), pp. 457-89.

Locke, J., *An Essay Concerning Human Understanding* (ed. P.H. Nidditch; Oxford: Clarendon Press, 1975).

Longacre, R.E., 'The Paragraph as a Grammatical Unit', in T. Givón (ed.), *Syntax and Semantics*. XII. *Discourse and Syntax* (New York: Academic Press, 1979), pp. 115-34.

Luelsdorff, P.A. (ed.), *The Prague School of Structural and Functional Linguistics* (Linguistic and Literary Studies in Eastern Europe, 41; Amsterdam: John Benjamins, 1994).

Lyons, J., *Introduction to Theoretical Linguistics* (Cambridge: Cambridge University Press, 1968).

Minsky, M., 'A Framework for Representing Knowledge', in P.H. Winston (ed.), *The Psychology of Computer Vision* (New York: McGraw–Hill, 1975), pp. 211-77.

Nesbitt, C., and G. Plum, 'Probabilities in a Systemic-Functional Grammar: The Clause Complex in English', in R.P. Fawcett and D. Young (eds.), *New Developments in Systemic Linguistics. II. Theory and Application* (Open Linguistics Series; London: Pinter Publishers, 1988), pp. 6-38.

Ochs, E., 'Planned and Unplanned Discourse', in T. Givón (ed.), *Syntax and Semantics. XII. Discourse and Syntax* (New York: Academic Press, 1979), pp. 51-80.

Rickheit, G., and C. Habel (eds.), *Focus and Coherence in Discourse Processing* (New York: W. de Gruyter, 1995).

Robins, R.H., *A Short History of Linguistics* (London: Longman, 2nd edn, 1979).

Schank, R.C., and R.P. Abelson, *Scripts, Plans, Goals and Understanding* (Hillsdale, NJ: Lawrence Erlbaum, 1977).

Schank, R.C., and M. Burstein, 'Artificial Intelligence: Modeling Memory for Language Understanding', in T.A. van Dijk (ed.), *Handbook of Discourse Analysis. I. Disciplines of Discourse* (London: Academic Press, 1985), pp. 145-66.

Sinclair, J.McH., and R.M. Coulthard, *Towards an Analysis of Discourse: The English Used by Teachers and Pupils* (London: Oxford University Press, 1975).

Sperber, D., and D. Wilson, *Relevance: Communication and Cognition* (Oxford: Basil Blackwell, 2nd edn, 1995).

Stubbs, M., *Discourse Analysis: The Sociolinguistic Analysis of Natural Language* (Language in Society, 4; Oxford: Basil Blackwell, 1983).

Vachek, J. (ed.), *Praguiana: Some Basic and Less Known Aspects of the Prague Linguistic School* (Prague: Academia, 1983).

Van Dijk, T.A., *Text and Context: Explorations in the Semantics and Pragmatics of Discourse* (Longman Linguistics Library, 12; London: Longman, 1977).

Van Dijk, T.A., and W. Kintsch, *Strategies of Discourse Comprehension* (New York: Academic Press, 1983).

Wallace, S., 'Figure and Ground: The Interrelationships of Linguistic Categories', in P.J. Hopper (ed.), *Tense-Aspect: Between Semantics and Pragmatics* (Amsterdam: John Benjamins, 1982), pp. 201-23.

Weaver, C.A., S. Mannes and C.R. Fletcher (eds.), *Discourse Comprehension: Essays in Honor of Walter Kintsch* (Hillsdale, NJ: Lawrence Erlbaum Associates, 1995).

B. *Discourse Connectives*

Bestgen, Y., 'Segmentation Markers as Trace and Signal of Discourse Structure', *Journal of Pragmatics* 29 (1998), pp. 753-63.

Bestgen, Y., and W. Vonk, 'The Role of Temporal Segmentation Markers in Discourse Processing', *Discourse Processes* 19 (1995), pp. 385-406.

Blakemore, D., *Semantic Constraints on Relevance* (Oxford: Basil Blackwell, 1987).

Fraser, B., 'An Approach to Discourse Markers', *Journal of Pragmatics* 14 (1990) pp. 383-95.

—'Contrastive Discourse Markers in English', in A.H. Jucker and Y. Ziv (eds.), *Discourse Markers: Descriptions and Theory* (Pragmatics and Beyond NS 57; Amsterdam: John Benjamins, 1998), pp. 301-26.

—'What Are Discourse Markers?', *Journal of Pragmatics* 31 (1999), pp. 931-52.

Georgakopoulou, A., and D. Goutsos, 'Conjunctions versus Discourse Markers in Greek: The Interaction of Frequency, Position, and Functions in Context', *Linguistics* 36 (1998), pp. 887-917.

Hansen, M.-B.M., *The Function of Discourse Particles: A Study with Special Reference to Spoken Standard French* (Pragmatics and Beyond NS 53; Amsterdam: John Benjamins, 1998).

—'The Semantics Status of Discourse Markers', *Lingua* 104 (1998), pp. 235-60.

Kroon, C., *Discourse Particles in Latin: A Study of* nam, enim, autem, vero *and* at (ASCP, 4; Amsterdam: J.C. Gieben, 1995).

—'Discourse Markers, Discourse Structure and Functional Grammar', in J.H. Connolly, R.M. Vismans, C. Butler and R.A. Gatward (eds.), *Discourse and Pragmatics in Functional Grammar* (Berlin: W. de Gruyter, 1997), pp. 17-32.

—'A Framework for the Description of Latin Discourse Markers', *Journal of Pragmatics* 30 (1998), pp. 205-23.

Millis, K.K., and M.A. Just, 'The Influence of Connectives on Sentence Comprehension', *Journal of Memory and Language* 33 (1994), pp. 128-47.

Millis, K.K., J.M. Golding and G. Barker, 'Causal Connectives Increase Inference Generation', *Discourse Processes* 20 (1995), pp. 29-49.

Murray, J.D., 'Connectives and Narrative Text: The Role of Continuity', *Memory & Cognition* 25 (1997), pp. 227-36.

Redeker, G., 'Ideational and Pragmatic Markers of Discourse Structure', *Journal of Pragmatics* 14 (1990), pp. 367-81.

—'Linguistic Markers of Discourse Structure', *Linguistics* 29 (1991), pp. 1139-72.

Risselada, R., and W. Spooren (eds.), 'Special Issue on: "Discourse Markers and Coherence Relations" ', *Journal of Pragmatics* 30 (1998).

Rouchota, V., 'Discourse Connectives: What Do They Link?', *UCL Working Papers in Linguistics* 8 (1996), pp. 199-212.

Schenkeveld, D.M., 'From Particula to Particle—The Genesis of a Class of Words', in I. Rosier (ed.), *L'Héritage des grammairiens latins de l'antiquité aux lumières: Actes du Colloque de Chantilly, 2-4 Septembre 1987* (Paris: Société pour l'information grammaticale, 1988), pp. 81-93.

Schiffrin, D., 'Functions of *And* in Discourse', *Journal of Pragmatics* 10 (1986), pp. 41-66.

—*Discourse Markers* (Cambridge: Cambridge University Press, 1987).

Schleppegrell, M.J., 'Paratactic *because*', *Journal of Pragmatics* 16 (1991), pp. 323-37.

Segal, E.M., J.F. Duchan and P.J. Scott, 'The Role of Interclausal Connectives in Narrative Structuring: Evidence From Adults' Interpretations of Simple Stories', *Discourse Processes* 14 (1991), pp. 27-54.

Shoroup, L., 'Discourse Markers', *Lingua* 107 (1999), pp. 227-65.

Unger, C., 'The Scope of Discourse Connectives: Implications for Discourse Organization', *Journal of Linguistics* 32 (1996), pp. 403-38.

Wierzbicka, A., 'Introduction', in *idem* (ed.), 'Special Issue on "Particles" ', *Journal of Pragmatics* 10 (1986), pp. 519-34.

Wilson, D., and D. Sperber, 'Linguistic Form and Relevance', *Lingua* 90 (1993), pp. 1-25.

C. *Corpus Linguistics and Quantitative Analysis*

Aijmer, K., and B. Altenberg (eds.), *English Corpus Linguistics: Studies in Honour of Jan Svartvik* (London: Longman, 1991).

Barnbrook, G., *Language and Computers: A Practical Introduction to the Computer Analysis of Language* (ETEL; Edinburgh: Edinburgh University Press, 1996).

Biber, D., S. Conrad and R. Reppen, *Corpus Linguistics: Investigating Language Structure and Use* (Cambridge Approaches to Linguistics; Cambridge: Cambridge University Press, 1998).

Chase, W., and F. Brown, *General Statistics* (New York: John Wiley & Sons, 2nd edn, 1992).

Christensen, L.B., and C.M. Stoup, *Introduction to Statistics for the Social and Behavioral Sciences* (Pacific Grove, CA: Brooks/Cole, 2nd edn, 1991).

Garside, R., G. Leech and A. McEnery (eds.), *Corpus Annotation: Linguistic Information from Computer Text Corpora* (London: Longman, 1997).

Halliday, M.A.K., 'Corpus Studies and Probabilistic Grammar', in K. Aijmer and B. Altenberg (eds.), *English Corpus Linguistics: Studies in Honour of Jan Svartvik* (London: Longman, 1991), pp. 30-43.

—'Language as System and Language as Instance: The Corpus as a Theoretical Construct', in J. Svartvik (ed.), *Directions in Corpus Linguistics: Proceedings of Nobel Symposium 82, Stockholm, 4-8 August 1991* (Berlin: Mouton de Gruyter, 1992), pp. 61-77.

Leech, G., 'The State of the Art in Corpus Linguistics', in K. Aijmer and B. Altenberg (eds.), *English Corpus Linguistics: Studies in Honour of Jan Svartvik* (London: Longman, 1991), pp. 8-29.

—'Corpora and Theories of Linguistic Performance', in J. Svartvik (ed.), *Directions in Corpus Linguistics: Proceedings of Nobel Symposium 82, Stockholm, 4-8 August 1991* (Berlin: Mouton de Gruyter, 1992), pp. 105-22.

McEnery, T., and A. Wilson, *Corpus Linguistics* (ETEL; Edinburgh: Edinburgh University Press, 1996).

Nerbonne, J., 'Introduction', in *idem* (ed.), *Linguistic Databases* (Stanford, CA: CSLI Publications, 1998), pp. 1-12.

Oakes, M.P. *Statistics for Corpus Linguistics* (ETEL; Edinburgh: Edinburgh University Press, 1998).

Sigurd, B., 'Comments', in J. Svartvik (ed.), *Directions in Corpus Linguistics: Proceedings of Nobel Symposium 82, Stockholm, 4-8 August 1991* (Berlin: Mouton de Gruyter, 1992), pp. 123-25.

Svartvik, J. (ed.), *Directions in Corpus Linguistics: Proceedings of Nobel Symposium 82, Stockholm, 4-8 August 1991* (Berlin: Mouton de Gruyter, 1992).

Woods, A., P. Fletcher and A. Hughes, *Statistics in Languages Studies* (CTL; Cambridge: Cambridge University Press, 1986).

II. *Greek Language*

A. *Grammars, Lexicons, Critical Texts and Other Reference Works*

Abbott, E.A., *Johannine Grammar* (London: Adam & Charles Black, 1906).

Aland, B., K. Aland and J. Karavidopoulos, C.M. Martini and B.M. Metzger (eds.), *The Greek New Testament* (Stuttgart: United Bible Societies, 4th edn, 1993).

Black, D.A., *Learn to Read New Testament Greek* (Nashville: Broadman & Holman, expanded edn, 1994).

—*It's Still Greek to Me: An Easy-to-Understand Guide to Intermediate Greek* (Grand Rapids: Baker, 1998).

Blass, F., *Grammatik des Neutestamentlichen Griechisch* (Göttingen: Vandenhoeck & Ruprecht, 1896).

—*Grammar of New Testament Greek* (trans. H.StJ. Thackeray; London: Macmillan, 1898).

—*Grammatik des neutestamentlichen Griechisch* (revised F. Rehkopf; Göttingen: Vandenhoeck & Ruprecht, 15th edn, 1979).

Dana, H.E., and J.R. Mantey, *A Manual Grammar of the Greek New Testament* (Toronto: Macmillan, 1927).

Deissmann, A., *Bibelstudien: Beiträge, zumeist aus den Papyri und Inschriften, zur Geschichte der Sprache, des Schrifttums und der Religion des hellenistischen Judentums und des Urchristentums* (Marburg: Elwert'sche Verlagsbuchhandlung, 1895).

—*Neue Bibelstudien: Sprachgeschichtliche Beiträge, zumeist aus den Papyri und Inschriften, zur Erklärung des Neuen Testaments* (Marburg: Elwert'sche Verlagsbuchhandlung, 1897).

—*Bible Studies: Contributions Chiefly from Papyri and Inscriptions to the History of the Language, the Literature, and the Religion of Hellenistic Judaism and Primitive Christianity* (trans. A. Grieve; Edinburgh: T. & T. Clark, 1901).

—*Licht vom Osten: Das Neue Testament und die neuentdeckten Texte der hellenistisch-römischen Welt* (Tübingen: J.C.B. Mohr [Paul Siebeck], 1908).

—*Light from the Ancient East: The New Testament Illustrated by Recently Discovered Texts of the Graeco-Roman World* (trans. L.R.M. Strachan; London: Hodder & Stoughton, 1910).

Dik, H., *Word Order in Ancient Greek: A Pragmatic Account of Word Order Variation in Herodotus* (ASCP, 5; Amsterdam: J.C. Gieben, 1995).

Dionysius Thrax, *Grammatike*, in I. Bekkeri, *Anecdota Graeca*, II (Berlin: Georg Reimer, 1816).

Donaldson, J.W., *A Complete Greek Grammar for the Use of Students* (Cambridge: Deighton Bell, 3rd edn, 1862).

Dover, K.J., *Greek Word Order* (Cambridge: Cambridge University Press, 1960).

Fanning, B.M., *Verbal Aspect in New Testament Greek* (Oxford Theological Monographs; Oxford: Clarendon Press, 1990).

Hawkins, J.C., *Horae Synopticae* (Oxford: Clarendon Press, 1909).

Kühner, R., and B. Gerth, *Ausführliche Grammatik der griechischen Sprache*. II. *Satzlehre* (Leipzig: Hahnsche, 1904).

Louw, J.P., and E.A. Nida (eds.), *Greek–English Lexicon of the New Testament Based on Semantic Domains* (New York: United Bible Societies, 2nd edn, 1989).

Mayser, E., *Grammatik der Griechischen Papyri aus der Ptolemäerzeit*. II/3. *Satzlehre, Synthetischer Teil* (Berlin: W. de Gruyter, 1934).

McKay, K.L., *A New Syntax of the Verb in New Testament Greek* (SBG, 5; New York: Peter Lang, 1993).

Morgenthaler, R., *Statistik des Neutestamentlichen Wortschatzes* (Zürich: Gotthelf-Verlag, 1958).

Moule, C.F.D., *An Idiom Book of New Testament Greek* (Cambridge: Cambridge University Press, 2nd edn, 1959).

Moulton, J.H., *A Grammar of New Testament Greek*. I. *Prolegomena* (Edinburgh: T. & T. Clark, 3rd edn, 1908).

Nestle, E., and K. Aland (eds.), *Novum Testamentum Graece* (Stuttgart: Deutsche Bibelstiftung, 27th edn, 1993).

Nida, E.A., and J.P. Louw, *Lexical Semantics of the Greek New Testament: A Supplement to the Greek–English Lexicon of the New Testament Based on Semantic Domains* (SBLRBS, 25; Atlanta: Scholars Press, 1992).

Porter, S.E., *Verbal Aspect in the Greek of the New Testament, with Reference to Tense and Mood* (SBG, 1; New York: Peter Lang, 2nd edn, 1993).

—*Idioms of the Greek New Testament* (Biblical Languages: Greek, 2; Sheffield: Sheffield Academic Press, 2nd edn, 1994).

Robertson, A.T., *A Grammar of the Greek New Testament in the Light of Historical Research* (Nashville: Broadman Press, 4th edn, 1934 [1906]).

Schwyzer, E., *Griechische Grammatik auf der Grundlage von Karl Brugmanns Griechischer Grammatik. II. Syntax und Syntaktische Stilistik* (ed. A. Debrunner; Munich: C.H. Beck, 5th edn, 1988).

Smyth, H.W., *Greek Grammar* (revised G. Messing; Cambridge, MA: Harvard University Press, 1956).

Swanson, R.J. (ed.), *New Testament Greek Manuscripts: Matthew: Variant Readings Arranged in Horizontal Lines against Codex Vaticanus* (Sheffield: Sheffield Academic Press, 1995).

Turner, E.G., *Greek Papyri: An Introduction* (Oxford: Clarendon Press, 1968).

Turner, N., *A Grammar of New Testament Greek. III. Syntax* (Edinburgh: T. & T. Clark, 1963).

—*A Grammar of New Testament Greek. IV. Style* (Edinburgh: T. & T. Clark, 1976).

Wallace, D.B., *Greek Grammar Beyond the Basics: An Exegetical Syntax of the New Testament* (Grand Rapids: Zondervan, 1996).

Winer, G.B., *Grammatik des neutestamentlichen Sprachidioms* (Leipzig: F.C.W. Vogel, 7th edn, 1867).

—*A Treatise on the Grammar of New Testament Greek* (trans. W.F. Moulton; Edinburgh: T. & T. Clark, 3rd edn, 1882).

Young, R.A., *Intermediate New Testament Greek: A Linguistic and Exegetical Approach* (Nashville: Broadman & Holman, 1994).

Zerwick, M., *Biblical Greek* (Rome: Scripta Pontificii Instituti Biblici, 1963).

B. *Greek Particles and Conjunctions*

Allen, E., 'Greek Syntactical Analysis: An Investigation into the Relationship between Conjunctions and Contextual Variables in the Gospel of Matthew' (unpublished MSc thesis, University College London, September 1999).

Bakker, E.J., 'Boundaries, Topics, and the Structure of Discourse: An Investigation of the Ancient Greek Particle *De*', *Studies in Language* 17 (1993), pp. 275-311.

Bird, C.H., 'Some γάρ Clauses in St Mark's Gospel', *JTS* 4 (1953), pp. 171-87.

Black, D.A., 'The Article, Conjunctions and Greek Word Order [Greek for Bible Readers]', *BR* 9 (October 1993), pp. 23, 61.

Blass, R., 'Constraints on Relevance in Koine Greek in the Pauline Epistles' (prepublication draft; first presented at the SIL Exegetical Seminar, Nairobi, Kenya, 29 May–19 July 1993; slightly revised March 1998).

Blomqvist, J., *Greek Particles in Hellenistic Prose* (Lund: C.W.K. Gleerup, 1969).

—*Das Sogennante KAI Adversativum: Zur Semantik einer griechischen Partikel* (Studia Graeca Upsaliensia, 13; Uppsala: Almqvist & Wiksell, 1979).

Buth, R., 'Semitic Καί and Greek Δέ', *START* 3 (1981), pp. 12-19.

—'On Levinsohn's "Development Units" ', *START* 5 (1981), pp. 53-56.

—'Perspective in Gospel Discourse Studies, with Notes on Euthus, Tote and the Temptation Pericopes', *START* 6 (1982), pp. 3-14.

—'⁻Edayin/Tote—Anatomy of a Semitism in Jewish Greek', *Maarav* 5-6 (1990), pp. 33-48.

—'Οὖν, Δέ, Καί, and Asyndeton in John's Gospel', in D.A. Black *et al.* (eds.), *Linguistics and New Testament Interpretation: Essays on Discourse Analysis* (Nashville: Broadman, 1992), pp. 144-61.

Callow, K., 'The Disappearing Δέ in Corinthians', in D.A. Black *et al.* (eds.), *Linguistics and New Testament Interpretation: Essays on Discourse Analysis* (Nashville: Broadman, 1992), pp. 183-93.

De Jong, I.J.F., 'Γάρ Introducing Embedded Narratives', in A. Rijksbaron (ed.), *New Approaches to Greek Particles* (ASCP, 7; Amsterdam: J.C. Gieben, 1997), pp. 175-86.

Denniston, J.D., *The Greek Particles* (rev. K. Dover; Oxford: Clarendon Press, 2nd edn, 1954).

Edwards, R.A., 'Narrative Implications of *Gar* in Matthew', *CBQ* 52 (1990), pp. 636-55.

Elliott, J.K., 'The Position of Causal Ὅτι Clauses in the New Testament', *FN* 3 (1990), pp. 155-57.

Güting, E.W., and D.L. Mealand, *Asyndeton in Paul: A Text-Critical and Statistical Enquiry into Pauline Style* (Studies in the Bible and Early Christianity, 39; Lewiston, NY: Edwin Mellen, 1998).

Heckert, J.A., *Discourse Function of Conjoiners in the Pastoral Epistles* (Dallas: Summer Institute of Linguistics, 1996).

Larsen, I., 'Notes on the Function of γάρ, οὖν, μέν, δέ, καί, and τέ in the Greek New Testament', *Notes on Translation* 5 (1991), pp. 35-45.

Levinsohn, S.H., *Textual Connections in Acts* (SBLMS, 31; Atlanta: Scholars Press, 1987).

—*Discourse Features of New Testament Greek: A Coursebook* (Dallas: Summer Institute of Linguistics, 1992).

—*Discourse Features of New Testament Greek: A Coursebook on the Information Structure of New Testament Greek* (Dallas: Summer Institute of Linguistics, 2nd edn, 2000).

McNeile, A.H., 'Τότε in St Matthew', *JTS* 12 (1911), pp. 127-28.

Morpurgo Davies, A., 'Particles in Greek Epigraphical Texts. The Case of Arcadian', in A. Rijksbaron (ed.), *New Approaches to Greek Particles* (ASCP, 7; Amsterdam: J.C. Gieben, 1997), pp. 49-73.

Poythress, V.S., 'The Use of the Intersentence Conjunctions *De, Oun, Kai*, and Asyndeton in the Gospel of John', *NovT* 26 (1984), pp. 312-40.

Rijksbaron, A., 'Introduction', in *idem* (ed.), *New Approaches to Greek Particles* (ASCP, 7; Amsterdam: J.C. Gieben, 1997), pp. 1-14.

Rijksbaron, A. (ed.), *New Approaches to Greek Particles* (ASCP, 7; Amsterdam: J.C. Gieben, 1997).

Ruijgh, C.J., *Autour de 'Te Épique'* (Amsterdam: Adolph M. Hakkert, 1971).

Sicking, C.M.J., 'Devices for Text Articulation in Lysias I and XII', in C.M.J. Sicking and J.M. van Ophuijsen, *Two Studies in Attic Particle Usage: Lysias and Plato* (Leiden: E.J. Brill, 1993), pp. 1-66.

Sicking, C.M.J., and J.M. van Ophuijsen, *Two Studies in Attic Particle Usage: Lysias and Plato* (Leiden: E.J. Brill, 1993).

Thrall, M., *Greek Particles in the New Testament* (NTTS, 3; Leiden: E.J. Brill, 1962).

Titrud, K., 'The Overlooked Καί in the Greek New Testament', *Notes on Translation* 5 (1991), pp. 1-23.

—'The Function of Καί in the Greek New Testament and an Application to 2 Peter', in D.A.
    Black *et al.* (eds.), *Linguistics and New Testament Interpretation: Essays on Discourse
    Analysis* (Nashville: Broadman, 1992), pp. 240-70.
Van Ophuijsen, J.M., 'ΟΥΝ, ΑΡΑ, ΔΗ, ΤΟΙΝΥΝ: The Linguistic Articulation of Arguments
    in Plato's Phaedo', in C.M.J. Sicking and J.M. van Ophuijsen, *Two Studies in Attic
    Particle Usage: Lysias and Plato* (Leiden: E.J. Brill, 1993), pp. 67-164.
Vargas-Machuca, A., '(Καὶ) ἰδού en estilo narrativo de Mateo', *Bib* 50 (1969), pp. 233-44.

C. *Other*

Achtemeier, P.J., '*Omne verbum sonat*: The New Testament and the Oral Environment of Late
    Western Antiquity', *JBL* 109 (1990), pp. 3-27.
Bakker, E.J., *Poetry in Speech: Orality and Homeric Discourse* (Ithaca, NY: Cornell
    University Press, 1997).
Barr, J., *The Semantics of Biblical Language* (Oxford: Oxford University Press, 1961).
Black, D.A., 'The Study of New Testament Greek in the Light of Ancient and Modern
    Linguistics', in D.A. Black and D.S. Dockery (eds.), *New Testament Criticism and
    Interpretation* (Grand Rapids: Zondervan, 1991), pp. 379-406.
Black, D.A., K. Barnwell and S. Levinsohn (eds.), *Linguistics and New Testament
    Interpretation: Essays on Discourse Analysis* (Nashville: Broadman, 1992).
Botha, J.E., *Jesus and the Samaritan Woman: A Speech Act Reading of John 4:1-42*
    (NovTSup, 65; Leiden: E.J. Brill, 1991).
—'Style in the New Testament: The Need for Serious Reconsideration', *JSNT* 43 (1991), pp.
    71-87 (reprinted in S.E. Porter and C.A. Evans [eds.], *New Testament Text and
    Language: A Sheffield Reader* [The Biblical Seminar, 44; Sheffield: Sheffield Academic
    Press, 1997], pp. 114-29).
Botha, P.J.J., 'Greco-Roman Literacy as Setting for New Testament Writings', *Neot* 26 (1992),
    pp. 195-215.
Charlesworth, R.H., *The Apocrypha and Pseudepigrapha of the Old Testament in English.* I.
    Apocrypha (Oxford: Clarendon Press, 1913).
Coggins, R.J., and M.A. Knibb, *The First and Second Books of Esdras* (Cambridge Bible
    Commentary on the New English Bible; Cambridge: Cambridge University Press, 1979).
Danove, P., 'The Theory of Construction Grammar and Its Application to New Testament
    Greek', in S.E. Porter and D.A. Carson (eds.), *Biblical Greek Language and Linguistics:
    Open Questions in Current Research* (JSNTSup, 80; Sheffield: JSOT Press, 1993), pp.
    119-51.
—*The End of Mark's Story: A Methodological Study* (Biblical Interpretation Series, 3;
    Leiden: E.J. Brill, 1993).
Dewey, J., 'Introduction', in *idem* (ed.), *Orality and Textuality in Early Christian Literature*,
    Semeia 65 (1995), pp. 1-4.
Duhoux, Y., 'Études sur l'aspect verbal en grec ancien, 1: présentation d'une méthode',
    Bulletin de la Société de Linguistique de Paris 40 (1995), pp. 241-99.
Gilliard, F.D., 'More Silent Reading in Antiquity: *Non omne verbum sonabat*', *JBL* 112
    (1993), pp. 689-96.
Horrocks, G., *Greek: A History of the Language and its Speakers* (Longman Linguistics
    Library; London: Longman, 1997).

Hoyle, R., 'The "Scenario" Theory of Cognitive Linguistics, Its Relevance for Analysing New Testament Greek and Modern Parkari Texts, and Its Implications for Translation Theory' (PhD thesis, University of Surrey Roehampton, in preparation).

Longacre, R.E., 'Mark 5.1-43: Generating the Complexity of a Narrative from its Most Basic Elements', in S.E. Porter and J.T. Reed (eds.), *Discourse Analysis in the New Testament: Approaches and Results* (JSNTSup, 170; SNTG, 4; Sheffield: Sheffield Academic Press, 1999), pp. 169-96.

Louw, J.P., 'New Testament Greek—The Present State of the Art', *Neot* 24 (1990), pp. 159-172.

Martín-Asensio, G., 'Hallidayan Functional Grammar as Heir to New Testament Rhetorical Criticism', in S.E. Porter and D.L Stamps (eds.), *The Rhetorical Interpretation of Scripture: Essays from the 1996 Malibu Conference* (JSNTSup, 180; Sheffield: Sheffield Academic Press, 1999), pp. 84-107.

Metzger, B.M., *The Text of the New Testament: Its Transmission, Corruption, and Restoration* (Oxford: Oxford University Press, 3rd edn, 1992).

Neufeld, D., *Reconceiving Texts as Speech Acts: An Analysis of I John* (Biblical Interpretation Series, 7; Leiden: E.J. Brill, 1994).

O'Donnell, M.B., 'The Use of Annotated Corpora for New Testament Discourse Analysis: A Survey of Current Practice and Future Prospects', in S.E. Porter and J.T. Reed (eds.), *Discourse Analysis in the New Testament: Approaches and Results* (JSNTSup, 170; SNTG, 4; Sheffield: Sheffield Academic Press, 1999), pp. 71-117.

Palmer, M., *Levels of Constituent Structure in New Testament Greek* (SBG, 4; New York: Peter Lang, 1995).

Porter, S.E., 'Studying Ancient Languages from a Modern Linguistic Perspective', *FN* 2 (1989), pp. 147-72.

—'Word Order and Clause Structure in New Testament Greek: An Unexplored Area of Greek Linguistics Using Philippians as a Test Case', *FN* 6 (1993), pp. 177-205.

—'Discourse Analysis and New Testament Studies: An Introductory Survey', in S.E. Porter and D.A. Carson (eds.), *Discourse Analysis and Other Topics in Biblical Greek* (JSNTSup, 113; Sheffield: Sheffield Academic Press, 1995), pp. 14-35.

—'The Case for Case Revisited', *Jian Dao* 6 (1996), pp. 13-28.

Porter, S.E., and M.B. O'Donnell, 'Semantic Patterns of Argumentation in the Book of Romans: Definitions, Proposals, Data and Experiments', in S.E. Porter (ed.), *Diglossia and Other Topics in New Testament Linguistics* (Sheffield: Sheffield Academic Press, 2001).

—*Discourse Analysis and the New Testament* (in preparation).

Porter, S.E., and J.T. Reed, 'Greek Grammar since BDF: A Retrospective and Prospective Analysis', *FN* 4 (1991), pp. 143-64.

Porter, S.E., and J.T. Reed (eds.), *Discourse Analysis in the New Testament: Approaches and Results* (JSNTSup, 170; SNTG, 4; Sheffield: Sheffield Academic Press, 1999).

Reed, J.T., *A Discourse Analysis of Philippians: Method and Rhetoric in the Debate over Literary Integrity* (JSNTSup, 136; Sheffield: Sheffield Academic Press, 1997).

Reiser, M., *Syntax und Stil des Markusevangeliums im Licht der hellenistischen Volksliteratur* (Tübingen: J.C.B. Mohr [Paul Siebeck], 1984).

Schmidt, D.D., *Hellenistic Greek Grammar and Noam Chomsky: Nominalizing Transformations* (SBLDS, 62; Chico, CA: Scholars Press, 1981).

—'The Study of Hellenistic Greek Grammar in the Light of Contemporary Linguistics', in
    C.H. Talbert (ed.), *Perspectives on the New Testament: Essays in Honor of Frank Stagg*
    (Macon, GA: Mercer University Press, 1985), pp. 27-38.
Wong, S., 'What Case Is This Case? An Application of Semantic Case in Biblical Exegesis',
    Jian Dao 1 (1994), pp. 49-73.
—*A Classification of Semantic Case-Relations in the Pauline Epistles* (SBG, 9; New York:
    Peter Lang, 1997).

III. *The Gospel of Matthew and Related Topics*

Allen, W.C., *A Critical and Exegetical Commentary on the Gospel According to S. Matthew*
    (ICC; Edinburgh: T. & T. Clark, 3rd edn, 1912).
Bacon, B.W., *Studies in Matthew* (London: Constable, 1930).
Bauer, D.R., *The Structure of Matthew's Gospel: A Study in Literary Design* (JSNTSup, 31;
    Bible and Literature Series, 15; Sheffield: Almond Press, 1988).
Black, S.L., 'The Historic Present in Matthew: Beyond Speech Margins', in S.E. Porter and
    J.T. Reed (eds.), *Discourse Analysis in the New Testament: Approaches and Results*
    (JSNTSup, 170; SNTG, 4; Sheffield: Sheffield Academic Press, 1999), pp. 120-39.
Bornkamm, G., 'The Stilling of the Storm in Matthew', in G. Bornkamm, G. Barth and H.J.
    Held, *Tradition and Interpretation in Matthew* (trans. P. Scott; London: SCM Press,
    1963), pp. 52-57.
Bornkamm, G., G. Barth and H.J. Held, *Tradition and Interpretation in Matthew* (trans. P.
    Scott; London: SCM Press, 1963).
Bultmann, R., *The History of the Synoptic Tradition* (trans. J. Marsh; Oxford: Basil Blackwell,
    1972).
Burger, C., 'Jesu Taten nach Matthäus 8 und 9', *ZTK* 70 (1973), pp. 272-87.
Combrink, H.J.B., 'The Structure of the Gospel of Matthew as Narrative', *TynBul* 34 (1983),
    pp. 61-90.
Davies, W.D., and D.C. Allison, *A Critical and Exegetical Commentary on the Gospel
    According to Saint Matthew*. I. *Introduction and Commentary on Matthew I–VII* (ICC;
    Edinburgh: T. & T. Clark, 1988).
—*A Critical and Exegetical Commentary on the Gospel According to Saint Matthew*. II.
    Commentary on Matthew VIII–XVIII (ICC; Edinburgh: T. & T. Clark, 1991).
—*A Critical and Exegetical Commentary on the Gospel According to Saint Matthew*. III.
    Commentary on Matthew XIX–XXVIII (ICC; Edinburgh: T. & T. Clark, 1997).
Dibelius, M., *From Tradition to Gospel* (trans. B.L. Woolf; London: Ivor Nicholson and
    Watson, 1934).
Dobschütz, E. von, 'Matthew as Rabbi and Catechist (1928)', in G.N. Stanton (ed.), *The
    Interpretation of Matthew* (Studies in New Testament Interpretation; Edinburgh: T. & T.
    Clark, 2nd edn, 1995), pp. 27-38.
Edwards, J.R., 'The Use of ΠΡΟΣΕΡΧΕΣΘΑΙ in the Gospel of Matthew', *JBL* 106 (1987),
    pp. 65-74.
Farmer, W.R., *The Synoptic Problem: A Critical Analysis* (New York: Macmillan, 1964).
France, R.T., *The Gospel According to Matthew: An Introduction and Commentary* (TNTC;
    Leicester: Inter-Varsity Press, 1985).
Fuller, R.H., and P. Perkins, *Who Is This Christ? Gospel Christology and Contemporary Faith*
    (Philadelphia: Fortress Press, 1983).

Gatzwieler, K., 'Les récits de miracles dans L'Évangile selon Saint Matthieu', in M. Didier (ed.), *L'Évangile selon Matthieu: Rédaction et théologie* (BETL, 29; Gembloux: Duculot, 1972), pp. 209-20.

Gerhardsson, B., *The Mighty Acts of Jesus According to Matthew* (Lund: C.W.K. Gleerup, 1979).

Grayston, K., 'The Translation of Matthew 28.17', *JSNT* 21 (1984), pp. 105-109.

Gundry, R.H., *Matthew: A Commentary on his Handbook for a Mixed Church under Persecution* (Grand Rapids: Eerdmans, 2nd edn, 1994).

Hagner, D.A., *Matthew 1–13* (WBC, 33A; Dallas: Word Books, 1993).

—*Matthew 14–28* (WBC, 33B; Dallas: Word Books, 1995).

Heil, J.P., 'Significant Aspects of the Healing Miracles in Matthew', *CBQ* 41 (1979), pp. 274-87.

Held, H.J., 'Matthew as Interpreter of the Miracle Stories', in G. Bornkamm, G. Barth and H.J. Held, *Tradition and Interpretation in Matthew* (trans. P. Scott; London: SCM Press, 1963), pp. 165-299.

Kingsbury, J.D., *Matthew: Structure, Christology, Kingdom* (Philadelphia: Fortress Press, 1975).

—'Observations on the "Miracle Chapters" of Matthew 8–9', *CBQ* 40 (1978), pp. 559-73.

—'The Developing Conflict between Jesus and the Jewish Leaders in Matthew's Gospel: A Literary-Critical Study', *CBQ* 49 (1987), pp. 57-73.

—*Matthew as Story* (Philadelphia: Fortress Press, 2nd edn, 1988).

Krentz, E., 'The Extent of Matthew's Prologue', *JBL* 83 (1964), pp. 409-14.

Lagrange, M.-J., *Évangile selon Saint Matthieu* (Paris: Librairie Lecoffre, 7th edn, 1948).

Larsen, I., 'A Semantic Structure Analysis of Matthew 4:1-11', *Notes on Translation* 112 (1986), pp. 33-41.

Lohmeyer, E., *Das Evangelium des Matthäus* (Göttingen: Vandenhoeck & Ruprecht, 1956).

Louw, J.P., 'The Structure of Mt 8:1–9:35', *Neot* 11 (1977), pp. 91-97.

Luz, U., *Das Evangelium nach Matthäus*. I. *Mt 1–7* (EKKNT, 1.1; Zürich: Benziger Verlag, 1985).

—'Die Wundergeschichten von Mt 8–9', in G.F. Hawthorne and O. Betz (eds.), *Tradition and Interpretation in the New Testament* (Grand Rapids: Eerdmans, 1987), pp. 149-65.

—*Matthew 1–7* (trans. W.C. Linss; Minneapolis: Augsburg, 1989).

—*Das Evangelium nach Matthäus*. II. *Mt 8–17* (EKKNT, I.2; Zürich: Benziger Verlag, 1990).

—*The Theology of the Gospel of Matthew* (trans. J.B. Robinson; Cambridge: Cambridge University Press, 1995).

McNeile, A.H., *The Gospel According to St Matthew* (London: Macmillan, 1938).

McKay, K.L., 'The Use of *hoi de* in Matthew 28.17', *JSNT* 24 (1985), pp. 71-72.

Moiser, J., 'The Structure of Matthew 8–9: A Suggestion', *ZNW* 76 (1985), pp. 117-18.

Neill, S., and T. Wright, *The Interpretation of the New Testament, 1861–1986* (Oxford: Oxford University Press, 2nd edn, 1988).

Neirynck, F., 'ΑΠΟ ΤΟΤΕ ΗΡΞΑΤΟ and the Structure of Matthew', in F. Van Segbroeck (ed.), *Evangelica II, 1982–1991. Collected Essays by Frans Neirynck* (Leuven: Leuven University Press, 1991), pp. 141-82.

Powell, M.A., *What Is Narrative Criticism?* (Minneapolis: Fortress Press, 1990).

Reedy, C.J., 'Rhetorical Concerns and Argumentative Techniques in Matthean Pronouncement Stories', in K.H. Richards (ed.), *Society of Biblical Literature 1983 Seminar Papers* (Chico, CA: Scholars Press, 1983), pp. 219-22.

Robbins, V.K., 'Chreia and Pronouncement Story in Synoptic Studies', in B.L. Mack and V.K. Robbins, *Patterns of Persuasion in the Gospels* (Sonoma, CA: Polebridge Press, 1989), pp. 1-29.

—'Apophthegm', in D.N. Freedman (ed.), *The Anchor Bible Dictionary*. I. *A–C* (New York: Doubleday, 1992), pp. 307-309.

Schweizer, E., 'Matthew's Church', in G.N. Stanton (ed.), *The Interpretation of Matthew* (Studies in New Testament Interpretation; Edinburgh: T. & T. Clark, 2nd edn, 1995), pp. 149-77.

Senior, D., *What Are They Saying about Matthew?* (New York: Paulist Press, revd edn, 1996).

Stanton, G.N. (ed.), *The Interpretation of Matthew* (Studies in New Testament Interpretation; Edinburgh: T. & T. Clark, 2nd edn, 1995).

Stendahl, K., 'Quis et Unde? An Analysis of Matthew 1–2 (1960)', in G.N. Stanton (ed.), *The Interpretation of Matthew* (Studies in New Testament Interpretation; Edinburgh: T. & T. Clark, 2nd edn, 1995), pp. 69-80.

Stonehouse, N.B., *The Witness of Matthew and Mark to Christ* (London: Tyndale, 1944).

Tannehill, R.C., 'Introduction: The Pronouncement Story and Its Types', *Semeia* 20 (1981), pp. 1-13.

Taylor, V., *The Formation of the Gospel Tradition* (London: Macmillan, 1933).

Theissen, G., *The Miracle Stories of the Early Christian Tradition* (Philadelphia: Fortress Press, 1983).

Thompson, W.G., 'Reflections on the Composition of Mt 8.1–9.34', *CBQ* 33 (1971), pp. 365-88.

Twelftree, G.H., *Jesus the Miracle Worker* (Downers Grove, IL: InterVarsity Press, 1999).

Van der Horst, P., 'Once More: The Translation of οἱ δέ in Matthew 28.17', *JSNT* 27 (1986), pp. 27-30.

Vledder, E.-J., *Conflict in the Miracle Stories: A Socio-Exegetical Study of Matthew 8 and 9* (JSNTSup, 152; Sheffield: Sheffield Academic Press, 1997).

INDEX OF REFERENCES

BIBLE

JOURNAL FOR THE STUDY OF THE OLD TESTAMENT
SUPPLEMENT SERIES